Representing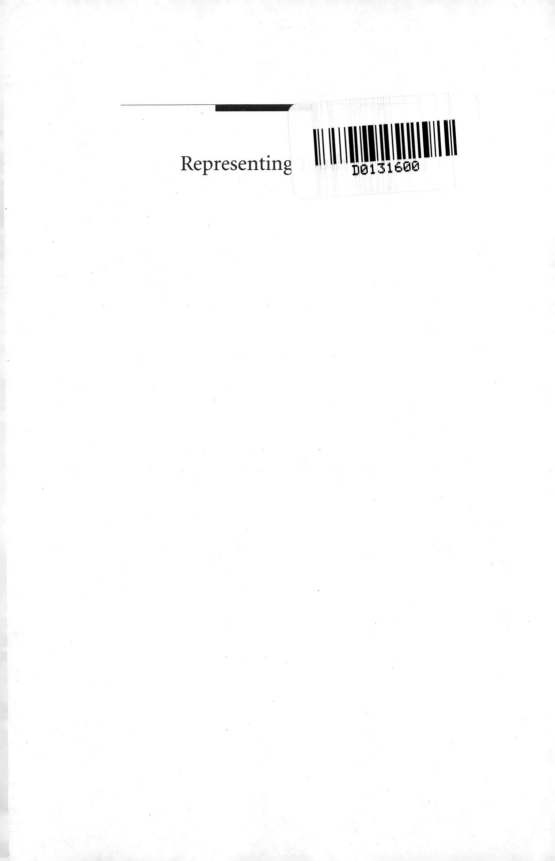

D0131600

Representing Youth

*Methodological Issues in
Critical Youth Studies*

EDITED BY

Amy L. Best

New York University Press

NEW YORK AND LONDON

NEW YORK UNIVERSITY PRESS
New York and London
www.nyupress.org

© 2007 by New York University

Library of Congress Cataloging-in-Publication Data

Representing youth : methodological issues in critical youth studies /
edited by Amy L. Best.
p.   cm.
Includes bibliographical references and index.
ISBN-13: 978-0-8147-9952-9 (cloth : alk. paper)
ISBN-10: 0-8147-9952-3 (cloth : alk. paper)
ISBN-13: 978-0-8147-9953-6 (pbk. : alk. paper)
ISBN-10: 0-8147-9953-1 (pbk. : alk. paper)
1. Youth—Study and teaching. 2. Children—Study and teaching.
3. Youth—Research. 4. Children—Research.   I. Best, Amy L., 1970–
HQ796.R484 2006
305.235072—dc22   2006023124

New York University Press books are printed on acid-free paper,
and their binding materials are chosen for strength and durability.

Manufactured in the United States of America
c 10 9 8 7 6 5 4 3 2 1
p 10 9 8 7 6 5 4 3 2 1

For my parents, Natalie Best and Gary Best

Contents

Acknowledgments

A debt of gratitude is owed to many people who provided support during the various stages of this project. I offer a most sincere thanks to the contributors to this volume for their patience and diligence as this project moved forward. I am truly appreciative of the support I received from the Sociology Department at San Jose State University, where I began this project, and the Department of Sociology and Anthropology at George Mason University, where I finished it. A faculty research leave provided by George Mason University was most appreciated. A special thanks to Ilene Kalish, my editor at NYU Press, who supported this project when it was just an idea and gently nudged me along to its end. Susan Murray, Elena Klaw, Dan Cook, Laura Fingerson, Mark Jacobs, Greg Guagnano, Nancy Hanrahan, Linda Seligmann, Steve Vallas, Jessica Greenebaum, Tom Williams, and Peter Chua provided fruitful comments on this project at different stages. Chris McCauley has provided much support during this project and all the others. For that I am grateful. Finally, I'd like to thank my teachers, Marj DeVault, Sari Biklen, Judy Long, Mike Yarrow, and Judith Barker, who inspired in me a deep interest in and lasting commitment to qualitative and feminist approaches to social research.

Introduction

Amy L. Best

I begin with a researcher's parable. Several years ago, I undertook a qualitative study examining youth and the high school prom (Best, 2000). I was interested in understanding the intersection of youth identity formation, schooling, and popular culture and the dynamic ways race, class, sexuality, and gender come to bear on these social forms and collective practices. I drew on a range of materials for analysis—in-depth interviews, participant observation of four public high schools, prom narratives written by college students, archival documents, and various media—to explore the rich meanings and subtle complexities of the prom as an iconic social event for today's American youth. Of the four schools I studied, two had significant immigrant student populations. In one of the schools, nearly 20 percent of the students were either immigrants or descendants of immigrants. I noted in my field notes, though only in passing, that one of the schools did not require students to have a prom date to attend the prom; students were permitted to go "stag." In my field notes I wrote that this was because a number of the students were Muslim or Hindu and their parents forbade their dating. Wanting all students to be able to participate in this "great coming-of-age American ritual," school administrators adjusted what had once been a hard-and-fast rule of the prom, the senior faculty adviser explained to me. In my field notes from my investigation of the second school, I noted that the Hmong student population was nearly absent from the prom, even though they represented well over 10 percent of the school's student body. The year I visited, only two Hmong students attended the prom.

These two facts, both remarkable, received only passing mention in the book I wrote, and one only as a footnote. Somehow these two points had fallen outside my purview, slipping off my radar screen only to become part of the repository of unused and unanalyzed material that qualitative researchers collect in the field but do nothing with. In fact, these were points I did not give any sustained consideration to until well after the study was concluded and I had moved on to another qualitative study, also involving young adults and the ways they (re)create the importance of race, gender, and class to their everyday lives (Best, 2006). Looking back, this point seems a glaring omission.

It is nearly impossible to know in retrospect what sense I would have made of these points then had I given them more serious attention while in the field. What is clear is that I failed to provide an account of a group of kids whose sense of the prom, and by extension their engagement with school and its cultural dynamics, differed from the kids I ended up writing about. It is likely that had I paid them their due, I would have been left with a different and probably more complicated picture of the prom and what it means in American cultural life. As feminist scholars have repeatedly demonstrated, the standpoints or perspectives we privilege shape our understandings of the social worlds we study (Collins, 1990; DeVault, 1990; Harding, 1987; Smith, 1987, 1990b). When we fail to recognize this, we not only render particular groups invisible but also obscure and distort our understandings of the everyday worlds they occupy *and* their social organization.

Why did these points fail to inspire a researcher's curiosity? Immigrant youth represent an ever-expanding portion of the larger U.S. population, yet often they remain invisible in studies of American youth culture. Although there are plenty of investigations that center on immigrant youths' social experiences,[1] those qualitative research projects that investigate youth as a broad and diverse category of identity and experience regularly fall short in seriously examining the lives of immigrant youth, just as I had done. Certainly this may be explained by our shortcomings as researchers. That I am a white woman who grew up in a community without a visible immigrant population no doubt played a role in the way I conducted the research. But might other explanations be equally plausible? What aspects of research and its social organization render some groups of youth invisible to researchers? Might it be that the conceptual and interpretive schemes that have historically organized the study of youth create blinders? Might there be a significant time lag between the shifts and transformations to the groups we study (as a group, youth have grown increasingly diverse and their diversity has grown increasingly complex in the past decade) and our acknowledgment of those changes?

Might the worlds we occupy matter to the worlds we study and how we study them? In the case I described, all these possibilities seem likely to have influenced how I proceeded with my research.

When I reflect on what precipitated my eventually giving consideration to this loosely connected group of young people, I think first of the changes to my own life. Just as I was finishing the prom project, I moved to a California community where 60 percent of the population are descendants of immigrants or are immigrants themselves. For the first time, immigrants represented a visible slice of the everyday worlds I traveled in and around: the students who sat before me as I taught sociology, the person sitting beside me as I rode the bus to the university each day, the bagger who helped me with my groceries, and my neighbors in the apartment complex where I'd created a home.[2] Everyday I watched young Chicanos on the cusp of thirteen in crisp white shirts and neatly pressed blue pants descend from the bus outside their school as I traveled to school myself. When I returned home in the early evenings, as I sat writing at my computer, I would watch a young Chinese mother and her three-year-old daughter feed the ducks outside my bedroom window, the mother speaking a mix of Mandarin and English to her daughter. I regularly observed Indian women in saris and salwars kameez cradle their babies as they walked beside similarly dressed older women around the blocks just beyond my door. I began to *see* and *sense* the world in a dramatically different way from how I had once *thought* of that world. As John Berger (1977) noted long ago in his classic *Ways of Seeing,* seeing is a situated practice; above all else, it is profoundly social. That contextual circumstances pattern how researchers see the worlds we study is not an especially new insight among qualitative researchers. Indeed, this is a point that has generated decades of reflection among qualitative practitioners of various stripes. Yet the precise ways the social worlds we occupy shape those we study, such that some realities become visible to us while others slowly fade, still eludes us on a very basic level. The world out there and our perceptions of it, despite our best reflexive efforts, are not so easily accessed or so transparent.

In time, I came to see a conceptual rift between my everyday world and the youth worlds I studied. This emerging awareness led me to reflect on and eventually to interrogate the very construction of "American youth culture" on which much of my work rested and to ask questions about the conceptual schemes researchers use as they study youth. Now, I can see how the construction of "youth culture" in "America" in academic and popular literature is presented as an essentially "American" culture. And even while representations of "American youth culture" are increasingly attentive to differences rooted in relations of race, class, gender, and sexuality, they continue to eclipse differences of citizenship, immigrant status, and nationality despite the growth and visibility of transnational communities. The use of the term "American youth culture" may invoke images of urban hipsters, suburban wiggas, cheerleaders, graffiti writers, skater kids, youth of the African Diaspora with oversized pants slung low on the hips, or lesbian zine writers, but rarely does such a term invoke images of girls donning burkas, even if they are also in sequined prom dresses, or of young Muslims praying to Allah in a meditation room in a university student union. An increasingly global economy and the steady stream of bodies moving across ever-shifting borders have produced a sea of changes to American youth cultures. These changes bear upon the framing of research questions and problems, how we define the groups we study and ultimately how we study them.

In retrospect, it is clear that the conceptual schemes and constructs I worked with produced their own failings. The jarring disconnect between the world I traveled in and the world I studied and read about led to my eventual awareness of immigrant youth and my rethinking of the conceptual tools I used to frame the worlds around me. From there, I began to engage a different set of questions that arose from my actively looking at my own world and those worlds I was studying for their differences and similarities in an attempt to generate alternative understandings to those I already had. This active attention to these points of commonality and difference between the world I thought in and the world I existed in helped me to trace the outlines of my own interpretive schemes, identifying their shortcomings and their promise.

This research experience, among others, led to my thinking more systematically about the varied ways age intersects with other axes of power and difference and its consequence for research practice, for how our lived worlds inform our conceptual worlds, for how we see, understand, and interact with youth, and for the knowledge we produce and disseminate. These questions, in large part, inspired this volume on youth and research methods.

In this spirit, this collection of writing aims to flesh out a number of key conceptual and methodological considerations in the study of youth and children. Although by no means exhaustive, this volume brings together the work of scholars across the social sciences and the humanities to address some of the distinct methodological problems and issues that qualitative practitioners confront in studying children and youth, and it draws from and extends the important insights generated by other collections dedicated to such matters. The authors ask important questions of the disciplines to which they belong, at times calling for radical shifts in the intellectual order of things. In this sense, this volume represents an interdisciplinary inquiry into the complex intersections of youth and social research methods. That this volume is interdisciplinary seems especially appropriate since the study of children and youth has never had one disciplinary home but many.

The study of children and youth is a rapidly growing area of research within a variety of disciplines including sociology, anthropology, social work, psychology, women's studies, ethnic studies, education, history, and cultural studies, giving rise to an emerging set of methodological concerns specific to the study of this diverse group. Yet, while this area of study has flourished in recent years, researchers have perhaps not given the sort of sustained and systematic attention to the complexity of issues relating to data collection and analysis of youth worlds that it warrants. The questions that arise in studying youth and children have not received the same detailed consideration as in the study of other groups. Consider the extensive body of writing and reflection dedicated to questions arising from the study of women by feminist scholars or investigations of third-world communities by first-world scholars, for instance. All of this is not to suggest that childhood and youth researchers have ignored such methodological concerns. Fine and Sandstrom's *Knowing Children: Participant Observation with Minors* (1988), Holmes's *Fieldwork with Children* (1998), Christensen and James's *Research with Children: Perspectives and Practice* (2000), Graue and Walsh's *Studying Children in Context: Theories, Methods, and Ethics* (1998), Waksler's *Studying the Social Worlds of Children* (1991), and most recently *Doing Research with Children and Young People* by Fraser et al. (2004) and *Researching Youth* by Bennett, Cieslik, and Miles (2003) serve as important engagements with questions relating to the study of youth and children. This collection builds from these critical engagements as it aims to both broaden and focus the discussion of queries and dilemmas that emerge when studying young people. A central objective here is to initiate a serious dialogue about what might be considered the methodological, ethical, practical, and conceptual boundaries for a more critical youth studies that is attentive to the changing social realities of youth and children as they come of age in a historical moment mediated by advanced communication systems and increasingly sophisticated media, economic change, and deepening inequalities. As others have noted, the contemporary cultural landscape of childhood and adolescence is changing rapidly on several fronts, political, economic, and social. This requires us to reflect on the methods and strategies, conceptual frames and analytical categories youth researchers commonly use as we study and represent children's and youths' cultures.

Qualitative Methods and Critical Youth Studies

Social researchers recognized long ago that excavation of the social dimensions of research practice and sustained and critical reflection on the role of the researcher in collecting and analyzing empirical materials are critical parts of sound qualitative research (Bogdan and Taylor, 1984; Clifford, 1983; R. Emerson, 2001: Emerson, Fretz, and Shaw, 1995; Glassner and Hertz, 1999; Lofland and Lofland, 1995; Tierney, 1998; Van Maanen, 1995). Much writing by qualitative research practitioners has been dedicated to exploring the relationship between researchers and the researched (Anderson, 1976; Harrington, 2003; Liebow, 1967; Thorne, 1983; Vanderstaay, 2005; Whyte, 1955). Negotiating the researcher role, issues relating to the outsider or insider status of the researcher, membership roles, matters of rapport, trust, and acceptance have long concerned qualitative researchers (Adler and Adler, 1987; Duneier, 1999; M. Fine, 1992; Harden et al., 2000; Nairn, Munro, and Smith, 2005; Norum, 2000; Reinharz, 1992; Twine and Warren, 2000; Van Maanen, 1988, 1995).

Over the past several decades, contemporary practitioners have directed attention to the situated nature of social research, considering the multiple ways a researcher's biography and social position (with specific regard to race, nationality, sexuality, class, and gender) not only are relevant to the relations of research while in the field but also shape the interpretive and theoretical claims we make after leaving the field (Arendell, 1997; Best, 2003; Bowles and Klein, 1983; De Andrade, 2000; DeVault, 1999; M. Fine, 1992; Horowitz, 1986; Long, 1999; Neilsen, 1990; Reich, 2003; Roberts, 1981; Russel y Rodriguez, 1998; Shope, 2005; Stacey, 1988; Wesley, 2005; Wolf, 1996). Matters of writing and representation, the authority of the researcher, and the interpretive practices that constitute the research enterprise have received much consideration (Clifford, 1983; Geertz, 1973; Koro-Ljungberg and Greckhamer, 2005; Lather, 1993: Minh-ha, 1989; Tierney 2002). Central to these discussions has been an effort to flesh out how the researcher's position of power within the field (e.g., white/"of color," "first world"/"third world," middle class/poor, man/woman, adult/child) mediates the collection and analysis of empirical materials (Behar and Gordon, 1995; Blee, 2000; Brooks, 2005; Collins, 1990; DeVault, 1990, 1999; Gallagher, 2000; Harding, 1987; Kenny, 2000; Kondo, 1990; Minh-ha, 1989; Mueller, 1995; Nespor, 1998; Oakley, 1981; Punch, 2002; Roberts, 1981; Thorne, 1993; Twine and Warren, 2000; Williams, 1996). For example, Michelle Fine's seminal call for critical researchers to better "work the hyphens" between self and other, researcher and researched helped to transform how researchers thought about research methods as "tools of domination" and generated alternative modes of representation to the "colonizing discourse of the 'Other'" that has prevailed across the social sciences (1994:70).

Contemporary practitioners have shed much light on the problems that emerge within even the best-intentioned research undertakings, impelling researchers to develop more innovative research strategies to address and circumvent such problems (Christensen and Prout, 2002; Cree, Kay, and Tisdall, 2002; DeVault, 1995; Edward and Alldred, 1999; Fine and Weis, 1998; Grover, 2004; Leyshon, 2002; Oakley, 1981; Patai, 1991; Stacey, 1988; Visweswaran, 1997; Young and Barrett, 2001; Yuen, 2004). Efforts to reduce the power imbalance inherent in the qualitative research endeavor and to conduct nonexploitative research have given rise to a more self-conscious and critical mode of inquiry and analysis (Denzin, 1992; Denzin and Lincoln, 2003a, 2003b; M. Fine, 1992; Gubrium and Holstein, 1997; Kreiger, 1991; Marcus, 1998). The growing popularity of autoethnography, personal narrative and storytelling, visual methods such as documentary film and photo essays, and social action research serve as meaningful examples of this direction (Berger and Quinney, 2004; Brooks, 2005; Ellis, 1995, 2001; Gordon, 1993; Kenny, 2000; Reinharz, 1992; Vidal-Ortiz, 2004). This collection stands as an important extension of these investigations. It represents new directions in critical youth studies as it utilizes frameworks emerging from cultural studies, queer studies, critical race studies, feminist studies, and postmodernism to engage questions of writing and representation, youth agency, research collaboration and social change, and the politics of the field. The essays in this volume reflect ongoing engagements with an established body of writing but also attempt to respond to and in some sense move beyond them. Enduring questions related to power and authority, the researcher's insider/outsider status, the relationship between rapport building and knowledge and understanding, representational practices and "Othering" are explored in the pages that follow, all with attention to the dynamics of age.

A range of concerns comes to the fore when thinking about how adults study youth and their social and symbolic worlds. As readers will immediately realize as they move through the essays, there are several critical points of intersection among the readings as the authors help to frame this undertaking by identifying key questions: How can investigators successfully negotiate the role of adult researcher as they work to gain access to youth worlds, break through "fronts," and develop meaningful rapport? In addition to age, what issues emerge when adult researchers also consider the significance of race, nationality, gender, class, and sexuality to our social experiences and interactions in the field? How can adults interpret and write about youth realities given the distance that exists between their worlds and our own? What role does adult memory play in research and in what ways does it limit understanding of the complex facets of youths' worlds today? How can researchers develop more sensitive and empowering ways to study youth and children, while also addressing key ethical considerations? How have prevailing conceptualizations of and cultural assumptions about youth and children narrowed our understanding of them, the social organization of the worlds they traverse, and the social relations therein?

Representing Youth, as it draws together different scholars studying diverse and in some cases divergent aspects of children's and youths' experiences and cultures, attempts to advance our understanding of old concerns and identify new ones. As readers moves through this volume, they will find a cross-fertilization of methods and theories not simply across disciplines. Taken together, the essays attempt to bridge other old divisions: the divide between microanalysis and macroanalysis, between the study of youth culture by subcultural and post-subcultural theorists and the study of children by the new developmental theorists, for instance. I am often struck by how salient these divisions sometimes are, and the insularity that is manifest, despite the concerted efforts to bridge them in the past decade. For example, I have frequently observed that those studying young people in the upper-age brackets are often tied to very different literatures, theoretically and methodologically, from those studying very young people. This is to our detriment I think, since similar queries and thematics have been addressed by these scholars. I also have observed that a growing number of researchers have recognized the value of this cross-fertilization and successfully integrated differing perspectives and literatures into their own research. For this reason, I chose to include essays that address concerns with young children and essays that focus on the study of young adults. The volume gives relatively even consideration to young children and young adults. For some this might feel like a odd pairing since the methods and theories involved in research with young children and young adults are in fact quite different, and in some instances they should be because the social realities, lived experiences, and cultural competencies of these groups differ. Nevertheless, my aim is to clarify the unifying threads in the study of children and young adults, seeing them as axes for coordinates on a methodological base of conceptual and practical considerations for a more critical youth studies. Although I am reluctant to offer any formal principles that distinguish a critical youth studies, fearing conceptual and methodological rigidity and closure of innovative thinking on these matters, a critical youth studies should involve the following as part of its methodological agenda:

a. A sustained concern for and consideration of the complexities of power and exploitation in the research encounter.
b. An acknowledgment of the connection between power and knowledge. Such an acknowledgment requires that we recognize that the accounts we provide shape and construct reality as much as they describe it. Youth researchers play a significant role in shaping the social experiences of children and youth through the discursive constructions or accounts we provide.
c. A desire to conduct sound ethical research that empowers youth and children and to find ways to improve the conditions under which their lives unfold.
d. A commitment to a radical reflexivity that interrogates the varied points of difference that intersect in our own lives and those we study.

The chapters in this collection flesh out these core considerations.

Paradigm Shifts and the New Childhood Studies

In large part, the essays in this collection take as their starting point the insights arising from what is often called the "New Childhood Studies," a set of perspectives that arrived on the scene nearly two decades ago and presented a well-organized and thoughtful challenge to the reigning developmental paradigms that had largely directed studies on children and adolescence (Adler and Adler, 1998; Christensen and James, 2000; Corsaro, 1997; James and James, 2004; Qvortrup, 1994). The New Childhood Studies sought to replace the adult-centered studies that dominated much research on children and youth with more child and youth-centered and socio-centered research approaches. As youth scholar Virginia Caputo remarked, "methodologically and conceptually children must be freed from the process of containment that produces them as 'other' and in turn continues to silence them" (1995:33). Highlighting the perspectives and activities of children and youth in the contexts of school, peer group, family, and market, the New Childhood Studies provided a more complex portrait of young people as meaningfully engaged, independent social actors whose activities and practices influence a variety of social contexts and settings (Adler and Adler, 1998; Chin, 2001; Corsaro, 1985; Eders, Evans, and Parker, 1995; G. Fine, 1987; Gaines, 1990; Jans, 2004). These emerging perspectives generated a cataclysmic shift in thinking about youth as they challenged the prevailing characterization of children as passive actors and instead emphasized children's autonomy and competence as actors in their own right. Youth researchers became increasingly disinterested in children's *becoming* (that is, what they might be) and far more interested in children's *being* (what they are) (Qvortrup, 1994).

In large part, the New Childhood Studies paved a new course for studying youth and children conceptually and practically. I can recall this shift having direct bearing on how I proceeded with the research I conducted on youth and their high school proms in the 1990s. When I began collecting empirical materials for the project I was very aware of how the prom is commonly defined as a "rite of passage" and saw this as an illustration of how cultural events in which youth participate are defined through the adult-centered rhetoric of "becoming." Indeed, images of the prom as a coming-of-age rite permeate our culture. In conducting the interviews for the project I was concerned that the kids would invoke this adult-centered discourse of the prom as they responded to my questions and that this would prevent my uncovering the varied and layered meanings of the event. This concern influenced the interview strategies I used. To work against what Barrie Thorne (1993) has called "adult ideological standpoints," I avoided broad questions like why they thought the prom was meaningful. I tried instead to uncover meanings from their talk about specific events, activities, and practices that emerged around the prom (e.g., shopping for the dress, renting the tuxedo, getting ready the evening of the prom). This interview strategy enabled me to move beyond the rendering of youth perched at the threshold of adulthood and uncover the contested meanings of the prom as they were reflexively articulated by kids themselves.[3]

In addition to demonstrating a deep respect for children's and youths' views and competencies, the New Childhood Studies drew our attention to the socially constructed nature of childhood and adolescence over and against the universalizing and naturalizing propensities of long-standing research paradigms in child development and adolescent studies (Corsaro, 1997; James, Jenks, and Prout, 1998; Lesko, 2001; Van Ausdale and Feagin, 2002). The result has been a methodological shift, a remapping of definitional boundaries, and a far greater awareness of the role social science inquiry plays in constituting the very groups we study. One tangible consequence of this is that we have witnessed an explosion of ethnographies and participant-observation studies on youth and children in the past two decades. In *The First R*, Debra Van Ausdale and Joe Feagin (2002) offered a compelling critique of the embeddedness of Piaget's developmental stages in everyday thought on youth and its limits for understanding the complex ways children as young as three and four use abstract racial constructs, for example. Their ethnographic research on children's use of racial constructs to define the self and others, to dominate, to include and exclude others in the context of a Florida day-care center provided in-depth understanding of the sociocultural worlds young children construct with peers that (re)produce racial meanings. Similarly, Paul Connolly (1998) examined the process of racial meaning-making among five- and six-year-old, low-income students in an ethnically diverse English elementary school using participant observation and interviewing. Immersing himself in the very young children's school-based peer interactions, Connolly demonstrated their ability to harness racial ideas to construct identities as feminine and masculine, showing the different contexts in which race and gender notions are deployed.

For some time now, youth studies scholars have treated children and youth as reflexive social agents and producers of culture, active in the complex negotiations of social life and contributing in significant ways to the everyday construction of the social world, not as subjects-in-the-making but as subjects in their own right (Best 2000; Brown 1999; Chin, 2001; Corsaro, 1985, 2003; G. Fine, 1987; Fine and Sandstrom, 1988; Hey, 1997; Giroux and Simon, 1989; Graebner, 1990; Lareau, 2003; McRobbie,

1991; Perry, 2002; Roman and Christian-Smith, 1989; Skelton and Valentine, 1998; Thorne 1993; Willis, 1977). Yet greater reflexive attention needs to be given to this outpouring of research and the new set of methodological issues it has raised.

Power and Adult Authority

The issue of adult authority and power has been a core concern among youth studies scholars because studying children and youth involves what social researchers have colloquially called "studying down"; thus, the subject is given extensive consideration in this volume. As Fine and Sandstrom observe, in an age-segregated society such as ours, "legitimate adult-child interaction depends on adult authority. The taken-for-granted character of this authority structure and the different worldviews that are related to it create unique problems for participant observation with children" (1988:13). The authority adults command and structures of power are deeply entangled, inasmuch as their authority flows from and is bolstered by a set of institutional and ideological arrangements. Any examination of adult authority, then, must also acknowledge and account for the structural and institutional relations that legitimate that authority, that produce differences in the roles adopted by children and adults in social settings and in the research encounter, and that create a vast gulf between the resources each group collectively holds. Consideration of the robust ways power is present as an active force at every stage of research— from the early conceptual stages, through data collection, to analysis— necessitates sustained and rigorous reflection on the part of the researcher. An acknowledgment of the imbalance of power in research requires careful attention to the ways our methods, our definitional boundaries, and our claims making construct a world and the groups in it as much as they express it.

Many youth researchers have explored how best to engage in ethical, nonexploitative research in the situation of "studying down." For instance, critical psychologist Lyn Mikel Brown (1999) became keenly aware of the power she held as an upwardly mobile middle-class, academic, adult woman as she investigated white middle-school girls from working-class and middle-class backgrounds and their struggles to move around, make sense of, and sometimes angrily resist conventional feminine constructs in their daily lives. As someone with contradictory class leanings, Brown was also conscious of her own struggle to understand these two different groups of girls in ways that did not reproduce the narrow fictions about them, to empower and not disempower them. She writes, "Throughout the course of listening to and interpreting the girls' thoughts and feelings I remain conscious of the fact that, as an observer and narrator of their lives, I too become, in Foucault's terms, a 'Surveillant Other' not simply listening, watching, and describing, 'but also producing a knowledge that feeds into the discursive practices regulating' girls' voices and class consciousness" (38).

Attention to power and authority and their role in shaping both time spent in the field and a broad range of representational practices might be thought of as a guiding principle of a critical youth studies. Each of the essays in this volume addresses fundamental concerns with power. But the authors engage these questions differently, making visible the complexities of power and investigating the different registers through which power and adult authority operate. Although youth scholars have long examined the deep division between adults and young people in research settings, how these dynamics are informed by other axes of difference has gained attention in recent years. As Rebecca Raby argues in this collection, "we are, as researchers, socially located and frequently privileged. Yet we all occupy multiple identifications. Age is one such subject position, and it is a salient feature of insider-outsider distinctions." Several essays in this collection ground their research inquiries of youth in queer theory, feminist theory, critical race theory, and cultural studies and, in doing so, complicate the adult-youth couplet by attending to other social relations of power such as those formed around race, gender, nationality, class, and sexuality.

Drawing on the insights from critical race scholars and feminist methodology, Jessica Taft, in her essay, "Racing Age: Reflections of Antiracist Research with Teenage Girls," examines how the dynamics of age in the research encounter are organized and shaped by other lines of power and difference, notably race. Taft explores how her own position as "a young-looking (but not teenaged) white woman" influenced relations in the field, her ability to develop rapport and to collect "good" data as she studied two groups of young women in different organizational settings, one largely white and middle class, the other composed primarily of urban, low-income Latinas and Black Americans. While Taft found that her "adult status precluded some forms of participation and discouraged some kinds of honest discussion," much of this depended on the dynamics of race. Taft found herself embroiled initially in an internal struggle to move beyond the desire to be seen by the girls of color she studied as "wise" and "cool" as a means to overcompensate for her position as an older white woman. She recognized that this precluded her asking the girls the types of questions she needed to ask. Taft observes that building rapport and forging meaningful connections in a situation where the constraints imposed by power and difference were palpable required her to relinquish this longing to belong as a racial and generational outsider. Like Taft's observations, this collection as a whole represents an extended investigation into the varied ways enduring social inequalities inspire the research we do but also structure it.

Focusing on how power and inequality inform our research undertakings and our attempts to conduct nonexploitative research also directs our attention to the larger institutional, political, and economic contexts in which knowledge about youth and children is produced and disseminated. Children and youth, despite being the subject of nearly a century of research, are largely excluded from the very social processes through which knowledge about them is created. As a means to counter this situation, a growing number of child and youth researchers have explored the possibilities of collaborative or participatory research protocols to promote what Michael Ungar in this volume calls youths' "discursive empowerment"; otherwise, either children and youth remain voiceless or, more commonly, the presentation of their voices is controlled by the researcher. These collaborative and participatory efforts have taken various forms. In some instances youth participate in the research design by helping to identify research questions; in other instances they collaborate in the collection of empirical materials; and in still other instances they coauthor written accounts (Cahill et al., 2004; Lobestine et al., 2004; Percy-Smith and Weil, 2003; Theis, 2001; Young and Barrett, 2001). In my own research on youths' engagements with American car cultures (Best, 2006), the boundaries between researcher and researched blurred as I recruited undergraduate students from the university where I was teaching to serve as youth researchers. These youth researchers, whom I trained in qualitative research methods, were also insiders to the popular youth car scenes in California, where the study was conducted. They served as informants for me but also helped coordinate interviews and conducted and transcribed some of the interviews themselves. These insider youth researchers served as important sounding boards, often directing and redirecting the way I collected materials and the analysis I developed of their symbolic worlds.

In this volume, Stephani Etheridge Woodson, Elizabeth Chin, and Susan Driver each examine the possibilities of collaborative research projects in which youth are active in the research process. These researchers explicitly seek to create programs of research where youth serve as agents of knowledge about their own lives. Their work raises questions about the very basis on which we assign value to research. Do we and can we value knowledge created by children or youth in the same way we value knowledge generated by adults? (For those of us who spend much of our time in college classrooms this question is highly salient.) Chin asks, "If we value only what adults do, and define the worthwhile as being fundamentally adult, have we created a field of value from which children are barred by definition?" Susan Driver's essay, which focuses on "do-it-yourself media projects" by queer youth, can be seen as a theoretical intervention that attempts to wrestle with these very questions of value, knowledge, and representation. Her investigations are explicitly political in nature in that they enable young people to produce their own creative visions of sexuality, to be subjects of investigation and co-creators of ideas about their own situations and circumstances. Driver imagines this approach as a means by which queer youth might overcome their objectified status in social research, while also pushing adult researchers to reflect on how they undertake their craft and the assumptions with which they work. Driver notes, "studying queer youth compels reflexive forms of knowledge" that can engage "researchers in a process of dialogue, interpretation, and activism." Much in the same way, Woodson explores the promise of community-based performance collaborations with youth using visual methods (digital storytelling in this case) as a strategy to mobilize youth and promote greater community involvement among youth. Woodson sees these community performance collaborations, because they are visually based, as a means to disrupt the cultural and behavioral tropes—"child as cute," "child as innocent"—through which childhood is performed in a deeply polarized, age-segregated culture such as ours, and to reveal in a tangible way childhood as a social construct. Woodson sees community art performance as a relevant methodology that engages youth as knowing subjects, stating that "art is a way of knowing" that can promote democratic dialogue, social connection across differences, and social justice. "Community-based arts allow a group to express their way of life, interests, and anxieties both to outsiders and, not least of all, to themselves." This, according to Woodson, has particular significance for youth as a group since youth are often denied voice and excluded from the public life of their communities. Drawing from her ethnographic research on low-income children of color and their consumption practices, Elizabeth Chin's "Power-Puff Ethnography/Guerrilla Research: Children as Native Anthropologists" considers the specific challenges children pose to the edifice of anthropology when they are mobilized as "native anthropologists." Chin observes, "doing collaborative research with children challenges the assumption that to be an anthropologist is also to be a grown up." Chin argues that while children are largely defined as "pre-political, pre-sexual, pre-powerful, and pre-agential, treating them as co-researchers challenges [these] notions of childhood." Like Woodson's and Driver's essays, Chin's essay compels us to look beyond children as passive objects of study and instead see them as active producers of ideas.

But drawing youth into the social relations that produce knowledge in more active ways is far from uncomplicated. As Woodson reflects in this volume, "The nature of collaborative work is that it is messy and variable." Indeed, the mantra of "research for, by, and about," which had been so easily harnessed by feminist researchers (i.e., research *for* women, *by* women, and *about* women) as they generated a meaningful critique of social research on the grounds of its systematic exclusion and objectification of women, does not translate easily to youth given both the differences in cultural and communicative competencies between adults and children and the ethics and politics surrounding informed consent and children's rights as a protected class (Alderson, 2000). As child researcher Adele Jones cautions,

> There are good and there are bad ways for children to be engaged in research. "Good" research requires careful attention to epistemological and methodological issues and the adoption of a critical reflective approach to research practice. . . . Critical reflective practice in studies that involve children as researchers includes analysis of "adult"-self as researcher [and] scrutiny of theory. . . . reflection must be both precursor to children's involvement and also concurrent with children's involvement. (2004:115)

Critical and reflexive collaborative research projects in their varied forms open the possibility to engage youth and children in ways that destabilize power formations that are often cemented, whether intentionally or not, through our research undertakings. This is a point that Chin came to see in her own research, as children began to play increasingly central roles as researchers in her work: "In my own work with developing child researchers, I have had to seriously rethink the relationship between researcher and researched and critically understand my own investment in maintaining my expertise as a source of power and control over my young colleagues." Indeed, if we ignore these dimensions, we risk resecuring relations of domination through our research.

The Power to Define and Represent

How children and youth and their worlds are conceptualized, defined, and represented has emerged as a core concern for youth and childhood scholars as critical debates and dialogues with the New Childhood Studies has led to a turning inward to examine the research practices themselves and their role in constructing "children" and "adolescents" as distinct social groups and "childhood" and "adolescence" as distinct stages in the life course. Youth studies scholars Jones, Starkey, and Orme observe that "decisions with regard to research questions, the focus on inquiry and channels of dissemination are often shaped by dominant cultural representations of youth. These representations have tended to frame young people as, for instance, "troubled," "in trouble," "at risk," "less rational" or "delinquent." . . . much research has tended to rehearse, or even amplify, constructs of youth that are present in other cultural spheres such as politics and media" (2003:55–56). Similarly, Robyn Holmes (1998) notes that popular characterizations of children as "copycats" and "primitives," for instance, direct and influence how child researchers interact with children in the field, write their field notes, generate codes and categories for analysis, and write accounts of kids' everyday lives. For youth, this is arguably the legacy of early youth studies' ties to an emerging field of juvenile delinquency, and for younger children it is a legacy of early developmental perspectives. In many ways, consideration of these representational practices as they relate to the business of research reflects the postmodern turn in social science research and what some scholars have regarded as a crisis of representation (Lincoln and Denzin, 1994). In recent years far greater attention has been given by youth scholars to the discursive constructions of social reality, the productive powers of discourse, and the role of discourse as a mechanism of regulation for marginalized populations. Nancy Lesko, for example, asks in her book *Act Your Age: The Social Construction of Adolescence*, "What are the systems of ideas that make possible the adolescence that we see, think, feel, act upon?" (2001:9). Using Foucault's genealogy method, Lesko traces the discursive formation of adolescence in the sciences over the past century and its relationship to Western colonial rule. In a similar fashion, Nicholas Sammond's *Babes in Tomorrowland* (2005) traces the shifting conceptions of the American child in sociology, anthropology, and the child study movement of the past century. Sammond maps a set of distinct but complementary scholarly discourses about consumption, media effects, and citizenship that have circulated around the American child and through which the child has been socially constructed. Such critical approaches to the connection between power and knowledge created by the social sciences are similarly utilized by many of the contributors to this collection and might be situated within what Alison James and Adrian James (2004) have recently called the "cultural politics of childhood," a mode of analysis that focuses on the cultural processes and discourses through which the child and childhood are socially constructed and on the way children respond to, manage, and influence these cultural determinants.

Several contributors to this volume zero in on these conceptual and representational matters. They give pause, raise questions, and formulate alternatives as they differently consider that stretch of time before the researcher enters the field *and* the period after the researcher leaves the field and begins to make sense of her or his empirical materials and writes, mindful of the role of social sciences in disempowering youth and defining them in narrow and limiting ways. The legacy of adult-centered conceptual schemes remains with us, as many of the authors attest.

In this volume, Rebecca Raby and Sari Knopp Biklen explore key dilemmas that stem from the complex relationship between adult authority and the way we conceptualize and represent our research. Both authors implicitly raise the question of whether and under what conditions adults may authorize themselves to construct accounts of a group of people who not only sit in a position subordinate to their own but also are rarely given the opportunity to represent themselves. In her essay, "Across a Great Gulf? Conducting Research with Adolescents," Raby addresses the complex coordinates of power in research with children and adolescents as she considers the historical legacy of developmental models in the framing of research undertakings and the interpretations of research materials. As the first essay in the volume, Raby introduces us to an ongoing conversation shared among youth and child researchers about how we should undertake our craft. She says, "we must acknowledge our access to resources that most children and adolescents do not have, the danger of constructing them as objects, not subjects of study, and the need to be particularly attentive to the authority of the adult researcher's voice and interpretation in the research process" (this volume, ooo). Raby entertains the possible ways researchers might negotiate power and tensions arising from the shifting positions researchers occupy as they design research protocols and attempt to develop rapport, manage their outsider status, and respect young people's independent culture while also recognizing its embeddedness in adult culture.

Sari Knopp Biklen's "Trouble on Memory Lane: Adults and Self-Retrospection in Researching Youth" (the only essay in this volume that has been previously published) tackles many of these same questions as she examines memory as a concern for ethnographers who study young people. Biklen says that "an adult conducting research with young people is an outsider who may imagine insider status based on memories of adolescence" (this volume, ooo). Biklen demonstrates how the use of childhood memories as a rhetorical strategy regularly invoked by authors heightens the narrator's authority and authenticity as it creates a sense of "having been there." Biklen laments the limits of such a rhetorical move as she shows the ways such a device not only draws attention away from youth informants and their own accounts but also ignores power relations between adults and youth. Biklen reframes our understandings of memory, persuasively arguing that "memory is not a form of bias but a problematic that must be addressed in order to provide adequate attention to the youthful informant's legitimacy and authority as an interpreter of experience." Building from Biklen's insights, several of the contributors in this volume also attempt to unravel this treacherous terrain of memory, dispelling the authority of "having been there." Alyssa Richman's "The Outsider Lurking Online: Adults Researching Youth Cyberculture" also raises questions about the uses of memory by adults. Richman argues that adults lack an "intuitive knowledge" about the social organization of Internet spaces because they are unable to access the repository of youthful memories that materialize in other sites since most adults spent their youth without the Internet. Richman considers the complexities of this issue as she details the difficulty she had in trying to follow the template for online communication exchange between young people.

In Michael Ungar's, Marc Flacks's, and Yvonne Vissing's essays, conceptual concerns also take center stage. These authors identify shortcomings and offer alternatives as they explore how adult-centered perspectives have informed and shaped the topics they study. What is particularly noteworthy in Ungar's and Flacks's essays is that both authors attempt to identify and redress long-standing problems of research on youth stemming from the conceptual schemes researchers have historically used. Both authors take as their topics of inquiry subjects that have been studied extensively, but often in adult-centered ways and not from the perspectives and experiences of youth themselves. "Youth civic engagement," the subject of Flacks's essay, and "youth risk and resilience," the subject of Ungar's, are well-traveled roads, widely studied by social scientists. Advancing a contextually and culturally sensitive research protocol, Ungar explores ways to better understand the resilience of young people across cultures using more child-centered approaches. Ungar notes in this line that the "tendency to psychopathologize children's behavior within a Western discourse focused on illness has neglected to document the adaptive and health-enhancing nature of children's behaviors that are frequently strategically employed for their survival." Ungar proposes a model for overcoming this conceptual shortcoming and other methodological and conceptual failings through the "rigorous application of qualitative methods," recognizing this to be essential to understanding the multiple pathways to health for children facing war, abuse, cultural disintegration, and other calamities arising from deepening structural inequalities. Like Ungar, Flacks examines the methodology that underlies a much studied topic, youth civic (dis)engagement. How are young people's democratic engagements to be conceptualized, defined, and measured? "As with any social scientific problem, one cannot really begin to adequately address questions of causation and solution until one has ensured that the relevant data are reliable and valid," Flacks writes. To understand the complex, varied, and sometimes downright surprising ways youth engage in public life and think about their engagement, Flacks draws our attention to the importance of recognizing the shifting historical realities for youth as he steers us away from the reified conceptualization of "youth civic engagement" that has dominated much of the research on youth and public life. Flacks argues in this volume that "as structural and cultural forces conspire to reshape the experience of growing up, researchers need to rework not just our study designs and techniques of data collection but also our basic conceptions of youth/adulthood, our theories of how and why growing up is being transformed and what consequences this might have, and the questions we ask when analyzing our data."

Ungar and Flacks demonstrate the limits of previous work as they each

separately sketch alternative framings that might serve as guides to study
these topics in ways that yield more robust and nuanced understandings
of not only the subjects they consider but other subjects that are relevant
to the unfolding lives of young people. Both authors situate their topics
within broader structural changes—eroding economic opportunities and
a changing cultural logic in a postindustrial society for Flacks and a shifting global order for Ungar—and thus implicitly acknowledge the bundle
of social, political, and economic forces that serve as a backdrop for young
people's lives, forces that are often overlooked in youth studies but war-
rant our scrutiny.

Vissing's applied work on studying homeless youth also explores conceptual challenges that arise in research involving youth, in this case a
group of youth who are understudied and largely invisible. Vissing writes
in this volume, "the study of invisible populations of children and youth is
especially challenging because of the interface of complex structural, emotional, conceptual, and methodological issues." Vissing's essay centers on
homeless youth, a group whose experiences of homelessness differ significantly from their adult counterparts. For Vissing, a chief problem is that
most research attempting to study homelessness among youth has used
research templates that have emerged in studying adult homeless populations. The outcome, Vissing observes, is that homelessness among youth is
not only undercounted but also misunderstood. Vissing considers how
these conceptual difficulties and definitional ambiguities in the context of
applied research can be exacerbated by the demands, constraints, and
expectations of public funding sources.

Power and Politics of the Field

A central concern among qualitative researchers studying children and
youth has been understanding the social dynamics in the field. What happens in the field as we undertake the messy work of collecting empirical
materials: interviewing young people about the intimate details of their
lives and forging meaningful ties with them as we observe their activities
and goings-on? As a rule, qualitative practitioners recognize that gaining
acceptance, establishing trust, and developing rapport are central to the
ability to embed oneself within the lives and social worlds of those they
study and that this in turn yields richer and more complete understanding. While adult researchers select from a range of participant roles when

conducting ethnographic research in children and youth worlds, they also recognize the slippery slope in selecting the right roles. As Sari Biklen observes in this volume, "the adult's role as an outsider may prevent trust and decrease shared understanding between researcher and participant, depending on the salience of age."

Of all the methodological issues that emerge in studying youth and children and their worlds, the membership roles available to researchers and issues of access have arguably received the most significant and sustained attention by youth researchers. Patricia and Peter Adler (1998) in *Peer Power* consider at length the merits and pitfalls of the parent-as-researcher, what they see as a "naturally occurring role" since parents are usually already immersed in the routine activities that constitute their children's lives. They write, "parents can readily gain entry to the world of children through their own children. They can also capitalize on this 'complete membership role' by 'opportunistically' making the community of youth to which their children belong a focus of study" (19). Parents, they note, are often better able to sail past gatekeepers than are unknown adult researchers since parents are granted an almost automatic trust, at least at some level. While largely recognizing the promise of this research role, Adler and Adler also explore ethical considerations, the risk of role confusion, and the sense of betrayal that could be experienced in managing this "dual-research-membership focus" (20). Similarly, Gary Alan Fine (1987; Fine and Sandstrom 1988) and William Corsaro (1985, 2003) have explored the membership roles available to adult researchers, seeing "the friend" role in many instances as the most effective and realistic way to diminish adult authority in the field, while also being advantageous in other ways. Nancy Mandell (1988) in her research on preschool children adopted what she referred to as a "least-adult" role, an observational strategy characterized by minimizing one's authority as an adult through deep participation in children's interactional routines, distancing oneself from other adults, and refusing to invoke one's power as an adult. Mandell recognized that although the least-adult role heightened teachers' suspicions of her research intentions and legitimacy, more importantly it facilitated easy entry into preschoolers' peer worlds.

As many scholars have demonstrated, differences in the age of the group under study matter to which membership role is most feasible. Although Mandell's least-adult role can be quite effective in researching very young children, Fine and Sandstrom (1988) and Raby (this volume) note that trying to be too much like participants in an adolescent setting is likely to undermine the researcher's ability to develop rapport. In this case, the researcher runs the risk of being defined as a "wannabe," a most undesirable label within adolescent peer groups.

Gender and sexuality, race, ethnicity, and class also shape the membership roles researchers are able to adopt and the ability of the researcher to gain access and develop rapport with children and youth. Feminist researchers have noted the increased difficulties in studying girls' worlds in comparison to boys', for instance. The lives and culture of girls, because of their historical exclusion from public spaces, play out in far more private settings (e.g., girls' bedrooms) than those of boys, who generally have greater access to public spaces. This is often further compounded by the fact that the boundaries of girls' intimate and tightly knit peer groups are carefully guarded and often well protected from interlopers. As sociologists Angela McRobbie and Jennifer Garber rightfully observe, girls' lives are "well insulated" (1980:222). In her research investigating middle-school girls' friendship patterns, Valerie Hey details the difficulties she encountered in trying to gain access to the girls' world because of these very reasons, noting the "fragility of rapport" (1997:44). Hey's access to the girls' lives and their intricate friendship networks largely depended on a series of tradeoffs and exchanges, mostly of goods she provided them. Hey writes, "As a 'new girl' in the field and as a new girl at school I made mistakes . . . which taught me a great deal about how girls exercise power through the veto of exclusion" (46). Like other researchers, Hey had to contend with two different types of gatekeepers, the girls and then the teachers and administrators, who largely saw her research as "subversive" because it had been identified as "feminist research" by them early on in the study. Teachers and administrators assumed that anyone studying girls in a school setting was there to document the various injustices committed by the school against the girls. Interestingly, although Hey notes the girls' marginalization in school settings, her primary interest was in understanding girls as actors in their own right.

Membership roles, access, trust, and acceptance are differently discussed in several of the essay in this volume, all with attention to the dynamics of power and authority. C. J. Pascoe and Kathryn Gold Hadley both draw on Mandell's notion of the least-adult as they reflect on the membership roles and rapport-building strategies that they adopted. Drawing from ethnographic work on peer cultures in Taiwanese children's public kindergarten and first-grade classrooms in Taipei City, Hadley's essay, "Will the Least-Adult Please Stand Up? Life as "Older Sister Katy" in a Taiwanese Elementary School," examines how language difficulties and ethnic gaps shaped her ability to fully participate in the children's routines and private culture as a least-adult. She examines her ability to gain acceptance and develop rapport as "a linguistically challenged and culturally incompetent member" and the ways in which this reality in some instances allowed for and in other instances forestalled meaningful connection with the kids in the classroom and on the playground. Like Hadley's essay, several other essays revisit concerns adult researchers have raised in the study of children, with the aim of complicating these previous discussions about the least-adult as a legitimate and feasible participatory role for adults.

Other essays in the volume focus on the social organization of the research encounter, giving thoughtful consideration to the ways research relations mirror the very social relations under study. C. J. Pascoe's essay, "What If a Guy Hits on You? Intersections of Gender, Sexuality, and Age in Fieldwork with Adolescents," considers how sexuality mediates and illuminates researcher-respondent interactions in adolescence as she investigates the production of masculinity among teenage boys. She explores how sexuality organizes and flows through researcher-respondent interactions as she guides her readers through a world in which boys demonstrate their physical dominance through sexualized interactions with girls and storytelling contests about their sexual triumphs. She zeroes in on how boys defined her alternately as a possible sexual conquest and as an "honorary guy," thereby drawing her into the same sexualizing processes boys engage in within their own age group. Using Mandell's model of the least-adult, Pascoe examines how a woman studying all-male worlds can adopt what she refers to as a "least gender identity," defined in large part by minimizing her social status as a woman. Pascoe explores the consequences for developing rapport, gaining access to the masculine world of talk normally closed to women, and ultimately yielding more complete understandings of young men and the role masculinity plays in organizing their lives. Pascoe's reflections about her own fieldwork experiences demonstrate how research encounters themselves influence the worlds we study and hope to change in studying them.

While critical youth studies researchers have acknowledged as a general rule the authority the adult researcher holds, they also recognize the fluidity, complexity, and porousness of power in cultural fields where children and youth are concentrated. Sometimes the power of other adults leaves researchers with little negotiating power. This is a point that Madeline Leonard demonstrates in her essay, "With a Capital 'G': Gatekeepers and Gatekeeping in Research with Children," as she explores the ongoing influence of adult gatekeepers in the research process when the respondents are children. Drawing on two research projects involving children, Leonard explores the ways adults not only shape access to particular youth but also exercise influence over how we frame, define, and undertake our studies. As Leonard notes, "gatekeepers may sometimes be encountered when the respondents are adults, but their influence is much more extensive when children are the respondents." This fact requires a more intensive consideration of gatekeepers' role in mediating the research process and its outcomes. Leonard insightfully observes how these very negotiations both highlight and "reflect the ongoing power imbalance between adults and children in contemporary society." Leonard also explores situations in which researchers themselves must be moral gatekeepers, filtering the information we collect as it is presented to different adult audiences. Leonard considers long-held ideas about the "best interest of the child," and although she does not take for granted its meaning, she does identify situations in which researchers must sometimes invoke this standard. Hadley, too, examines gatekeepers, considering the gatekeeping role adults and children play in research involving children. Hadley shows how teachers, who typically operate as gatekeepers, can differently facilitate entry and rapport. For example, one teacher, who was a graduate student herself and sympathetic to Hadley's research aims, facilitated easy access and rapport in a way that other teacher gatekeepers, though interested and supportive of her research, did not. Hadley's research also details the ways youth themselves serve as powerbrokers, carefully policing the symbolic and physical boundaries of their worlds in ways that can either preclude or provide access.

This shifting dynamic of power that plays out between the researcher and the researched is also captured in Richman's essay, as she examines the roles adult researchers adopt in studying visual communities and online chat rooms composed of youth. As the Internet becomes an increasingly central aspect of contemporary life in the United States, particularly for young people, social researchers are beginning to recognize the importance of online research in the study of youth culture, Richman argues. This new terrain requires careful reflection and reexamination of the issues that arise when adults research youth in a setting where youth are far more likely to be navigational experts than are adults. Richman writes, "while those who study other sites of childhood research (e.g., schools, malls) bring their own expertise and memory work about the spaces, the relatively recent proliferation of online sites precludes first-hand adult knowledge of an Internet childhood." Her discussion compels us to revisit key debates surrounding the role of insider and outsider in research with youth. These are concerns that have long vexed qualitative researchers, and Richman, like other authors in this volume, reveals the malleability of the insider/outsider continuum along which we move. Like Richman, many of the contributors push us to move beyond the conventional either/or conceptualization of insider/outsider as we understand and strategize time spent in the field, showing how the insider/outsider relation is ultimately a fragile one, subject to change as interactions unfold. The essays in this volume, as they give attention to how we structure our time in the field and how participants also structure it for us, call on us to be sensitive to the shifting positions we occupy and the role context plays in generating these shifts.

Conclusion

The ethnographer John Van Maanen wrote in the foreword to Fine and Sandstrom's *Knowing Children* (the double entendre of the book's title should not be lost on us), "Ideology, proximity, concern and, of course, memory all contribute to what we make of our daily experience with children. While such practical theorizing about children rarely hardens into a formal sort, it does seem the case that most of us probably share the conceit that we understand children at least as well as they understand themselves. Such a conceit is not unlike one carried by cultural snobs everywhere who think of culture as something they have plenty of but others lack" (1988:7). In writing this, Van Maanen draws our attention to the ways in which the status of young people in broader American culture, and indeed in researchers' own culture, complicate the research we do with, for, and about them. As the essays in this collection address a variety of conceptual, practical, and ethical matters involved in studying young people, they examine conventional ways in which youth and children are known, the role our off-handed and everyday understandings of youth and children have played in how we proceed with our research, and the struggles and dilemmas that arise in such undertakings. All of the authors reflect on how they undertook the craft of qualitative research, from the framing of questions to experiences in the field to interpreting their materials. Nonetheless, *Representing Youth* does not provide a comprehensive investigation of methodological issues in studying youth and children. Indeed, such an undertaking is too vast for one volume. A number of considerations either have been addressed elsewhere or await critical comment. As with all volumes of this kind, certain themes are privileged over others, but not because they are somehow intrinsically more important. Certain obvious omission might be noted here: less attention is given to the analysis of empirical materials than to their collection, and interviewing strategies are less of a focus than participant observation. How researchers manage the ever-tightening institutional constraints of universities' institutional review boards, as protections for youth and children grow increasingly stringent in what Mark Cieslik and Gary Pollock (2002) see as the risk society of late modernity, warrants more serious attention and perhaps even action as youth researchers find themselves in situations where their research is forestalled or significantly redirected. Although attention is given here to some of the dynamic aspects of difference and power as they are refracted by race, gender, sexuality, and social class, the diversity of situations and settings in which these dynamics play out deserves further consideration and specification.

These points aside, the contributors in this volume identify concrete and innovative research strategies for studying youth and analyzing and representing young peoples' social experiences. They begin with an implicit awareness that the task of the reflexive researcher is to continue to flesh out the social dynamics of research, to develop more innovative ways of doing social research, and to understand more specifically how the social organization of research (re)produces the very hierarchies and inequities we seek to explain. In this sense, the arguments and insights drawn from these essays have meaning for not only the study of youth but the study of any group where social differences and social hierarchies structure the relationship between our reality and their own. As ethnographers Koro-Ljungberg and Greckhamer recently remarked, "researchers must acknowledge that disciplinary power, contests over labels, and methodological tensions always remain within any evolving field of research" (2005:302). True enough. It is my hope that we might all have something to gain from the lessons offered here.

NOTES

1. See, for example, Maira, 2002, and Olsen, 1997.

2. It is also interesting that during several of the years I conducted the prom research I lived in New York City, also a city with a large immigrant population. The difference, however, was the extent to which I engaged daily with immigrants. In New York City, I had limited genuine interaction with individuals who had migrated to the United States, in contrast to when I lived in Northern California.

3. A fairly significant body of research has been dedicated to matters related to interviewing children and young adults. See, for example, Eder and Fingerson, 2002; Fingerson, 2005, Irwin and Johnson, 2005; Keddie, 2004; and Nespor, 1998. For other strategies to collect accounts, see Hessler et al., 2003.

REFERENCES

Adler, P., and P. Adler. 1998. *Peer Power.* New Brunswick, NJ: Rutgers University Press.

Adler, P., and P. Adler. 1987. *Membership Roles in Field Research.* Newbury Park, CA: Sage.

Alderson, P. 2000. "Children as Researchers: The Effects of Participation Rights on Research Methodology." In *Research with Children: Perspectives and Practices,* ed. P. Christensen and A. James. London: Falmer.

Anderson, E. 1976. *A Place on the Corner.* Chicago: University of Chicago Press.

Arendell, T. 1997. "Reflections on the Researcher-Researched Relationship: A Woman Interviewing Men." *Qualitative Sociology* 20:3 (341–368).

Behar, R., and D. Gordon. 1995. *Women Writing Culture.* Berkeley: University of California Press.

Bennett, A., M. Cieslik, and S. Miles. 2003. *Researching Youth.* London: Palgrave.

Berger, J. 1977. *Ways of Seeing.* London: Penguin.

Berger, P., and T. Luckmann. 1967. *The Social Construction of Reality.* New York: Doubleday.

Berger, R., and R. Quinney. 2004. *Storytelling Sociology: Narrative as Social Inquiry.* Boulder, CO: Lynne Rienner.

Best, Amy L. 2006. *Fast Cars, Cool Rides: The Accelerating World of Youth and Their Cars.* New York: Routledge.

Best, Amy L. 2003. "Doing Race in the Context of Feminist Interviewing: Constructing Whiteness through Talk." *Qualitative Inquiry,* 9:6 (895–914).

Best, Amy L. 2000. *Prom Night: Youth, Schools, and Popular Culture.* New York: Routledge.

Blee, K. 2000. "White on White: Interviewing Women in U.S. White Supremacist

Groups." In *Racing Research, Researching Race: Methodological Dilemmas in Critical Race Studies,* ed. F. W. Twine and J. W. Warren. New York: New York University Press.

Blumer, H. 1969. *Symbolic Interactionism: Perspective and Method.* Englewood Cliffs, NJ: Prentice Hall.

Bogdan, R., and S. Taylor. 1984. *Introduction to Qualitative Methods: The Search for Meaning.* New York: Wiley/Interscience.

Bowles, G., and R. D. Klein. 1983. *Theories of Women's Studies.* London: Routledge and Kegan Paul.

Brooks, M. 2005. "Man to Man: A Body Talk between Male Friends." *Qualitative Inquiry,* 12:1 (185–207).

Brown, L. M. 1999. *Raising Their Voices: The Politics of Girls' Anger.* Cambridge, MA: Harvard University Press.

Cahill, C., E. Arenas, J. Contreras, J. Na, I. Rios-Moore, and T. Threatts. 2004. "Speaking Back: Voices of Young Urban Womyn of Color Using Participatory Action Research to Challenge and Complicate Representations of Young Women." In *All about the Girl: Culture, Power, and Identity,* ed. A. Harris. New York: Routledge.

Caputo, V. 1995. "Anthropology's Silent 'Others': A Consideration of Some Conceptual and Methodological Issues for the Study of Youth and Children Cultures." In *Youth Cultures: A Cross-Cultural Perspective,* ed. V. Amit-Talai and H. Wulff. London: Routledge.

Carspeken, P., and P. Cordiero. 1995. "Being, Doing, Becoming: Textual Interpretations of Social Identity and a Case Study." *Qualitative Inquiry,* 1:1 (87–109).

Chin, E. 2001. *Purchasing Power: Black Kids and American Consumer Culture.* Minneapolis: University of Minnesota Press.

Christensen, P., and A. James (eds.). 2000. *Research with Children: Perspectives and Practices.* London: Falmer.

Christensen, P., and A. Prout. 2002. "Working with Ethical Symmetry in Social Research with Children." *Childhood: A Global Journal of Child Research,* 9:4 (477–497).

Cieslik, M., and G. Pollock (eds.). 2002. *Young People in Risk Society: The Restructuring of Youth Identities and Transitions in Late Modernity.* London: Ashgate.

Clifford, J. 1983. "On Ethnographic Authority." *Representations,* 1:2 (118–146).

Collins, P. H. 1990. *Black Feminist Thought: Knowledge, Consciousness, and the Politics of Empowerment.* New York: Routledge.

Connolly, P. 1998. *Racism, Gender Identities, and Young Children: Social Relations in a Multi-Ethnic, Inner-City Primary School.* London: Routledge.

Corsaro, W. 2003. *We're Friends Right? Inside Kids' Culture.* Washington, DC: Joseph Henry Press.

Corsaro, W. 1997. *The Sociology of Childhood.* Thousand Oaks, CA: Pine Forge.

Corsaro, W. 1985. *Friendship and Peer Culture in the Early Years.* Norwood, NJ: Ablex.

Cree, V., H. Kay, and K. Tisdall. 2002. "Research with Children: Sharing the Dilemmas." *Child and Family Social Work,* 7:1 (47–57).

De Andrade, L. L. 2000. "Negotiating from the Inside: Constructing Racial and Ethnic Identity in Qualitative Research." *Journal of Contemporary Ethnography,* 29:3 (268–391).

Denzin, N. K. 1992. *Symbolic Interactionism and Cultural Studies: The Politics of Interpretation.* Oxford, UK: Blackwell.

Denzin, N., and Y. Lincoln (eds.). 2003a. *Strategies of Qualitative Inquiry.* Newbury Park, CA: Sage.

Denzin, N., and Y. Lincoln (eds.). 2003b. *The Landscape of Qualitative Research: Theories and Issues.* Newbury Park, CA: Sage.

DeVault, M. 1999. *Liberating Methods: Feminism and Social Research.* Philadelphia: Temple University Press.

DeVault, M. 1995. "Ethnicity and Expertise: Racial-Ethnic Knowledge in Sociological Research." *Gender and Society,* 9:5 (612–631).

DeVault, M. 1991. *Feeding the Family: The Social Organization of Caring as Gendered Work.* Chicago: University of Chicago Press.

DeVault, M. 1990. "Talking and Listening from Women's Standpoint: Feminist Strategies for Interviewing and Analysis." *Social Problems,* 37:1 (96–116).

Duneier, M. 2000. "Race and Peeing on Sixth Avenue." In *Racing Research, Researching Race: Methodological Dilemmas in Critical Race Studies,* ed. F. W. Twine and J. W. Warren. New York: New York University Press.

Duneier, M. 1999. *Sidewalk.* New York: Farrar, Straus, and Giroux.

Eder, D., C. C. Evans, and S. Parker. 1995. *School Talk: Gender and Adolescent Culture.* New Brunswick, NJ: Rutgers University Press.

Eder, D., and L. Fingerson. 2002. "Interviewing Children and Adolescents." In *Handbook of Interview Research,* ed. J. Gubrium and J. Holstein. Thousand Oaks, CA: Sage.

Edward, R., and P. Alldred. 1999. "Children and Young People's Views of Social Research: The Case of Research on Home-School Relations." *Childhood: A Global Journal of Child Research,* 6:2 (261–281).

Ellis, C. 2001. "Shattered Lives: Making Sense of September 11th and Its Aftermath." *Journal of Contemporary Ethnography,* 31 (375–410).

Ellis, C. 1995. *Final Negotiations: A Story of Love, Loss, and Chronic Illness.* Philadelphia: Temple University Press.

Emerson, J. P. 1970. "Behavior in Private Places: Sustaining Definitions of Reality of Gynecological Examinations." In *Recent Sociology,* ed. P. Dreitsel. New York: Macmillan.

Emerson, R. (ed.). 2001. *Contemporary Field Research: Perspectives and Formulations,* 2nd ed. Prospect Heights, IL: Waveland.

Emerson, R. M., R. I. Fretz, and L. Shaw. 1995. *Writing Ethnographic Fieldnotes.* Chicago: University of Chicago Press.

Fensternmaker, S., and C. West. 2002. *Doing Gender, Doing Difference: Inequality, Power, and Institutional Change.* New York: Routledge.

Fine, G. A. 1987. *With the Boys: Little League Baseball and Preadolescent Culture.* Chicago: University of Chicago Press.

Fine, G. A., and K. Sandstrom. 1988. *Knowing Children: Participant Observation with Minors.* Qualitative Research Methods 15. Newbury Park, CA: Sage.

Fine, M. 1994. "Working the Hyphens: Reinventing Self and Other in Qualitative Research." In *Handbook of Qualitative Research,* ed. N. Denzin and Y. Lincoln. Thousand Oaks, CA: Sage.

Fine, M. 1992. *Disruptive Voices: The Possibilities of Feminist Research.* Ann Arbor: University of Michigan Press.

Fine, M., and L. Weis. 1998. *The Unknown City: The Lives of Poor and Working-Class Young Adults.* Boston: Beacon.

Finc, M., L. Weis, L. C. Powell, and L. M. Wong (eds.). 1997. *Off White: Readings on Race, Power, and Society.* New York: Routledge.

Fingerson, L. 2005. " 'Yeah, Me Too!' Adolescent Talk Building in Group Interviews." *Sociological Studies of Children and Youth,* 11 (261–287).

Frankenberg, R. 1993. *White Women, Race Matters: The Social Construction of Whiteness.* Minneapolis: University of Minnesota Press.

Fraser, S., V. Lewis, S. Ding, M. Kellett, and C. Robinson (eds.). 2004. *Doing Research with Children and Young People.* London: Sage.

Gaines, D. 1990. *Teenage Wasteland: Suburbia's Dead End Kids.* Chicago: University of Chicago Press.

Gallagher, C. 2000. "White Like Me? Methods, Meaning, and Manipulation in the Field of White Studies." In *Racing Research, Researching Race: Methodological Dilemmas in Critical Race Studies,* ed. F. W. Twine and J. W. Warren. New York: New York University Press.

Geertz, C. 1973. *The Interpretation of Cultures.* New York: Basic Books.

Giroux, Henry, and Roger Simon (eds.). 1989. *Popular Culture, Schooling, and Everyday Life.* Westport, CT: Bergin and Garvey.

Glassner, B., and R. Hertz (eds.). 1999. *Qualitative Sociology as Everyday Life.* Thousand Oaks, CA: Sage.

Gordon, D. 1993. "Worlds of Consequence: Feminist Ethnography as Social Action." *Critique of Anthropology,* 13:4 (429–443).

Graebner, W. 1990. *Coming of Age in Buffalo: Youth and Authority in the Post-War Era.* Philadelphia: Temple University Press.

Graue, M. E., and D. Walsh. 1998. *Studying Children in Context: Theories, Methods, and Ethics.* Thousand Oaks, CA: Sage.

Grover, S. 2004. "Why Won't They Listen to Us? On Giving Power and Voice to

Children Participating in Social Research." *Childhood: A Global Journal of Child Research,* 11:1 (81–93).

Gubrium, J. F., and J. A. Holstein. 1997. *The New Language of Qualitative Method.* New York: Oxford University Press.

Guillamine, C. 1995. *Racism, Sexism, Power, and Ideology.* London: Routledge.

Harden, J., S. Scott, K. Backett-Millburn, and S. Jackson. 2000. "Can't Talk, Won't Talk? Methodological Issues in Researching Children." *Sociological Research Online,* 5:2 (84–94).

Harding, S. 1987. *Feminism and Methodology: Social Science Issues.* Bloomington: Indiana University Press.

Harrington, B. 2003. "The Social Psychology of Access in Ethnographic Research." *Journal of Contemporary Ethnography,* 32:5 (512–534).

Hessler, R., J. Downing, C. Beltz, A. Pelliccio, M. Powell, and W. Vale. 2003. "Qualitative Research on Adolescent Risk Using Email: A Methodological Assessment." *Qualitative Sociology,* 26:1 (111–124).

Hey, V. 1997. *The Company She Keeps: An Ethnography of Girls' Friendships.* Buckingham, UK: Open University Press.

Holmes, R. 1998. *Fieldwork with Children.* Thousand Oaks, CA: Sage.

Horowitz, Ruth. 1986. "Remaining an Outsider: Membership as a Threat to Research Rapport." *Urban Life,* 14 (409–430).

Irwin, L. G., and J. Johnson. 2005. "Interviewing Young Children: Explicating Our Practices and Dilemma." *Qualitative Health Research,* 15:6 (821–831).

James, A., and A. James. 2004. *Constructing Childhood: Theory, Policy, and Social Practice.* London: Palgrave.

James, A., C. Jenks, and A. Prout. 1998. *Theorizing Childhood.* Cambridge, UK: Polity.

Jans, M. 2004. "Children as Citizens: Towards a Contemporary Notion of Child Participation." *Childhood: A Global Journal of Child Research,* 11:1 (27–44).

Jones, Adele. 2004 "Involving Children and Young People as Researchers." In *Doing Research with Children and Young People,* ed. S. Fraser, V. Lewis, S. Ding, M. Kellett, and C. Robinson. London: Sage.

Jones, M., F. Starkey, and J. Orme. 2003. "Framing Youth: Reviewing Locally Commissioned Research on Young People, Drug Use, and Drug Education." In *Researching Youth,* ed. A. Bennett, M. Cieslik, and S. Miles. London: Palgrave.

Keddie, A. 2004. "Research with Young Children: The Use of an Affinity Group Approach to Explore the Social Dynamics of Peer Culture." *British Journal of Sociology of Education,* 25:1 (35–51).

Kenny, L. D. 2000. *Daughters of Suburbia: Growing Up White, Middle Class, and Female.* New Brunswick, NJ: Rutgers University Press.

Kondo, D. 1990. *Crafting Selves: Gender, Power, and Discourse of Identities in a Japanese Workplace.* Chicago: University of Chicago Press.

Koro-Ljungberg, and T. Greckhamer. 2005. "Strategic Turns Labeled 'Ethnography': From Description to Openly Ideological Production of Culture." *Qualitative Research,* 5:3 (285–306).

Kreiger, S. 1991. *Social Science and the Self.* New Brunswick, NJ: Rutgers University Press.

Lareau, A. 2003. *Unequal Childhoods: Race, Class, and Family Life.* Berkeley: University of California Press.

Lather, P. 1993. "Fertile Obsession: Validity after Post-Structuralism." *Sociological Quarterly,* 34:4 (673–693).

Lesko, N. 2001. *Act Your Age: The Cultural Construction of Adolescence.* New York: Routledge.

Leyshon, M. 2002. "On Being 'in the Field': Practice, Progress, and Problems in Research with Young People in Rural Areas." *Journal of Rural Studies,* 18:2 (179–191).

Liebow, E. 1967. *Tally's Corner.* Boston: Little, Brown.

Lincoln, Y., and N. Denzin. 1994. "The Fifth Moment." In *Handbook of Qualitative Research,* ed. N. Denzin and Y. Lincoln. Thousand Oaks, CA: Sage.

Lobestine, L., Y. Pereira,, J. Whitley, J. Robles, Y. Soto, J. Sergeant, D. Jimenez, E. Jimenez, J. Ortiz, and S. Corino. 2004. "Possible Selves and Pasteles: How a Group of Mothers and Daughters Took a London Conference by Storm." In *All about the Girl: Culture, Power, and Identity,* ed. A. Harris. New York: Routledge.

Lofland, J., and L. H. Lofland. 1995. *Analyzing Social Settings.* Belmont, CA: Wadsworth.

Long, J. 1999. *Telling Women's Lives: Subject, Narrator, Reader, Text.* New York: New York University Press.

Lugones, M., and E. Spelman. 1983. "Have We Got a Theory for You! Feminist Theory, Cultural Imperialism, and the Demand for 'the Woman's Voice.'" *Women's Studies International Forum,* 6 (573–581).

Maira, Sunaina Marr. 2002. *Desis in the House: Indian American Youth Culture in New York City.* Philadelphia: Temple University Press.

Mandell, Nancy. 1988. "The Least-Adult Role in Studying Children." *Journal of Contemporary Ethnography,* 16 (433–467).

Marcus, G. 1998. *Ethnography through Thick and Thin.* Princeton, NJ: Princeton University Press.

McRobbie, A. 1991. *Feminism and Youth Culture: From Jackie to Just Seventeen.* London: Unwin Hyman.

McRobbie, A., and J. Garber. 1980. "Girls and Subcultures." In *Resistance through Ritual: Youth Subcultures in Post-war Britain,* ed. S. Hall and T. Jefferson. London: Routledge and Kegan Paul.

Minh-ha, T. T. 1989. *Women, Native, Other: Writing Postcoloniality and Feminism.* Bloomington: Indiana University Press.

Miron, L. F., and J. X. Inda. 2000. "Race as a Kind of Speech Act." *Cultural Studies: A Research Annual,* 5 (85–107).

Mueller, A. 1995. "Beginning in the Standpoint of Women: An Investigation of the Gap between Cholas and 'Women in Peru.'" In *Knowledge, Experience, and Ruling Relations: Studies in the Social Organization of Knowledge,* ed. Marie Campbell and Ann Manicom. Toronto: University of Toronto Press, 96–105.

Nairn, K., J. Munro, and A. Smith. 2005. "A Counter-Narrative of a Failed Interview." *Qualitative Research,* 5:2 (221–244).

Neilsen, J. M. 1990. *Feminist Research Methods: Exemplary Readings in the Social Sciences.* Boulder, CO: Westview.

Nespor, J. 1998. "The Meaning of Research: Kids as Subjects and Kids as Inquirers." *Qualitative Inquiry,* 4:3 (369–388).

Norum, K. 2000. "Black (w)Holes: A Researcher's Place in Her Research." *Qualitative Sociology,* 23:3 (319–340).

Oakley, A. 1981. "Interviewing Women: A Contradiction in Terms." In *Doing Feminist Research,* ed. H. Roberts. London: Routledge and Kegan Paul.

Olsen, L. 1997. *Made in America: Immigrant Students in Our Public Schools.* New York: New Press.

Patai, D. 1991. "U.S. Academics and Third World Women: Is Ethical Research Possible?" In *Women's Worlds: The Feminist Practice of Oral History,* ed. Sherna B. Gluck and Daphne Patai. New York: Routledge.

Percy-Smith, B., and S. Weil. 2003. "Practice-Based Research as Development: Innovation and Empowerment in Youth Intervention Initiatives Using Collaborative Action Inquiry." In *Researching Youth,* ed. A. Bennett, M. Cieslik, and S. Miles. London: Palgrave.

Perry, P. 2002. *Shades of White: White Kids and Racial Identities in High School.* Durham, NC: Duke University Press.

Proweller, A. 1998. *Constructing Female Identities: Meaning Making in an Upper-Middle-Class Youth Culture.* Albany: State University of New York Press.

Punch, S. 2002. "Research with Children: The Same or Different from Research with Adults?" *Childhood: A Global Journal of Child Research,* 9:3 (321–341).

Qvortrup, J. 1994. "Childhood Matters: An Introduction." In *Childhood Matters: Social Theory, Practice, and Politics,* ed. J. Qvortrup, M. Bardy, G. Sgritta, and H. Wintersberger. Aldershot, UK: Avebury.

Reich, J. 2003. "Pregnant with Possibility: Reflections on Embodiment, Access, and Inclusion in Field Research." *Qualitative Sociology,* 26:3 (351–367).

Reinharz, S. 1992. *Feminist Methods in Social Research.* New York: Oxford University Press.

Reisman, C. K. 1987. "When Gender Is Not Enough: Women Interviewing Women." *Gender and Society,* 1:2 (172–207).

Roberts, H. 1981. *Doing Feminist Research.* London: Routledge and Kegan Paul.

Roman, L., and L. Christian-Smith (eds.). 1989. *Becoming Feminine: The Politics of Popular Culture.* London: Falmer.

Russel, L. 2005. "It's a Question of Trust: Balancing the Relationship between Students and Teachers in Ethnographic Fieldwork." *Qualitative Research*, 5:2 (181–199).

Russel y Rodriguez, M. 1998. "Confronting Anthropology's Silencing Praxis: Speaking of/from a Chicana Consciousness." *Qualitative Inquiry*, 4:1 (15–40).

Sammond, N. 2005. *Babes in Tomorrowland: Walt Disney and the Making of the American Child, 1930–1960.* Durham, NC: Duke University Press.

Schwartzman, H. 2001. *Children and Anthropology: Perspectives for the Twenty-First Century.* Westport, CT: Bergin and Garvey.

Shope, J. 2005. "You Can't Cross a River without Getting Wet: A Feminist Standpoint on Dilemmas of Cross-Cultural Research." *Qualitative Inquiry*, 12:1 (163–184).

Skelton, T., and G. Valentine (eds.). 1998. *Cool Places: Geographies of Youth Culture.* London: Routledge.

Smith, D. 1990a. *Texts, Facts, and Femininity: Exploring the Relations of Ruling.* New York: Routledge.

Smith, D. 1990b. *The Conceptual Practices of Power: A Feminist Sociology of Knowledge.* Boston: Northeastern University Press.

Smith, D. 1987. *The Everyday World as Problematic: A Feminist Method.* Boston: Northeastern University Press.

Stacey, J. 1988. "Can There Be a Feminist Ethnography?" *Women's Studies International Forum*, 11 (21–27).

Stack, C. 1996. "Writing Ethnography: Feminist Critical Practice." In *Feminist Dilemmas in Fieldwork*, ed. D. Wolf. Boulder, CO: Westview.

Stanley, B., and J. Sieber (eds.). 1992. *Social Research on Children and Adolescents.* Newbury Park, CA: Sage.

Theis, J. 2001. "Participatory Research with Children in Vietnam." In *Children and Anthropology: Perspectives for the Twenty-First Century*, ed. H. Schwartzman. Westport, CT: Bergin and Garvey.

Thorne, B. 1993. *Gender Play: Girls and Boys in School.* New Brunswick, NJ: Rutgers University Press.

Thorne, B. 1983. "Political Activist as Participant Observer: Conflicts of Commitment in a Study of the Draft Resistance Movement of the 1960s." In *Contemporary Field Research: A Collection of Readings*, ed. R. Emerson. Prospect Heights, IL: Waveland.

Tierney, W. G. 2002. "Writing Matters." *International Journal of Qualitative Studies in Education*, 15:4 (427–430).

Tierney, W. G. 1998. "Life History's History: Subjects Foretold." *Qualitative Inquiry*, 4:1 (49–70).

Twine, F. W., and J. W. Warren (eds.). 2000. *Racing Research, Researching Race: Methodological Dilemmas in Critical Race Studies.* New York: New York University Press.

Van Ausdale, D., and J. R. Feagin. 2002. *The First R: How Children Learn Race and Racism.* New York: Rowman and Littlefield.

Vanderstaay, S. 2005. "One Hundred Dollars and a Dead Man: Ethical Decision-Making in Ethnographic Fieldwork." *Journal of Contemporary Ethnography,* 34:4 (371–409).

Van Maanen, J. (ed.). 1995. *Representation in Ethnography.* London: Sage.

Van Maanen, J. 1988. *Tales of the Field.* Chicago: University of Chicago Press.

Vidal-Ortiz, S. 2004. "On Being a White Person of Color: Using Autoethnography to Understand Puerto Ricans' Racialization." *Qualitative Sociology,* 27:2 (179–203).

Visweswaran K. 1997. *Fictions of Feminist Ethnography.* Minneapolis: University of Minnesota Press.

Waksler, F. C. (ed.). 1991. *Studying the Social Worlds of Children: Sociological Readings.* London: Falmer.

Wesley, J. 2005. "Negotiating Myself: The Impact of Studying Female Exotic Dancers on a Feminist Researcher." *Qualitative Inquiry,* 12:1 (146–162).

Whyte, W. F. 1955. *Street Corner Society.* Chicago: University of Chicago Press.

Williams, B. 1996. "Skinfolk, Not Kinfolk: Comparative Reflections of the Identity of Participant Observation in Two Field Situations. In *Feminist Dilemmas in Fieldwork,* ed. D. Wolf. Boulder, CO: Westview.

Willis, P. 1977. *Learning to Labour.* Aldershot, UK: Saxon House.

Wolf, D. (ed.). 1996. *Feminist Dilemmas in Fieldwork.* Boulder, CO: Westview.

Young, L., and H. Barrett. 2001. "Adapting Visual Methods: Action Research with Kampala Street Children." *Area,* 33:2 (141–152).

Yuen, F. C. 2004. "It Was Fun . . . I Liked Drawing My Thoughts: Using Drawing as Part of the Focus Group Process with Children." *Journal of Leisure Research,* 36:4 (461–482).

Zavella, P. 1996. "Feminist Insider Dilemmas: Constructing Ethnic Identity with Chicana Informants." *Feminist Dilemmas in Fieldwork,* ed. D. Wolf. Boulder, CO: Westview.

Part I

Framing Youth
Definitional Boundaries and Ambiguities

Chapter 1

Across a Great Gulf?
Conducting Research with Adolescents

Rebecca Raby

Over the past two decades there has been an increase in reflection on, and engagement with, children's active involvement in research projects, fueled by the recognition that young people are social actors who have important things to tell us about their lives. This work comes primarily, though not exclusively, from those within the new sociology of childhood (e.g., Christensen and James 2000a, Fraser et al. 2004, Holmes 1998, James, Jenks, and Prout 1998; Mayall 2000). I enter into these discussions by focusing on adolescence, with specific attention to questions of distance and power. Our conceptualizations of adolescence influence how we approach research on or with teenagers. This chapter concentrates on such conceptualizations as they relate to perceptions of distance between adults and young people, reflecting on such distance in terms of power and inequality. Must adults cross a "great gulf" of development, culture, and inequality in order to learn about the lives of adolescents? If so, what tools might assist us?

First, I consider the role of developmentalism in research with young people, a position that implies that there is a distance between adults and young people but that this distance is negotiable through the position of the knowing adult. Recently, researchers in critical psychology and the new sociology of childhood have been critical of developmental approaches for homogenizing young people across cultural, gender, and economic locations, constructing them as passive and producing them as inherently incomplete compared to the fully developed adult (Caputo 1995, Dannefer 1984, Graue and Walsh 1998, James, Jenks, and Prout 1998, Lesko 1996, Mayall 2000). Yet when we attempt to work with young people in research, do we implicitly rely on developmental logic as we adjust our language, methods, and analysis to presumptions of age (Mauthner 1997, O'Kane 2000)? Is there a developmental distance to cross in research with adolescents, and can it be done without constructing them as objects of research?

Second, it has been argued that there is a cultural gap between adults and young people because children and teenagers occupy distinct cultural locations from those of adults, locations in part defined through inequality but also through the institutionalization of age-based distinctions (James, Jenks, and Prout 1998). How do we accommodate this distinct position in research without assuming that we can directly access this culture or approaching adolescents as entirely Other (James, Jenks, and Prout 1998, Lesko 1996, Morrow and Richards 1996)? In addressing this latter question, I specifically consider how research with adolescents is similar to, and different from, research with those who occupy other kinds of marginalized identity positions and how these positions complicate the shifting ground of insider-outsider statuses.

The category of adolescence, in itself, can be considered a legacy of developmental approaches. Yet historians and constructionists situate adolescence as a predominantly twentieth-century phenomenon that has taken on significant cultural meaning in the North American context (Adams 1997, Best 2000, Lesko 1996). Adolescence is perceived as a distinct category, one that is part of, but separate from, childhood. It is constructed through distinct discourses, representations, and expectations, which suggests a need for researchers to reflect on the specific location of teenagers. At times in this chapter I discuss children and adolescents together, occasionally referring to them collectively as "young people." At other times, I distinguish between the two groups in order to explore adolescence as a unique social location. Finally, this is not a "how-to" essay that comprehensively addresses specific research methods; rather, it presents a broader discussion of distance and power in research about and with teenagers.

Addressing Development: Blueprints and Explanations

Developmental approaches commonly typologize changes from infancy to adulthood into a series of discrete steps or stages at the physical, cognitive, and emotional levels.[1] As Hogan explains, "If there is a core mission in the field of developmental psychology, it is to understand the processes of change, with age, in the psychological functioning of individuals" (2005: 24). From this position, young people's development of competencies can be charted, compared, and addressed in instances of "deficiency" (or, commonly in the case of adolescents, instances of risk). For the most part, developmental research has been conducted on children and "has not sought to understand children's subjective experience" (Hogan 2005:22), with young people's reports generally presumed to be less reliable than adults' (Hogan 2005). An underlying implication is that young people are inherently incomplete as they progress toward adulthood (Mayall 2000) and that adults know and understand children and teenagers much better than young people know and understand themselves (Lesko 1996). Similarly, John Morss explains that developmental approaches presume unidirectional, progressive change whereby adults are framed as "more rational or complex in their thinking than children" (1996:49). Adults are thus assumed to be able to knowledgeably conduct reliable research on young people and explain the results.

From such a position, a developmental gulf between adults and adolescents is not necessarily a cause for concern; the researcher is an outsider who can know young people. For example, extensive research has identified "normal" patterns of development, which can then be drawn upon when doing research with both children and adolescents. This knowledge can thus become a *blueprint* for designing programs of research with children and adolescents and later become an *explanation* for their behavior. Thus, if a researcher designs a survey for seven-year-olds and omits any questions that are thought to be inaccessible to seven-year-olds because they require abstract thinking, then developmental knowledge has been used as a blueprint. Similarly, if a young person has trouble with a question about how their experiences of being a child compare to those of their parents, this difficulty may be explained as childhood egocentricity, undeveloped language skills, or undeveloped abilities to perform abstract thought, thus drawing on developmental theory for explanation. In reflecting on the process of conducting interviews with adolescents, Weber, Miracle, and Skehan (1994) advise readers on how to interview adolescents based on their developmental location. For example, they suggest that chronological age should direct how a questionnaire is to be constructed. They also caution that "an interviewee experiencing emotional conflict (associated with adolescence) may project this conflict onto the interviewer" (43). Developmental logic thus filters what information is collected and, in turn, how it is explained.

Such an approach also has limitations, however. The concern is that researchers assume developmental features to be inevitable and universal. These features therefore become a blueprint assumed to adequately discover knowledge about young people. "Facts" of childhood and adolescence are thus produced through a particular regime of domination (Adams 1997, Lesko 1996, 2002). Rather than an active agent with a unique social location and life path to share and reflect upon, the participant is then, first and foremost, an object of analysis that serves as an example of a previously established category (Hogan 2005) and evidence to confirm models (Graue and Walsh 1998). Individual, cultural, historical, and contextual specificity are elided (Morrow and Richards, 1996), and the child's potential involvement in the research process is compromised. Through such an approach it may be difficult to take children seriously as social actors, and their lives are potentially misunderstood as "data collected from children," which "may be quite out of line with what the children meant" (Morrow and Richards 1996:98).

Alternatives?

How can researchers mitigate against a tendency to explain young people's experiences through such blueprints and through our own social location of adults who have finished "growing up"? Do we reject developmental findings altogether? Some researchers working within the new sociology of childhood argue that any gulf between young people and adults is a result of adults' cultural assumptions about children and adolescents, social inequalities, and young people's negotiation of such assumptions and inequalities. For example, Fraser (2004) argues that "child-friendly" research techniques are really participant-friendly techniques, "not 'friendly' because they are relevant to a developmental stage but because they have been negotiated between the researcher and researched" (24). Thus, vocabulary and the research process must make sense to both the young person and the researcher, with "special techniques" as negotiated compromises. Fraser is rightly concerned that "*any* theoretical framework which makes predictions and which lies outside the direct experience of the child may be imposed" (23). From this position, no assumptions should be made in advance.

Alternatively, a variant of developmentalism can be used as a *flexible guide* rather than a blueprint. As such, developmental models can be used to recognize that research participants within certain contexts are at ages that may roughly indicate language, experience, and cognitive skills that may guide the creation of interview questions, questionnaires, experiments, or interactive research tools. In this way we can draw on generalized knowledge that has been created about young people's locations without letting this knowledge rigidly determine tools to shape a study, interact with participants, or interpret what young people say and do. For example, recurring patterns in the skills of twelve-year-old boys from suburban North America can guide research with similar cohorts of twelve-year-old boys. Thus, we draw on research that has come before us, but carefully, thoughtfully, strategically, and critically, as we try to understand and engage with young people's lives through means that are valuable and accessible to those young people themselves.

A reader might now pause to wonder whether constructionist and developmental positions are nonetheless incompatible, with one embedded in a positivist tradition and the other in critical interpretivism. Hogan (2005) has pointed to areas of compatibility, arguing for example that although the universalism and determinism of developmental approaches is problematic, attention to context is not incompatible with them and that the meaning of life experiences to those involved can also be explored. More theoretically, cultural studies icon Stuart Hall contends that the material world is always both filtered through, and constituted by, its representation (Hall 1996). But rather than suggesting that "nothing exists outside of discourse," he argues that "nothing *meaningful* exists outside of discourse" (Hall, in Jhally 1997). Such a view opens up a space in which the developmental and constructionist positions can loosely coexist. One can argue that concrete changes do indeed occur as children grow up, changes that can be framed as linguistic, cognitive, physical, emotional, and/or psychological. Yet we do not have transparent access to these material changes; they are always filtered through our cultural, historical, linguistic, and theoretical locations. Bodies are part of the material world but embedded in the social, so how we think about bodies shifts contextually (Morgan and Scott 1993). Furthermore, a constructionist position recognizes that features of childhood and adolescence have been shaped, identified, and given priority within our cultural landscape, a landscape that includes developmental approaches whose dominance has shaped the very skills and experiences of young people involved in research (Caputo 1995, Lesko 1996). Young people may be in different cognitive locations than adults, for example, but it is how (or whether) such differences get shaped, prioritized, framed, or represented that concerns researchers and, in turn, influences how researchers need to work with young people. From this position, developmental findings can be considered relevant and valuable to working with children and adolescents *within this particular sociohistorical moment,* with researchers also attentive to the potential homogenizing effects of our interpretations and the way knowledges in themselves construct how we see children and adolescents.

Research across Cultural Difference?

Researchers such as Fraser (2004), James, Jenks, and Prout (1998), Lesko (1996), and Mandell (1988) emphasize a separate cultural location for children and adolescents and/or emphasize power differences between adults and young people as much more relevant than development. Do culture and inequality thus entail two other great gulfs that adult researchers face in their work with young people? What are some ways for researchers to negotiate adolescents' distinct cultures while recognizing their embeddedness in wider social structures, for example? And how is such negotiation complicated by young people's marginality?

James, Jenks, and Prout (1998) suggest that research on children has conceptualized the child in four distinct ways, each influencing how research is conducted with them: the socially developing child, the tribal child, the minority child, and the socially constructed child. I will draw on this typology to frame the following discussion of adolescent cultures and marginality. The model of the "socially developing child" is embedded in a developmental process in which young people's abilities gradually develop toward the ideal norm of adulthood. This conceptualization has already been discussed, although it seems more salient in reflecting on childhood than adolescence. The model of the "tribal child," in contrast, "acknowledges children's different social status [from adults] in celebration of the relative autonomy of the cultural world of children" (James, Jenks, and Prout 1998:180). The "tribal child" concept recognizes that young people develop their own hierarchies, uses of language, humor, rituals, and so forth, all of which contribute to the creation of their independent, separate cultures. This approach has been particularly valuable in ethnographic research that studies children's cultures (Punch 2002), although the term "tribal child" also invokes a conceptualization of children's cultures as Other: different, separate, exotic, mysterious, and potentially in need of control. It is within this conceptualization of separate cultures that adolescent subcultures have received a fair bit of research attention (e.g., Hebdige 1979, Leblanc 2001, McRobbie 1978, Widdicombe and Wooffitt 1995). As subcultures have tended to be marked by visible symbols and actions, this inclination has some logic to it. Although earlier subcultures theorists in particular have a legacy of speaking *for* adolescents (France 2004), some work on subcultures has been "from the inside" and committed to young people's self-representations (e.g., Leblanc 2001).

Similar to the model of the social developing child, the "tribal child" model thus provides a lens through which research with or on children and adolescents is organized. Consider Nancy Mandell's well-known, innovative research role of the "least-adult" (1988). The least-adult role involves participant observation with children through attempting to become an insider, or as "least-adult" as possible. Through this research role, "the researcher suspends all adult-like characteristics except physical size" (Mandell 1988:435), and even physical size is minimized. Mandell draws on Meadian research approaches to suggest that by employing such techniques, children are treated as social members who have knowledge that we need to learn. She argues that the exchange of meaning is of key importance to research and to developing joint action, which is possible through such techniques, even when children and adults experience such different social worlds. Notably, however, the least-adult role has rarely been used when researching the lives of teenagers, a pattern that will be examined shortly.

Mandell (1988) has provided us with insight into children's distinct relationships with one another. Alternatively, James, Jenks, and Prout (1998) caution that the tribal child model may create a false gap between adults' and children's social worlds and is in danger of treating young people's cultures as separate and exotic. Furthermore, this position elides the connections between young people's cultures and adults', in that it overlooks how deeply young people's lives are delimited through adult social structures. As Valerie Hey observes in her work on friendships among adolescent girls in England (1997), young people may create a social world out of language, for example, but the language that is drawn upon emerges from the wider, adult-involved world. The organization of time, the allocation of resources, the rule of law, and architectural structures are all aspects of adult culture that directly affect the lives of young people (see, e.g., Amit-Talai 1995 on the role of schools in shaping peer culture).

Exploring the tribal child model through ethnographic approaches also has some interesting implications in terms of power. Fine and Sandstrom (1988) remind us that although we may think we come to know young people's worlds and thinking, we may not actually do so, which suggests that their worlds are not wholly accessible. Also, young people are experts in and remain gatekeepers of their own cultures. Other scholars feel that investigating the tribal child through a least-adult approach downplays the power differentials that exist between young people and adults. While children may warm to an adult who is a participant observer in the role of least-adult, this adult will always be in a position that sets her or him apart from the participants: the adult usually has access to institutional resources and decides how to analyze and present findings, and the adult may always leave (Robinson and Kellett 2004). Even in cases where the researcher draws on techniques such as participant action research or feminist research methods to redress such imbalances (discussed below), such inequality remains present because the researcher is the one with the ultimate choice about how to represent others.

In contrast to the "tribal child," the concept of the "minority-group child" envisions children "as competent participants in a shared, but adult-centred world" (James, Jenks, and Prout 1998:184), a world in which they are oppressed. The minority-group child is a participant in the wider adult culture, but in a minority role within that culture—acknowledged but not given full status or influence. This position seems particularly relevant to adolescents, who are perceived to be on the threshold of adulthood. It recognizes power inequalities that these young people experience and recognizes them as embedded within broader institutional structures, but it downplays their agency as participants within this adult culture and the possibility that young people have their own cultures. Morrow and Richards argue that this position has failed to adequately address "the differences between adult researchers and child subjects in terms of social status" (1996:100), for from such a position, research with children and adolescents can be understood as quite similar to that with adults.

James, Jenks, and Prout's (1998) final category of the "socially constructed child" recognizes that there is no essential child but, rather, that young people are part of shifting social structures. They argue that children and adolescents are constructed through history, material conditions, and dominant discourses. Regarding research, this approach suggests that adults and children are similar as research subjects but that children have different (rather than inferior) knowledge, abilities, and areas of strength that our research methods must address. This position brings us back to our engagement with developmental approaches. For example, through experience, social location, and/or age, young people may have particular skills in drawing, storytelling, or journaling. Adjustments in methods are not about addressing developmental deficits, therefore, but about addressing strengths. The model of the socially constructed child is advocated by James, Jenks, and Prout for its recognition that young people are shaped by structural forces and are not inherently undeveloped or inadequate cultural participants. Rather, they are creative agents with unique contributions to offer: both in shaping their own cultures within wider structures and in shaping those wider structures themselves.

Power and Inequality

A common feature to the minority-child and socially constructed child is an emphasis on power and inequality. Some scholars consider inequality between young people and adults to be harmless and necessary. James Scott asserts, "The asymmetry of power in this situation is extreme— hence the possibility for abuses—but it is typically benign and nurturant rather than exploitative, and it is a biological given" (1990:82). As already noted, others see such inequalities as problematic and see attention to them in research as vital. There are inequalities of representation, size, access to resources, and decision making, for instance, all of which suggest that there are indeed vast differences between adults and young people that must be bridged in research. As Lansdown (1994) suggests, children are vulnerable because they lack political and economic power, and, despite the UN Convention on the Rights of the Child, they frequently lack civil rights in practice. This vulnerability in turn affects how children get treated in research projects, both for and with them, an issue addressed by those studying research with children (e.g., Christensen and James 2000a, Graue and Walsh 1998, James, Jenks, and Prout 1998) more so than those studying research with adolescents.

With adolescence, power relations may become more complicated because teenagers are in a social position that shifts frequently between areas of dependence and independence. Furthermore, adolescents may be seen to be particularly powerful in societies that value and celebrate youth (Danesi 2003), and adult anxieties about the perceived dominance and influence of adolescent subcultural peer groups (such as gangs) may suggest to adults that adolescents are not unequal to them. Yet in research with adolescents, young people's dependence, low social status, lack of access to institutional resources, and different social skills tip the balance in favor of the researcher.[2] Adolescence is a subject position heavily laden with normative assumptions and social meaning (Griffin 1993, Lesko 1996). While youth is valorized in North American culture, teenagers are routinely subject to discourses that construct them as being at-risk, as social problems, and as incomplete, discourses that are in turn used in their regulation and control (particularly in schools) and that provide them with little room in which to represent themselves (Griffin 1993, Lesko 1996, Raby 2002). France suggests the most dominant assumption regarding youth is that they are a social problem (2004). Adolescents thus have similarities with other marginalized groups in that, as we have seen, there is a potential separateness to them, despite their embeddedness in wider cultures, and discourses circulating about them deepen that marginalization.

Adolescence, however, is obviously occupied as a temporary position, a factor that potentially complicates it. On the one hand, if youth are perceived to be occupying a temporary "irrationality" on the way to what they will become, then their current position is marginal by its very negation. If what teenagers *will be* is what is important, then how they are constructed in the present is significantly less so, and a gap with adults is greater. On the other hand, adults' concern with this process of becoming may also decrease adolescent marginality because young people are viewed through a lens that sees them as adults-to-be. Their location in the present is of vital, central concern because it *shapes* what they will become, which in turn may shrink a perceived gulf between adults and teenagers.

There is also a danger in framing structural inequalities in terms of young people's vulnerability, victimhood, and incompetence, all of which ignore their agency, fail to identify the ways that children and adolescents control access to their worlds, and undermine the ability (and perceived ability) of young people to represent themselves. Furthermore, although such inequalities are important to consider in conducting research with young people, we cannot assume that we know how they will play out across contexts. The diversity of structural locations *within* childhood and adolescence complicate easy assumptions about the relations of dominance and subordination they occupy. We must be cautious not to assume we know in advance what configurations that power will take.

Identity and Insider-Outsider Distinctions

I have examined positions that explore a potential gulf between research-ers and young people of development, culture, and power. With each of these disparities, the focus is on what separates the adult researcher from the child and adolescent participants. In the remainder of this chapter, I discuss these differences through the lens of insider-outsider distinctions, starting from the position that although developmental, cultural, and power differentials may lead to an understanding of age as an identity location that separates adults, children, and teenagers, age is one identity among many others that people may have in common.

Subjectivity provides us with a sense of self and a site through which to make "sense of our relation to the world" (Brah 1996:123), and identity is integral to this sense of self. Stuart Hall (1996) argues that we are consti-tuted through shared, constructed, available subject positions with which we identify in order to give our unstable identities coherence (also see Brah 1996). Identity thus arises through identifications with (and against) other people, based on shared characteristics that are often presumed to be essential, but need not be: "Identities are thus points of temporary attachment to the subject positions which discursive practices construct for us" (Hall 1996:6). The experience of identity not only is the configura-tion of a sense of self internally but also is conferred upon us by others. Identifications arise from socially created categories that are occupied in concrete conditions and with material effects and consequences. Age can be seen as one such subject position.

An investigator's shared identifications can be understood as shared insider status. There are a number of advantages to insider status, partic-ularly in situations where an identity is marginalized (Tewksbury and Gagne 1997). It may facilitate access to a group of participants, increase levels of trust, and allow for a shared understanding of language and cul-ture (Merriam et al. 2001). Certainly a perception of shared insider status can assist with research, for although assumptions of shared identity may not be reliable, they nonetheless occur. For example, in my interviews with teenage girls and their grandmothers on their perceptions and experiences of adolescence (Raby 2002), my insider status as a woman facilitated cer-tain aspects of the research process. I was often invited to meet with the teenage girls and grandmothers while they were alone in their homes. A shared vocabulary between women (based on assumed heterosexuality) also facilitated dialogue. Some of the teenagers talked to me in detail about having crushes on boys, and several interviewees discussed puberty with assumed insider knowledge about menstruation. Similarly, Frosh, Phoenix, and Pattman (2002) found that boys talked about having rapport with their interviewer because he was male.

Stuart Hall (1996) argues that all identity positions are fluid and temporary attachments, but many tend to be experienced as far more permanent than age, such as identifications based on race or gender. Furthermore, the researcher has already been an insider (i.e., an adolescent), which makes this quite a distinct category compared to others. As Hendrick states (2000), the "Other" of childhood is different because we have all occupied it. Does this provide insider knowledge? A source of connection? Distortion as we project our own past experiences of adolescence onto the young people we research? What role does memory play in our configurations of adolescence today? Perhaps the experience of the researcher having already been a young person decreases the possibilities of difference and Othering because there is a sense of familiarity and sameness. Yet, as a result of this sense of familiarity, the potential to Other may increase as we think we know young people's experiences and therefore more actively colonize them. In either case, how does this shifting status influence insider-outsider distinctions?

An adult conducting research with young people is an outsider who may imagine insider status based on memories of adolescence. Yet for the participant, the adult's role as an outsider may prevent trust and decrease shared understanding between researcher and participant, depending on the salience of age to the interview topics, how adolescence and adulthood are both conceptualized, and possibly on how far the adult is perceived to have aged away from adolescence. Yet outsider status is not always a problem. An insider can have disadvantages, and outsider status can be an asset. Shared insider status may generate false perceptions of a common outlook or similar interpretations of social patterns, affecting both participants' and researchers' expectations and researchers' interpretations of data. Participants may pay more attention to these processes when working with a researcher who is perceived to be an outsider. An outsider may ask naïve but important questions (Tewksbury and Gagne 1997), and he or she also has the advantage of being outside community relationships and tensions.

How then have researchers attempted to negotiate their roles as adults doing research with or on adolescents? Many scholars have been involved in some form of participant-observation research with teenagers, but this tends to be from an overt position of outsider. Peter McLaren (1993) and Dan Yon (2000) have both observed students in high schools in Toronto. Amy Best's (2000) investigation of the prom included hanging out with young people as they prepared for and attended their proms. Valerie Hey (1997) has conducted an in-depth study of girls' friendships in English high schools, and Amira Proweller (1998) spent a significant amount of time as a participant observer in a Northeastern American private high school for girls. In none of these studies did the researcher attempt to take on a least-adult role of the young person, the tactic that attempts to share insider status, discussed earlier. Why might this be? In North America, adolescence is a category that prioritizes peer relationships and a separation from adult culture. Whereas for teenagers size and language differences that we see between children and adults may be less relevant, the insider-outsider gulf between teenagers and adults can seem greater, which is supported by popular commentary on teens as suddenly foreign to us and by the greater likelihood that teenagers will see adults as imposters. Perhaps for this reason it seems harder to envision the cultural immersion of an adult researcher into the lives of adolescents as a welcomed peer.

James, Jenks, and Prout (1998) argue that we do not need to take a least-adult role, or to adopt a kind of temporary insider status, in order to learn from young people. These scholars are interested in exploring when it is that the differences between children and adults are more important and when they are less relevant. I would add that we need to specifically address the moments when power imbalances become more salient and what the consequences of such imbalances might be. The least-adult role is one option in research, but as James, Jenks, and Prout suggest, other kinds of research relationships may be equally productive: friend, adult interviewer, or fellow worker, for instance. This may be a particularly fruitful approach to consider in research with teenagers. As young people leave childhood, the potential increases for nonhierarchical relationships with adults in nonschool settings, like work or community organizations, providing unique opportunities to disrupt a clear, hierarchical division between adults and teenagers. At the same time, as I have discussed, the role of adult researcher can have added value as an outsider who is therefore beyond the subcultural power dynamics of young people and who can therefore ask "ignorant" questions (Fine, in James, Jenks, and Prout

1998:183). This does not mean that power imbalances disappear, but it does suggest that age inequalities are not the only relevant manifestations of inequality.

An insider-outsider distinction privileges one subject position over others, but people do not occupy one subject position at a time. Our fluid, changing identifications intersect, complement, and contradict (Hall 1996). Neither cultures (Merriam et al. 2001) nor identities are monolithic. For example, Merriam et al. focus on interview relationships across and between global cultures to illustrate how insider status can shift based on intersecting, changing identifications. Adolescence is not an exception, and as an identity it intersects with class, gender, race, ethnicity, ability, and sexuality, among other identifications. Similarly, the researcher is not coming "from nowhere" but is embedded in identity categories that are complicated by unequal power relations. Such intersections, in turn, can either exacerbate or significantly decrease the marginality of an adolescent participant in an adult-initiated project. For example, earlier I discussed how my interviews with teenage girls and their grandmothers were facilitated by my shared insider status based on gender, which eased interactions despite age differences between the interview participants and me. As acknowledged by Reinharz (1992), such identifications can become further complicated. Gender can be performed in many different ways, such that identification with a researcher might depend not on sex but on specific performances of femininity or masculinity and on intersections of sexuality, class, and ethnicity. Such attention to the complexity of identifications disrupts an easy insider-outsider dichotomy. It reminds us that we cannot easily "read off" one identity position and assume ease in a research relationship as a consequence. By privileging other identity positions besides age, particularly shared, marginal positions, a perceived gulf between adults and teens may sometimes be partially bridged. An exclusive focus on age as *the* salient identification in a research situation elides these other deeply significant locations that can contribute to connection (or division) between adult researchers and adolescent participants.

This position, in turn, raises a new set of questions. In research between adults and adolescents, how do researchers and participants negotiate these diverse identifications? Which hold more importance at various moments in time and with differing modes or methods of inquiry? To what extent are differences in identification mitigated by strong research skills (Tewksbury and Gagne 1997)? Finally, in what ways does the salience of age as it interacts with other identifications change when we are conducting research with adolescents rather than children? Adolescence has been constructed as a pivotal time for the development of distinct personal identities and a sense of self as embedded in larger social structures (Erikson 1968). Does this mean that among adolescents non-age-based identifications take on added importance that are less salient in childhood?

Bridging through Methodology

Janneli Miller's article "I Have a Frog in My Stomach" (1996) is one that I have used in research methods courses. Miller tells the story of Lucia, a Mayan American woman whose life is significantly transformed when her boyfriend's mother puts a spell on her, putting a frog into her stomach—a frog that later needs to be removed by a shaman. Miller reflects on the challenge she experienced in trying to reconcile Lucia's story with her own Western beliefs about the nature of reality and how we can access it. Miller's strategy in her article is to advocate a "beginner's mind," which involves suspending preconceived notions and recognizing different conceptual locations when we enter into the research relationship, to meet participants on their own terms and to understand their locations. In the case of young people, this does not mean encountering them with set, preconceived notions about their developmental location, treating them as small adults, or presuming that we will always be outsiders to their worlds. Rather, researchers need to come into the research relationship both informed by previous work and open to the possibilities that participants and their context present.

Some have advocated Participant Action Research (PAR) as an ideal approach to more fully meet and include young people in research about them. PAR is appealing for a researcher who is concerned with the treatment of young people as subjects and participants rather than objects of study (Alderson 2000; O'Kane 2000). Assuming that we occupy different locations in society in terms of power and resources, advocates of PAR try to work with, and empower, oppressed or marginal groups through "constructing and using their own knowledge" (Reason 1994:328), producing knowledge and action that is useful to them, and through Paulo Freire's concept of *conscientization*, "a process of self-awareness through collective self-inquiry and reflection" (Fals-Borda and Rahman, in Reason 1994:328). The PAR approach attempts to draw on a diversity of methods to honor the lived experiences of oppressed groups through a genuine commitment to collaboration—working with participants, from the choice of research questions to the dissemination of research results. Rather than "deny the hyphen" between self and Other by writing about those who have been Othered, in this case young people, Michelle Fine argues that we need instead "to engage in social struggles with those who have been exploited and subjugated" (1994:72). PAR is one strategy through which to accomplish this.

PAR addresses some of the concerns discussed in this chapter. Rather than overlaying a blueprint of developmentalism onto participants, PAR attempts to meet participants where they are and in terms of what is interesting to them. It constructs young people as social agents rather than objects of study. Furthermore, PAR allows for recognition that young people occupy distinct cultural locations but within wider social structures. PAR also helps to negotiate this question of insider-outsider statuses in that it creates a dynamic in which the participants are both asking the questions and responding to them.

Some scholars have been cautious about how central children can be to such a research relationship, however. Pole, Mizen, and Bolton warn that "despite the best intentions of [PAR] researchers, the structure and organization of research inevitably reduces children to the status of at best participants rather than partners and at worst objects of the researcher's gaze" (1999:39). Barrie Thorne comments that although children may help with research, they "will never be in central positions of knowledge-creation" (1987:102). Alderson (2000), however, argues that children and adolescents *can* be active participants in all aspects of the research process. PAR may be of particular benefit to adolescents because they may be in a stronger social position than young children to articulate and reflect on their lives and yet therefore experience their disenfranchisement more acutely.

Feminist methodologies also address some of the power relations involved in research processes (see Fine 1992, Lather 1991, and Reinharz 1992), through advocating open-ended interviews, an acceptance of participants' experiences, disclosure of research aims, researcher reflexivity, and returning transcripts to interviewees for comments.

In addition to the specific research techniques used, it is important to develop a philosophical approach to adolescence that attempts to explore teenage lives and concerns without filtering them through our previously developed lenses for where and what they should be—not just with regard to language or cognitive skills but to social and emotional locations as well. Discourses that define teenagers as "at risk," as "social problems," or as tossed on the sea of hormonal/emotional change reify preconceived notions about adolescent experiences. Attention to young people's independent cultures and unequal social locations is also necessary, but not sufficient, for engaging with young people as active participants in their own and the wider culture. Finally, we may reflect on the structural and developmental locations of the young people we research, and adjust our approach as a consequence, but great care must be taken in how we apply preconceived notions and theories of childhood and adolescence such that their voices are not molded merely to fit our own positions.

We are, as researchers, socially located and frequently privileged. We must acknowledge our access to resources that most children and adolescents do not have, the danger of constructing them as objects rather than subjects of study, and the need to be particularly attentive to the authority of the adult researcher's voice and interpretation in the research process. But we all occupy multiple identifications, and age is just one such subject position. Age is a salient feature of insider-outsider distinctions, but it is at the same time intersected by other identifications that may provide points for connection across age.

NOTES

1. In this chapter I discuss dominant, mainstream developmental approaches, specifically developmental psychology. It is important to note, however, that some work within developmental theory has sought to contextualize developmental processes in terms of history and culture and to represent children as relevant social actors (Hogan 2005).

2. Of course, this is not always the case. The discussion of insider and outsider statuses in the next section of this chapter reminds us that power relations can reconfigure in many different ways. Relations may be different in a situation where a young, working-class woman conducts interviews with private-school boys, for example.

REFERENCES

Adams, Mary-Louise. 1997. *The Trouble with Normal: Postwar Youth and the Making of Heterosexuality.* Toronto: University of Toronto Press.

Alderson, Priscilla. 2000. "Children as Researchers: The Effects of Participation Rights on Research Methodology." In *Research with Children: Perspectives and Practices*, ed. Pia Christensen and Allison James. London: Falmer, 241–257.

Amit-Talai, Vered. 1995. "The Waltz of Sociability: Intimacy, Dislocation, and Friendship in a Quebec High School." In *Youth Cultures: A Cross-Cultural Perspective,* ed. Vered Amit-Talai and Helena Wulff. London: Routledge, 144–165.

Best, Amy. 2000. *Prom Night: Youth, Schools, and Popular Culture.* New York: Routledge.

Brah, Avtar. 1996. *Cartographies of Diaspora: Contesting Identities.* London: Routledge.

Caputo, Virginia. 1995. "Anthropology's Silent 'Others': A Consideration of Some Conceptual and Methodological Issues for the Study of Youth and Children's Cultures." In *Youth Cultures: A Cross-Cultural Perspective,* ed. Vered Amit-Talai and Helena Wulff. London: Routledge, 43–62.

Christensen, Pia, and Allison James. 2000a. "Introduction: Researching Children and Childhood: Cultures of Communication." In *Research with Children: Perspectives and Practices,* ed. Pia Christensen and Allison James. London: Falmer, 1–8.

Christensen, Pia, and Allison James. 2000b. "Childhood Diversity and Commonality: Some Methodological Insights." In *Research with Children: Perspectives and Practices,* ed. Pia Christensen and Allison James. London: Falmer, 160–178.

Danesi, Marcel. 2003. *Forever Young: The Teen-Aging of Modern Culture.* Toronto: University of Toronto Press.

Dannefer, Dale. 1984. "Adult Development and Social Theory: A Paradigmatic Reappraisal." *American Sociological Review,* 49, 100–116.

Erikson, Erik. 1968. *Identity, Youth, and Crisis.* New York: Norton.

Fine, Gary Alan, and Kent L. Sandstrom. 1988. *Knowing Children: Participant Observation with Minors.* Qualitative Research Methods 15. Newbury Park, Calif.: Sage.

Fine, Michelle. 1994. "Working the Hyphens: Reinventing Self and Other in Qualitative Research." In *Handbook of Qualitative Research,* ed. Norman K. Denzin and Yvonna S. Lincoln. Thousand Oaks, Calif.: Sage, 70–81.

———. 1992. "Passions, Politics, and Power: Feminist Research Possibilities." In *Disruptive Voices: The Possibilities of Feminist Research,* ed. Michelle Fine. Ann Arbor: University of Michigan Press, 205–232.

France, Alan. 2004. "Young People." In *Doing Research with Children and Young People,* ed. Sandy Fraser, Vicky Lewis, Sharon Ding, Mary Kellett, and Chris Robinson. London: Sage, 175–190.

Fraser, Sandy. 2004. "Situating Empirical Research." In *Doing Research with Children and Young People,* ed. Sandy Fraser, Vicky Lewis, Sharon Ding, Mary Kellett, and Chris Robinson. London: Sage, 15–26.

Fraser, Sandy, Vicky Lewis, Sharon Ding, Mary Kellett, and Chris Robinson, eds. 2004. *Doing Research with Children and Young People.* London: Sage.

Frosh, Stephen, Ann Phoenix, and Rob Pattman. 2002. *Young Masculinities: Understanding Boys in Contemporary Society.* London: Palgrave.

Graue, M. Elizabeth, and Daniel. J. Walsh. 1998. "Ethics: Being Fair." In *Studying Children in Context: Theories, Methods, and Ethics,* ed. M. Elizabeth Graue and Daniel J. Walsh. Thousand Oaks, Calif.: Sage, 55–69.

Griffin, Christine. 1993. *Representations of Youth: The Study of Youth and Adolescence in Britain and America.* Cambridge, U.K.: Polity.

Hall, Stuart. 1996. "Who Needs Identity?" In *Questions of Cultural Identity,* ed. Stuart Hall and Paul du Gay. London: Sage, 1–17.

Hebdige, Dick. 1979. *Subculture: The Meaning of Style.* London: Methuen.

Hendrick, Harry. 2000. "The Child as a Social Actor in Historical Sources: Problems of Identification and Interpretation." In *Research with Children: Perspectives and Practices,* ed. P. Christensen and A. James. London: Routledge-Falmer, 36–61.

Hey, Valerie. 1997. *The Company She Keeps.* Buckingham, U.K.: Open University Press.

Hogan, Diane. 2005. "Researching 'the Child' in Developmental Psychology." In *Researching Children's Experience: Methods and Approaches,* ed. Sheila Green and Diane Hogan. London: Sage.

Holmes, Robyn. 1998. *Fieldwork with Children.* Thousand Oaks, Calif.: Sage.

Hood, Suzanne, Peter Kelley, and Berry Mayall. "Children as Research Subjects: A Risky Enterprise." *Children and Society,* 10(2), June, 117–128.

James, Alison, Chris Jenks, and Alan Prout. 1998. *Theorizing Childhood.* Cambridge, U.K.: Polity.

Jhally, Sut. 1997. *Representation and the Media.* Northampton, Mass.: Media Education Foundation.

Lansdown, G. 1994. "Children's Rights." In *Children's Childhoods: Observed and Experienced,* ed. B. Mayall. London: Falmer, 33–44.

Lather, Patti. 1991. *Getting Smart: Feminist Research and Pedagogy with/in the Postmodern.* New York: Routledge.

Leblanc, Lorraine. 2001. *Pretty in Punk: Girls' Gender Resistance in a Boys' Subculture.* New Brunswick, N.J.: Rutgers University Press.

Lesko, Nancy. 2002. *Act Your Age! A Cultural Construction of Adolescence.* New York: Routledge.

———. 1996. "Denaturalizing Adolescence: The Politics of Contemporary Representations." *Youth and Society,* 28(2), 139–161.

Mandell, Nancy. 1988. "The Least-Adult Role in Studying Children." *Journal of Contemporary Ethnography,* 16(4), January, 433–467.

Mauthner, Melanie. 1997. "Methodological Aspects of Collecting Data from Children: Lessons from Three Research Projects." *Children and Society,* 11, 16–28.

Mayall, Berry. 2000. "Conversations with Children: Working with Generational Issues." In *Research with Children: Perspectives and Practices,* ed. Pia Christensen and Allison James. London: Falmer, 120–135.

McLaren, Peter. 1993. *Schooling as a Ritual Performance: Towards a Political Economy of Educational Symbols and Gestures,* 2nd ed. London: Routledge.

McRobbie, Angela. 1978. "Working-Class Girls and the Culture of Femininity." In *Women Take Issue: Aspects of Women's Subordination.* Women's Studies Group, Centre for Contemporary Cultural Studies. London: Hutchinson, 96–108.

Merriam, Sharan B., Juanita Johnson-Bailey, Ming-Yeh Lee, Youngwha Kee, Gabo Ntseane, and Mazanah Muhamad. 2001. "Power and Positionality: Negotiating Insider/Outsider Status within and across Cultures." *International Journal of Lifelong Education,* 20(5), September-October, 405–416.

Miller, Janneli. 1996. "'I Have a Frog in My Stomach': Mythology and Truth in Life History." In *Unrelated Kin: Race and Gender in Women's Personal Narratives,* ed. Gwendolyn Etter-Lewis and Michele Foster. New York: Routledge, 103–119.

Morgan, D., and S. Scott. 1993. "Bodies in a Social Landscape." In *Body Matters: Essays on the Sociology of the Body,* ed. S. Scott and D. Morgan. London: Falmer, 1–21.

Morrow, Virginia, and Martin Richards. 1996. "The Ethics of Social Research with Children: An Overview." *Children and Society,* 10(2), June, 90–105.

Morss, John R. 1996. *Growing Critical: Alternatives to Developmental Psychology.* New York: Routledge.

O'Kane, Clare. 2000. "The Development of Participatory Techniques: Facilitating Children's Views about Decisions That Affect Them." In *Research with Children: Perspectives and Practices,* ed. Pia Christensen and Allison James. London: Falmer, 136–159.

Pole, Christopher, Philip Mizen, and Angela Bolton. 1999. "Realising Children's Agency in Research: Partners and Participants?" *International Journal of Social Research Methodology,* 2(1), 39–54.

Proweller, Amira. 1998. *Constructing Female Identities: Meaning Making in an Upper-Middle-Class Youth Culture.* Albany: State University of New York Press.

Punch, Samantha. 2002. "Research with Children: The Same or Different from Research with Adults?" *Childhood,* 9(3), 321–341.

Raby, Rebecca. 2002. "A Tangle of Discourses: Girls Negotiating Adolescence." *Journal of Youth Studies,* 5(4), December, 415–450.

Reason, Peter. 1994. "Three Approaches to Participative Inquiry." In *Handbook of Qualitative Research,* ed. Norman K. Denzin and Yvonna S. Lincoln. Thousand Oaks, Calif.: Sage, 324–339.

Reinharz, Shulamit. 1992. *Feminist Methods in Social Research.* Oxford: Oxford University Press.

Robinson, Chris, and Mary Kellett. 2004. "Power." In *Doing Research with Children and Young People,* ed. Sandy Fraser, Vicky Lewis, Sharon Ding, Mary Kellett, and Chris Robinson. London: Sage, 81–96.

Scott, J. C. 1990. *Domination and the Arts of Resistance: Hidden Transcripts.* New Haven: Yale University Press.

Tewksbury, Richard, and Patricia Gagne. 1997. "Assumed and Presumed Identities: Problems of Self-Presentation in Field Research." *Sociological Spectrum,* 17(2), April-June, 127–156.

Thorne, Barrie. 1987. "Re-visioning Women and Social Change: Where Are the Children? *Gender and Society,* 1(1), 85–109.

Weber, Linda R., Andrew Miracle, and Tom Skehan. 1994. "Interviewing Early Adolescents: Some Methodological Considerations." *Human Organization,* 53(1), 42–47.

Widdicombe, Sue, and Robin Wooffitt. 1995. *The Language of Youth Subcultures: Social Identity in Action.* New York: Harvester Wheatsheaf.

Yon, Daniel A. 2000. *Elusive Culture: Schooling, Race, and Identity in Global Times.* Albany: State University of New York Press.

Chapter 2

"Label Jars Not People"
How (Not) to Study Youth Civic Engagement

Marc Flacks

When it comes to political engagement, it often seems that young people are damned if they do and damned if they don't. In periods when youthful political action has been relatively widespread (e.g., the 1930s and 1960s), young activists are often condemned as naively rebellious at best, and as dangerously deluded at worst. Yet in periods of relative youthful quiescence, young Americans have been admonished for being disengaged, or lazy, or idiotic (in the original sense of that term). Scholars have thus approached youth politics as a "problem" and have typically sought "causes" for the problem (whether too much politics or too little) in young people's backgrounds. We can readily see the drawbacks of such an approach when we consider that "permissive parenting" has been used as an explanation both for wild-eyed youthful rebellion and for youthful disaffection and apathy. Recently, though, critical youth scholars have begun to rethink both youth and adulthood and to construct new concepts, theories, and methods for approaching the study of young people, including their politics. My own work has followed a parallel trajectory: Whereas I began my research on youth politics armed with the concepts and theories and methods developed during the heyday of social scientific research on youthful political engagement (i.e., the 1960s and early 1970s), the data I have worked with have compelled me to adopt different ways of thinking about, studying, and explaining young people and their politics. In this essay, I aim to examine three related methodological/conceptual issues that I have confronted in my own research: (1) the phenomenon of "emerging adulthood," and how it leads to a reconsideration of concepts like "youth," "adulthood," and "transition to adulthood"; (2) the possibility that researchers have misunderstood and mischaracterized young people's political engagement by paying insufficient methodological attention to the phenomenon of "emerging adulthood"; (3) the growing sense among youth researchers that broad categorical terms like "youth," "subculture," and even "emerging adulthood" may be inadequate for the challenges of studying contemporary young people.

Reluctant Patriotism?

Let me begin by relating a problem I encountered while conducting research (for my Ph.D. dissertation) on young men's decisions to enlist in the military. The overall goal of this research was to analyze enlistment "conversion," that is, the process by which individuals who are initially uninterested in military service eventually become willing volunteers. This was a compelling research topic at the time because for several years the military had experienced a steady decline in enlistment and enlistment "propensity" (i.e., interest in enlisting) on the part of young men, and military officials were highly concerned about, as well as at a loss to explain, the trend. The quantitative survey data collected by the military clearly demonstrated a broad-based decline in young men's military enlistment propensity, but these data were not very useful for understanding *why* this was the case. Nevertheless, despite the absence of richer, more explanatory data, military officials had concluded that the problem was "Generation X"—that is, lazy, apathetic, undisciplined youth who are not interested in or prepared for military service (Department of Defense, 1996). As a critical youth studies scholar as well as a member of the putative "Generation X," I was unsatisfied with this analysis, and so I designed a qualitative study that employed depth interviews with recent "reluctant" enlistees, in order to learn more about their initial unwillingness to enlist and about the factors that eventually pushed them toward the decision to do so.

According to the conventional wisdom on military enlistment, young men tend to volunteer for military service for two main types of reasons: first, for material goals like pay, benefits, training, money for college, and so on, and second, for normative goals like service to one's country, defending one's homeland, or continuing a family tradition (cf. Orvis, Sastry, and McDonald, 1996). Among the first findings generated from my own research, however, was that only one of the young men I interviewed mentioned patriotic reasons as a motivation to enlist. Perhaps more surprising, though, was that very few of them said that monetary/ material goals were their main motivation to enlist either. Rather, most of these young men explained that they had decided to enlist as a means of escaping a sense of being "stuck," or "blocked," on their paths to adulthood. For most of the young men, what the military offered them that civilian life did not was a ready opportunity to prove themselves as capable, respectable, adult men (Flacks, 2000). Although they did not always articulate this in so many words, their explanations, for example, that they chose the Marine Corps because it is the "hardest" service to go through and that "people respect you when you're a Marine" or that "at Wal-Mart I was just a stocker, but in the Army I'll be able to prove that I can do stuff that other guys can't" indicate that the military promised to fulfill their "identity needs" (as opposed to their normative or material needs). For some of them, especially those who had never gone to college, this search for a satisfying adult identity was tinged with notions of machismo and tough masculinity. But even those who did not choose the Marines, or who never alluded to a desire for tough physical challenges or proving their manhood, explained how civilian life was moving "too slowly" for them, either in the sense of being "stuck in a dead-end job" or being caught in an educational credentialing process that could take six, eight, even ten years to complete (and which still might not guarantee them a secure middle-class career). Most of these young men came from blue-collar middle-class families, but in their view, because of downsizing and the loss of industrial jobs due to globalization, they could not follow the same routes to middle-class comfort that their parents had traveled. In short, almost all the young men appeared to be experiencing what some social scientists have recently begun to call "emerging adulthood" (Arnett, 2000b; Arnett, 2004) or simply "early adulthood" (Furstenberg et al., 2004) —that is, an extended period between adolescence and adulthood, wherein young people are no longer seen as "youth" but have nevertheless not yet attained the conventional markers of adulthood like marriage, independence from their parents, a full-time career, their own home, and so on. For most of these young men, the military offered them a path of almost instantaneous adulthood, where, after a few months of training, they would have new and satisfying identities as Marines, soldiers, sailors, or airmen, and they would have the uniforms to prove it. Military service would allow them to move out of their parents' homes, to have a "real job" as opposed to a dead-end one stocking shelves or flipping burgers, and, above all, to present themselves to their parents, peers, and their wider communities as fully mature adults on a concrete life trajectory.

However, when my interviews shifted from questions about why the young men decided to enlist to questions about their attitudes about the military, politics, and social issues, nearly all of them proclaimed their deep sense of patriotism, their commitment to democratic ideals, and their interest in staying abreast of domestic and foreign political affairs (this was well before 9/11/01). That is, when asked about why they enlisted, almost none of them mentioned a word about patriotism or politics, but when asked to describe their political views, nearly all of them described themselves as patriots and as engaged citizens (emphatically stating that the label "Generation X" did not apply to them or most of their peers), and indeed, some of them even asked me, "What do you mean, do I care about politics? I enlisted in the military, didn't I?"

Methodologically, then, my study design had presumed that the question of why the young men had enlisted was conceptually and empirically distinct from questions about their political and social beliefs, and at first, my data appeared to confirm this. However, in analyzing my data as a whole, it became clear that, in the young men's own minds, these issues were deeply entwined. True, almost none of them initially mentioned politics as a reason for enlisting, but it was clearly inaccurate, in the final analysis, to conclude that political considerations played no role in their decision. Thus, it is clear to me now that it is impossible to fully and accurately understand either these young men's enlistment decisions or their orientation to politics and civic engagement without simultaneously attending to their lived experience as "emerging adults." My research initially grew out of the conviction that survey data, relying as they typically do on forced-choice, closed-ended questions, were inadequate for getting at questions of why young men do or do not enlist, but it is now clear to me that my qualitative methodology was also flawed to the extent that it neglected to permit the young men to describe their decision-making in their own terms, using their own voices. In other words, in the absence of an appropriate conceptualization and theorization of "emerging adulthood," my methodology for studying contemporary young men's enlistment decisions was flawed and incomplete.

Whereas I had been laboring under the assumption that young men who had graduated from high school and had enlisted in the military were for all intents and purposes adults, and that their career decisions could therefore be analyzed intelligibly separately from their politics and ideology, I now understand that they did not see themselves as full adults and that their political and ideological views were highly contingent on achieving a stable sense of adulthood. Although I had been expecting to elicit their political and ideological views and, from there, to analyze their respective backgrounds in order to make sense of these aspects of their selfhood, it became clear to me that in many ways their "foregrounds," perhaps more than their backgrounds, had the potential to be the determining factor in their sense(s) of self and therefore their worldviews. Put another way, although these young men came from fairly diverse backgrounds (different ethnic groups, different regions of the country, different families with differing socioeconomic status, and so on), they all expressed a sense that they were not yet who they hoped to be (to the extent that they could even articulate such hopes), and it became clear that their lack of certainty with respect to their futures translated into a lack of conviction with respect to their political and ideological positions. In a sense, these young men were telling me, "Ask me about my politics later, once I've established myself on a concrete career and identity trajectory; right now I am not sure who I am, or what I believe, exactly." If circumstances had permitted it, I would have at that point redesigned the study to include a follow-up set of interviews to be conducted after the young men had completed their basic training, or even after they had served their terms in the military, in order to substantiate whether their worldviews were contingent on achieving a stronger sense of adulthood. This did not prove practical, but the experience has pushed me further to investigate the phenomenon of "emerging adulthood" and to examine its conceptual/methodological implications. I now turn to a fuller discussion of these issues.

"Emerging Adulthood"

One reason that the phenomenon of emerging adulthood may sometimes catch youth researchers by surprise, as it did me, is that "the events that make up the transition to adulthood have generally been studied separately rather than in conjunction with one another" (Furstenberg et al., 2004:898). Moreover, "relatively little in-depth or even survey data on the processes of identity formation and the establishment of goals and commitments [of young people] is available" (ibid.:899). Thus, Furstenberg and colleagues raise a theoretical and programmatic challenge that echoes the challenges presented by my research on military enlistees:

> Just how young people construct their identities in a world in which attaining the traditional markers of adult status has become more difficult (or at least considerably delayed) is an issue worth pursuing in future research.... All too little work provides thick description of how adolescence appears to those going through it. (ibid.:899).

Although psychologist Jeffrey Jensen Arnett coined the term "emerging adulthood" and has probably produced the most voluminous and sustained work on the subject, sociologists have generally expressed dissatisfaction with Arnett's relative lack of attention to historical and social structural factors in the transformation of the transition to adulthood. In many ways, Arnett's causal analysis of the emergence of emerging adulthood is basically identical to 1960s-era youth scholars Erikson's and Keniston's analyses of the emergence of the "youth" lifestage. That is, because advanced technological societies require longer apprenticeship periods for young workers, and more intensive education, individuals are increasingly constrained to put off adult transitions (e.g., full-time career, marriage, establishing a household, childbearing, and childrearing) until later in life than previous cohorts have done. According to this view, this "moratorium" on adulthood may be structurally imposed, but it is nevertheless beneficial to individuals and to society as a whole. Arnett, for example, posits that the "explorations in the areas of love, work, and worldviews" (Arnett, Ramos, and Jensen, 2001:69) made possible by emerging adulthood allow individuals to "expand their range of personal experiences," and, he implies, this will help them to be more effective in making "the more enduring choices of adulthood" (Arnett, 2000b:469).

Yet the military enlistees I interviewed did not appear to embrace their status as emerging adults and instead seemed to be searching for ways to escape it and to enter the status of fully socially recognized men/adults. Likewise, other sociologists, while agreeing that the moratorium on adulthood has indeed grown longer for many individuals, have also called attention to the ways in which this can be a source of stress, anxiety, and tension for young people and sometimes their parents as well. Importantly, although these sociologists agree with Arnett that emerging adulthood is increasingly shared by young people in industrialized societies, they maintain that young people's "life chances" continue to be structured and differentiated by traditional boundaries of race, class, and gender. For British sociologists Furlong and Cartmel, for example, the most significant transformation of the transition to adulthood is not structural or demographic but subjective—it is harder to become an adult than it once was because the social landscape has fewer social formations available in which young people can forge a stable and meaningful subjectivity. That is, as "collectivist traditions" like trade unionism and other social movements have weakened, young people have been increasingly forced to understand their biographical trajectories in individualistic terms (Furlong and Cartmel, 1999). According to Furlong and Cartmel, this means that many young people misunderstand their lives and experiences because they are operating under an "epistemological fallacy" that blames individuals for problems that are in fact social and structural in nature. By comparison, whereas the "committed youth" whom Keniston (1968) studied were able to channel their relative freedom of exploration into positive and fulfilling activities like full-time work as social movement activists, today's "emerging adults" have few collective or social outlets for their transient status, and so they cope with the challenges of growing up on their own, seeing it as their own heroic struggle. For example, whereas the young men in my dissertation research saw their "dead-end" jobs as a personal problem, and enlisting in the military as a personal solution that demonstrated their own gumption, young people in previous decades were relatively more able to draw on collective traditions like the labor movement in order to understand their "private troubles" as "public issues" and to join collective efforts to address such problems. Had the military enlistees I interviewed come of age in, say, the 1960s, this line of argument suggests, they might have understood their predicaments in more political terms and might have joined a social movement, rather than the military, as a way of addressing them. Furlong and Cartmel therefore conclude that understanding how the transition to adulthood has changed in recent decades requires understanding larger social trends such as globalization, economic restructuring, the shift from "Fordist" to "Post-Fordist" social systems, the growth of corporate culture, and the decline of progressive social movements.

Moreover, this more sociological understanding of emerging adulthood forces us to consider that the changes associated with late capitalism may be more consequential for adulthood than for youth per se. That is, the "risks and uncertainties" Furlong and Cartmel point to (e.g., unemployment, downsizing, loss of social safety nets) may be things that young people anticipate in the future but are perils that many adults face in the present (see also Moore, 1998). Thus, whereas the young people who were the focus of study during the 1960s heyday of youth research were generally confident that their periods of "moratorium" would (or could) be followed by relatively secure careers in stable, affluent welfare states (Keniston, 1968), today's emerging adults are much less certain of what lies ahead of them. As I suggested earlier, this foreground uncertainty may at times be more theoretically and methodologically significant than young people's backgrounds, especially if political views and behavior are the objects of analysis.

Relatedly, Australian sociologists Wyn and White argue that scholars should stop conceiving of youth in "categorical" terms and instead should "rethink youth" in relational ones (Wyn and White, 1997). Drawing on feminist theories of gender as socially constructed and relational as opposed to absolute and categorical, they suggest that "youth is a relational concept because it exists and has meaning largely in relation to the concept of adulthood" (ibid.:11), and they argue that a relational conceptualization of youth permits greater understanding of how youth experiences are shaped by specific social, political, and economic conditions. In other words, "youth scholars" also need to be "adulthood scholars" and continuously ask how young people's present views, beliefs, and behavior are being shaped in relation to their anticipated futures (and/or lack thereof). If youth is relationally defined by adulthood, then researchers ought to ask where a concept like "emerging adulthood" fits into the traditional youth/adulthood binary opposition. That is, if "youth" is that which "adulthood" is not (and vice versa), then what meaning can be ascribed to "emerging adulthood," which would appear to sit uncomfortably in the liminal space between youth and adulthood?

If "emerging adulthood" is to be a useful analytical concept, then, one must not neglect the material and social circumstances behind its emergence. Arnett, for his part, seems willing to accept causal analyses developed in the 1950s and 1960s, whereas more sociologically oriented scholars have been attempting to understand how fairly recent transformations associated with late capitalism and "late modernity" are affecting the transition to adulthood for people in Western societies. This distinction is important, for whereas youth scholars of the 1950s and 1960s assumed that the "psychosocial moratorium on adulthood" (i.e., "youth") was functionally necessary for modern society and that it was more or less welcomed by individuals themselves, there is evidence (including my own dissertation findings) that many of today's "emerging adults" feel trapped and stifled by "prolonged" adolescent statuses and that various forms of problematic behavior can flow from this feeling (Cote and Alahar, 1995).

Emerging Adulthood and Youth Engagement

To date, there is very little scholarship that examines how a prolonged transition to adulthood may affect political consciousness and civic engagement. In light of the previous discussion, we can see that this lacuna is not merely a substantive one but may reflect a disconnect between concepts, theories, and methods of studying young people. For example, survey researchers have generally concluded that contemporary young people are simply "apathetic" or "cynical" or "disaffected," while paying little if any attention to the changing lived experience of coming of age (i.e., "emerging adulthood"). Even qualitative researchers who have consciously attempted to uncover "subterranean" forms of youth politics have found that adult researchers may not always communicate effectively with "emerging adults," which can lead to research findings that are inconclusive at best (Andolina et al., 2002). There is thus a clear need for attention to be paid to finding appropriate methods for studying the politics of contemporary youth, and such a task requires taking account of the concepts and theories relating to the "emerging adulthood" thesis.

This need became especially clear to me during a research project wherein I was analyzing college students' qualitative responses to a large-scale survey on student engagement that consisted primarily of forced-choice, closed-ended questions. In the open-ended responses I was analyzing, students offered criticisms and commentary about the survey itself; collectively, these comments point to the methodological importance of taking account of the phenomenon of "emerging adulthood." The data I was analyzing, and on which I will be drawing in the sections to follow, come from an ongoing study of "student engagement" in the University of California system. This study, known as Student Experiences in the Research University in the 21st Century (SERU21), is unique in a number of respects: First, although it is primarily a survey that elicits information about students' experiences in the UC system, the principle investigators who designed the survey also intended it to gather data on students' overall engagement with civic, political, and social institutions and issues (http://ishi.lib.berkeley.edu/cshe/seru21/). As such, the survey asks a variety of questions about students' ideological orientations, political affiliations, voting behavior, membership in voluntary associations, sympathies toward social movements and social causes, and so on. Second, unlike most large-scale surveys of this kind, SERU21 provides ample opportunities for respondents to provide open-ended, qualitative responses in their own words and with minimal constraints. Because the data I will be drawing on come from Phase One of the SERU21 study, the open-ended responses were elicited primarily to help the researchers refine and improve their survey instrument prior to Phase Two, but they were also included in the survey in order to give respondents a chance to vent any concerns they might have about their university experiences, including their experiences in taking the survey itself. In this way, the survey provides an excellent and unusual opportunity to examine both young people's engagement per se and their attitudes toward the research techniques used to elicit such information.

A few caveats about this data are in order: First, since the data are drawn from Phase One of the SERU21 survey, it only includes responses from first-year students and seniors in the UC system. In Phase Two, the survey will be targeted to a random, representative sample of all UC students. Second, because the data are drawn only from UC students, it is not representative of American youth as a whole (i.e., it excludes nonstudents, students at less selective universities, students at urban and/or teaching universities as opposed to research universities, and students from other regions of the United States). And since it is a survey of students, some respondents are transfer students and "reentry" students who are not "young," though I have tried to exclude such respondents from my analysis. These caveats aside, the data are very useful for examining how young people—especially those who are relatively well educated and articulate—respond when they are given a chance to discuss their engagement (and research on their engagement) in their own words and on their own terms. Because the existing quantitative data on youth civic disengagement shows that students, on average, are as likely to be disengaged as nonstudents (Ehrlich, 2000), the insights derived from this data should be more or less applicable (in this sense at least) to young Americans in general. That is, although these respondents may be somewhat more thoughtful and literate than the average young American, their lived experience with respect to politics and civic engagement is probably not that far removed from their noncollege peers and their peers in other academic institutions.

Disengagement or Delayed Engagement?

One possible implication of the "emerging adulthood" phenomenon is that, if individuals are "delaying" their transition to adulthood in the domains of work, residence, and family formation, they may also be delaying their transition to becoming engaged citizens. If such is the case, the hand-wringing over the widely noted decline in voting and other forms of participation by eighteen- to twenty-five-year-olds may be somewhat misplaced. True, "emerging adults" who do not vote do themselves a disservice by allowing older voters to dominate the attention and agendas of elected officials, but if "emerging adults" begin to participate at higher levels as they achieve full adult status, then the democratic system as a whole may not be as imperiled as some observers have suggested. The SERU21 survey, unlike most quantitative studies of youth political participation, gave respondents an opportunity to explain *why* they did not vote in the last election. Although many of the qualitative responses to this prompt echo other studies showing that young Americans do not vote because they are apathetic or alienated or cynical or disaffected, there are also many responses that indicate that quite a few students see themselves as still developing and as not quite ready, either intellectually or emotionally, to be participants in the "real-world" political process. Indeed, quite a few respondents felt that it would be unethical for them to participate in an election, given their relative lack of political knowledge and experience. So although traditional measures of political participation would characterize the respondents who offered the following comments simply as "disengaged" or as "nonvoters," the respondents themselves seem to see their lack of participation as a kind of principled "abstention":

I was not well enough informed about each candidate's platform to submit an educated vote, and I did not want to participate otherwise.

I have begun to realize the complexities of Political [*sic*] process throughout history and have had little time/energy to become sufficiently informed about the various issues.

I didn't take the time to inform myself fully and I would have voted for Nader but knew he wasn't going to get the minimum votes he needed to make it a three party race.

I spend too many hours at school and work to make myself well enough informed to make educated decisions. I don't want to vote on national or local issues if I haven't heard all of the benefits and negative aspects of each proposition and candidate.

I never received a ballot, and I didn't know what to do since it was my first time being able to vote. I didn't know what needed to be done or where to obtain information about voting. I may also have been in the process of moving, which may have caused my mailing route to be disrupted.

Didn't feel I was educated enough on the issues to make a decision that would reflect my interests.

I didn't know what was going on and what the issues were. I had no background on what I was supposed to be voting on.

As mentioned before, my political views are very neutral, and I have a difficult time choosing between political extremes offered in most elections. I am also not very well informed about political issues by my own fault, but I feel this wouldn't allow me to make a truly informed decision. Furthermore, I am affiliated with people with a multitude of different views that they are happy to press on other people, and many of those views contradict those of other people. This also lends itself to making a poor decision in light of a lack of proper knowledge.

I did not receive anything in the mail notifying me of political dates or information pertaining to the election. I was uncomfortable making an uninformed vote.

I felt my vote was not that important, and felt that I was an uninformed voter that could do more harm than good.

I don't know enough about politics to make an educated relevant decision.

I did not register to vote because I didn't understand the importance of it.

I am not registered and I do not choose to involve myself in politics because I am not well educated on the issues. I don't believe people should vote to vote, they should be informed before they vote and I am not therefore I should not vote.

Whether respondents like these will participate more in the political process as they grow older and (presumably) gain knowledge and experience is of course an open question. From a methodological and conceptual standpoint, however, such comments suggest that scholars of youth engagement ought to pay more attention than they generally have to the ways in which individuals associate voting and other forms of political participation with "adulthood" and, to the extent that they do, whether this presents an opportunity for an interpretation of voting rates among eighteen- to twenty-five-year-olds not merely as "decline" or "disengagement" but perhaps also as "delay" and "emerging engagement." In future surveys of students, for example, it might make sense to ask respondents whether they consider themselves "adults" or not and then to examine whether self-identified "adults" exhibit higher levels of political participation than those who do not so identify themselves.

Researchers might also pay attention to how institutional practices shape youths' understandings of themselves as adults—do university policies, for example, encourage or discourage students' subjective understandings of themselves as "adults"? The student movement of the 1960s, it should be recalled, often complained of the "in loco parentis" policies pursued by administrators and, in effect, successfully demanded that students be treated more like adults (Bailey, 1998). To the extent that administrative paternalism has crept back into the university environment in the form of such things as fewer electives, increased general education requirements, increased pressure on "time to degree," and restrictions on dorm life, then we should perhaps not be surprised by students' perceptions of themselves as "not yet ready" to cast informed votes. Indeed, in view of the recent rise of policies like youth curfews, restricted high school campuses, "zero-tolerance" rules, and other efforts to enforce strictly the line between young people and adults (Dohrn, 2000), it may be appropriate to speak of a process of the "infantilization" of American youth that begins during the high school years and lasts well into their early twenties. In any case, young people's delayed transitions to adulthood would seem clearly to have implications for their political consciousness and behavior, and researchers need to be attentive to this fact when formulating study designs and measures and when attempting to establish rapport with young people.

The Declining Significance of Youth Subcultures?

As mentioned earlier, one of the unique advantages of the SERU21 survey instrument is that it gives respondents several opportunities to vent their concerns, both with respect to their university experiences and with respect to their experiences taking the survey itself. Not surprisingly, many of the student respondents took advantage of the opportunity to complain about a variety of issues, ranging from concerns about professors and teachers who speak with thick accents to parking difficulties to impacted majors to the declining social diversity on their campuses to the perception that the survey was too long. For the purposes of this essay, I will focus on the complaints that bear squarely on the methodological issues surrounding the study of emerging adults' civic engagement. There were quite a few of these types of complaints, which is probably not surprising given that many of these respondents are currently learning about research methodology, survey techniques, statistics, and the scientific method and thus have a keen eye for potential sources of bias introduced by the survey instrument. However, it appears that the survey item respondents most frequently chose to comment on and complain about was one that asked them to identify themselves with particular social groups and/or cliques at their institution. Here is the text of that item:

C2A. Thinking of who you are, which, if any, of the following types of UC students do you strongly identify with? CHECK ALL THAT APPLY

c2a_1 Students who are serious about getting good grades
c2a_2 Party-goers, fun-loving students
c2a_3 Students who are serious about social or political issues
c2a_4 Intellectuals
c2a_5 Religious students
c2a_6 Athletes/Jocks
c2a_7 Other students of my ethnic background
c2a_8 Other students in my major or field of interest
c2a_9 Fraternity/Sorority types
c2a_10 Students from affluent backgrounds/ "rich kids"
c2a_11 Artsy students
c2a_12 Liberal students
c2a_13 Conservative students
c2a_14 Other (write in below)

In general, respondents complained that this item was presumptuous in that it assumed, first, that such social groupings were clearly identifiable at their institutions and, second, that respondents would want to identify themselves with a particular group, whether or not such groupings were evident. Interestingly, respondents often went beyond merely criticizing the assumptions underlying the item and offered their own statements about social identification in general. Many respondents seemed to be sensitive to the idea that this survey item is politically charged and that the data generated from the item could potentially be used by policymakers dealing with highly contentious issues such as campus diversity, affirmative action and other admissions policies, the status of the Greek system, athletic programs, and so on. More broadly, respondents' complaints about this item seem to revolve around the idea that the question was not appropriate for individuals in an "emerging adult" status: on the one hand, identifying oneself strongly with a clique seemed to many respondents to be immature "high school stuff," but on the other hand, having one's social identity too narrowly defined was associated by many with the stultifying aspects of full adulthood. But although such complaints can perhaps be interpreted as reflecting a "lifecourse effect"—that is, that emerging adults are uncomfortable with narrow social identification—it might also be possible to interpret them as reflecting a "generation effect" —that is, that contemporary emerging adults have experienced a great deal of social diversity compared to previous cohorts and share an existential consciousness that sees identity in universalistic terms. Here is a sampling of the critical open-ended responses to question C2A:

I try not to categorize the people I identify with—can't we all just get along??

I identify with people who identify with me. Besides, why do I have to be identified with certain groups of people? I'm me and that's all that matters.

I get along with most people but don't strongly identify with a group.

Laid back, happy go lucky types, people who don't really have a category to fit into, salt of the earth people.

I pretty much associate with and hang out with people of all kinds. College has given me the opportunity to truly meet people from all walks of life.

From these experiences I have learned more about myself and the type of person I want to be.

In college I learned to like a much wider variety of people than I was used to identifying with in high school. One category not on here is those interested in extracurriculars. Working on the school newspaper and radio station were a huge part of my education.

People who don't like categories.

I identify with people as individuals, not by specific types.

Underachievers/procrastinators, people dedicated to not being too dedicated to one thing.

People who are thoughtful and mature in being with other people, who are not egoistic and have a good brain and ear, too. Interesting people cannot be put in a box where we can check off of. They can be from all kinds of backgrounds. The essential thing is he who thinks beyond the surface of life and is explorative and curious.

I [would] rather not be categorized into specific groups because it limits my opportunities.

My identity is developing because I am being influenced by everyone I meet.

Students who don't assume stupid labels like those listed above.

Individuals uninterested in associating themselves with a group.

I find your "rich kids" mildly offensive, nowhere else in the above list is any category or "stereotype" mentioned in quotation. Really. Is that necessary??

You probably already know that this question is a bit offensive, in terms of putting people in boxes. Is anyone going to admit that they're looking for rich friends?? Maybe I'm naïve, but I think this is limiting.

I am none of the above but a little of them all.

I don't think any of these are me. I don't like thinking of myself as any of these, nor do my behaviors really fit in these categories. If you must classify, put me under "computer geeks."

I do not strongly identify with any of the above groups, in fact I have found it extremely difficult to find a "group" that I can identify [with]. Quite possibly I would have to say those that have to pay their way through college by working would be the group I identify with.

I don't really identify with any specific group. There are many different types of people on campus and in the world and I enjoy getting to know a different variety of people.

People who think the categorizations on this survey are lame.

Students who hate being categorized by banal labels such as these.

For questions C2A and C2B, I think they are a bit inaccurate in judging students because all students are different and may or cannot give a real judgment of answers about who they do or do not identify with on the campus. A student may be all of the above or none when in different moods or different periods of time. Personally, I think it's a bit biased and does not consider all of the variances in the campus environment. Students may identify with these but are more strong with one.

I don't associate with any distinct group. I feel like those are all stereotypes and drastic, I feel like I'm a little bit of some but by all means none of those come close to how I am—those are just stereotypes and I am much more than a stereotype.

I would have clicked the third box from the top, but all the forms of leftists on campus came to mind and I would have clicked the fifth box, but all the forms of Evangelicals come to mind. That being said I am serious about politics and religion, but not in the stereotypical college way. [Respondent continued later at open-ended prompt.] Biologically and anthropologically there is no such thing as race and since you all claim to be scientists after a fashion you should know that and hence, not use the word race when all that it does is cause division between people. So, when I answered the first question, I answered it based on ethnicity only.

Why do you group party goers with fun loving students? Can't you be fun loving without being a partier?

Anyone who is laid back and open-minded, not into having one specific group to hang out with, people who are willing to hang out with anyone that happens to be around at that time . . . no clicks (sp?)

Tend NOT to associate with groups or group mentality; Be my own person and have my own ideas with as little influence as possible by groups.

Generally people who are aware that they do not need to fit into a category in order to exist. The contradictions are intentional.

I do not think that any of these categories can define me as a person. There are bits and pieces of maybe every single one of the categories that have affected my life in some aspect or another, but I felt that I should comment on this rather than check off every single one.

Students who melt across categories because they want to take advantage of the diverse population and learn more about how human beings work.

Smart people who can see through the bullshit behind every category on that list, people with their heads screwed on straight.

I find myself identifying with members from every group, it really depends on the individual's personality. Label jars not people.

The notion that young people often form distinct subcultures is one of the foundations of the sociology of youth (Widdicombe and Wooffitt, 1995) and can be traced at least as far back as Karl Mannheim's seminal essay, "The Problem of Generations." However, in light of contemporary emerging adults' experiences with multicultural education, growing social diversity in America, and globalization and with a dominant popular culture that increasingly appropriates aspects of youth subcultures for commercial purposes, there may well be a need to challenge or at least reassess the utility of the youth subculture concept. The comments just presented surely lend credence to the growing chorus of scholars who are calling on youth researchers to reassess the subculture concept (see Muggleton and Weinzierl, 2003).

What is perhaps most striking about the students' comments on group identification is how broad-based they apparently are: students from all walks of life seem to resist the notion that they could or should identify themselves with particular groups. On one hand, this could reflect the "epistemological fallacy" discussed earlier whereby many young people are essentially blind to the ways their lives are structured by their membership in various collectivities, but on the other hand, it can just as plausibly be interpreted as a reflection of a particular kind of political/social *consciousness,* as opposed to ignorance. In the context of their other responses to this survey, it would be inaccurate to say that these young people are unaware of the politics of race, gender, class, and nationality and therefore reject collective labels out of naïveté. Instead, they appear to be searching for ways to transcend such fault lines and to forge novel forms of social and political solidarity. Ironically, although the formation of youth subcultures has often been theorized as precisely an effort by young people to establish social bonds that diverge from their ascriptive origins, the respondents quoted here seem to reject even youth subcultural identifications. Clearly, researchers need to find out more about contemporary young people's subcultural identifications or lack thereof, but the data presented here strongly suggest that researchers ought to be methodologically circumspect when pursuing such questions. For example, rather than presenting survey respondents with a predetermined list of subgroups and subcultures, it might be preferable to simply ask respondents whether they do or do not identify with any particular groups and, if they do, prompt them for a list of such groups. Alternatively, it might be useful to pose more pointed questions to respondents, such as whether they identify with other members of their race, and why this is or is not the case.

Conclusion

From a conceptual and methodological standpoint, the preceding discussion perhaps leads to one overarching conclusion: in order to fully understand the attitudes and behaviors of contemporary emerging adults, we may need to resist the temptation to conceive of them using generalized terms like "generation," "youth disengagement," "subculture," and even "emerging adults." Although it is indeed the case that today's younger cohorts face what might be called obstacles on their paths to adulthood, their responses to this shared predicament appear to be quite multiple and varied. So although youth scholars have had a tendency, at least since the 1960s, to presume that youth share a collective identity as youth, and have typically sought to describe and theorize this shared identity, it would appear that the more relevant task for contemporary youth scholars is to grasp the different adaptations young people are making to their shared circumstances.

With respect to civic engagement in particular, accomplishing this task presents several methodological requirements. First, studies should be designed in such a way as to maximize subjects' ability to articulate their own conceptions of politics, participation, political identity, and political engagement. Forced-choice and closed-ended designs, of course, risk blinding us to the variety of forms of engagement that young people may be exploring. Second, studies should allow subjects to place themselves on the developmental continuum between childhood and adulthood, rather than presuming, on the basis of age alone, that they fall into one or another fixed category. That is, in order to learn more about how the changing transition to adulthood may be affecting young people's civic behavior, we need to pay more attention to how individuals define themselves and, in turn, examine how their definitions of engagement relate to their perceptions of their own developmental progress.

The analysis presented here also suggests that the realities of emerging adulthood present researchers with challenges that go beyond relatively straightforward methodological issues of conceptualization, study design, and data collection and that bear more broadly on the matter of how researchers analyze the data they have collected. For although a survey instrument like the one used in the SERU21 study could certainly be improved by rewording and restructuring certain items and prompts, the higher-quality data that could be produced thereby would be of little value if they were not analyzed in a manner that is sensitive to the lived experiences of emerging adulthood. In short, we need to ask better questions of young respondents, but we also need to ask the right questions about the data that we produce.

Relatedly, when analyzing our data, critical youth studies scholars ought to be mindful of the "relational" nature of youth (Wyn and White, 1997) and emerging adulthood. By this I mean to suggest that researchers should be more attentive to the ways in which the definitions and experience of youth are entwined with and dependent on society's definitions and experiences of adulthood in a particular historical moment. As suggested by my analysis, there are instances when young people's responses to researchers' questions appear to be rooted less in the background of the individual youth and more in the youth's foreground, that is, in the kind of adulthood the individual anticipates experiencing in the future. This is also a data-collection issue, in that quantitative approaches tend to focus on background variables (e.g., race, gender, income of one's family-of-origin) for explanations of young people's current attitudes and behavior, whereas qualitative approaches are in a much better position to detect the ways in which young people's actions today may be explicable by reference to their anticipated futures. But whether one is analyzing quantitative data, qualitative data, or a combination of the two, the apertures of our analytical lenses need to be open wide enough to allow us to see the interconnections among childhood, youth, emerging adulthood, and adulthood (and perhaps even later life stages), and our lenses need to be sensitive enough to detect the different ways that young people respond to their shared predicaments.

Postscript

Since writing the bulk of this essay, the notion of "emerging adulthood" has gained greater currency in both academic and popular discourses. Arnett, who coined the term, has now published a book with that title (Arnett, 2004). More recently, the American Sociological Association's new magazine, *Contexts,* ran a cover story on the subject of "delayed" adulthood (Furstenberg et al., 2004), and *Time* magazine also did a cover story on "twixters" (Grossman, 2005), that is, individuals caught "betwixt and between" youth and adulthood. In the past several years, there has been a growing number of representations of "emerging adulthood" in the popular culture, in movies like *Punch-Drunk Love, The Good Girl, About a Boy, School of Rock, Lost in Translation, Garden State,* and *Along Came Polly.* These films can be added to the list of films about emerging adults that were made previously like *Slacker, Reality Bites, Swingers, Party Girl, Clerks, Chuck and Buck, Grosse Pointe Blank, Flirting with Disaster, Bottle Rocket, Chasing Amy,* and *High Fidelity.* Meanwhile, America's armed forces continue to report difficulty in meeting their recruitment needs, despite a brief bump in enlistment immediately after 9/11/01, and despite (or because of) America's ongoing "war on terror" (cf. Grimm, 2004). Youth turnout in the 2004 presidential election was "up sharply" (9.3 percent) from the 2000 election, and voters under thirty were the only age group to favor the Democratic ticket of Kerry-Edwards (http://www.civic youth.org/PopUps/Release_Turnout2004.pdf). These developments suggest that there is now an even greater need for critical youth studies and for analyses that critically interrogate generalized labels like "twixters" and other mass-media representations, while at the same time paying serious attention to the ways that the transition to adulthood is being transformed and how this affects the lived experiences of young people. There is also clearly a greater need for examinations of youth/adulthood in a global context, including the ways in which popular culture's representations may be helping to redefine the transition to adulthood both in the United States and abroad. As I have tried to demonstrate throughout this essay, the methodological dilemmas faced by youth studies scholars are really more than that: as structural and cultural forces conspire to reshape the experience of growing up, researchers need to rework not just our study designs and techniques of data collection but also our basic conceptions of youth/adulthood, our theories of how and why growing up is being transformed and what consequences this might have, and the questions we ask when analyzing our data. Just as feminist sociologists discovered that a full and accurate understanding of women's experiences required developing new ontological categories and new techniques for analyzing them, the challenge for youth scholars today is to move beyond the generic and often static concepts established during the 1960s heyday of youth research and to develop concepts and methods that are able to comprehend the lived experience of growing up in a postmodern world.

REFERENCES

Andolina, Molly W., Krista Jenkins, Scott Keeter, and Cliff Zukin. 2002. "Searching for the Meaning of Youth Civic Engagement: Notes from the Field." *Applied Developmental Science,* 6(4): 189–195.

Arnett, Jeffrey Jensen, 2000a. "High Hopes in a Grim World: Emerging Adults' Views of their Futures and 'Generation X.'" *Youth and Society,* 31(3): 267–286.

Arnett, Jeffrey Jensen. 2000b. "Emerging Adulthood: A Theory of Development from the Late Teens through the Twenties." *American Psychologist,* 55(5): 469–480.

Arnett, Jeffrey Jensen, 2002. "The Psychology of Globalization." *American Psychologist,* 57(10): 774–783.

Arnett, Jeffrey Jensen. 2004. *Emerging Adulthood.* New York: Oxford University Press.

Arnett, Jeffrey Jensen, Kathleen D. Ramos, and Lene Arnett Jensen. 2001. "Ideological Views in Emerging Adulthood: Balancing Autonomy and Community." *Journal of Adult Development,* 8(2): 69–79.

Asch, Beth J., and B. R. Orvis. 1994. *Recent Recruiting Trends and Their Implications: Preliminary Analysis and Recommendations.* Santa Monica, CA: RAND, MR-549–A/OSD.

Bailey, Beth. 1998. "From Panty Raids to Revolution: Youth and Authority, 1950–1970." In Joe Austin and Michael Nevin Willard, eds., *Generations of Youth: Youth Cultures and History in Twentieth-Century America.* New York: NYU Press, pp. 187–204.

Bucholtz, Mary. 2002. "Youth and Cultural Practice." *Annual Review of Anthropology,* 31: 525–552.

Camino, Linda, and Shepherd Zeldin. 2002. "From Periphery to Center: Pathways for Youth Civic Engagement in the Day-to-Day Life of Communities." *Applied Developmental Science,* 6(4): 213–220.

Chisholm, Lynne, and Klaus Hurrelmann. 1995. "Adolescence in Modern Europe: Pluralized Transition Patterns and Their Implications for Personal and Social Risks." *Journal of Adolescence,* 18: 129–158.

Cote, James E., and Anton L. Allahar. 1995. *Generation on Hold: Coming of Age in the Late Twentieth Century.* New York: NYU Press.

Delli Carpini, Michael X. 2000. "Gen.com: Youth, Civic Engagement, and the New Information Environment." *Political Communication,* 17: 341–349.

Department of Defense. 1996. *Population Representation in the Military Services.* Washington, DC: Department of Defense.

Dohrn, Bernadine. 2000. "Look Out, Kid, It's Something You Did": The Criminalization of Children." In Valerie Polakow, ed., *The Public Assault on America's Children: Poverty, Violence, and Juvenile Injustice.* New York: Teachers College Press.

Dorn, Edwin. 1999. "Students in Service: Why Not Tie College Financial Aid to Military Obligation?" Editorial. *San Jose Mercury News,* February 26, 7B.

Ehrlich, Thomas, 2000. *Civic Responsibility and Higher Education.* Phoenix, AZ: American Council on Education/Oryx Press.

Epstein, Jonathon S. 1998. *Youth Culture: Identity in a Postmodern World.* Malden, MA: Blackwell.

Flacks, Marc, 2000. "Reluctant Patriots? Youth, Politics, and Military Enlistment." Ph.D. dissertation, University of California–Santa Cruz.

Flacks, Marc, and Martin F. Wiskoff. 1998. *Gangs, Extremist Groups, and the Military: Screening for Service.* PERSEREC: SRC-TR-98-003.

Flanagan, Constance, and Lonnie R. Sherrod. 1998. "Youth Political Development: An Introduction." *Journal of Social Issues,* 54(3): 447–456.

Friedman, Milton. 1967. "Why Not a Volunteer Military?" In Sol Tax, ed., *The Draft: A Handbook of Facts and Alternatives.* Chicago: University of Chicago Press.

Furlong, Andy, and Fred Cartmel. 1999. *Young People and Social Change: Individualization and Risk in Late Modernity.* Philadelphia: Open University Press.

Furstenberg, Frank F. 2000. "The Sociology of Adolescence and Youth in the 1990s: A Critical Commentary." *Journal of Marriage and the Family,* 62: 896–910.

Furstenberg, Frank F., Sheila Kennedy, Vonnie C. McLoyd, Ruben G. Rumbaut, and Richard A. Settersten. 2004. "Growing Up Is Harder to Do." *Contexts,* 3(3): 33–41.

Galston, William A. 2001. "Political Knowledge, Political Engagement, and Civic Education." *Annual Review of Political Science,* 4: 217–234.

Goldscheider, Frances, and Calvin Goldscheider. 1994. "Leaving and Returning Home in Twentieth-Century America." *Population Bulletin,* 48(4): 1–35.

Grimm, Matthew. 2004. "The Army's Bitter Harvest." *Brandweek,* 45(40): 24.

Grossman, Lev. 2005. "Grow Up? Not So Fast." *Time,* 165(4): 42–53.

Hays, Carol E. 1998. "Alienation, Engagement, and the College Student: A Focus Group Study." In Thomas J. Johnson, Carol E. Hays, and Scott P. Hays, eds., *Engaging the Public: How Government and the Media Can Reinvigorate American Democracy.* New York: Rowman and Littlefield.

Keniston, Kenneth. 1968. *Young Radicals: Notes on Committed Youth.* New York: Harcourt, Brace, and World.

Lancaster, Anita, and Jerome Lehnus. 1996. "Declining Interest in Military Service: Quantitative Observations." *Proceedings of the 38th Annual Conference of the International Military Testing Association.* San Antonio, TX: IMTA, pp. 100–105.

Moore, Ryan. 1998. "'. . . And Tomorrow Is Just Another Crazy Scam': Postmodernity, Youth, and the Downward Mobility of the Middle Class." In Joe Austin and Michael Nevin Willard, eds., *Generations of Youth: Youth Cultures and History in Twentieth-Century America.* New York: NYU Press, pp. 253–271.

Muggleton, David, and Rupert Weinzierl, eds. 2003. *The Post-Subcultures Reader.* New York: Oxford University Press.

Niemi, Richard G. 1999. "Editor's Introduction to Special Issue on Political Socialization." *Political Psychology,* 20(3): 471–476.

Orvis, B. R., N. Sastry, L. L. and McDonald. 1996. *Military Recruiting Outlook: Recent Trends in Enlistment Propensity and Conversion of Potential Enlisted Supply.* Santa Monica, CA: RAND, MR-677-A/OSD.

Southwell, Priscilla Lewis. 2002. "The Politics of Alienation: Nonvoting and Support for Third-Party Candidates among 18–30-Year-Olds." *Social Science Journal,* 40: 99–107.

Widdicombe, Sue, and Robin Wooffitt. 1995. "Youth Subcultures and Sociology." In Sue Widdicombe and Robin Wooffitt, *The Language of Youth Subcultures: Social Identity in Action.* New York: Harvester Wheatsheaf.

Wyn, Johanna, and Rob White. 1997. *Rethinking Youth.* London: Sage.

Youniss, James, Susan Bales, Verona Christmas-Best, Marcelo Diversi, Milbrey McLaughlin, and Rainer Slbereisen. 2002. "Youth Civic Engagement in the Twenty-First Century." *Journal of Research on Adolescence,* 12(1): 121–148.

Chapter 3

Grow 'em Strong
Conceptual Challenges in Researching
Childhood Resilience

Michael Ungar

An increasing fascination with resilience among researchers and service providers concerned with enhancing the capacities of at-risk children, youth, and families has led many in the field of children's mental health to shift their focus from psychopathology to resilience. Despite this interest in health-related phenomena, however, the validity of the resilience construct remains a point of debate. Which child is resilient, and which not? To a large extent we have probed and discussed the lives of children facing multiple risks with the blinders of a culture deeply imbued with the perspective of a Western psychological discourse. That discourse arbitrarily designates some children as healthy and others as deviant, dangerous, delinquent, and disordered depending on the perceived social acceptability of children's behavior. Research with children has left largely unchallenged our thinking about children and the labels we adults place on them. We continue doing violence to them through our methodologically flawed and contextually irrelevant interpretations of their worlds.

In particular, there are two frequently noted shortcomings in studies of resilience that have yet to be addressed adequately. First, there is arbitrariness in the selection of outcome variables, with standardized testing more appropriate to discovering the etiology of illness than the building blocks of health. Similarly, there has been little attention paid to the social and cultural contexts in which resilience occurs. There is an implicit assumption that all children have access to the resources required to achieve the type of functioning synonymous with successful coping. For example, I was recently struck by the oddity of some of the items on the Behavioral and Emotional Rating Scale (Epstein and Sharma, 1998), a well-known measure used to assess health phenomena in children. Children and their caregivers are asked about individual children's "hobbies" and "favorite vacations." Implicit in the measure is the view that a child who has extra-curricular interests that are socially acceptable and a family with leisure time is healthier than one who does not. Questions such as these, typical of many instruments, demonstrate a cultural insularity that speaks more to the standpoint bias of the researcher than the lived experiences of a global community of children in both Northern (typically understood as economically developed, Western) and Southern (less economically developed) countries. Whatever are we to make, then, of the child soldier in Sierra Leone or the young street vendor in Colombia who have neither the time nor the resources to pursue socially acceptable pathways to resilience?

In this chapter, I will look at these issues and argue that we require methodologies that can engage with children in ways that promote their constructions of health being heard alongside that of their caregivers and elders. In an effort to make this concrete, I will discuss an ongoing program of research that is seeking to develop a mixed-method design to study children's resilience in ways that address these issues. These efforts have involved an interdisciplinary team of international researchers with expertise in both qualitative and quantitative methods, service providers, families, and youth. A multiyear project now under way in Canada, the United States, Colombia, Hong Kong, Palestine, Israel, The Gambia, South Africa, Tanzania, India, and Russia to develop and pilot a methodology to study resilience has generated an approach to research that is contextually relevant and more systematic in its selection of outcome criteria by which resilience is to be discovered rather than judged.

Competing Definitions of Resilience

An immense body of literature has helped us to understand some of the processes and characteristics associated with individuals who overcome great adversity and live healthy lives. However, as sweeping as some of these studies have been, the problem remains that definitional ambiguity continues for terms like "risk factors," "protective mechanisms," "vulnerability," and "resilience" (Anthony and Cohler, 1987; Cairns and Cairns, 1994; Fraser, 1997; Glantz and Sloboda, 1999; Luthar, 1993). At its simplest, a definition of resilience could be as succinct as that provided by Masten, who defines resilience as a "class of phenomena characterized by *good out-comes in spite of serious threats to adaptation or development*" (2001:228). Resilience, or an ability to bounce back following exposure to severe or prolonged stress, is understood to indicate both the state of a child's well-being and the characteristics and processes through which well-being is successfully achieved (Gilgun, 1999).

Although such definitions would seem to make resilience something easy to study, even quantitative researchers have been self-critical regarding the arbitrariness of their choice of outcome measures and the difficulties accounting for cultural and contextual variables that challenge us to say anything about the findings that is generalizable across contexts (Masten, 2001; McCubbin et al., 1998; Silbereisen and von Eye, 1999). According to Richman and Fraser, "resilience requires exposure to significant risk, overcoming risk or adversity, and success that is beyond predicted expectations. Of course, problems arise when researchers and practitioners attempt to agree on what constitutes *significant* risk and *successful* outcomes that are *beyond predicted* expectations" (2001:6). And Cohen and his colleagues note that "the variability in participants' subjective definitions of such terms as *benefits* or *gains*" means researchers must necessarily introduce their own bias and model of adjustment in order to draw conclusions from their data (1998:325). Quantitative researchers have responded with some healthy caution and methodological complexity, challenging one subject's self-report with the corroboration of significant others, and by using control groups to better understand the basis for normal functioning. It is not surprising, then, that quantitative researchers have refined their measures, expanded their data collection, and sought variability across cultural groups, as well as employed more powerful analytic tools to better account for the apparent arbitrariness in their findings. Sadly, they have seldom turned to colleagues across research paradigms for answers, largely ignoring complementary qualitative methods such as grounded theory, ethnographies, and hermeneutics (see, for some exceptions, Boehnke, 1999; Graham, 2001; Graham and Rockwood, 1998; Hauser, 1999; Kaplan, 1999; Luthar and Zigler, 1991; Magnus et al., 1999; Nesselroade and McCollam, 2000; Rutter, 2001; Thoits, 1995; Yellin, Quinn, and Hoffman, 1998).

Not surprisingly, without confronting the underlying methodological shortcomings of quantitative data collection, efforts to deconstruct the arbitrariness of what is and is not a good health-related outcome have fallen short of broadening our understanding of resilience. We have been unsuccessful in sustaining a more child-focused appreciation for how lives are lived well. There persists in this literature a reluctance by authors to present the voices of youth and their unique communities in a way that is appreciative of who they are and how they survive. In my own work, which has been more participatory and engaged with youth in the co-construction of a definition of resilience, youth naively labeled as deviant, dangerous, delinquent, and disordered have argued instead that *resilience is the outcome from negotiations between individuals and their environments to maintain a self-definition as healthy* (Ungar, 2002a, 2004). In other words, resilience is not something that can be arbitrarily designated without giving due consideration to the relative power of the one doing the defining and the one being defined. The self-other dichotomy, so aptly critiqued by Fine (1994), evaporates in a blur of competing discourses as we come to realize that infrequently are children's voices privileged when we label them as healthy or unhealthy. In the words of one participant working with me during a recent study, "sticks and stones may break my bones, but names will really hurt me." Defined this way, resilience becomes a question of one's degree of discursive empowerment. If I am convinced I am healthy despite the adversity I face, and I am capable of convincing others of my health status, then I am healthy.

Take for example a teenaged girl who gives birth to a child. We typically say that a teenager who has a child is more at risk than one who does not. But in this chaotic terrain of competing definitions of risk and resilience, we cannot say that a woman's being older when she first gives birth is necessarily a protective factor. There is evidence that for some teenagers, the birth of their first child is not a crisis. In fact, it brings them a sense of maturity and the social status they crave (for a good example of this, see Adrian LeBlanc's journalistic novel, *Random Family* [2003], or Ladner's study [1971]). In addition, this definitional ambiguity is further confounded by culture. As Luthar and Zelazo note, "There is a need for greater consideration of *cross-cultural variations* in resilience processes. The literature in this field is markedly lacking in international perspectives, and it will be useful to illuminate the types of risk modifiers that tend to be highly robust across widely disparate cultural contexts and those more idiosyncratic to particular settings" (2003:525).

With all these problems, it has come time to see qualitative methods as more than exploratory opening acts to the quantitative show. They can instead be a methodologically sound approach knitted into mixed-method designs or standing firmly on their own as robust knowledge-generating research tools for health researchers.

Contextualizing Resilience: Universal versus the Specific

Clearly, we need to understand children's worlds better, both through deconstruction and contextualization. As the social sciences philosopher Ian Hacking (1999) argues, it is important to do more than understand our experiences as socially constructed; we must also take into account the factual circumstances in which our lives unfold. A child who is labeled delinquent, but who has few other options for success, will do what he or she must to survive. Even Pulitzer Prize–winning novelist Frank McCourt demonstrated as much in his book *Angela's Ashes* (1996). The main character, Frankie, growing up in incredible poverty in Limerick, Ireland, nevertheless survives, not always doing what we would prefer a healthy young boy do. In one passage, McCourt writes,

> The Dominican church is just up Glentworth Street.
> Bless me, Father, for I have sinned, it's a fortnight since my last confession. I tell him the usual sins and then, I stole fish and chips from a drunken man.
> Why, my child?
> I was hungry, Father.
> And why were you hungry?
> There was nothing in my belly, Father.
> He says nothing and even though it's dark I know he's shaking his head. My dear child, why can't you go home and ask your mother for something?
> Because she sent me looking for my father in the pubs, Father, and I couldn't find him and she hasn't a scrap in the house because he's drinking the five pounds Grandpa sent from the North for the new baby and she's raging by the fire because I can't find my father. (184–185)

We run the risk of overlooking aspects of resilience in children like Frankie, and clues to help children heal, when we fail to note the hidden resilience evident in their lives (Ungar, 2002a, 2004). Instead, as Lesko (2001) explains, we seek to control them to keep our fear of them in check, without necessarily critiquing the world that *we offer* them as their salvation. Furthermore, Martineau (1999), in her look at the way resilience as a construct is used, explains, "The resiliency discourse imposes prescribed norms of school success and social success upon underprivileged children identified as at risk. The effect is that non-conforming individuals may be pathologized as *non-resilient.* Emphasis remains wholly on the individual and thus, *individualism* is a dominant ideology embedded in the mainstream resiliency discourse" (11–12) (for a similar critique see Massey et al., 1998).

The children who resist the hegemony imposed on them by a media that would have us believe everyone's life should look like a Walt Disney production are not likely to invite much praise. However, for many, especially those without access to the families or communities, personal competencies or motivation to make their lives over in the image of Walt's Utopia, they run the risk that their hyperactivity, adventure seeking, risk-taking, and pursuit of differentness will be overlooked as their only viable sources of resilience.

This can best be understood when one appreciates the complexity of understanding the qualities that support resilience. Jew, Green, and Kroger (1999), for example, developed a resiliency scale based on work by Mrazek and Mrazek (1987). The scale measures twelve skills and abilities people use to cope with stress: rapid responsivity to danger, precocious maturity, disassociation of affect, information seeking, formation and utilization of relationships for survival, positive projective anticipation, decisive risk-taking, the conviction of being loved, idealization of an aggressor's competence, cognitive restructuring of painful events, altruism, and optimism and hope. What is seldom acknowledged, however, is that all twelve characteristics are potentially available to some children through deviant pathways to health as well as pathways that are more socially acceptable. One need only think of how gangs offer youth a street family, a sense of belonging, even hope and opportunities for "decisive risk-taking" that impoverished families struggling with addictions and underfunded schools may not. Resilience, then, must be viewed in the context of the availability of resources, options, culture, politics, constructed meanings, and finally health discourses.

Qualitative methods have a natural edge when it comes to this kind of contextualized research. When we fail to listen to children's own stories we are likely to miss important details of their thriving. What I have called "narratives of resilience" are in fact children's healthy self-constructions hidden beneath chaotic behaviors in resource-poor environments (Ungar, 2001a, 2004).

Studying Children: Culture and Place

There is a tension in the resilience literature between the search for universal truths and tolerance for the heterogeneity of children's expressions of health and how that health is promoted globally. As Swartz (1998), a South African, explains, there are no universals when it comes to mental health, when we look at people's experiences of health or the phenomena of illness. Mental health is not just biological. Our current discourse that seeks to make it so seems sorely misguided when one inquires about mental health phenomena using non-Western and nonmedical models of health. Swartz's comments lead us squarely into a debate over hermeneutics, one component of qualitative research. How are we to understand another's experience within the context and constraints of another's life unless we get the individual to explain his or her life to us? We are challenged to understand an individual's emic (personal) construction of reality when blinded by the supposed veracity of our own etic (outsider) perspective. The more we do so, the more likely we will be able to methodologically handle the heterogeneity inherent in experiences of health and illness that we encounter through cross-cultural research.

In practical terms, Swartz shows how treating something like posttraumatic stress cannot be done using a cookie-cutter approach. Nor can we individualize trauma. For example, women who Swartz worked with who had suffered displacement and violence were reluctant to accept new homes provided by the government, even though they evidently needed the shelter. A psychopathologizing discourse might locate the source of their problems in a fear of attaching to one place or another or in an inability to make decisions. But Swartz shows that the women had good reason to be worried about their relocation: they feared that other services they had come to rely on such as food support and mental health counseling would be revoked once they were resettled. In other words, in treating these women's trauma, those who intervened needed to understand the very specific ways the women viewed their world and how each decision they made was both a reflection of their inner psychological state as well as an appraisal of the real-world threats to survival that they experienced.

Research to Address Cultural Pluralism and Resilience

One need only look globally at children's lives to know the necessity for contextualizing better how we understand children's expressions of health. Suppose an eighteen-year-old American youth (I will consider her a child despite her age, for reasons that will become clear later on) joins the Marines and dies fighting in Iraq. As is rightly her due, her tragic death is mourned by her country, and her courage is applauded by her family and friends. That this youth has access to a militarily advanced army to which she can dedicate her efforts to protect others speaks to the context in which she is able to express a desire to do something worthwhile. But what are we to make of the seventeen-year-old Palestinian youth who, having grown up in exile, finds no such easy path to the same expression of community consciousness? Instead, she straps explosives to her body and, believing in the righteousness of her cause, sacrifices her life (and the lives of innocent others) in what she perceives as the fulfillment of her role as a soldier in an undeclared war. There is simply no way to understand the actions of these youth as either a soldier or suicide bomber without appreciating the contextual specificity in which their decisions are made (see Awwad, 1999). These are very difficult critiques for us to accept, so certain have we been that one expression of resistance/protection/nationalism is healthy, the other the act of a child incapable of making an informed decision. In Booth's (2002) look at Arab adolescents, however, we are shown that fundamentalism might be adaptive when there are few choices for self-expression. A careful reading of international accounts of children's lives shows that they make due as best they can. Though they are often pulled toward internalizing the values handed to them as part of a hegemonic globalization, they also effectively resist, sustaining unique and culturally valid beliefs.

As an exemplar of what research can do, we can look at a study led by Lalonde (2004) on youth suicide among Canadian aboriginal populations. In trying to understand why Canada has the highest rates of youth suicide among aboriginal youth in the world, Lalonde looked beyond the individual for answers. He examined why some people in some communities kill themselves while others who share many demographic similarities, such as culture and socioeconomic level, but live in different communities do not. His research proves that some communities insulate youth from the risks of suicide. In other words, although Lalonde does not specifically talk about resilience, his work strongly supports the thesis of this chapter, that resilience is as much a quality of the child's community as an individual characteristic.

Lalonde reviews youth suicide rates over a fourteen-year period in two hundred Native bands in British Columbia on Canada's west coast. Though geographically and culturally linked, over half of all bands had no suicides in the past fourteen years. Lalonde hypothesizes, and then shows, that children in some communities do not navigate the transitions from simple to complex understandings of themselves as a unified self as they mature. The narratives or stories that youth tell about themselves in increasingly complex ways as they grow are not well supported in some communities. In communities where youth suicide is high, as many as 80 percent of the youth are unable to adequately answer the question of how they are still the same but different as they grow and mature. They have no dominant narrative or essentialist explanation for the paradoxical experience of change and sameness. Lalonde speculates that self-continuity "is not a private matter" and that we create a sense of ourselves through contact with others. In other words, something as individual as self-concept carried over time is extinguished in some communities and sustained in others. The fact of being a Native person is not the risk factor that predicts suicide. Continuity in language use, spirituality, traditional ways of life, engagement in collective political and legal fights, youth programs, and community control over natural resources and government bodies seem to produce a climate in which youth at the individual level experience more continuity in their identity development. In fact, so strong was the association that Lalonde showed that communities that had eight specific features—self-government, negotiated land claims, control over their children's education, control over health services, police and fire services, a building for cultural events, women participating in band governance, and control over their child and family services—had had no suicides occur among their youth during the fourteen-year period studied.

The Need for Qualitative Contributions to Resilience Research

Quantitative measures of health-seeking behavior cannot help but carry with them the bias of a cultural myopia. If we think back to the example of the soldier and the suicide bomber, we might speculate that the conceptual terrain separating the actions of those two young women is murky at best. Any examination bounded by a priori assumptions of each individual's health, decontextualized, would likely produce a biased picture. Typically, when quantitative researchers consider the problems they face in the arbitrariness of their designs, their tendency has been to simply do more of the same (Nesselroade and McCollam, 2000). Qualitative methods have the potential to present a more comprehensive picture of lives lived under adversity, but to date their use has been limited and their integration with more mainstream programs of research has been less than adequate (Galambos and Leadbeater, 2000). This argument for a need for contextualization is even more relevant when we include in studies participants from Southern-world contexts, whose lives are seldom reflected in the literature. If we look, for example, at a high-risk environment such as that found in Bogatá, Colombia, we require new explanations to document health phenomena. When Klevens, a researcher with the Centers for Disease Control in Atlanta, explored the life histories of forty-six young men from high-risk families in Bogatá, she found that the epidemiological factors she predicted would account for patterns of violence were not the ones the men themselves said were the most significant (Klevens and Roca, 1999). As Klevens explains, "We chose qualitative methods for data collection and analysis to avoid imposing foreign variables and hypotheses in this new context and to allow new variables to emerge from the data" (313). Such efforts to give voice to those marginalized from professional health discourses is not an argument for unhampered relativism but, instead, an honest effort to make health research a more political affair, one in which the power over how problems are defined and their etiologies explained is understood as part of people's negotiations for power. Those who control the naming of our lives also control the health resources we need to heal and the structures through which they are provided.

The Benefits of Qualitative Methods

In particular, five aspects of good qualitative research make it ideally suited to studies of health and resilience in children (Ungar, 2002b): its ability to discover unnamed processes, attend to the contextual specificity of health phenomena, increase the "volume" of marginalized voices, produce thick enough descriptions of lives lived for others to transfer findings between contexts, and challenge the researcher standpoint bias that orients findings toward an adult-centric perspective.

Discovery of Unnamed Processes

Children's health-seeking béhaviors are seldom seen through their own eyes. A poignant example is found scattered throughout the literature regarding children's own strategies to protect against risk as they move in and out of care (Garbarino, 2001; Ungar, 2001b). In a recent study during which I interviewed forty-three youth who had experienced multiple out-of-home placements, I found that

> the high-risk youth in this study talked about their behaviours before, during and after placement as efforts to construct a self-definition for themselves as resilient. These constructive efforts resisted the problem-saturated identities imposed on them both by their communities and caregivers while residents/clients/wards/patients. Contrary to what caregivers believe, youth see themselves as exercising a great deal of control (but not exclusive control) over several aspects of the placement process. They argue that they influence when they "get put inside," the way they "survive inside," and the way they cope when "going home." At each juncture, youth say they use placement as a way to negotiate continuities and discontinuities in their identity constructions in order to co-create the most powerful and health-enhancing identity available from the resources they have at hand. (Ungar, 2001b:143–144)

A process of institutionalization as negotiation for health resources is not typically what we imagine occurring among high-risk children. Such discoveries are typical of qualitative methods that have promoted lengthy engagement with participants and their files or that have had key informants make visible health-related patterns that might not otherwise have been obvious to outsiders (Felsman, 1989; Gilgun, 1996, 1999; Rodwell, 1998; Silverman, 2000; Strauss and Corbin, 1990).

Contextual Specificity

The above example demonstrates that even the children on our doorstep can remain incomprehensible to outside researchers who believe health is found in one pattern, such as through a secure attachment with family members. In order for research on children to be more truly inclusive, we must pay attention to different socioeconomic or sociocultural backgrounds. A recent article by Zimbabwean Elias Mpofu (2002) recounts the different meaning early-onset aggression has to youth in his country. It is highly improbable, he says, that such patterns are equivalent in their consequences to the same behaviors found among children in economically developed countries. We rarely see such qualifiers as this in reported findings published in reputable journals. Disclaimers that make explicit the very limited generalizability of findings beyond one community in one country are seldom seen.

Instead, we might better follow the lead of researchers like Johnson-Powell and Yamamoto, who approaches research on children with an explicit eye to context:

> A comprehensive assessment requires information from the school, the parents, significant family members, and the child; and it must also include the cultural factors related to the psychosocial environment, the cultural identity, and the cultural explanation or meanings given to the child's symptoms or behavior. The cultural assessment then becomes an essential part of the diagnostic process. (1997:350)

In practice this means creating work that resembles that of Dupree, Spencer, and Bell (1997), which builds on Spencer's phenomenological variant of ecological systems theory that has challenged culturally inappropriate assumptions such as those regarding the prevalence of suspected deviance in African American communities. Instead Dupree et al. urge us to see children's behavior as meaning different things in different cultural contexts. For example, in order to see resilience among African American youth and families, notably the healthy aspects of how children are raised in "fatherless" homes (a biased perspective at best), we need to look beyond outcomes and instead appreciate people's experiences of their oppression, their living situation, and other broad social forces rather than blame parents for what are likely highly adaptive coping strategies manifested as parenting practices.

The Power of Marginalized Voices

In her qualitative research with a group of fifteen adolescents attending a day treatment program at a state mental health facility in the United States, Flom (2002) notes what she terms the "resilience aspirations" of participants. Despite the problems they face, and their precarious mental health status, these youth still hold clear hopes for a better future and a critical perspective on the service gaps they experience, in opposition to the individualized claims of psychopathology in evidence in their clinical records and among the professionals who provide them with care. Within Flom's account of these adolescent voices, we find recognition of a perspective of health as resource dependent. This perspective is not unique (see Caputo, 2000). As Huang (2003) says, "We need to integrate the impact of disparities into our mental health care of children." It would seem the children agree. When heard through qualitative research, the marginalized voices of youth are frequently disturbing. Discoveries of health among those we assume to be unhealthy are best elicited through qualitative inquiry. Quantitative efforts tend to discover, but be unable to account for, the marginal discourses found among youth.

Such findings should not surprise us when we attend to the voices of children themselves. In fact, children can help to show us the ineffectiveness of the very interventions we adults employ to correct their behavior. For example, Salmivalli's (2001) quantitative work in Finland using a peer-led intervention in a school to address bullying found that results showed at best ambivalence about bullying and at worst that pro-bullying attitudes actually *increased* among boys following the intervention. If we are to move beyond the confusion such findings reveal, then we must adopt qualitative methods that can capture the perspectives of children themselves (see, for example, Lightfoot, 1992).

Transferability

As discussed earlier, qualitative research provides a way to thickly describe the lives of children, especially those from culturally diverse backgrounds who may be doubly marginalized by both age and social address. When we conduct qualitative research we are amply cautioned that the responsibility for interpreting results from one group in the context of another must be given to those who are consumers of the research. As Lincoln and Guba explain, the researcher "can provide only the thick description necessary to enable someone interested in making a transfer to reach a conclusion about whether transfer can be contemplated as a possibility" (1985:316).

To return to the example of bullying and other forms of violence between youth, we now know to approach the phenomenon with caution. As Garbarino found in his examination of youth violence among inmates at a maximum-security juvenile detention center, "all acts of violence express a need for justice. . . . Such behaviors may be warped and distorted and difficult to fathom from the outside, but if we dig deeply enough and listen openly enough, we may hear of the need to restore justice by personally acting on the feelings of shame that come from being rejected, denied, abused, and deprived" (2001:84–85). If we are to help children move toward pro-social behaviors (if that remains our goal), then starting with an understanding of how their behavior is motivated by a search for health and seeing part of their negotiations with others as healthy will arguably put us in a better position to intervene. In short, we need to proceed cautiously when distilling lessons from Garbarino's work or that of any other researcher. Children's stories, especially when compared across contexts, do not all mean the same thing.

Researcher Standpoint Bias

Although qualitative inquiry has the potential to explore these unheard stories, and has been demonstrated to be effective in doing so, it is important that researchers of all stripes attend to their biased standpoints. Qualitative investigations in which the researcher is the research instrument makes it easier to discern the adult-centric bias that many studies fail to control. Participatory work, for example, by Cheatham and Shen (2003) with Cambodian girls living in California made sure researchers checked their bias through participatory means of investigation. Explicit in the research was a focus on the relative power of the participants and the researchers: "Dealing explicitly with issues of power in [Community Based Participatory Research] does not mean that power is always equally shared but rather that power dynamics are not hidden and that efforts at democratizing power take place to the extent possible" (318–319). Ensuring the participation of research subjects, and the consciousness of researcher standpoint, is more easily accomplished when qualitative or mixed-method designs are employed in health-related research.

Qualitative Studies of Resilience

There are a growing number of studies of resilience that employ qualitative methods. Given the five strengths of qualitative studies in resilience-related research, it is becoming more apparent to the research community that qualitative research can complement quantitative methods. The two research paradigms form a dialectic, in which some combination of the two may produce the most informed findings. As discussed, the arbitrariness and contextual problems that plague resilience research can be addressed through the use of qualitative approaches.

The fit between qualitative methods and the study of phenomenon in which one must account for the contextual specificity of the construct under investigation is well established. Such inquiry does, however, bring with it hidden dangers amid the maze of confusion that occurs when qualitative inquiry takes place in settings that are less familiar with these methods (Miller and Crabtree, 1994; Morgan, 1998). Importantly, qualitative studies of childhood resilience have shown that there are very specific ways health is understood based on the standpoints of those involved in the research (Gilgun, 1999; Klevens and Roca, 1999; Taylor, Gilligan, and Sullivan, 1995; Ungar and Teram, 2000). To the studies already discussed we can add work by Todis and her colleagues (2001) that followed fifteen adolescents for five years as they moved in and out of placements, demonstrating that according to the youth themselves, it is the quality of attachments that makes the differences to health outcomes. Similarly, Schofield (2000) took a life-span perspective and interviewed forty adults about their childhood placement experiences with nonkin families, highlighting again the mechanisms that best protect children but that are too complex to capture in any one quantitative study. De Antoni and Koller (2000) documented the lives of Brazilian street children and their ingenious ways of surviving, again through attachments to one another and to caring adults. Likewise, two psychoanalysts from Israel, Apfel and Simon (2000), used unstructured interviews to understand how ten Israeli and ten Palestinian children cope with the situation they currently experience. These examples, and many others, are beginning to break new conceptual and methodological terrain in the study of resilience.

A Program of Research

In order to address the many issues discussed in this chapter, members of an international team of researchers, direct service providers, administrators, and students in eleven countries on five continents are collaborating to address shortcomings in the study of resilience (Ungar et al., in press; Ungar and Liebenberg, 2005). Specifically, the International Resilience Project is working from the following hypotheses:

1. Hypothesis One: Resilience is a multidimensional construct, the definition of which is negotiated between individuals and their communities.
2. Hypothesis Two: In order to overcome the arbitrariness in the choice of outcomes associated with resilience and to produce contextually sensitive research methods and tools for its study, a methodologically diverse interdisciplinary global community of researchers, service providers, and participants/advisers (both elders and youth) is needed.

This research endeavor is, to the best knowledge of my colleagues and me, the first attempt to design and pilot research that addresses the challenges of comparing resilience-related data from a mixed-methods study across diverse domestic and international cultural and environmental contexts. This pilot work is committed to resolving the apparent contradictions between the demands for contextual specificity, construct validity across settings, and generalizability or transferability of findings in the study of resilience. Each of the communities involved in this work have come on board with the express purpose of gaining access to the tools to study resilience in their specific contexts in order to understand the pathways to health that high-risk children and families travel.

This international team brings together academics and community leaders with disciplinary and methodological diversity and cross-cultural expertise. Represented are experts from the fields of social work, health statistics and measurement, psychology, medical anthropology, education, medicine, and epidemiology. Methodological diversity has been assured through the combination of well-recognized quantitative researchers and equally well-known qualitative researchers. Finally, research partners from many different global communities not only add methodological expertise but also offer cultural awareness and diversity. Equally important are the selected domestic and international research sites that have enthusiastically embraced this project, lending their organizational support and capacity.

Each community has been selected for the diversity it brings to understanding children and youth in high-risk environments. Sheshatshiu in Labrador is a northern Canadian aboriginal community struggling with cultural disintegration and high rates of suicide and substance abuse among young people; Hong Kong provides access to children and youth in a country undergoing vast sociopolitical change; both Palestine and Israel, two separate sites, provide access to high-risk children and youth experiencing war; Medellin, Colombia, brings to the research the voices of children and youth struggling for health in one of the most violent cities on earth; Moscow brings access to child and youth populations experiencing the turmoil of social and economic upheaval and related mental health problems; India provides access to children and youth living in poverty, coping with an economy in transition, and confronted by sectarian violence; The Gambia, Tanzania, and South Africa all struggle with epidemics of AIDS, poverty, and violence; South Florida provides a cohort of racially diverse children and youth with a range of mental and family-related health issues; Halifax provides access to children and youth with mental and emotional challenges more typical of resilience research done to date, and Winnipeg provides the diversity of a street population and of youth and children in care facilities in North America.

The project has taken a unique approach to combining methodologies, rather than using qualitative methods as exploratory, with the implicit assumption that the real work is then done quantitatively. In designing the initial study across all sites, a Child and Youth Resilience Measure (CYRM) and concurrent qualitative approaches were developed through electronic and face-to-face discussions in small groups and during complete team meetings together in March 2003 and June 2005. The CYRM includes thirty-two topic areas nominated for inclusion by the group as a whole and questions related to each area jointly generated by youth, elders, academics, and service providers in each community. The team then integrated at least one "local" question from each research site into the final instrument being administered across all sites. Each site also has the opportunity to include in its administration of the CYRM questions that it thinks useful but that were not selected for cross-site testing.

Qualitatively, a tool kit of possible qualitative methods are being shared among team members in order to allow narratives of resilience to be gathered in different cultural contexts. These tools include the use of cameras and other audio and visual equipment to document children's lives; vignettes that participants can comment on, with responses compared between sites; the exchange between sites of children's stories told in culturally appropriate ways and recorded to allow comparative coding and interpretation; sentence-completion exercises that fit well in cultures where expectations regarding privacy are high; talking circles conducted in cultural contexts where there are strong oral traditions; the sharing of games or outdoor challenges as a way to stimulate reflection and comment; as well as other indigenous techniques being developed as the research advances and as challenges to data collection are encountered.

In order to develop a combined methodology numerous challenges had to be overcome. A series of steps were taken to bring consensus among group members. We began by asking one representative from each research site to answer the following questions:

- What are the most significant challenges faced by children and youth in your community?
- What are the most common factors that help children and youth cope with the challenges they face?
- What does the term resilience mean to people in your community?

Following the sharing of this information, the team addressed four methodological issues.

1. Who do we study? There was widespread recognition and agreement that any transitions from one developmental stage to another are important events in children's lives but that the timing of these transitions would vary in terms of which life events are considered to be important. For example, in Labrador twelve- to thirteen-year-olds are well along in their decisions regarding smoking, drugs, and sexual relationships. In Hong Kong the decision about which school a youth will attend changes the youth's outcome and prospects: school selection carries an important meaning in a child's life and therefore this transition occurs at quite a young age (eleven to twelve years). In Florida, eleven- to twelve-year-olds are engaging in risk-taking behaviors. In the more violent communities in Medellin, Colombia, it is not uncommon to encounter twelve-year-old boys who have been involved in three or four serious assaults and weapons offenses. It was decided to sample youth at the age at which they make the transition to a more adult-like status within their communities, even if this age was different in different research sites. Even with this ideal criteria for selection, the final sample still varied even by communities' definitions of transitional ages due to issues of accessibility to youth in contexts where such research is not typically performed. The final sample of 1,451 youth completed the CYRM, and another eighty-seven participated in qualitative data collection activities. These youth included those "doing well" and those "not doing well" based on community norms. Both males and females are being studied. In addition, community elders who could speak to the phenomenon of resilience in their community were also included in the study.

2. *What do we study?* In discussing the many factors that could potentially affect resilience, there were a number of worries expressed. Chief among them was that many of the cultural items did not translate well into English. For example, while trying to translate the idea of "self-betterment" from Chinese into English, the following phrases were used: self-reliance, to regenerate oneself, to improve oneself, trying to obtain excellence, having a personal philosophy, living harmoniously, and not fighting it; but none of these phrases adequately expressed the construct. In deciding which aspects of resilience to study, both quantitatively and qualitatively, a lengthy list of potential areas of study were ranked by team members, and then items not specified in the literature were added. Most notable is the identification of items related to culture that were largely overlooked in the mainstream literature. These include questions such as the following:

- To what extent do you know where your parent(s) and/or grandparents were born?
- To what extent does the older generation understand and tolerate the ideas and strong beliefs of people your age?
- To what extent does your culture teach you to become a better person?
- To what extent are members of your family or community who do unacceptable things accepted afterward?
- To what extent can you openly disagree with your parent(s) and elders when you believe things different from what they believe?

3. *What are the best qualitative and quantitative approaches for this kind of research?* Quantitatively, it was recognized that the team required a semi-structured measure that accommodates well to language and literacy differences. It was proposed that a conceptually driven skeleton be created and distributed to all the sites. Each site would then contribute items it felt necessary to understand resilience in its particular context. The qualitative methods allow the team to look at more than just the statistical significance of each item, but to understand the most important attributes of resilience in context. Some of these questions include, "Do you trust your parents to choose the person you will marry?" (The Gambia), "Does your family's economic and social background influence your peers' attitudes

toward you?" (Russia), and "Do you have any knowledge in suicide intervention?" (the Innu of Sheshatshiu, Labrador, who have a rate of suicide at least five times the Canadian average).

As already noted, a toolbox of qualitative tools has also been in development. Guiding their implementation are "catalyst" questions that are being used in all sites to stimulate conversations and other forms of data collection. These questions included the following:

- What would one need to know to grow up well here?
- How do you describe people who grow up well here despite the many problems they face?
- What does it mean to you, to your family, and to your community, when bad things happen?
- What do you do, and others you know do, to keep healthy, mentally, physically, emotionally, spiritually?
- Can you share with me a story about another child who grew up well in this community despite facing many challenges?

For both sets of researchers, the goal has been to find indigenous methods of data collection that are novel and fit well with particular contexts.

4. What are the major ethical issues in this research? There are both site-specific issues and issues that all sites shared in common. Among the most pressing issues confronting this research are confidentiality and safety, the consent process, and the usefulness of the research to each community.

Regarding confidentiality, it was noted that in some communities youth may not want to share information with others, nor would they trust adults not to share information with their parents and other caregivers. There are also significant differences regarding the interviewers' obligation to report abuse across sites. How are interviewers to respond to instances when children are being exposed to domestic violence or when youth may be returning to a dangerous community or home? It has been the explicit belief of the team that in all such instances confidentiality and safety concerns must be discussed at the local level before proceeding with the study.

Gaining written or verbal consent is similarly complicated. In Canada and the United States, with younger children, parental consent is required. However, in Russia, Colombia, and India, people are suspicious about signing a consent form and have been similarly reluctant to agree to audio or video recordings. Also, it may be difficult to get more than oral consent from street youth in Western settings. In other settings such as China, it can be inappropriate to ask parental permission if the school where data collection is taking place has already given its permission for a child to participate in the study. Across all sites it has been important to emphasize that participation remains voluntary and that participants retain the right to withdraw from the study at any time. Such issues have been addressed by local ethics committees, when available. In settings where such structures do not exist, a protocol has been developed clearly stating where participants can go to discuss any problems that arise during the research.

Finally, the team felt strongly and discussed at length the need to ensure that communities receive something tangible for their participation. Some partner communities have a history of being the objects of research and therefore have needed to have it made clear how information is interpreted, how meaning is ascribed, and who has ownership of the research about the community and its people. In most cases, developing the communities' research capacity, returning results to key stakeholders, providing training through exchanges of researchers, coauthoring reports, and assisting in future funding proposals to seed new program development were all felt to be sufficient gains by the communities involved.

Breaking Barriers

There is little precedent for this interdisciplinary, mixed-method approach to studying resilience. This fact is well documented in the recent National Institute of Mental Health *Report on Child and Adolescent Mental Health*, which cites "discipline insularity" as a major threat to our "prospects for gaining a deeper understanding of the complexities of child and adolescent mental illnesses" (2001:5). Researchers studying resilience in culturally distinct settings have employed designs that typically integrate established test instruments with demonstrated reliability and validity from studies of mental functioning more typically used in research on illness and seldom validated with populations outside Northern or economically developed settings. A few attempts at constructing resilience instruments have shown promise, though they vary greatly in their content and reported validity and reliability (Cohen et al., 1998; Kaplan, 1999; O'Neal, 1999). As discussed earlier, past attempts to study resilience have included a variety of retrospective, longitudinal, and prospective designs with a large and varied number of factors being studied, without consensus across disciplines of which are the most appropriate or of how best to measure them.

The study outlined above, developed to address the methodological and contextual shortcomings facing resilience researchers, is an exemplar of what can be accomplished when paradigmatically and culturally diverse teams of researchers and community stakeholders come together. Far from utopian, these efforts are similar to that of other teams internationally that are striving to achieve the same fit between methods and contexts. The cultural myopia of Western-based research that assumes homogeneity is no longer sufficiently robust to understand the complexity of children's lives and the multiple pathways they travel toward resilience.

REFERENCES

Anthony, E. J., and Cohler, B. J. (eds.) (1987). *The invulnerable child.* New York: Guilford.

Apfel, R. J., and Simon, B. (2000). Mitigating discontents with children in war: An ongoing psychoanalytic inquiry. In A. Robben and M. Suarez-Orozco (eds.), *Cultures under siege: Collective violence and trauma* (pp. 102–130). New York: Publications of the Society for the Study of Psychological Anthropology.

Awwad, E. (1999). Between trauma and recovery: Some perspectives on Palestinian's vulnerability and adaptation. In K. Nader, N. Dubrow, and B. H. Stamm (eds.), *Honoring differences: Cultural issues in the treatment of trauma and loss* (pp. 234–266). Philadelphia: Brunner/Mazel.

Boehnke, K. (1999). Is there social change? Photographs as a means of contrasting individual development and societal change in the new states of Germany. In R. K. Silbereisen and A. von Eye (eds.), *Growing up in times of social change* (pp. 31–50). New York: Walter de Gruyter.

Booth, M. (2002). Arab adolescents facing the future: Enduring ideals and pressures to change. In B. Bradford, R. W. Larson, and T. S. Saraswathi (eds.), *The world's youth: adolescence in eight regions of the globe* (pp. 207–242). New York: Cambridge University Press.

Cairns, R. B., and Cairns, B. D. (1994). *Lifelines and risks: Pathways of youth in our time.* Cambridge: Cambridge University Press.

Caputo, T. (2000). *Hearing the voices of youth: Youth participation in selected Canadian municipalities.* Ottawa: Health Canada.

Cheatham, A., and Shen, E. (2003). Community-based participatory research with Cambodian girls in Long Beach, California: A case study. In M. Minkler and N. Wallerstein (eds.), *Community-based participatory research for health* (pp. 316–331). San Francisco: Jossey-Bass.

Cohen, L. H., Cimbolic, K., Armeli, S. R., and Hettler, T. R. (1998). Quantitative assessment of thriving. *Journal of Social Issues,* 54(2), 323–335.

de Antoni, C., and Koller, S. (2000). Vulnerability and resilience: A study with adolescents who had suffered intrafamilial maltreatment. *PSICO,* 31(1), 39–66.

Dupree, D., Spencer, M. B., and Bell, S. (1997). African American children. In G. Johnson-Powell and J. Yamamoto (eds.), *Transcultural child development: Psychological assessment and treatment* (pp. 237–268). New York: Wiley.

Epstein, M. H., and Sharma, J. M. (1998). *Behavioral and emotional rating scale (BERS).* Austin, TX: PRO-ED.

Felsman, J. K. (1989). Risk and resiliency in childhood: The lives of street children. In T. F. Dugan and R. Coles (eds.), *The child in our times: Studies in the development of resiliency* (pp. 56–80). New York: Brunner/Mazel.

Fine, M. (1994). Working the hyphens: Reinventing self and other in qualitative research. In N. K. Denzin and Y. S. Lincoln (eds.), *Handbook of qualitative research* (pp. 70–82). Thousand Oaks, CA: Sage.

Flom, B. L. (2002). Just don't shut the door on me: Aspirations and resilience characteristics of adolescents in day treatment. *Dissertation Abstracts,* 62(10-B), 4782.

Fraser, M. (ed.) (1997). *Risk and resilience in childhood: An ecological perspective.* Washington, DC: NASW Press.

Galambos, N. L., and Leadbeater, B. J. (2000). Trends in adolescent research for the new millennium. *International Journal of Behavioral Development,* 24(3), 289–294.

Garbarino, J. (2001). Making sense of senseless youth violence. In J. M. Richman and M. W. Fraser (eds.), *The context of youth violence: Resilience, risk, and protection.* Westport, CT: Praeger.

Gilgun, J. F. (1996). Human development and adversity in ecological perspective, Part 1: A conceptual framework. *Families in Society,* 77(7), 395–402.

Gilgun, J. F. (1999). Mapping resilience as process among adults with childhood adversities. In H. I. McCubbin et al. (eds.), *The dynamics of resilient families* (pp. 41–70). Thousand Oaks, CA: Sage.

Glantz, M. D., and Sloboda, Z. (1999). Analysis and reconceptualization of resilience. In M. D. Glantz and J. L. Johnson (eds.), *Resilience and development: Positive life adaptations* (pp. 109–128). New York: Kluwer Academic/Plenum.

Graham, J. (2001). If meaning counted: Measuring e/affect in antidementia therapies. *Gerontology,* 47(supp. 1), 572–573.

Graham, J., and Rockwood, K. (1998). Treatment expectations for Alzheimer's disease: The ACADIE study. *Gerontologist,* 38(1), 99.

Hacking, I. (1999). *The social construction of what?* Cambridge, MA: Harvard University Press.

Hauser, S. T. (1999). Understanding resilient outcomes: Adolescent lives across time and generations. *Journal of Research on Adolescence,* 9(1), 1–24.

Huang, L. N. (2003). Plenary address. Presented at Sixteenth Annual Research

Conference: A System of Care for Children's Mental Health: Expanding the Research Base. University of South Florida, Tampa, March.

Jew, C. L., Green, K. E., and Kroger, J. (1999). Development and validation of a measure of resiliency. *Measurement and Evaluation in Counseling and Development,* 32(2), 75–89.

Johnson-Powell, G., and Yamamoto, J. (eds.) (1997). *Transcultural child development: Psychological assessment and treatment.* New York: Wiley.

Kaplan, H. B. (1999). Toward an understanding of resilience: A critical review of definitions and models. In M. D. Glantz and J. L. Johnson (eds.), *Resilience and development: Positive life adaptations* (pp. 17–84). New York: Kluwer/Plenum.

Klevens, J., and Roca, J. (1999). Nonviolent youth in a violent society: Resilience and vulnerability in the country of Colombia. *Violence and Victims,* 14(3), 311–322.

Ladner, J. A. (1971). *Tomorrow's tomorrow: The Black woman.* Garden City, NY: Anchor Books.

Lalonde, C. (2004). Identity formation and resilient communities. Paper presented at the Sixth International Looking After Children Conference, Ottawa, ON, August.

LeBlanc, A. N. (2003). *Random family.* New York: Scribner.

Lesko, N. (2001). *Act your age: A cultural construction of adolescence.* New York: Routledge Falmer.

Lightfoot, C. (1992). Constructing self and peer culture: A narrative perspective on adolescent risk taking. In L. T. Winegar and J. Valsiner (eds.), *Children's development within social context, vol. 2* (pp. 229–245). Hillsdale, NJ: Lawrence Erlbaum.

Lincoln, Y. S., and Guba, E. G. (1985). *Naturalistic inquiry.* Newbury Park, CA: Sage.

Luthar, S. S. (1993). Annotation: Methodological and conceptual issues in research on childhood resilience. *Journal of Child Psychology and Psychiatry,* 34(4), 441–453.

Luthar, S. S., and Zelazo, L. B. (2003). Research on resilience: An integrative review. In S. S. Luthar (ed.), *Resilience and vulnerability: Adaptation in the context of childhood adversities,* (pp. 510–549). Cambridge: Cambridge University Press.

Luthar, S. S., and Zigler, E. (1991). Vulnerability and competence: A review of research on resilience in childhood. *American Journal of Orthopsychiatry,* 61(1), 6–22.

Magnus, K. B., Cowen, E. L., Wyman, P. A., Fagen, D. B., and Work, W. C. (1999). Correlates of resilient outcomes among highly stressed African-American and White urban children. *Journal of Community Psychology,* 27(4), 473–488.

Martineau, S. (1999). Rewriting resilience: A critical discourse analysis of childhood resilience and the politics of teaching resilience to "kids at risk." Ph.D. dissertation, University of British Columbia, Vancouver, BC.

Massey, S., Cameron, A., Ouellette, S., and Fine, M. (1998). Qualitative approaches to the study of thriving: What can be learned? *Journal of Social Issues,* 54(2), 337–355.

Masten, A. S. (2001). Ordinary magic: Resilience processes in development. *American Psychologist,* 56(3), 227–238.

McCourt, F. (1996). *Angela's ashes.* New York: Simon and Schuster.

McCubbin, H. I., Fleming, W. M., Thompson, A. I., Neitman, P., Elver, K. M., and Savas, S. A. (1998). Resiliency and coping in "at risk" African-American youth and their families. In H. I. McCubbin, E. A. Thompson, A. I. Thompson, and J. A. Futrell (eds.), *Resiliency in African-American families* (pp. 287–328). Thousand Oaks, CA: Sage.

Miller, W., and Crabtree, B. F. (1994). Clinical research. In N. K. Denzin and Y. S. Lincoln (eds.), *Handbook of qualitative research* (pp. 340–352). Thousand Oaks, CA: Sage.

Morgan, D. L. (1998). Practical strategies for combining qualitative and quantitative methods: Applications to health research. *Qualitative Health Research,* 8(3), 362–376. Available at http://proquest.umi.com/.

Mpofu, E. (2002). Types and theories of aggression in an African setting: A Zimbabwean perspective. *International Society for the Study of Behavioural Development Newsletter,* 2(42), 10–13.

Mrazek, P. J., and Mrazek, D. A. (1987). Resilience in child maltreatment victims: A conceptual exploration. *Child Abuse and Neglect,* 11(3), 357–366.

National Institute of Mental Health (2001). *Blueprint for change: Research on child and adolescent mental health.* Bethesda, MD: National Institute of Mental Health.

Nesselroade, J. R., and McCollam, K. M. (2000). Putting the process in developmental processes. *International Journal of Behavioral Development,* 24(3), 295–300.

O'Neal, M. R. (1999). Measuring resilience. Paper presented at the Annual Meeting of the Mid-South Educational Research Association, Point Clear, Alabama. Retrieved online from EDRS, document #ED436574.

Richman, J. M., and Fraser, M. W. (eds.) (2001). *The context of youth violence: Resilience, risk, and protection.* Westport, CT: Praeger.

Rodwell, M. K. (1998). *Social work constructivist research.* New York: Garland.

Rutter, M. (2001). Psychosocial adversity: Risk, resilience, and recovery. In J. M. Richman and M. W. Fraser (eds.), *The context of youth violence: Resilience, risk, and protection.* Westport, CT: Praeger.

Salmivalli, C. (2001). Peer-led intervention campaign against school bullying: Who considered it useful, who benefited? *Educational Research,* 43(3), 263–278.

Schofield, Gillian. (2000). Resilience and family placement: A lifespan perspective. *Adoption and Fostering,* 25(1), 6–19.

Silbereisen, R. K., and von Eye, A. (eds.) (1999). *Growing up in times of social change.* New York: Walter de Gruyter.

Silverman, D. (2000). *Doing qualitative research: A practical handbook.* Thousand Oaks, CA: Sage.

Strauss, A., and Corbin, J. (1990). *Basics of qualitative research: Grounded theory procedures and techniques.* Newbury Park, CA: Sage.

Swartz, L. (1998). *Culture and mental health: A southern African view.* Cape Town, South Africa: Oxford University Press.

Taylor, J. M., Gilligan, C., and Sullivan, A. M. (1995). *Between voice and silence: Women and girls, race and relationship.* Cambridge, MA: Harvard University Press.

Thoits, P. A. (1995). Identity-relevant events and psychological symptoms: A cautionary tale. *Journal of Health and Social Behavior,* 36(1), 72–82.

Todis, B., Bullis, M., Waintrup, M., Schultz, R., and D'Ambrosio, R. (2001). Overcoming the odds: Qualitative examination of resilience among formerly incarcerated adolescents. *Exceptional Children,* 68(1), 119–139.

Ungar, M. (2001a). Constructing narratives of resilience with high-risk youth. *Journal of Systemic Therapies,* 20(2), 58–73.

Ungar, M. (2001b). The social construction of resilience among "problem" youth in out-of-home placement: A study of health-enhancing deviance. *Child and Youth Care Forum,* 30(3), 137–154.

Ungar, M. (2002a). *Playing at being bad: The hidden resilience of troubled teens.* Lawrencetown Beach, NS: Pottersfield.

Ungar, M. (2002b). Qualitative contributions to resilience research. *Qualitative Social Work,* 2(1), 85–102.

Ungar, M. (2004). *Nurturing hidden resilience in troubled youth.* Toronto: University of Toronto Press.

Ungar, M., Lee, A. W., Callaghan, T., and Boothroyd, R. (in press). An international collaboration to study resilience in adolescents across cultures. *Journal of Social Work Research and Evaluation.*

Ungar, M., and Liebenberg, L. (2005). The International Resilience Project: A mixed methods approach to the study of resilience across cultures. In M. Ungar (ed.), *Handbook for working with children and youth: Pathways to Resilience across cultures and contexts* (pp. 211–226). Thousand Oaks, CA: Sage.

Ungar, M., and Teram, E. (2000). Drifting towards mental health: High-risk adolescents and the process of empowerment. *Youth and Society,* 32(2), 228–252.

Yellin, E. M., Quinn, M. M., and Hoffman, C. C. (1998). Heavy mettle: Stories of transition for delinquent youth. *Reaching Today's Youth,* Summer, 4–8.

Chapter 4

A Roof over Their Head

Applied Research Issues and Dilemmas in the Investigation of Homeless Children and Youth

Yvonne Vissing

Sociologists have often been asked to conduct research in order to solve social problems (Dahrendorf 1959; Eitzen and Smith 2003; Kornblum and Julian 2005). As public attention to the social problem of child and youth homelessness has increased in recent years, so have opportunities to conduct applied research. During the past fifteen years, I have learned that researching invisible populations, such as homeless children and teens, is often made more difficult because of complex structural, emotional, conceptual, and methodological obstacles that must be overcome. Homelessness in general is a politically sensitive topic, and its existence among children is a hot-button issue among politicians and service providers alike. This chapter focuses on common definitional and methodological challenges encountered by applied researchers who study controversial problems that children experience. The content is specific to studying homeless children, but its implications are generalizable for all hard-to-find populations of children. Suggestions are given about how to overcome applied research obstacles in order to conduct high-quality research that has both scholarly credibility and utility for practitioners and policy makers.

Funding Priorities Guide Applied Research Directions

Sociologists find that their research programs are often dictated by the organizations that fund their projects. Public funding sources provide support for projects because they envision a specific benefit from doing so. For instance, my first homeless research project was funded by the New Hampshire State Department of Education (NHSDE). All states were required by the Stewart B. McKinney Act (Public Law 100-77) to conduct a yearly count of homeless students. The NHSDE announced a Request For Proposals (RFP) in 1989 for projects that would investigate the causes and consequences of homelessness among students in five selected communities across the state. Each community was to provide a sample of homeless students to be interviewed in case-study format. The state hoped that by knowing more about the needs of their homeless students they could better serve them.

My area of specialty is in the sociology of children, so this proposal was of interest. But at that time I knew nothing more about homelessness than the average person, and I had no knowledge of homeless children. As a former human-services worker, I appreciated the service component of the grant, but this project also appealed to me as an academic because I thought it would be possible to integrate sociological theory and constructs. Believing that a child's reality is socially constructed and that early socialization experiences influence how a child views him- or herself and the world, it seemed logical that housing and financial distress would influence a child's sense of self and well-being (Bassuk 1990; Berger and Luckman 1966). The process delineating how children's perception of reality is shaped by their homelessness experience was unknown, since the existing literature on homelessness focused on adults, not children. I felt that this grant would enable me to make scholarly contributions that far exceeded the service agenda of the NHSDE. Although there could be many different ways to design a project about homeless students, I was comfortable in following the design selected by the NHSDE. Since that project, I have worked with many different funders and organizations to develop projects to study child homelessness; some have given me freedom to design the project as I see fit, and others have maintained rigid control of it.

All applied researchers are confronted with the scholarly and ethical decision of whether to accept funding to produce a particular type of research project. When researchers are hired to conduct applied research, they may have a theoretical position imposed on them that is in concert with political, agency, or logistic factors, whether they want to admit it or not. Anytime a researcher receives funding to conduct a study, the funders have overt and covert agendas that influence why they are supporting the project and what they hope to receive from it. In this respect, applied research may be a delicate area for investigators who want to conduct good-quality research but who feel constrained to look at the problem, like homelessness, in a particular way or lose the contract.

Challenges of Defining Homelessness

One of the largest problems in studying homelessness in children is deriving a definition that clearly describes their housing dilemma. It is difficult to design a project on an understudied topic, such as child homelessness, because key concepts may not have been clearly defined in previous research. Although poverty has long been a topic of inquiry for sociologists and policy makers, financial distress and housing dislocation have been studied primarily as adult phenomena (Harrington 1997; Lewis 1961; Matza 1996; Myrdal 1969; Payne 2005; Riis 1997; Simmel 1972 [1908]; Whitake 1999). Homelessness was originally analyzed as part of the context of poverty in general, and children's housing plight was given no extraordinary distinction. For instance, during the Industrial Revolution, multiple immigrant families would share living space until they were able to afford their own housing accommodations; during the Great Depression of the 1930s, many families would live doubled-up together because they could not afford housing otherwise. There was often a social-problems focus underlying the analysis of these living conditions; the impact of housing distress on children was not usually a specific area of inquiry.

The bulk of contemporary literature about homeless people continues this legacy of focusing on adults, especially those in impoverished urban areas (National Coalition for the Homeless 1999). When the Census Bureau studied homeless people, their methodology resulted in gross undercounts of homeless people in general and families and children in particular (Burt 1991). The lack of previous research on homeless youth in suburbs and rural areas was an especially big problem for me since my study focused on children in a rural state. The lack of data reflected the field's more general focus on the concentration of poverty in urban areas at the expense of understanding poverty in rural areas. When child homelessness was studied, it was almost always in the context of family homelessness, in which children are analyzed as part of the larger family structure. This clouded both their numbers and experiences. Literature on teen homelessness was hard to find because homeless youth are often not identifiable (Link 2001; National Coalition for the Homeless 1999; Toomey and First 1993; United States Conference of Mayors 2005). As a result, there has been little emphasis on housing distress of rural children in either scholarly or public literature.

Researchers, like the public, are not immune from stereotypes of skid-row bums and bag ladies as representative of the homeless population. Studies of homeless adults often tend to "blame the victim" (Ryan 1971), implicitly or explicitly, for conditions leading up to their housing distress, and some authorities go so far as to blame youth for their housing problems (Limbaugh 1993). Initially, I did not know exactly what homeless children looked like or how they acted. Stereotypes continue to portray homeless people as old, alcoholic, mentally ill drug abusers despite the fact that the largest population of homeless people now consists of families and children. Because homeless children had not been well studied, the lack of child-oriented data reinforced the perception that homelessness was an adult problem. Stereotypes of homeless adults do not fit homeless children, who are not visible, partly because their distress is strategically hidden and partly because the public does not want to believe that significant numbers of children have no place to live. Because children are not "supposed" to be homeless, especially in suburbs and rural areas, researchers have frequently ignored the study of them. They are often "out of sight and out of mind" (Bassuk 1990; Children's Defense Fund 2005; National Coalition for the Homeless 1999; Vissing 1996).

The NHSDE had provided for our use a definition of homelessness from the McKinney Act, which defined homeless children as "those who lack a fixed, regular night-time residence." This definition, I soon learned, seemed written with urban children in mind, and it was not particularly useful for defining children in rural areas. Urban adults may be identified when they are living on the street, but homeless children in rural areas are not visible and do not fit the homeless urban adult stereotype. The definition of homelessness became key to the study and measurement of child homelessness in this study. School administrators were conflicted, because they knew they had children in the school who were homeless but who almost always had some place to stay. When the administrators tried to apply the McKinney definition, they counted few students who they felt met the strict definition; when they talked about children who had no home, the numbers mushroomed. So which definition should they use?

One elementary principal pointed out how the official definition of homelessness got in the way of her serving housing-displaced children. If attention was given only to children who were defined as homeless, the children who were living a marginal existence, who had housing distress, who were poor, and who had been homeless in the past but not at this precise moment could all be overlooked. These are children who do not fit tightly into the McKinney definition, but they do not fall entirely outside it either (Vissing 1996). Because of the nature of rural homelessness, children who lack housing are, in many ways, indistinguishable from rural children who are poor but not homeless (Patton 1987; Snow and Bradford 1994). Having a place to stay overnight is quite different from having a home. Living through the brutal winters of rural New Hampshire would be almost impossible without some form of shelter; parents go out of there way there to make sure their children are protected from the weather and are creative in finding living accommodations. Just because children had a roof over their head did not imply that they had a home, which has symbolically and emotionally much greater meaning. Therefore, it was challenging to come up with a definition of who is homeless that was in accordance with that of the McKinney Act but that still allowed school administrators to identify housing-distressed students in a flexible manner.

Designing the Projects

Methodologically, the study of homeless children is complicated because of significant sampling, data-gathering, and measurement obstacles. Ethical concerns in researching hard-to-find populations of children are enhanced because of their young age, marginal social status, fragile social networks, and high-risk living situations. The study of homeless children and youth is a researchable topic, but investigators are advised to be aware of common pitfalls so that high-quality research can result. It is imperative to do good research when investigating understudied but emotionally charged social phenomena because such research will shape contemporary understanding of the phenomena's dynamics.

Most applied researchers select a clear direction for their projects, and they have lots of choices about how to study a phenomenon like youth homelessness. They can develop projects to *explore* to what degree homelessness is a problem for children and youth, they can *describe* the demographic and behavioral attributes of those who are homeless, they can choose to *explain* why they experience housing distress, or researchers may use data to *predict* which children will become homeless. Each of these decisions—to explore, describe, explain, or predict—will take a researcher in very different directions (Babbie 2003; Neuman 2003). Thanks to the efforts of previous researchers who explored child homelessness and identified it as a problem, investigators now are able to develop more descriptive and analytical studies about youth housing distress. Organizations need descriptive research to document the numbers and kinds of people who are homeless; if few youth are identified to be in need, child homelessness is then not seen as a problem, and no program development, services, or funding will be provided. There is also pressure to develop explanatory research, since it is difficult to prevent child and family homelessness without understanding why it exists. By accumulating explanatory information about what kinds of people experience homelessness for what reasons, it may be possible to develop predictive models about who is at risk of becoming homeless. Applied research may also take forms such as needs assessments and process or outcome evaluations. Although the emphasis of applied research may be on obtaining data that funders can apply, I have found that it is still possible to incorporate basic research questions that will enable the researcher to develop explanatory frameworks. A well-designed applied study can still incorporate essential elements of basic research.

Benefits of the Mixed-Method Approach. I have conducted both qualitative and quantitative studies of homeless children over the past fifteen years and have sometimes used both approaches together in a single multitmethod-design study. Each type of study has unique contributions to make to our understanding of the lives of homeless children. Quantitative studies allow for researchers to enumerate actual numbers of children at risk, as well as to identify their demographic characteristics (Vissing 2000; Vissing and Diament 1993). It is possible to determine, through the use of statistical analyses, behavioral patterns and causal sequences that would otherwise be difficult to ascertain, as will be shown later in this chapter. On the other hand, qualitative studies provide researchers with the opportunity to enter into the otherwise unknown world of homeless children and youth. The socioemotional data derived from interviews, observations, and case studies enable researchers to integrate the totality of the child's experience into the research.

When both types of methods are used within a single study, the results can be confirming and powerful (Denzin 1978). The use of a mixed-methodological approach is particularly useful when investigating problems and populations that have been understudied. It is easy to think one understands "reality" when using only one methodology, but when using several different approaches, it is possible to gain a broader view of the phenomenon. Mixed-method approaches also provide a system of checks and balances; competing findings help researchers to keep up their investigation until they are sure that their conclusions are correct. Use of qualitative research can provide contextual understanding that would be unavailable in a single-method design. The mixed-methodology approach is particularly important when trying to understand the lives of children, since adults view the experience one way and children may view it differently. Use of both qualitative and quantitative data will help researchers to identify patterns and understand experiences that would be difficult otherwise.

Access to Informants. Securing a representative sample is important in studies of this kind, especially in instances where there has been little baseline data available. When researching homeless children and youth, the traditional research conventions of random sampling often go out the window. Use of convenience samples, snowball samples, and social-network samples may be more realistic. For the purposes of doing this type of research, nonparametric samples are respectable and appropriate for data gathering. But in the scholarly world, random-sampling designs are considered much better since they yield more generalizable findings. Both types of studies yield rich results that help researchers to understand the world of homeless children.

The purpose of one's research dictates what kind of sample should be used; conversely, what type of access to subjects one has may influence the type of project that can be developed. When I could access students through large, random samples, I had the analytical benefit of enumerating homeless children and found some fascinating aggregated trends that I did not expect. On the other hand, my limited subject access enabled me to focus on ethnographic studies into the private lives of homeless children and youth. The subject design of the NHSDE study enabled me to learn about how children construct their social reality as homeless individuals. Qualitative data enhanced my quantitative data because it allowed me, as a researcher, to find out their views about what caused them to become homeless, the process they had gone through to deal with their housing troubles, and what kinds of outcomes their housing distress had caused. I concluded that in applied research it is not always possible, or desirable, to use random samples. For instance, in a study that I conducted for the Greater Piscataqua Foundation, we explored what happens to homeless children in the summer when they do not have access to the resources of school. This study enabled me to have a snapshot picture into experiences of children that would otherwise go unnoticed.

The NHSDE study enabled me the benefit of interviewing several dozen homeless children, but finding a sample was complicated because homeless children often seemed like "normal" children (Vissing 1996). What I learned as a result of this study was that only a fraction of homeless children ever go to shelters; parents are likely to double-up with others to afford housing or create alternative living arrangements to avoid having their children "on the street." Aware of the negative stigma of homelessness, many parents, children, and youth do not define themselves as homeless and prefer to define their housing dislocation as temporary and due to "hard times." Learning how hard parents work to conceal their being homeless was one finding of the study, as well as being a sampling issue. In a form of impression management, children may be recruited by their parents to conceal the fact that they are homeless (Goffman 1959). Schools often do not know which students are homeless because parents often keep housing problems well hidden from the gaze of those with authority and power. Even the most loving and caring parents fear that they could be reported to welfare authorities because they cannot afford housing. In the past, children were removed from parents because they lacked housing, so homeless parents who keep silent because they are afraid their children could be taken away do have some legitimate concerns (Gil 1970; Knudsen 2005; Pelton 1991). These type of parents were the norm, but I also interviewed youth who had become homeless because of family conflict or abuse. When youths are estranged from their parents, it is difficult to receive parents' permission for the children to participate in a study. However, we were usually able to avoid this problem because the school either assisted us with getting parental permission or they obtained authorization for us to speak with independent students. We found this assistance from the schools to be very helpful in gaining us access to homeless students, since I found it difficult to obtain samples from welfare and social service agencies. The agencies were often unable to identify older teens who live on their own because they cannot legally serve them without parental consent; unemancipated youth are reluctant to ask agencies for help. If students were not in school or emancipated, it was almost impossible to gain access to them or to include them in our studies (Vissing 1996).

Children are sometimes hesitant to talk to strangers about private matters. Gaining the children's trust to talk is yet another obstacle to be overcome, because they are very sensitive to issues of social class and exploitation. For instance, I found that I had to wear extremely casual clothes; otherwise homeless teens would focus too much on what I was wearing. I also had to monitor my interaction style to encourage them to give honest answers and avoid giving me what they thought would be acceptable answers "for the professor." In another incident, when an inexperienced interviewer became visibly uncomfortable while a homeless girl was talking about sexual activities, the girl immediately quit talking and the interview essentially ended. When applied researchers interact with children and youth, they must be extremely careful to monitor even subtle behaviors that may contaminate the research process, since getting good data essentially depends on developing good rapport.

Getting Reliable Data. It is important to get reliable data in any project, but especially when dealing with an understudied population involving a controversial topic. It is possible to get reliable data from either well-designed qualitative or quantitative studies. From my experience researching homeless children and youth, I have found young people to be accurate informants of their experiences (Corsaro 2002). They do not seem to lie or embellish information about their lives and housing distress if they feel they can trust the interviewer. In my experience, older students serve as better informants in most instances than younger ones because they have a more sophisticated conceptual and cognitive framework from which to explain events. Reliability is enhanced when age-appropriate questions are asked; children cannot be asked to provide information about things that they may know little about, such as their parents' income or employment history.

Parents can also be reliable sources of information about children's experiences of homelessness, but this is not without pitfalls. During interviews, I found that many parents were initially hesitant to talk about the intimate details of their housing distress and problems, but they provided much useful information once they felt they could trust the interviewer. They had usually told their life story to social service providers before and sometimes perceived researchers to be "another do-gooder," according to one father. Although there are many different good interview techniques, the style that worked best for me was to use a semistructured interview schedule that enabled parents to talk about their experiences at length. I tried to interject neither sympathy nor anger for what they had experienced; rather, I told them that I would tell their stories to help teachers and policy makers so that they could better help other children and families. Once they understood that I was not a social worker but an information conduit to policy makers, most subjects seemed to relax and disclose details about their housing problems. I found that parents of younger children were more willing informants than were parents of teens. Young children are more likely to live with their parents, who have a better idea about where the children are and who they are with when they are apart. Teens, on the other hand, have more independent lives and more private emotions. Parents may not be accurate informants about how housing distress affects older youth. Also, as tensions grow between teens and parents, as can be the case, parents cannot be relied on to provide the quality of data necessary to understanding the causes and consequences of homelessness on youth from the perspective of the youth themselves. Relying on parents to interpret children's understandings of events or situations always runs the risk of producing misunderstanding and silencing children since it privileges adult standpoints.

Some studies rely on data about homeless children from informants such as social workers, shelter providers, welfare officials, police officers, or soup-kitchen staff. Collecting data from professionals who work with homeless youth is convenient since they are an easily identifiable group, and researchers may feel comfortable negotiating a study with them. Researchers can also avoid the problem of getting parental consent to speak with them. However, the reliability of the data is only as good as the informant. In one study I conducted (Vissing and Diament 1993), eighty human-service organizations in the seacoast region of Maine and New Hampshire were sent a questionnaire, which asked them to identify how many adolescents they served, according to eleven different categories of housing distress. Despite having a broad range of housing conditions from which to choose, most of the agencies were unable to identify teens in any category. As part of a triangulated study, youth from the same communities were also surveyed, and they indicated that up to 20 percent of teens experienced some form of housing distress. This suggests that agencies and teens may have very different ideas about how many teens are in housing-distressed situations. When it comes to obtaining certain kinds of information, such as ascertaining how many children live in distressed housing conditions or what it is like to be without housing, children may actually be better informants than the adults who work with them.

Developing Findings

Some funders only want research findings and do not care if a theoretical framework is provided. Professionally, I find that it is my job to provide a contextual framework for whatever findings I glean from the data. Work by Barney Glaser (2001) and Robert K. Merton (1949) insist that any social phenomenon's causes must be deduced from the data that surrounds it. In this way, theory must be grounded so that it can be understood and applied by others. William Corsaro proposes the theoretical use of interpretative sociology in order to gain perspective into how children actively engage in interpreting and creating new meanings to social realities. In developing my findings, I selected a grounded methodology and interpretative child-oriented theoretical approach to my research of homeless children because this seemed to provide a useful framework for me to explain how homelessness impacted them. The homeless causal typology I created by looking at the intersection of structural and individualistic factors is shown in figure 4.1.

This model proposes that when children live in communities where there is inadequate housing and few well-paying jobs and where there are few services to catch people who are falling into poverty, homelessness results as a manifestation of structural problems that are beyond an individual's control. If structural problems go unaddressed, they can foist a variety of personal problems on even the most well-adjusted individuals. If children do not have personal problems, they may be able to move to another community or double-up with people who have resources, thereby avoiding homelessness. Homelessness is a result of the community's failure to address the basic needs of their citizens. If children in structurally inadequate communities have parents who cannot or will not take care of them, or if kids are in trouble and have individual problems that spiral out of control in environments in which there is no help, these children are victims of the "double whammy," which makes it very challenging

		Structural Factors	
		YES	NO
Personal Factors	YES	Double Whammy	Individual Woes
	NO	Community Failure	Accidental Homeless

Fig. 4.1

TABLE 4.1
Explained Variance

Factor	Eigenvalue	% Variance
1	5.984	15.343
2	2.374	6.087
3	2.150	5.514
4	1.723	4.417

to help them. They will need many resources in order to bring them into a functional lifestyle.

My findings led me to assume that when children who experience personal problems live in rich environments that have plenty of affordable housing, jobs, and services, once they tap into those resources, they should be able to do well. Children who do not have personal problems can still become homeless, as we have learned from news about victims of fires, floods, tornadoes, and other unexpected catastrophes and as we recently saw in the case of devastation wrought by Hurricane Katrina. But if the children have a support system, both individually and within the community, their homelessness should be short-lived.

Use of a mixed-method approach to collecting data on invisible populations of children provides researchers with different ways to convey their findings. For instance, when trying to explain the complex world of homeless children to scholars and policy makers, use of well-analyzed quantitative data is recommended. In another study I conducted (Vissing 2000), 1,912 students were randomly selected through a sampling design developed by the Centers for Disease Control in conjunction with the New Hampshire Youth Risk Behavior Survey (YRBS). Sixty-four high schools in New Hampshire participated in this study, and two classes per high school were randomly selected to be included in this survey. A variety of data was collected that enabled both descriptive and inferential analyses to be conducted. Factor analysis proved to yield fascinating results about the nature of youth homelessness. Four factors occurred that indicated there may be different dynamics to the homeless experience (see table 4.1). When looking at these four factor loadings more closely, it is clear that all homeless youth are not alike. Table 4.2 shows that variables clustered in patterns that indicated different causations of homelessness.

Factor 1 implies the existence of a Multiproblem Youth. These multiproblem youth may have run away from home or been abused, and they may have housing distress of multiple types, use substances, have mental

TABLE 4.2
Factor Loadings

Factors	1	2	3	4
# Places lived/yr.	−.402	.308		
Unsafe home	−.498			
Runaway	.604			
Need counseling	.474			
Need MD care	.417			
Need DDS care	.372			
Rate health	−.453			
Suicidal thoughts	.494			
Alcohol	−.429		.408	.331
Marijuana	−.436		.399	.373
Other drugs	−.392			.326
Intercourse	−.481		.402	
Relationship with parents	−.489			
Health problems	.326			
Mental health problems	.488			
Financial problems	.428			
Physical abuse	.477			
Sexual abuse	.417			
Emotional abuse	.574	.403		
Verbal abuse	.552	.373		
School problems	.487			
Homeless this year	.487	−.440	.340	
Ever homeless	.358	−.368	.470	

health problems and suicidal ideation, have poor relationships with parents, have unmet physical and mental health needs, and have financial and school problems. Factor 2, on the other hand, shows housing-distressed youth who feel emotionally and verbally abused but not physically abused. They do engage in risky behaviors such as substance use. These kids are transient—they may be homeless this year or may have been homeless previously—and have experienced emotional and verbal abuse, but the abuse may be correlated with the parental stress of having financial and housing problems. These kids have housing problems and have suffered emotionally, but otherwise they seem to be keeping their lives in good control and are not subject to mental or behavioral difficulties that plague the previous category of youth. Factor 3 indicates that some youth use alcohol or marijuana and are more likely to be sexually active, behaviors that are well within the norm for most high school students. These youth differ from others, however, in that they have been homeless this year and homeless previously as well. Factor 4 indicates a group of youth who have been homeless in the past and are involved with alcohol, marijuana, and other drug use. These youth tend to be more involved with substances than with sexual experimentation or suicidal ideation, perhaps to escape the difficulties of a lifestyle in which homelessness occurred and could occur again.

Combining the factor-analysis data with chi-square data, descriptive analyses, and qualitative data, homeless students could be categorized as belonging to the following types: (a) students who are well cared for by their parents and who have positive relationships with them—these students tend to be physically and emotionally healthy, to get good grades in school, and to be minimally involved in high-risk behavior; (b) students with many problems who do not have access to care and assistance; (c) students who have economic problems that result in housing distress, who have mental and physical health problems, and who engage in more high-risk behaviors as a result; (d) students who engage in normal adolescent experimentation of substance use and sexual experimentation; and (e) students with multiple problems who seem to have everything going wrong—they have economic, health, school, and abusive-family problems, they engage in high-risk behaviors, and they do not get help.

Through the use of mixed methods, my data indicate that most child and youth homelessness is intermittent or sporadic in nature. Usually they, or their parents, experience specific problems that make it difficult to maintain stable housing. Usually children are not chronically homeless. They are more likely to experience a sudden problem that results in not having stable, regular housing for a period of time. They may live with others until they get their feet on the ground. Even though they are homeless, children and youth have some aspects of their lives that are similar to any other child. Most will never become homeless again, although some may float in and out of an unstable housing situation. These findings are diametrically different from the stereotype of homeless adults.

Presenting Research

Once data are collected about homeless children, it is important to get the information into the hands of people who can help homeless children, as well as to scholars who benefit from the information. There are regular presentation and publication outlets for scholarly dissemination of knowledge; however, it takes time to find the right professional venue for presentation, and it can take a year after submission before an article is printed in an academic journal. Scholarly information may not necessarily be disseminated to the general public without the researcher's concentrated effort. Making the information available to the public can be difficult for a variety of reasons, which I learned when I contacted two dozen newspapers with press releases about my studies of teen homelessness, and only one published an article about my work—and that was a newspaper disseminated to the housing-advocacy community. Radio presentations are typically news bites that last only minutes.

Funding agencies are inclined to hold news conferences or otherwise promote the findings of the research project in which they have invested. This is a wonderful opportunity for the investigator to promote key findings, but it also provides a sociological context for the information. Human-service providers want data to better serve children in their communities. They are also looking for documentation of needs that they can use to justify program development, the hiring of new staff members, or requests for more funding. It is often difficult to get existing information into the hands of practitioners who could implement recommendations for prevention of homelessness.

Applied research may be better received by practitioners and the public when portrayed in visual formats. Tables, figures, and graphs that explain a great deal of information at a glance are appreciated by practitioners who do not have much time to digest reports of complicated studies. In my experience of putting qualitative findings into a video called "I Want to Go Home," I found that the short video moved hearts and minds great distances among people who would not otherwise be inclined to be interested in a topic such as child homelessness. As part of a team for the University of Massachusetts's homeless video project, "Give Us Your Poor," I have found that the visualized presentation of research on a variety of the causes and effects of homelessness in television, web, and DVD format is a great way to take complex data and present it in a way that will capture audience and then educate them.

The presentation of information on homelessness must be put into an appropriate context; otherwise it may not be well received. For instance, when a school counselor in New Hampshire who really knew her students reported accurate numbers of homeless students, newspaper comparisons of her data with data from other school districts made it seem as though there were more homeless youth in her community than in others. The probable reality, according to my 1993 study, is that approximately the same number of homeless youth exists in most communities. But when this counselor reported that homeless youth existed in her community, her good research was met with assertions of inflation and inaccuracy, since community leaders were embarrassed that they looked like they had more homeless children there than anywhere else in the state. Community leaders were afraid that others would perceive their town to be a homeless "magnet" and that tourism would suffer as a result. Ironically, the next year, the counselor was not allowed to conduct the school's count of homeless students. Not surprisingly, the new study indicated that the number of homeless youth had decreased. Findings that substantiate the existence of homeless children means that a community may feel politically and ethically obligated to do something about homelessness. Feeling compelled to help, they may realize that helping costs money, takes personnel, and ruffles the feathers of those who would prefer to believe that homelessness does not exist in their community.

Sometimes in their reporting of data, researchers may wish to become advocates for homeless individuals. It is difficult to witness dire economic conditions and problems that could be prevented, avoided, and eliminated with the use of community resources. Researchers must be clear on their role and help when appropriate. Balancing research commitments and advocacy when dealing with issues like child homelessness can be a challenge for applied researchers, for whom the line between responsible scholarship and responsible humanity is sometimes thin. Researchers cannot promise any individual or community that the research results will improve their quality of life. Government, social, moral, and economic factors influence whether a community will help homeless children.

Recommendations

In order to conduct research on groups of invisible, vulnerable children and youth, the following actions are recommended.

Stay grounded in the use of systematic methods of inquiry to ensure credibility and legitimacy in an applied world where a commitment to scientific rigor prevails.

Create theory. Many of the traditional theories, though useful, have limitations as they pertain to the study of children. Just as children are active interpreters of their social world as their personalities are being shaped by it, the dynamic nature of childhood requires that researchers be open to more creative, integrative understandings of the nature of reality.

Use a mixed method of data collection and analyses in order to enhance the contextual understanding of the lives of poorly understood groups of children and youth.

Be clear on one's role when conducting applied research and reporting results. All applied researchers have to decide how to manage themselves as they present findings. Professional and more dispassionate modes of communication might lend greater legitimacy to findings, but on the other hand, they might compromise the researcher's sense of ethical commitment to the topic.

Whether they seek to explore, describe, explain, or predict a phenomenon, all researchers have assumptions or theories about why an event like child homelessness occurs. Child and youth homelessness is an emotionally charged topic. It evokes the long-standing sociological debate: should we, like Max Weber, be "value-free" when we study such topics, or should we, like Howard Becker, be upfront about "whose side we are on" (Weber 2001 [1921]; Becker 1963)? I struggled with this question as I developed my work; obviously I did not believe that homelessness was good for children, and yet I knew a child-advocacy position could weaken the presentation of my work. I believe that I have straddled the world of science and application well, but it has been a challenge from both sides.

Summary

It may be difficult to research invisible populations of children and youth, such as those who are homeless, but the use of applied methodological approaches can result in good applied research projects that will have uses in the public realm. Vulnerable groups of children pose a delicate area of inquiry. Emotional, economic, and political factors actively complicate studying them. At every point in the applied research process, investigators are forced to consider how the research will affect the lives of some of the most vulnerable people in society. Researchers have an obligation to research homeless children in an ethical way that has intellectual integrity.

Although adult-centered approaches provide valuable insight into the world of children, they are limited because they do not analyze a phenomenon's etiology or outcome from a child's point of view (Corsaro 2002). The study of children and youth is especially challenging because of the complex interface of theoretical, structural, perceptual, and methodological issues.

This chapter has focused on homeless children, but it also provides a typology of research factors that assist in the study of all hard-to-find groups of children and youth. It encourages the use of mixed methodologies and child-focused contextual analyses that incorporates both phenomenological and positivist research approaches to help professors, researchers, policy makers, and service providers, especially when they use applied research for public funding agencies. Use of sophisticated research designs and analyses create a scholarly basis for understanding homelessness in children and youth. The greatest gift that researchers can give is good-quality work, from start to finish. With the strength of their findings, those who advocate, fund, and create policy will have the information they need to conduct a battle that will more effectively counter the war against children in the United States (Vissing 2003).

REFERENCES

Babbie, Earl. 2003. *The Practice of Social Research.* Belmont, CA: Wadsworth.

Bassuck, Ellen. 1990. "The Impact of Homelessness on Children." *Children and Youth Services,* 141, 19–33.

Becker, Howard. 1963. *Outsiders: Studies in the Sociology of Deviance.* New York: Free Press.

Berger, Peter, and Thomas Luckman. 1966. *The Social Construction of Reality: A Treatise in the Sociology of Knowledge.* Garden City, NY: Doubleday.

Burt, Martha. 1991. *Alternative Methods to Estimate the Number of Homeless Children and Youth.* Washington, DC: Urban Institute Press.

Children's Defense Fund. 2005. *The State of Children in the United States 2005.* Washington, DC: Children's Defense Fund.

Corsaro, William. 2002. *The Sociology of Childhood.* Thousand Oaks, CA: Pine Forge.

Dahrendorf, Ralf. 1959. *Class and Class Conflict in Industrialized Society.* Stanford, CA: Stanford University Press.

Denzin, Norman K. 1978. *The Research Act.* Englewood Cliffs, NJ: Prentice Hall.

Ehrich, L. C. 1996. "The Difficulties of Using Phenomenology: A Novice Researcher's Experience." In P. Willis and B. Neville, eds., *Qualitative Research Practice in Adult Education.* Ringwood, Victoria: David Lovell.

Eitzen, D. Stanley, and Kelly Eitzen Smith. 2003. *Experiencing Poverty: Voices from the Bottom.* Belmont, CA: Thompson/Wadsworth.

Gil, David. 1970. *Violence against Children: Physical Child Abuse in the United States.* Cambridge, MA: Harvard University Press.

Glaser, Barney. 2001. *The Grounded Theory Perspective: Conceptualization Contrasted with Description.* Mill Valley, CA: Sociology Press.

Goffman, Erving. 1959. *The Presentation of Self in Everyday Life.* New York: Doubleday.

Harrington, Michael. 1997. *The Other America,* reprint ed. New York: Scribner.

Hein, Serge, and Wendy Austin. 2001. "Empirical and Hermeneutic Approaches to Phenomenological Research." *Gestalt,* 5(2), 35–41.

Kimmel, Allan. 1988. *Ethics and Values in Applied Research.* Applied Social Research Methods 12. Newbury Park, CA: Sage.

Knudsen, Dean. 2005. *Child Maltreatment.* Thousand Oaks, CA: Pine Forge.

Kornblum, William, and Joseph Julian. 2005. *Social Problems,* 11th ed. Englewood Cliffs, NJ: Prentice Hall.

Kuhn, T. S. 1970. *The Structure of Scientific Revolutions,* 2nd ed. Chicago: University of Chicago Press.

Lewis, Oscar. 1961. *The Children of Sanchez.* New York: Random House.

Liazos, Alexander. 1996. "The Poverty of the Sociology of Deviance: Nuts, Sluts, and 'Perverts.'" *Radical Criminology,* 12(28), 372–395.

Limbaugh, Rush. 1993. *The Way Things Ought to Be.* New York: Pocket Books.

Link, Bruce. 2001. "Conceptualizing Stigma." *Annual Review of Sociology,* 27, 363–385.

Link, Bruce. 1993. *Lifetime and Five-Year Prevalence of Homelessness in the United States.* New York: Columbia University Press.

Matza, David. 1966. "The Disreputable Poor." In R. Bendix and Seymour Lipset, eds., *Social Stratification.* New York: Free Press.

Merton. Robert K. 1949. *Social Theory and Social Structure.* New York: Free Press.

Myrdal, Gunnar. 1969. *Challenge to Affluence.* New York: Pantheon.

National Association of State Coordinators for the Education of Homeless Children and Youth. 1993. *Opening the Doors.* Baton Rouge, LA: NAEHCY.

National Coalition for the Homeless. 1999. *The Essential Reference on Homelessness.* Washington, DC: National Coalition for the Homeless.

National Commission for Children. 1991. *Beyond Rhetoric: A New American Agenda for Children and Families.* Washington, DC: U.S. Government Printing Office.

Neuman, Lawrence. 2003. *Social Research Methods.* Boston: Allyn and Bacon.

Palmer, Richard E. 1997. *The Philosophy of Hans-Georg Gadamer.* Library of Living Philosophers 24. Peru, IL: Open Court.

Patton, L. T. 1987. *The Rural Homeless.* Washington, DC: Health Resources and Services Administration.

Payne, Ruby. 2005. *A Framework for Understanding Poverty.* Highlands, TX: aha! Process.

Pelton, L. H. 1991. "Poverty and Child Protection." *Protecting Children,* 7, Winter, 35.

Proctor, Bernedette, and Joseph Daleker. 2003. "Poverty in the United States: Current Population Reports." Washington, DC: U.S. Department of Commerce, Census Bureau.

Riis, Jacob. 1997. *How the Other Half Lives,* reprint ed. New York: Penguin.

Ryan, William. 1971. *Blaming the Victim.* New York: Vintage.

Simmel, Georg. 1972 [1908]. "The Poor." In Donald Levine, ed., *Georg Simmel on Individuality and Social Forms.* Chicago: University of Chicago Press.

Snow, D. A., and G. M. Bradford. 1994. "Broadening Perspectives of the Homeless." *American Behavioral Scientist,* 34(4), 451–585.

Toomey, Beverly, and Richard First. 1993. "Counting the Rural Homeless: Political and Methodological Dilemmas." *Social Work Research and Abstracts,* 29(4), 23–27.

United States Conference of Mayors. 2005. "Hunger and Homelessness Survey." Washington, DC.

United States Department of Health and Human Services, Administration for Children and Families, National Center on Child Abuse and Neglect. 1996. *The Third National Incidence Study of Child Abuse and Neglect* (NIS-3). September. Chapter 5, pp. 2–17; Summary: Chapter 8, pp. 10–11.

United States Department of Housing and Urban Development. 1999. "Homeless Teens." Available at www.huduser.org.

van Manen, M. 1990. *Researching Lived Experience: Human Science for Action Sensitive Pedagogy.* Albany: State University of New York Press.

van Manen, M., and Levering, B. 1996. *Childhood's Secrets: Intimacy, Privacy, and the Self Reconsidered.* New York: Teachers College Press.

Vissing, Y. 2003. "The $ubtle War against Children." *Fellowship,* 69(3–4), March–April, 20–23.

Vissing, Y. 2001. "Homelessness Is a Problem in Rural Areas." In Jennifer Hurley, ed., *The Homeless: Opposing Viewpoints.* San Diego: Greenhaven.

Vissing, Y. 2000. "Homelessness in Middle School Students." In James Stronge and Evelyn Reed-Victor, eds., *Educating Homeless Students: Promising Practices.* Newbury Park, CA: Sage.

Vissing, Y. 1999. "High School Students at Risk." New Hampshire State Department of Mental Health and Department of Education.

Vissing, Y. M., D. Schroepfer, and F. Bloise. 1994. "Homeless Students, Heroic Students." *Phi Delta Kappa* (Indiana University), March, 535–539.

Vissing, Y. 1996. *Out of Sight, Out of Mind: Homeless Children and Families in Small-Town America.* Lexington: University Press of Kentucky.

Vissing, Y., and J. Diament. 1997. "Homeless Youth in My Community?" *International Journal of Social Distress and Homelessness,* 2(2), 27–33.

Vissing, Y., and J. Diament. 1996. "Counting Homeless Adolescents." *Social Work,* 1(3), 39–42.

Vissing, Y., and J. Diament. 1993. "Enumeration of Homeless Adolescents in the Seacoast." Prepared for the Greater Piscataqua Community Foundation.

Vissing, Y., and Sharon Peer. 2003. *Researching Children.* Hauppauge, NY: Nova.

Vissing, Y., Dorothy Schroepfer, and Fred Bloise. 1994. "Homeless Students, Heroic Students." *Phi Delta Kappa,* March, 535–539.

Wallace, Walter. 1971. *The Logic of Science in Sociology.* Chicago: Aldine-Atherton.

Weber, Max. 2001 [1921]. *The Protestant Ethic and the Spirit of Capitalism.* New York: Routledge.

Whitake, Philips. 1999. *Child Social Well-Being in the U.S.: Unequal Opportunities and the Role of the State.* New York: Garland.

Part II

From the Field
Adults in Youth Worlds

Chapter 5

With a Capital "G"

Gatekeepers and Gatekeeping in Research with Children

Madeline Leonard

It is only recently that researchers into the everyday worlds of childhood have adopted practices that place the child at the center of the research process. This involves acknowledging that doing research with children based on active partnership is much more likely to produce rich, meaningful data than research done on children. Moving from research *on* to research *with* children necessitates involving children in an informed way at all stages of the research process. But this brings up an initial problem concerning access to children as respondents. It is a well-established procedure in sociological research that at the outset the researcher must actively obtain the consent of those being researched. However, as is now widely documented, in research involving children, consent is commonly sought from adults in the first instance, and only after this has been secured are children given the opportunity to agree to being researched. Access to children has to be negotiated through multiple layers of gatekeepers, and the process provides important clues to the nature of social relations within the research setting. Childhood researchers are immediately confronted with the power imbalance that exists between adults and children, and indeed the fact that researchers are themselves adults has implications for all stages of the fieldwork. The role of gatekeepers renders children voiceless during the initial stages of the research when access is being negotiated. One set of adults (usually parents or teachers) undertakes to assess the intentions of another set of adults (researchers). This initial dialogue takes place among adults, and agreement is commonly reached in the absence of children. Hence, the first stages of doing research with children is characterized by their invisibility and passivity irrespective of the subsequent approaches the researcher later intends to adopt to render the child an active subject of the research process.

Of course, the practice of gatekeeping reveals the differing power relationships between adults in the research process because gatekeepers in their role as protectors of children have the power to grant or refuse access to adult researchers. Negotiating access through adult gatekeepers involves different sets of adults entering into relationships based on bargaining and compromise. These relationships have consequences for all stages of the subsequent research process. Yet the role of gatekeepers in research with children often receives insufficient coverage. Rather, the consequences for obtaining children's informed consent are prioritized, which renders invisible the ongoing influence that a range of gatekeepers may have at different stages of the research. The purpose of this chapter is to highlight the role of gatekeepers in research with children by drawing on the author's experience in relation to two research projects. Although gatekeepers do influence research with adults, their impact is much more pronounced when the research subjects are minors. Moreover, on occasion, researchers themselves become gatekeepers, which will be illustrated in relation to media interest in the findings of the research and the researcher's role as gatekeeper to the data.

Background to the Research Projects

The first project (Leonard, 1999) was concerned with examining children's participation in term-time employment. The methodology was based on a questionnaire filled in during class time by children aged fourteen to fifteen. The researcher negotiated directly, distributing the questionnaire to the children, with the teacher being absent for the time period allocated for the research. There were 567 children who took part in the research, and the sample was drawn from twelve schools located in Belfast, selected to include gender, class, and religion as potentially significant variables. The researcher was able to secure an additional time period to hold discussions with the children on the general theme of benefits and disadvantages associated with term-time employment. Finally, two focus groups of working children were interviewed and tape-recorded. Seven children took part in the first focus group interview, and eight children took part in the second. The second project (Leonard, 2001) examined children's experiences of doing the transfer test in Belfast known colloquially as the "11 plus." This test is taken by around 90 percent of children in Northern Ireland between the ages of ten and eleven, and the results are used to determine the child's post-primary-school destination. Eight schools participated in the research. One primary-seven class was selected from each school to take part in the research. A total of 143 children participated in the research. Each primary-seven class was divided into focus groups comprising between six and eight children in each group. The children were interviewed three times over a period of three months in the same focus groups. It is not my intention to discuss the findings of each project. Rather, the remainder of the chapter focuses on the access process and the role played by gatekeepers in the projects.

Initial Access: Hierarchies of Power

As indicated, the research sites for both projects were schools. Within educational establishments children and adults are located in highly structured relationships with one another. Although the primary purpose of schools is to educate children, they are also arenas characterized by discipline and control. Parents relinquish their responsibility for children to teachers who assume a superior status in relation to children within the confines of the schooling system. Access to children within schools has to be negotiated with adult gatekeepers who control entry to children's worlds within the school environment. In Burgess's view, "gatekeepers are those individuals within an organization that have the power to grant or withhold access to people or situations for the purposes of research" (1993: 48). His methodological insights refer mainly to adults who wish to gain access to other adults within organizational settings based on hierarchy. As Dingwall (1980) points out, within stratified research settings, there is a hierarchy of consent whereby those at the top grant permission for researchers to gain access to those located further down in the organization. In relation to the two projects discussed here, school principals made the crucial gatekeeping decision, sometimes but not always in consultation with teachers. Although I had asked for the involvement in the consent-negotiation stage of the teachers whose classes I wanted to access, in the majority of cases, the school principal felt that his or her permission was all that was necessary. This meant that I was often imposed on the adult teachers located further down the hierarchy of the school system. In some cases, teachers were resentful of their own powerlessness in the decision-making process regarding the research, and I had to work hard to assure them that I did not equate the principal's consent with their consent. This suggests that it is too simplistic to simply highlight unequal power relationships between adults and children, as adults themselves are located within different power structures. Powerful gatekeepers who grant access may make it difficult for subordinates to subsequently refuse to participate (Atkinson, 1981; Dingwall 1977).

Having secured consent from a variety of adults to conduct the research, it was then necessary to secure consent further down the hierarchy, of the children themselves. I made it clear to all the school principals and teachers that I did not equate their consent with that of the children's. However, it was clear from their reactions that the majority of them assumed that their consent was all that was necessary. Even teachers who resented my initial presence because of their own powerlessness in relation to the principal's giving his or her consent seemed unable to extend their feelings of powerlessness to the children whose consent they monopolized. Some schools additionally sought parental consent by sending consent letters home to parents to fill in, and I left this as a matter of school policy. This adds a further complication to the research process because one set of adults (teachers) may agree to the child's participating in research, while another set of adults (parents) may refuse to give consent. This may prove even more problematic if the child indicates a willingness to take part. In one instance, when I was researching children's participation in term-time employment, one fourteen-year-old girl's parents either refused or forgot to sign the consent form. The girl begged me to give her permission to participate but was removed from the class by the teacher and given extra work to do while I engaged the rest of the class for two school time periods lasting eighty minutes. In this instance the adults and child were positioned against each other, with the parent as unwilling, the researcher as enthusiastic, the teacher as ambivalent, and the pupil as powerless.

This example suggests that access is an ongoing aspect of the research process rather than a one-off event. It is not just a matter of getting past the initial gatekeeper but a process of continuous negotiating and building up trust and rapport with individuals at a number of different levels. In recognizing this difficulty, Burgess suggests that "there are likely to be multiple points of entry that require a continuous process of negotiation and renegotiation" (1993:49). One outcome of this state of affairs is that we tend to know more about the powerless in society than the powerful. Indeed, the recent burgeoning literature on children's lives suggests that their relatively powerless position in society renders them amenable to adult researchers' requests to understand their daily lives. On the other hand, dominant discourses surrounding childhood have increasingly positioned children as under threat from adults and have facilitated a move toward a more and more protectionist stance by those rendered as gatekeepers to their everyday lives. But despite these constraints, the everyday lives of children remain more open to scrutiny than are the gatekeepers who grant access to their worlds.

Of course, subordinates may decide not to cooperate with the researcher. Superiors' giving support for the research in the first place may produce distrust in the subordinates that carries over to the research (Flick, 1998). In Brewer's (1991) study of policing in Northern Ireland, police officers were worried that the data might be used by management against their interests and in many cases tried to avert the researcher. According to Woods (1998), much organizational research illustrates superiors' disregard for subordinates. In Woods's experience, gatekeepers assumed that subordinates would have no objection to being studied and that their permission was therefore unnecessary. Others have differentiated between "physical" access and "social access" (Lee, 1993) in order to indicate how access to the research site through a powerful gatekeeper by no means ensures subsequent access to subjects. This suggests that research subjects may maintain some element of control over their participation in the research process even when consent to the field has already been made on their behalf. Lee (1993) draws on a range of studies whereby participants impeded the researcher's progress through obfuscation, concealment, and deception.

Children may also retain some power over the research process by their subsequent involvement in the research, despite their initial marginalization by adult gatekeepers. As Mandell (1991) points out, children are the ultimate gatekeepers to their worlds. Hence, they may have some leeway in relation to their level of cooperation despite their initial powerlessness at the access stage. Ball points out that "pupils are able to exclude the researcher from certain areas, to draw lines, to keep certain issues or topics private" (1985:44). This is reflected in the primary-school-aged girls interviewed by B. Davies (1982); the girls went to great lengths to curtail the breadth of discussion topics, and there were clear limits to the extent to which they would make disclosures about certain parts of their everyday lives. Fine and Sandstrom (1988) argue that children, like adults, have mastered the art of impression management and that therefore, like adults, they will tend to edit their answers. Similarly, Lewis and Lindsay (2000) argue that children are skilled at controlling what they reveal.

However, the crucial role that adults play in allowing children to take part in research is potentially problematic as it may make it difficult for children to refuse to take part in research or to practice disclosure. The adult-pupil relationship reflects wider disparities in power between adults and children. In Lee's view, "the 'finished' standard adult has powers over and responsibilities towards the 'unfinished' child" (2001:19). This may make it extremely difficult for pupils to withhold consent when other adults, especially those in a superior relationship to them within the educational system, have already consented on their behalf. Hence, Morrow and Richards (1996) point out, researchers need to pay as much attention to informed dissent as they pay to informed consent. This means that when researchers negotiate access through adult gatekeepers, they must recognize the constraints to which children may be subject. Since these gatekeepers have already consented on children's behalf, they may make it very difficult for children to subsequently refuse to participate in research. The freedom that children have to opt out of school-based research may be particularly limited given the taken-for-granted power relationships that exist within schools, which locate adult teachers as key decision makers. Hence, rather than simply requiring children to affirm their consent, researchers should explore ways in which children are enabled to practice active dissent.

In the research projects that I conducted, I tried to give children, without the teachers' knowledge, opportunities not to participate. Hence, I discussed nonparticipation only when I was left alone with the children. In relation to the first project on term-time employment, I suggested to children that if they did not want to take part in the research they did not have to fill in the questionnaire and could read a book or do their homework while others engaged in the task. In all, twenty-two questionnaires were not filled in. In relation to the focus-group interviews with younger children, I suggested to the children that they could refuse to talk or that they could do some other activity during the focus-group interviews. In this case, they could leave the class with the group, suggesting to the teacher that their cooperation was unproblematic, but decide not to participate when part of the actual group. Of course, their not talking could be due to shyness or disinterest rather than active refusal, and it is difficult to gauge when to draw children into conversation or leave their voices silent. This necessitates the researcher's making judgments, which may reflect mistaken adult assumptions about children's behavior. In one instance, I was talking to children in a library setting that was being utilized for focus-group discussions. One boy appeared unwilling to participate in the research, looking noisily through a book during conversations. However, he later contributed to the discussion in a way that indicated that he had been listening to the earlier dialogue. This is a reminder that children, like adults, can engage in multiple simultaneous activities. My interpretation of the boy's behavior as one of active dissent was unfounded in this particular case, but the example illustrates the continual tightrope researchers need to negotiate between active consent and dissent in research with children that initially relies on adult gatekeepers who control researchers' access and children's opportunities to express their views. Good practice should include a continual review of consent to ensure that children remain willing to be involved. Children should continually be made aware that they have the right to withdraw from the research at any time (Stanley and Sieber 1992). Moreover, although the researcher may have some leeway in diluting the influence of the gatekeepers at one stage of the research, at other times the research process may provide more limited opportunities for flexibility.

This discussion suggests broad similarities between gaining access to children within schools and to employees within organizations. Both are located as subordinates within hierarchical structures. Both may be expected to take part in research through a process whereby powerful gatekeepers have consented on their behalf. Both may find it difficult to subsequently refuse to cooperate, but both may adopt strategies of resistance and erect barriers to their everyday worlds. However, fundamental differences remain. The power imbalance between teachers and pupils in schools is much more pronounced than between adult employers and employees. Children must legally attend school and do not have the same choices or autonomy that employees have in the workplace. Schools are much more extensive sites of discipline and control than the workplace. Indeed, Lee suggests that one of the primary purposes behind the establishment of an educational system based on compulsory attendance at schools was to transform "each pupil from an element of a disorderly mass, into a discrete docile individual" (2001:79). According to Cullingford, "the official framework for a school is simple. The head rules. Teachers carry out his or her wishes. Pupils obey" (2002:199). Although of course schools may also be sites of resistance, nonetheless pupils come to realize that their voices do not count for much. Even schools moving toward more democratic systems based on empowering pupils tend to allow them input to minor matters such as the school uniform rather than crucial issues such as the school curriculum. In Cullingford's view, "pupils are to all intents and purposes treated as children without a voice until they leave school" (2002:15). As children, they are seen as irrational, irresponsible, and incompetent. They are also regarded as vulnerable and in need of protection, and this places adult gatekeepers to children's worlds in a different position than adult gatekeepers to other adults.

Presentation of Self as Quasi-Adult–Quasi-Child Researcher

Appearance management is an important part of the research process. Researchers have to carefully consider how to present themselves at a number of different levels. In relation to school-based research, researchers need to present themselves to the top of the hierarchy and then sometimes change their self-presentation as they work downward toward the actual subjects of the research. This means that researchers might need to present themselves differently to gatekeepers and subjects. A number of studies have focused on the importance of dress (Delamont, 2002; Measor, 1985). For the initial meetings with school principals, I always dressed formally but moved toward more informal dress when meeting pupils. This is consistent with the strategies adopted by other researchers in order to promote acceptance among populations with different images of appropriate and inappropriate dress. Measor (1985) found that among teachers appearance carries tremendous importance. Wearing conservative dress was interpreted as demonstrating a serious nature and served to facilitate trust between outside researchers and school principals. However, much more casual attire is required to gain acceptance among pupils. Both Measor (1985) and Delamont (2002) found that their attempts to manage their appearance paid off because school pupils regarded them as adults who were not quite teachers.

Gender is also likely to have an impact on the willingness of gatekeepers to grant access to unknown adult researchers. Within school settings, teachers are placed as the promoters of children's well-being, and this means ensuring that they are safe in the company of strange adult visitors to the school. Gatekeepers may deny researchers the opportunity to gain access to child research subjects because of the typical positioning of children as a vulnerable group and the increasing location of adult males in particular as threats to the innocence of childhood. As Jenkins (1998) points out, there is an increasing "media crusade" against child sex abusers that turns uncommon childhood risks into ones that appear as everyday events and has an impact on the freedom adult males have to interact with children. Women are perceived as posing less of a threat to the sanctuary of childhood because the lives of women and children are commonly bound to one another in ways that are taken for granted culturally (Thorne, 1987:5). It could be argued that because of my gender I was able to negotiate more extensive access than a male researcher would have been able to do. As a middle-aged woman and a mother, I may have activated taken-for-granted assumptions about motherhood and nurturing. Hence, in allowing me access, gatekeepers may have constructed traditional images of femininity and in the process opened up school space and childhood space because of preconceived notions of shared links between children and the women who traditionally care for them.

Of course, outward appearance is only the first step in the process of gaining acceptance. Of much more importance is how the self is presented and managed during the build-up of rapport. Again this takes place at a number of different levels. At the initial access stage, researchers have to convince gatekeepers that they are competent to carry out the research. This necessitates giving the impression of being a "proper" researcher (de Laine, 2000). This may include indicating previous experience of working with children. For example, some researchers highlight their background as teachers as a way of demonstrating their ability to manage classrooms full of pupils (Hargreaves, 1967; Woods, 1979), though this assumes a particular kind of adult-child relationship. The role adopted by the researcher may influence the kind of data obtained. Some researchers recommend moving away from being adult-like by adopting more child-friendly roles. This finds expression in Mandell's (1991) notion of the "least-adult role" in child research. However, other researchers are wary of the extent to which this least-adult role can be accomplished. In the work of both Ball (1985) and L. Davies (1985), age differences between them and their respondents precluded their ability to "pass" as pupils. Their aim became one of not being quite teacher, parent, or adult but at the same time not quite being a pupil or child either. The various structures of schooling may compromise the researcher's ability to fully adopt a childlike role (Epstein, 1998). My own position is that moving away from established adult roles is important in building rapport with school pupils, so I opt for a middle ground between not being a proper adult and equally not being a proper child. As Fine and Glasner point out, "children seem to have a sense of whether a researcher looks like a good bet as a friend and will spot those who attempt to be something other than they are" (1979:167).

Gatekeepers may influence the attempts of researchers who try to adopt quasi-adult and quasi-child roles. Hence, childhood researchers need to reflect on how they are viewed by adults as well as by children. The school principals and teachers involved in my research projects clearly saw me as an experienced, mature researcher and held an image of how research is conducted. They implicitly expected my adult status to be a dominant feature of my interaction with the pupils. This expectation emerged at various points during the focus-group interviews with primary-school pupils. In some schools, an interview room had been set aside for talking with pupils, with a large chair set apart from the others for me as researcher and smaller chairs grouped together for the children. When I mentioned this to a colleague, he pointed out that since I was taller than the children, this seemed an obvious room layout. But it was not just the size of the chairs that mattered but their positioning in the room. My large chair was located in the center of the room and indeed dominated the room. The smaller chairs were a substantial distance from the large chair, and their grouping in relation to mine suggested subordination and conformity. Indeed, Lee (2001) points out that the traditional layout of classrooms, where individual desks all face the front, was designed to ensure that the teacher at the top of the classroom could maintain control over pupils. Although a number of schools had different classroom layouts, with desks or tables grouped together, in two schools the traditional layout remained in place. In all cases, I chose to change the layout of the interview room. In some cases, I dispensed with the chairs and sat on the floor with the children. In others, I sat on one of the small chairs and left the large chair vacant. This was followed by the children taking turns sitting on the large chair and adopting the role of teacher, which they accomplished by wagging their fingers at the group and speaking in a disapproving tone. However, some children appeared uneasy with my attempts to negotiate space, as the initial layout was more familiar to them. This suggests more complex patterns of interaction between adult researchers and children than advocates of child-friendly methods imply. Children themselves may have certain expectations of adult roles within schools and may respond uneasily if researchers try to change the status quo. As Epstein (1998) suggests, some children may remain unconvinced, despite the researcher's attempt to perform the least-adult role, that the researcher is not an adult. In some cases, it was not until my third meeting with children that they played an active role in changing the room layout.

The children were told to address me respectfully as "Miss," and my attempts to be on first-name terms aroused disapproval and in some cases reprimand from teachers when pupils called me by my first name in their presence. In one instance, the school principal became involved in repri- manding pupils. In this particular case, children were showing me some of the items on display in the library. On being shown a stuffed bat in a jar, I expressed fear, to the delight of the children, who proceeded to chase me around the library with the jar. We were having a great laugh at this, although I was trying to hide my genuine fear when it was suggested that the bat be removed from the jar and placed in my pocket. In this midst of this commotion, the teacher entered the room and began to reprimand the children. Though I was not included in the reprimand, I was consid- ered an ineffective researcher who could not control even a small group of children rather than being seen as a participant in a game attempting to build rapport. Afterward, I explained to the teacher that I had encouraged the children's behavior and was equally responsible for making the noise. The teacher was very dismissive of my explanation and indicated that the children should not have behaved in the way they did. On returning for the next interview with the children, I learned that the school principal had talked to the children about how much they had let the school down in front of a university lecturer.

This incident helped me bond with the children (although they had to endure a reprimand), as it was reported throughout the other groups and was constantly referred to amid much giggling in subsequent interviews. This event placed me outside the teacher role. The teacher's estimation of my incompetence as a researcher allied me with the children, who were often also considered incompetent in other respects. Yet the incident also highlights the problems of transgressing the boundaries between adult and child by adopting the least-adult role in that often the literature on this issue focuses on the adult-child relationship and leaves unexplored the reaction of other adults who are used to clear boundaries between adulthood and childhood. This brings up issues related to the dual alle- giances that researchers often confront in the field. In this particular case, the impression-management techniques that I employed were basically in contradiction with one another. Displaying competency, in terms of how adult teachers viewed competency, would have distanced me from the children whose views I sought, but displaying "incompetence" invoked the possibility of the research field being closed to me as a consequence of teacher-gatekeepers protecting children from an adult that appeared to be unable to do her job properly.

Confidentiality

In my research projects, I employed the standard procedure of assuring children that the data would be treated as confidential. Of course, confidentiality is problematic in relation to children in cases where accounts of abuse may be raised, even when this issue is outside the purview of the research project. In these circumstances, researchers in the United Kingdom are under obligation to report allegations to other adults who can sensitively deal with the situation. Childhood researchers have developed a number of strategies for dealing with this issue and with its impact on the confidentiality relationship between researchers and researched (Stanley and Sieber 1992).

This issue did not emerge in either of the projects I conducted, but there are other problematic aspects to the confidentiality relationship when research is located in a school setting. Maintaining privacy within a school environment is no easy task. Pupils' close proximity to one another presents difficulties regardless of the methodology used. This means that even if pupils are engaged in individual tasks such as filling in questionnaires, there is no guarantee that answers will not be seen by peers because of the tendency in some schools for desks to be grouped closely together. Focus groups create additional problems because all group members hear one's answers, and although the researcher may assure pupils that he or she will treat responses confidentially, this guarantee cannot be extended to other participants, who may divulge information to others outside the group. In my experience, pupils' main concern is that information not be disclosed to teachers, and it is this aspect that I want to focus on here. Of course, some researchers carry out research with teachers present. In these circumstances I assume that children place some limitations on what they say, and confidentiality takes on a different meaning from instances such as the two projects under discussion here, where no adults other than the researcher were present.

A number of issues emerged during the research process that rendered confidentiality problematic. On many occasions, principals and teachers asked about what the children had said during my interactions with them. Although these adults respected my declarations of confidentiality, in some cases the probing was extensive. On some occasions, the space allocated for my meetings with pupils was not very private, and I had to continually negotiate and renegotiate private space. These examples may not differ much from superiors' questioning of researchers who are studying subordinate adults, the following example suggests much more intrusive behavior by gatekeepers when the research subjects are children. In relation to studying children's participation in term-time employment, I had negotiated with gatekeepers to allow me to distribute questionnaires without any teachers being present. This was to try to dilute and renegotiate the typical power imbalance that lies within the teacher-pupil relationship. Moreover, some schools disapproved of children working during term time because of a perceived negative impact on study time and exam performance. Indeed the majority of teachers and principals were surprised at the age group I was concentrating on because they felt that there would not be much evidence of children working. The data analysis subsequently revealed that one in three children held a current or previous term-time job but that many children kept their involvement hidden because they felt that their lives outside school were their private affair (Leonard, 2003). During the period when pupils were completing the questionnaire I assured them that their responses would remain confidential, that they would only be seen by me, and that the research would be written up in such a way that no pupil or school could be individually identified. In one school, the teacher returned to the classroom at the end of the session. At one point he walked over to the desk of a pupil and lifted the questionnaire and began to read the responses. The boy in question had a term-time job in a pub, and the teacher expressed surprise at this revelation in the following way: "Well, well, I didn't think anybody as lazy as you would have a part-time job. So that's why you're always falling asleep during lessons." I failed to react adequately to this situation. I was collecting questionnaires and chatting to other pupils, and the incident happened so quickly that I was not in a position to immediately remove the questionnaire from the teacher's hands. The incident left me feeling extremely uneasy about my inability to guarantee such a basic level of confidentiality. It is unlikely that such an incident would occur between adult gatekeepers

and adult respondents. The incident revealed the intricacies of power relations between adults and children that goes far beyond the power relations
between adults located at different levels in adult-only organizations.

Anonymity

Confidentiality and anonymity go hand in hand. Research confidentiality
usually extends to disclosing information in such a way that protects the
identity of those taking part in the research. Hence, although the researcher may know details about respondents and gatekeepers may have general
information about groups who take part in the research, research is written up in such a way that no individual can be identified. This is usually
achieved by ensuring that identities are anonymous and by using pseudonyms when referring to comments made by individual research participants. Access is often best facilitated by reassuring gatekeepers that anonymity will be maintained (de Laine, 2000). Indeed, access is often con-
ditional on certain assurances being given at the initial consent stage.
Assuring anonymity enhances the likelihood of gatekeepers' consenting to
involvement in the research. The procedure often facilitates the willingness
of gatekeepers to give consent on other people's behalf, because at the end
of the day, individual identities remain concealed and known only to the
researcher. Anonymity also promotes the acquiescence of subordinates because assurances that their identities will remain unknown may enhance
their willingness to participate. However, children may have a different
conception of anonymity. In both research projects, I assured children that
their replies would be treated as anonymous. The majority of the children had problems with the concept of anonymity. For many children, it
seemed to contradict my claim that I wanted children's voices to be heard.
If this was the case, then why could they not be given credit for what they
said? As one child said, "You are expecting us to do all this work for you,
and then nobody even knows it was us. I want you to use my name if I did
the work for you." The assurance for anonymity had already been given to
school principals and was one of the conditions for gaining access, so I
had no leeway in withdrawing this assurance. Some childhood researchers
use the practice of allowing children to choose their own pseudonyms
(O'Kane, 2000). However, the younger children who took part in this research considered using their real names fundamentally superior to having
a choice of pseudonym. Lofland and Lofland (1995) point out that some

researchers feel that it is their personal ethical responsibility to give "voice" to their informants by using their real names. In one case, I tried to negotiate with the school principal to use the real name of a girl who had drawn a picture that I had decided to use for the cover of the report. The principal was unhappy with the contents of the report and refused permission. Given that anonymity was one of the conditions of access, I had no alternative but to accept the principal's refusal. This again highlights the disparities between children and adults in the research process. Indeed, my attempts to get the principal to change his mind and his outright refusal took place without the girl's knowledge, and she was given no role whatsoever in this negotiation process. This introduces a further dimension to the adult gatekeeper's role. Adults granted access to researchers based on guaranteed anonymity, but for children anonymity was an indication of their voices in part being heard through someone else, in this case, through their pseudonyms. In this sense the children were silenced. One could argue that their subjectivity was partly lost and that they were located as mere objects of study. Giving voice to children and indeed adults is always an interpretative process that emanates from the interaction that takes place between the researcher and the researched. Although the researcher can continually report back to respondents to ensure that their voices have been accurately heard, to these children, the standard practice of rendering subjects anonymous made some of them lose faith in the whole research process. Some children exhibited less interest in validating the voice of a pseudonym, seeing the practice as unjustifiable. For these children, maintaining one's own identity should be a fundamental part of the process whereby they can encourage adults to listen to their views.

Researcher as Gatekeeper

There are also moments in the research process when the researcher becomes the gatekeeper to the data. This is most likely to occur when the object of the research is to influence social policy and the findings are made public to a range of interested parties. Of course, an added dimension here is that although pupils may have some control over what they offer to the researcher as data, they have little control over the interpretation of their words. Most childhood research continues to be written by adults for other adults. One way to minimize misinterpretation is to report back to research subjects prior to publication to ensure that children's voices have been properly heard. This practice of reporting back was used in both of the research projects I conducted. But even when care is given to ensure accurate interpretation, the researcher has less control over the uses of the data by others because selective reporting may lead to misinterpretation. Quoting research out of context and based on partial information may encourage misunderstandings that would be unsubstantiated if the selected extracts were placed in the wider context of overall findings. Media reporting may be particularly problematic in relation to the researcher's role as gatekeeper to the data.

In both projects I conducted, dissemination of the findings was a fundamental aspect of the research from the outset. Both projects were funded by a children's organization whose intention was to use the knowledge generated to lobby and campaign for policy changes with local and national bodies. Both projects were launched during specially advertised conferences aimed at the media, politicians, policy makers, and those with a general interest in both topics and their relevance for children's lives. All the children who took part in the research were invited to attend both these events. Both projects attracted a great deal of media interest, and I was invited to appear on a number of radio and television programs. This was important to the funders of the projects because this type of dissemination ensured that the research reached a much wider audience. On a number of occasions I was placed under a great deal of pressure to produce "real" children from the reports whom the media could interview. The sponsor of the research gave me autonomy in deciding whether to agree to children being interviewed or not and did not influence me in any way in relation to making decisions on this issue. Hence, in terms of hierarchy, I was the crucial gatekeeper here, although obviously permission would need to be gained from the other gatekeepers and indeed from the children themselves. But my permission was necessary before the other multiple levels of access could be set in motion.

In relation to the research on children's participation in term-time employment, I was under considerable pressure from the media to produce a "working child." I was guaranteed extra airtime or wider coverage if I could produce actual respondents. During the period when the research was being carried out, child-employment legislation was being debated in the British Parliament; the dominant discourses at the time focused on the need to protect children from employment. The inclusion by the media of "real" children from the research would have enhanced policy debate about the topic. The majority of children felt that they had a right to work, and their stories converged around wanting legislation that would promote their right to work rather than legislation that would prohibit their employment. The majority of children demonstrated a mature, sensible approach to employment, and working had little negative impact on the health or educational potential of the majority of them. However, the media did not want an ordinary, average working child (the group that formed the majority of my sample) but one that would demonstrate the worst features of child employment. For the media, the ideal example would have been a child working in an occupation banned by the legislation, being paid exploitative wages, and working hours detrimental to the health and education of the child. Although I could have produced such examples, I declined to do so, seeing this as exploitative in and of itself. I know the children who took part in the research would readily have consented to such media coverage. When I had broached this issue with two respondents who could fulfill the requirements of illustrating the negative features of child employment, upon telling them that their identities would be concealed, one turned to the other and stated, "Brilliant, we can be like real IRA men." This referred to a common practice of interviewing paramilitary members in darkened room with their faces concealed. The media's suggestion for dealing with the interviews in this clandestine way and the children's enthusiasm for this practice left me feeling very uneasy, and I made the decision not to go ahead with the interviews.

In the second research project on children's experiences of doing the 11 plus exam, the media again preferred a group of children who would emphasize extreme rather than common experiences. Prior to the launch of the report, I was involved in a radio interview to highlight the launch and discuss the findings. I was given a set of broad questions in advance, but in practice the interview took a completely different tone. The interviewer selected the following two quotations to open up the discussion:

> Do you know what it felt like? It felt like you were in a big cage with all dogs that you know are going to destroy you. Yeah, that's what all the stress is about. You think if you don't keep good you are going to die. The dogs are the 11 plus and you have to kill them. They are the ones that are trying to eat you and you're in the cage and you can't escape. If you do bad you fall out and they maul you.

Or you're on top of a volcano and if you don't keep good, you are going to fall in. You think you are in for it. You are going to die. Like you're not going to do this. You're not going to make it. It's pretty scary.

These two boys were referring to their experiences of doing the 11 plus and represented the two most extreme quotations from a report containing extensive quotation across eighty-four pages. The interviewer, upon reading both these quotations over the air, asked me, "So what you're saying in this report is that the 11 plus is a form of child abuse?" To some extent this form of extreme reporting backs up my concerns about children being interviewed by the media. Although the majority of children who took part in the second project were unhappy with the 11 plus system, they had developed strategies for dealing with the stress associated with doing the exam, and many of them practiced modes of resistance. The media coverage of the report focused by and large on adults' responsibility to protect children from the exam and left unexplored notions of children's agency and coping and resistance strategies. I remain unsure whether the active participation of children from the research in the media reporting of the event would have altered this approach. However, I took this decision without consulting the children who took part in the research. Instead, I positioned myself as an adult acting in their best interest.

Research always competes for attention with a number of other stories and events and often is only newsworthy when sensationalized (Cohen and Young, 1981; Golding and Elliot, 1979). This often leads to superficial or even misleading accounts of the actual research. There are a number of examples of media accounts that dramatize children's experiences (Messenger-Davies, 2001; Roberts, 2000). Although, of course, sensationalism may be unavoidable, the participation of "real-life children" may enable the media to make their point in a much starker way. Although my intention was to protect children from such potentially manipulative media attention, in doing so I could be accused of asserting my adult judgment as superior to those of the children, who would have welcomed the opportunity to engage in a radio or television program. Hence, I made this decision on the basis of assuming that I had the uninformed consent of children, that they were not fully aware of what they might be letting themselves in for, and that the media might misrepresent their views. I should add here that I have made this a condition of all research I undertake, whether with adults or children, that I will not seek their consent to take part in media interviews. Thus, my behavior does not differ between research with adults and with children in this respect. However, my own research experience suggests that children are much more likely to consent to such exposure than are adults. The question is whether their desire to be involved in dissemination in this way should override that of the researcher who does not concur with this type of dissemination.

Doing research with children necessitates that researchers confront and recognize the limits of children's effective participation in the wider society. Although children have been given the right to be heard as a fundamental right of childhood, to some extent this remains more symbolic than real. Roberts (2000) makes an important distinction between listening to the voices of children and providing for their genuine participation. This is illustrated in the growing media interest in children's everyday lives. The media plays an increasingly important role in constructing and disseminating representations of childhood, but in relation to social policy issues, the media often continues to portray children as inevitably vulnerable and in need of protection. In both research projects discussed here, locating children as vulnerable was evident in the media coverage of the two projects. The ongoing tendency of the media to contribute to passive images of children has been contested in the United Kingdom. The United Kingdom's Broadcasting Standards Commission commissioned a study on children's interaction with the media because of public concern about the use and claimed abuse of children in television news and documentaries (Messenger-Davies and Mosdell, 2005). The study found that although children were competent in giving opinions in their own right, their competency was interpreted "flexibly by producers and [varied] between different genres of programming and between different companies" (213). The authors conclude that more thought needs to be given to the ways in which the media represents childhood and the mechanisms that they have in place to ensure that children can assert and maintain their own views in discussions with adults.

These policy initiatives are laudable, but research projects with children will often place the researcher as gatekeeper to children's accounts of their everyday lives. Hence, researchers will be faced with decisions of what to make public and what to exclude, and if the research is topical and reflects wider policy debates, then they may be placed in situations where they have to make decisions about the extent to which children are involved in disseminating the findings. This brings up all sorts of contradictions between empowering research subjects and at the same time ensuring that media tendencies toward sensationalism are minimized. In relation to the two projects discussed here, I contributed to children's passivity by positioning myself as the speaker and interpreter of the children's voices. I placed myself as gatekeeper to their worlds and allowed media reporting of their voices to be channeled through my own adult voice. In this respect I contributed to a notion of children as vulnerable and in need of protection. The example highlights the ongoing dilemma that childhood researchers have to face between being committed to the best interests of the child and not assuming an overly protective stance. Enhancing children's subjectivity and empowering them means challenging their marginalization in the wider society rather than contributing to that marginalization by speaking on their behalf. Tackling and dismantling media notions of children's inherent vulnerability can only effectively be accomplished by challenging their structural vulnerability (Lansdown, 1994). This necessitates reexamining existing frameworks, which often prevent children from giving their opinion and having that opinion taken seriously. This also involves childhood researchers engaging in internal reflections about the ways in which children's voices are channeled through their words. At times researchers may be presented with opportunities to make children's voices heard by involving them more proactively in the dissemination stage. This necessitates adult researchers' confronting their own taken-for-granted assumptions regarding children and childhood and continually questioning the rationales they put forward to justify the often uncomfortable choices they subsequently make.

Opening the Gates of Gatekeepers

In doing research with children, researchers need to take note of a number of important issues that arise in the planning, carrying out, and dissemination stages of research. These methodological issues are not unique to research with children, but they present more acute problems because of the unequal power relationships between adults and children. This chapter has concentrated on the role gatekeepers play throughout the research process. Children are rarely free to decide for themselves whether or not to participate in research. Although children are keepers of the knowledge that researchers wish to access, they are surrounded by adults who act as gatekeepers controlling researchers' access and children's opportunities to participate in research.

Gatekeepers cannot be disregarded once access has been obtained.

Rather, they exercise influence over all stages of the research process. Hence, access should never be seen as a one-off event but as a continual process, which permeates all aspects of the research project. Although gatekeepers play a key role in enabling researchers to access other adults, their influence is much more extensive when the research subjects are children. The access process provides important clues to the nature of social relations within the research setting (Lee, 1993). Doing research with children necessitates recognizing the network of power relationships to which the child is already subject. Within schools, the inherent power relations between adults and children are clearly visible: children occupy in much more pronounced ways a subordinate and marginal position vis-à-vis adults. This finds expression in the ongoing influence that gatekeepers have at all stages of the research process. In setting up boundaries and justifying the inferior position of children within the school setting, gatekeepers expose some of the manifestations of the distribution of power between adults and children. Their expectations regarding adults' interaction with children may impose constraints on researchers who try to minimize these boundaries. Schools are often bounded and constrained social spaces. They provide a research context where the adult-child power imbalance is particularly acute. Within schools, children are to some extent "captive subjects," which means that they may have limited ability to exercise their rights to participate or not (Morrow and Richards, 1996). This means that attention needs to be paid throughout the research process to the child's right to dissent, and active steps need to be taken by the researcher not only to secure consent but also to provide safe space for children to make the decision not to cooperate without feeling obligated because of the power dynamics that already exist within the authoritarian context of the school setting.

However, researchers themselves are part of this "generational order" (Alanen, 1994; Mayall, 2000). Researchers are almost always adults and therefore are located in a dominant category in relation to children and childhood (Qvortrup, 2000). Sometimes researchers themselves may act as gatekeepers and control access to the data. This may involve them in confronting ethical dilemmas between giving voice to participants and simultaneously protecting their interests. Although protecting the interests of research participants is a fundamental aspect of any research project, the difficulties may be more pronounced when the research is with children. These difficulties operate on a number of levels. They partly reflect the relationship between the researcher and the researched, which itself is subject to relationships that exist between adults and children in the wider society. These relationships locate adults as protectors of children, and adult researchers may find themselves engaging in a series of internal dialogues in which the interplay between protecting children and promoting their interests places them in socially constructed contradictory roles. Researchers have to confront, suspend, and negotiate taken-for-granted assumptions that underpin the messy relationships that exist between promoting the best interests of the child and protecting children in ways that empowers them and does not undermine their subjectivity. There are no easy solutions to the difficulties associated with achieving a balance between these sometimes contradictory aims, but childhood researchers need to engage in an ongoing process of reflection and make public the rationales that underlie the compromises they subsequently make.

ACKNOWLEDGMENTS

I would like to thank Save the Children for funding the two research projects and the Department of Education for Northern Ireland for providing additional funding for the second project.

I would like to acknowledge the assistance of Ciara Davey, who worked as a research assistant for three months on the second project.

This chapter was completed during a sabbatical spent at the Center for Work and Family Research, Pennsylvania State University. I would like to thank Nan Crouter and Barbara King for their support during my visit.

REFERENCES

Alanen, L. 1994. "Gender and Generation." In *Childhood Matters: Social Theory, Practice, and Politics,* edited by J. Qvortrup, M. Brady, G, Sgritta, and H. Wintersberger. Aldershot, UK: Avebury.

Atkinson, P. A. 1981. *The Clinical Experience.* Farnborough, UK: Gower.

Ball, S. 1985. "Participant Observation with Pupils." In *Strategies of Educational Research: Qualitative Methods,* edited by R. G. Burgess. London: Falmer.

Brewer, J. D. 1991. *Inside the RUC: Routine Policing in a Divided Society.* Oxford, UK: Clarendon.

Burgess, R. G. 1993. *In the Field.* London: Routledge.

Cohen, S., and Young, J. 1981. *The Manufacture of News.* London: Constable.

Cullingford, C. 2002. *The Best Years of Their Lives? Pupils' Experience of Schooling.* London: Kogan Page.

Davies, B. 1982. *Life in the Classroom and Playground: The Accounts of Primary School Children.* London: Routledge and Kegan Paul.

Davies, L. 1985. "Ethnography and Status: Focusing on Gender in Education Research." In *Field Methods in the Study of Education,* edited by R. G. Burgess. London: Falmer.

de Laine, M. 2000. *Fieldwork, Participation, and Practice: Ethics and Dilemmas in Qualitative Research.* London: Sage.

Delamont, S. 2002. *Fieldwork in Educational Settings: Methods, Pitfalls, and Perspectives.* London: Routledge.

Dingwall, R. 1980. "Ethics and Ethnography." *Sociological Review* 28: 871–891.

Dingwall, R. 1977. *The Social Organization of Health Visitor Training.* London: Croom Helm.

Epstein, D. 1998. "Are You a Girl or Are You a Teacher? The 'Least Adult' Role in Research about Gender and Sexuality in a Primary School." In *Doing Research about Education,* edited by G. Walford. London: Falmer.

Fine, G. A., and Glasner, B. 1979. "Participant Observation with Children: Promise and Problems." *Urban Life* 8: 153–174.

Fine, G. A., and Sandstrom, K. L. 1988. *Knowing Children: Participant Observation with Minors.* Newbury Park, CA: Sage.

Flick, U. 1998. *An Introduction to Qualitative Research.* London: Sage.

Golding, P., and Elliot, P. 1979. *Making the News.* London: Longman.

Hargreaves, D. H. 1967. *Social Relations in a Secondary School.* London: Routledge and Kegan Paul.

Jenkins, P. 1998. *Moral Panic: Changing Conceptions of the Child Molester in Modern America.* New Haven, CT: Yale University Press.

Lansdown, G. 1994. "Children's Rights." In *Children's Childhoods: Observed and Experienced,* edited by B. Mayall. London: Falmer.

Lee, R. M. 2001. *Unobtrusive Methods in Social Research.* Buckingham, UK: Open University Press.

Lee, R. M. 1993. *Doing Research on Sensitive Topics.* London: Sage.

Leonard, M. 2003. "Children's Attitudes to Parents', Teachers', and Employers' Perceptions of Term-Time Employment." *Children and Society* 17: 349–360.

Leonard, M. 2001. *Thoughts on the 11 Plus.* Belfast: Save the Children.

Leonard, M. 1999. *Play Fair with Working Children.* Belfast: Save the Children.

Lewis, A., and Lindsay, G. 2000. *Researching Children's Perspectives.* Buckingham, UK: Open University Press.

Lofland, J., and Lofland, L. 1995. *Analyzing Social Settings: A Guide to Qualitative Observation and Analysis.* Belmont, CA: Wadsworth.

Mandell, N. 1991. "The Least-Adult Role in Studying Children." In *Studying the Social Worlds of Children: Sociological Readings,* edited by F. C. Waksler. London: Falmer.

Mayall, B. 2000. "Conversations with Children: Working with Generational Issues."

In *Research with Children: Perspectives and Practices,* edited by P. Christensen and A. James. London: Falmer.

Measor, L. 1985. "Interviewing: A Strategy in Qualitative Research." In *Strategies of Educational Research: Qualitative Methods,* edited by R. G. Burgess. London: Falmer.

Messenger-Davies, M. 2001. *Dear BBC: Children, Television-Storytelling, and the Public Sphere.* Cambridge: Cambridge University Press.

Messenger-Davies, M., and Mosdell, N. 2005. "The Representation of Children in the Media: Aspects of Agency and Literacy." In *The Politics of Childhood,* edited by J. Goddard, S. McNamee, A. James, and A. James. New York: Palgrave Macmillan.

Morrow, V., and Richards, M. 1996. "The Ethics of Social Research with Children: An Overview." *Children and Society* 10: 90–105.

O'Kane, C. 2000. "The Development of Participatory Techniques: Facilitating Children's Views about Decisions Which Affect Them." In *Research with Children: Perspectives and Practices,* edited by P. Christensen and A. James. London: Falmer.

Qvortrup, J. 2000. "Macroanalysis of Childhood." In *Research with Children: Perspectives and Practices,* edited by P. Christensen and A. James. London: Falmer.

Roberts, H. 2000. "Listening to Children and Hearing Them." In *Research with Children: Perspectives and Practices,* edited by P. Christensen and A. James. London: Falmer.

Stanley, B., and Sieber, J. 1992. *Social Research on Children and Adolescents: Ethical Issues.* Newbury Park, CA: Sage.

Thorne, B. 1987. "Re-visioning Women and Social Change: Where Are the Children?" *Gender and Society* 1: 85–109.

Woods, P. 1998. "Critical Moments in the Creative Teaching Research." In *Doing Research about Education,* edited by G. Walford. London: Falmer.

Woods, P. 1979. *The Divided School.* London: Routledge and Kegan Paul.

Chapter 6

Will the Least-Adult Please Stand Up?
Life as "Older Sister Katy" in a Taiwanese Elementary School

Kathryn Gold Hadley

On June 23, 2001, eighteen Taiwanese children and I graduated from a public kindergarten class in Taipei City, Taiwan. As we stood proudly on the stage under a banner congratulating the kindergarten class of academic year 2000–2001, parents and relatives applauded. When I, a thirty-year-old, white American woman, walked across the stage to receive my graduation certificate, my classmates' parents smiled while unfamiliar relatives turned to one another with puzzled expressions. Once the head of the kindergarten explained that Older Sister Katy was here conducting research, the confused expressions turned into cautious smiles. In my carefully prepared and memorized graduation speech, I thanked the teachers and students for making me feel like a member of the class. Little did I know that the acceptance I experienced in kindergarten foreshadowed the inclusion I would enjoy the following fall when I joined a first-grade class.

Over the course of my ethnographic field research investigating Taiwanese children's transition from kindergarten to elementary school, I became a special member of one kindergarten class and one first-grade class at Little Forest Elementary School.[1] After spending the final semester of kindergarten with these students and graduating with them, I made the transition to first grade in the same elementary school. As an ethnographer, my goal was to see the world from the children's points of view by experiencing life as they did as they interacted with one another in their own peer cultures. By joining students in their daily activities and responding to their invitations for interaction, I slowly learned about their collectively created peer worlds. Although I made daily decisions about how to behave, teachers and students served as important gatekeepers who shaped my level of participation. Indeed, the students played the most important role in accepting me as a special member of their peer cultures. The kindergarten and first-graders showed me what it meant to be a member of their peer cultures by including me, joking with me, instructing and reprimanding me, and also by leaving me out at times. The students' decisions to teach me, a linguistically challenged and culturally incompetent member, how to participate effectively afforded me rich data-collection opportunities.

Kindergarten and Elementary School in Taiwan

In Taiwan, "kindergarten" refers to early childhood education that is not a formal part of the elementary school system. Officially, kindergarten education is designed to foster good physical and mental health, good behavior and ethical practices, and strong social skills (Ministry of Education 1999). Students are typically four or five years old when they enter public or private kindergarten and often stay in kindergarten for two years (Ministry of Education 2002). In 2001 there were 1,230 public and 1,920 private kindergartens in Taiwan, and 2.3 times more students enrolled in private kindergartens compared to public ones (Ministry of Education 2002). After kindergarten, children enter elementary school. First grade marks the beginning of nine years of compulsory education in Taiwan (Bureau of Statistics 1998). Grades one through six are housed in elementary schools, and 99 percent of Taiwanese elementary schools are publicly run (Ministry of Education 2002).

Little Forest Elementary School Attached Kindergarten and First Grade

During the second semester of the 2000–2001 academic year, I conducted over 350 hours of participant observation at the Little Forest Elementary School Attached Kindergarten, a public kindergarten in Taipei City, Taiwan. This public kindergarten is attached to Little Forest Municipal Elementary School, a public elementary school in the city. At Little Forest Kindergarten, I spent four days per week (three full days and one half day) in the Blue Horse class,[2] a class composed of thirty four-, five-, and six-year-old students and two female teachers. Although all students spent class and play periods together, the teachers labeled the children according to age. Eighteen five- and six-year-old children were members of the *dàbān* (oldest class),[3] and twelve four- and five-year-old children were members of the *zhōngbān* (middle class). There was no *xiǎobān* (youngest class) in this classroom or kindergarten. Most students did or would attend this kindergarten for two years before entering elementary school, and most students came from working-class or middle-class backgrounds.

After the summer break, I returned to Little Forest Elementary School[4] for more than 315 hours of participant observation in one first-grade classroom. I spent five days per week (two full days and three half days) in First Grade Class One. There was one teacher and twenty six- and seven-year-old students in the class. I knew or recognized the majority of these new first-graders. Seven of these students had been members of the Blue Horse class in the attached kindergarten. Four other students in Class One were members of the other class in the attached kindergarten, and nine students came from kindergartens that were not affiliated with Little Forest Elementary School.

Selecting a Research Role

Most sociologists and anthropologists studying children and adolescents today adopt the position that children are worthy of study in their own right (James, Jenks, and Prout 1998). Such a theoretical position demands a research method that allows the adult researcher an opportunity to see the world from the child's perspective. Ethnography does just that. An ethnographer spends an extended period of time at the research site becoming a member of the group under study. Through active participation in the daily lives of the participants and systematic collection of observations, the ethnographer learns how the participants see and experience the world from their own points of view. This method is especially appropriate for studying children's lives. Because young children are not well skilled at self-reflection, methods such as surveys and interviews often fail to capture the complexity of children's early experiences (Corsaro 1996). In addition, ethnographic study is an excellent method for studying transitions. The long-term nature of the research allows the researcher to develop an understanding of unfolding processes rather than capturing a collection of snapshots at certain points before and after the actual transition has taken place.

Ethnographers studying young children's lives in educational settings are faced with the task of gaining entry to the peer cultures and establishing a participant status in each. The most important part of this process is the willingness to learn from children, coupled with the ability to put aside the assumption that as former children we adults already know what it means to be a child (Fine and Sandstrom 1988; Thorne 1993). Conducting research with children who do not share the researcher's native language and nationality forestalls the adult researcher's assumption of communicative competence and cultural familiarity. In the Taiwanese school setting, it was not difficult for me to relinquish aspects of adult power and control because I did not grow up in Taiwan and could not draw on early experiences to assume I understood the experiences of Taiwanese children. In admitting our incompetence and strong desire to learn the child's point of view, we enter the research setting and select from a range of roles within it.

In her work with preschool children, Nancy Mandell (1988) adopted a complete involvement role she called the "least-adult" role. As a least-adult, Mandell distanced herself from the other adults in the setting and engaged in joint action with kids during free-play periods in order to minimize her power and status as an adult. In trying to participate as children did, she learned about being a preschooler from both her failed and successful attempts at doing things as the kids did. Mandell did note that despite her efforts at becoming a complete member of the peer culture with equal status, there were times when she needed to step out of the play mode and back into a more adult-like role, such as when asked to assist the teacher with basic child-care tasks. The children in her study understood the dual nature of her participation in free play versus more structured settings. In sum, at times Mandell achieved an equal, peer-like status with the preschool children, and at other times she adopted a more adult-like role that placed her above the children in terms of power and control.

Most researchers who enter children's peer cultures adopt a semiparticipatory role, a more modified participation role than the one used by Mandell. Some researchers even argue that a semiparticipatory role is preferable to a complete involvement role (James, Jenks, and Prout 1998). Within this category there is a range in the degree to which adults participate in the activities and lives of the children. For example, in his work with American preschool children William Corsaro (1985) adopted a reactive method in that he placed himself in areas where children play but waited for them to draw him into their interactions. The children soon learned that he was a novice and a sort of incompetent adult/big kid. Debra Van Ausdale also chose to distance herself from an authoritative role when she became a "nonsanctioning, playmate-adult" in her study of children's racial-ethnic awareness in an American preschool (Van Ausdale and Feagin 2001:40).

As children grow older, the focus of their peer culture and routines shifts from one centered on play and shared activities to one centered on shared language and talk. Adult researchers entering the peer cultures of older children also have to make shifts in their level and type of participation. Fine and Sandstrom (1988) made the point that as kids grow older, they gain more power and ability to decide when to let adults into their peer cultures. Perhaps the combination of a new focus on talk and an increased power of the kids to exclude unwanted participants relegates adult researchers to a more marginal role in the peer cultures of older kids. Nevertheless, adult researchers still try to understand peer culture by aligning themselves with the children and distancing themselves from an adult status.

In an attempt to downplay his adult status, Gary Alan Fine (1987) adopted a semiparticipatory role in his study of preadolescent boys in Little League baseball. He became a "friend" (Fine and Sandstrom 1988) to the boys and worked to establish trust by refraining from taking a position of authority or from admonishing their sexist and racist talk. In her work with middle-school students, Donna Eder and her colleagues (1995) also took on semiparticipatory, "quiet friend" roles. They spent time at extracurricular activities and in the school lunchroom listening, asking some questions, and in general distancing themselves from adults in the setting. Barrie Thorne (1993) also adopted a more marginal participatory role in her study of elementary-school kids. Most times she hung on the edges of play during recess but did participate a bit more actively at lunchtime. In the classroom, she worked to avoid having an adult authority role and avoided aligning with teachers.

Adults who enter children's peer cultures free of previously established roles (such as parent or teacher) enjoy the ability to adopt a range of roles located at various distances from adult power and status. Only researchers who work with the youngest children go so far as to "do what the kids do," taking on a complete involvement role. As children grow older, their peer cultures focus on talk over activity so there is little for the adult researcher to do other than listen or join the conversation to varying degrees. Adopting a willingness to see the world from the kid's perspective and deliberately distancing oneself from adult figures in the setting affords adults the opportunity to see and hear what kids talk about and do when regular adults are not around.

Demonstrating eagerness to shed authoritative positions over children is important, but displaying "real" incompetence greatly facilitates the process of closing the gap between adult and child power and control. Conducting research with children who speak a native language and share a national identity different from that of the researcher swiftly diminishes the communicative competence and cultural confidence of the adult researcher. Indeed, displaying language difficulty and cultural incompetence can help narrow the gap between the adult researcher and child participants. Corsaro's cross-cultural research with preschoolers in Italy provides a good example of the positive role language barriers can play in helping adults achieve a participant status in children's peer cultures (Corsaro and Rizzo 1988).

In my own work, I too entered the classroom as a person who was familiar with the language but who struggled to communicate fluently. My labored efforts to communicate signaled my eagerness to learn more about the students but also marked my difference from adult authority figures in the school setting. Furthermore, my weak language skills placed the students in a position unique for many children. They became experts who could teach me, the least-adult, how to communicate more effectively in their peer world. In fact, I found that the students enthusiastically embraced this teacher-like role by listening patiently as I struggled to answer their questions and honestly agreeing when I described my own skills as weak. Here was a rare chance for young children to exhibit a level of competence and power higher than that of an adult. As I will discuss, there were times I clearly held a position even lower than that of a peer-like equal.

Certainly, adults can never become children or "pass" as children. No adult sheds all adult privileges when researching the lives of children (Graue and Walsh 1998), even those who have important language and cultural differences. Nor should adult researchers ignore or even downplay generational differences between adults and children (Mayall 2000). Clearly adult size and power inequalities set them apart from kids. Nevertheless, adults can put adult-like behaviors aside and make the commitment to join children in the activities that children themselves determine to be central to their peer culture. As Corsaro (1997) points out, preschool-age children experience their peer cultures in the moment. Standing off to the side provides only a distant and incomplete view of the preschool peer culture.

Becoming a Member of the Kindergarten and First-Grade Peer Cultures

Entering the Field: Teachers as Initial Gatekeepers

The kindergarten teachers served as the first and most direct gatekeepers for my entry into the kindergarten students' peer culture. Before the semester began, I first met with the school principal and the classroom teachers in order to introduce myself and explain my research goals. Throughout this initial meeting with the teachers I spoke passable Mandarin, which seemed to put them at ease. They looked relieved when I did not try to speak to them in English, and I felt them warm up to me immediately. I explained my desire to adopt a least-adult role and my goal to participate fully in the students' activities.

Before starting my first day of fieldwork, I considered how I hoped the teachers would introduce me to the children. Choosing an appropriate name for me was a very important issue in establishing a desirable role in the setting. In Chinese culture, children usually do not call adults by their full names. Instead, they use a form of address such as "Teacher" or "Principal" that marks the adult's higher status. If they address an adult who is not familiar to them, children often use the title "Aunt" or "Uncle." In her own study of Taiwanese preschool, Chung-Hui Liang (2000) discovered the importance of her title while conducting her own research. Over three different data-collection periods, students called her Teacher, Aunt, and Older Sister, and Liang found that she felt closest to the students when they called her Older Sister. Based on Liang's experience, I knew that I wanted to be called by a title more familiar than Teacher or Aunt in order to minimize the status difference between me and the students.

On my first day of participant observation in the Blue Horse class, Teacher Bai asked me what I wanted to be called, and I suggested a number of options including my full name, Jin KaiDi, or "older sister." She considered these options and decided on a combination of them: "Older Sister Katy." In contrast, the students were called by their full names, so this title set me apart from them, but I was thrilled that I avoided being labeled as Teacher or Aunt. Teacher Bai's decision to adopt this title provided the first indication that she understood my desire to minimize status differences between myself and the students. Indeed, many gatekeepers in other settings where adults study children do not understand this relationship so clearly or so early in the research process.

During the first class period of the day, Teacher Bai introduced me to the students as KaiDi JieJie (Older Sister Katy) and told them that I would play and eat with them. When she asked the students what else I would do in the class, several suggested that I would also take a nap and attend class with them. The students seemed to understand immediately that I would do what they do. In fact, several students helped me to sit in the correct place in the classroom and showed me how to cross my legs in the same way the other students did. From the outset, the kindergarten students understood my peer-like position and frequently adopted expert, teacher-like roles as they taught me how to behave correctly in their classroom. I felt well cared for, even on my first day in the classroom. Free-play time, an even more child-directed space in the school day, proved to be no exception.

During free-choice time, several students took me by the hand and included me in their activities and play. When I was invited into the free-play area of the kindergarten, I waited in line with several other kids before I received what turned out to be a full-service Taiwanese beauty salon treatment including an extensive shoulder massage, hair wash and cut, and complimentary cup of tea. The students quickly realized that I was a willing participant who followed their lead and accepted invitations to play whatever the students suggested. This set me apart from other adults in the setting since the teachers did not allow the kids to play with their hair, and they did not do activities like climbing up into the students' playground equipment or crawling on the floor with the kids during activities as I did.

Entering the first-grade class as a least-adult proved to be a smoother process than I anticipated. When I returned to Taiwan before the start of the school year in August, I learned that the first-grade teacher assigned to the class I would join had been one of the kindergarten teachers from the attached kindergarten. Although she was not one of the teachers in the Blue Horse class, Teacher Wang and I were already acquainted and had discussed my research. There was little for me to explain to her about my research goals and my desire to participate as a student in the class.

On the first day of school, the first-graders and their parents attended together. After the teacher explained the curriculum, she introduced me to the parents. Teacher Wang explained that I would participate with the students in class, and she told them that I am a *xiǎo péngyǒu* (little friend). Her use of this term, one teachers often use when referring to students of kindergarten and elementary-school age, demonstrated her understanding of the role I hoped to achieve.

On the first day of first grade, I was happy to see seven friends from the Blue Horse class. Several of the girls greeted me by name, and I did the same. One of the boys from the class, Deng RenQuan, ran by me and called out a silly but familiar name, KaiShan DaDi (Julius Caesar). He playfully called me by this name back in kindergarten, so I felt welcomed into First Grade Class One. Another one of my former classmates from the Blue Horse class, Huang YingMing, also made me feel like one of the group on the first day of school. She noticed that I had not yet received my textbooks and encouraged me to ask the teacher about this before she started to show me all her books. In addition, other kids from the Blue Horse class invited me to run through the school and visit the old kindergarten class. I gladly joined them during the break between classes.

Some of the first-grade students who were new to Little Forest looked at me with curiosity for the first few days, but they quickly saw my old classmates treating me like one of their peers. The students who did not recognize me started to interact with me gradually. One boy noticed that he and I had the same pencil box, and we made a connection that way. Another student joined in a brief jumping routine that a girl from the kindergarten had initiated with me. Some students and I got to know one another by playing side by side during breaks, and others approached me to ask questions. Overall, it was easier to enter the field for the second time because the teacher understood my research goals and some of the students knew me and drew me into interactions from the beginning of the school year. New students saw how I was being treated by their peers and often did the same.

Negotiating Participation: Students as Gatekeepers and Expert Teachers

Although entering the field on a positive note was important in kindergarten and first grade, research roles are not achieved on one day and then forgotten. Instead, the researcher's role is developed and shaped from the first day in the field to the last. I constantly worked with the teachers and students to define and redefine how deeply I was included in the peer and school culture. The kindergarten teachers included me in class activities, meals, nap time, and all outings with the students. Furthermore, the teachers afforded me the freedom to interact with the students throughout the school day. They did not talk with me about "adult" issues in front of the students. About a month into my field research, one of the teachers told me simply, "I envy you." When I asked her to explain what she meant, she said she envied the fact that I could just "be" with the students, whereas she had to be in charge. Her simple statement showed that she understood clearly how different my role was compared to hers. As a result, the teachers rarely asked me to take on a supervisory role. Once, when one of the teachers experienced a medical emergency, I was alone with the students for a few minutes. Although I did "keep an eye out" for problems, I felt relieved that I never had to control students' behavior or confront a dangerous situation.

Although the teachers understood my complete-involvement role, there were limits to how completely the teachers treated me like the kindergarten students. Specifically, I did not join the students at the start of the school year; therefore, I did not receive some of the resources that the students did. For example, each of the thirty students was assigned a class number. The kids also had textbooks for homework, school-issued silverware and bowls for lunch and snack, storage space for extra clothes, backpacks, and sleeping blankets for nap time. I did not receive any of these resources that would mark me as a more complete, official member of the class. Instead, I supplied my own silverware and bowls. I left my backpack and sleeping bag on a desk in a separate room, and I did not participate in most homework assignments. At first I worried that these differences would set me apart from the students. Although some students noticed these differences, they used them as tools of inclusion rather than exclusion.

Students served as important gatekeepers to my inclusion in some of the more formal aspects of school life that the teachers did not. First, the teachers labeled each student as a member either of the *dàbān* (older class) or the *zhōngbān* (middle class) according to age. The teachers did not refer to me using these labels, so the students named me as a member of the *dàbān,* and the teachers followed their lead. When Wang YaAo questioned my status as a member of the older class, Teacher Yang supported my membership in the *dàbān,* explaining that I was in the older class because

I was going to elementary school next year. Although the students and teachers agreed on my membership in the older class, it was the students who instigated discussions about my class number, as in the following episode.

Field note 1: 03/09/2001, discussing my "class number"

As I stood in line for snack, one of the kids, I think it was Wang HaoKe or Xi YangZao asked me what number I am. All the kids have numbers, and that's what they were talking about. I told him, "I don't have a number." Then I suggested number 31, as the last kid is number 30. He said that there is no number 31. Then he said, "Number 4," and I said, "Isn't there someone with that number?" Wang HaoKe told me that there is a kid with that number but he never comes to school. Then I said, "OK."

The discussion ended there, but soon after, some of the students began to use the number thirty-one to refer to me, as in the following episode.

Field note 2: 03/26/2001, using my "class number"

Teacher Yang took roll by calling out class numbers. After all the class numbers were called, the kids sitting near me asked, "What number are you?" Xia YiQi smiled and said, "31." Then he and a few other kids quietly called out the number "31," and I quietly raised my hand and said "You" like the kids did when the teacher called their number in class. Teacher Bai did not look at us during this exchange and did not say anything to us about it.

In fact, the students used my created school number so frequently that the teachers eventually used the number thirty-one to refer to me as well. Here, the students helped me achieve my research goals by initiating my inclusion in this structured aspect of school life.

As a special member of the students' peer culture, they held me to the same standards expected of all peers. In this spirit, kids would remind me to adhere to the rules that applied to students only, as in the following example.

Field note 3: 06/01/2001, reminding me about rules

It was time to clean up. I picked up a few scraps of paper from the floor. I started to walk behind Teacher Bai's desk to throw the paper in the small wastebasket under her desk. Yu HaoYi was standing nearby. She told me that we are not supposed to go behind the teacher's desk. I told her that I was throwing away some garbage. She said it did not matter and that I should take the garbage to the garbage can in the center of the kindergarten. The teachers said we are not allowed in the area behind their desks.

I deferred to Yu HaoYi's reminder and left the area behind the teacher's desk to throw out the garbage. Yu HaoYi's reminder marked her recognition of my participant, peer-like status, as one who had to behave like a kid in accordance with the teacher's rules. My mistake also became an occasion in which Yu HaoYi demonstrated her expert knowledge, highlighting my incompetent performance as a Taiwanese kindergarten student. I unintentionally afforded the students many such opportunities to exercise their role as "teachers" as I struggled to learn and then remember the students' rules for correct behavior.

In the first-grade classroom, I hoped to participate as fully as I had in kindergarten. Like in the previous semester, I was willing to do everything the students did including class activities and homework, cleaning duties, nap time, and eating together at meals. I was hopeful that the teacher would include me in these activities, but I also expected that I might have to take on a more detached observer role. Because the school day was now structured around academic work rather than play, I suspected that the teacher would allow me to watch but not participate as fully as the students. Much to my delight, my assumptions were wrong. Teacher Wang willingly included me in all aspects of first-grade life.

On the first day of class, Teacher Wang included me in all the routines that would become a regular part of the class without singling me out as a special case. First, she called the roll using each student's full name and assigned class number. In contrast to kindergarten, the first-grade teacher did not set me apart with the title "Older Sister Katy," nor did she wait for the students to assign me a school number. After receiving responses from all twenty students, she called out my full name and the number twenty-one. After calling roll, Teacher Wang asked each student to come to the front of the room to introduce her- or himself. Each student complied, saying each name, something they like to do, and the name of the kindergarten they attended. When it was my turn, I said my full name, stated that I went to Little Forest Attached Kindergarten, and declared that I like to walk my dogs.

Marking my inclusion in the formal structure of first grade, I received all eleven textbooks and homework books just like the other students. I even completed the daily entries in the *liánluò běn* (Contact Book) that the teacher used to assign homework and report information to parents. I squeezed into a student desk and sat in rows with the other students. My street shoes fit in a cubby outside the classroom door, and my extra books sat on a shelf labeled "21" in the back of the room. In short, the teacher assigned me all the resources afforded regular students in the class.

In contrast to the kindergarten teachers, who actively avoided asking me questions and talking with me about adult topics in front of the students, the first-grade teacher occasionally talked to me as an adult during the school day. She asked questions about my family and my graduate work back in the United States. At first I felt a bit nervous about these interactions. I feared that the students would think of me as less than a peer if they witnessed me talking with the teacher as an equal. Fortunately, the teacher did not initiate many of these interactions during the school day, and I soon realized that the students did not treat me differently as a result of these brief conversations. Because I had already established a least-adult role with some of the students back in kindergarten, they seemed to understand that these brief asides did not change my relationships with them.

In contrast, students did seem to regard me differently during the rare times when I spoke English in front of them. One older elementary student spoke very good English and occasionally initiated conversations with me. When this happened, some of the first-graders asked, "What were you talking about?" It seemed that speaking English with another student was more distancing than speaking Mandarin with another adult. This experience illustrates Mandell's (1988) point that children can understand the fact that the adult researcher acts differently at different times. Although I was not acting in an authoritative way, I was acting differently than usual in these situations, but this did not seem to affect my overall relationships with the students.

As the semester progressed, some students asked me for help with homework and other academic assignments. Although my adult status did endow me with manual dexterity and neat writing and drawing skills, the students quickly learned that my limited language skills and cultural knowledge rendered me quite useless in the area of homework help. In fact, I found myself turning to the first-graders for help when completing Chinese-language homework assignments. I had little trouble writing the phonetic spelling symbols clearly, but I struggled to choose correct answers when identifying vocabulary words. The following episode demonstrates my weakness.

Field note 4: 11/05/2001, identifying storybook characters

Next, Teacher Wang explained the homework assignment that we will complete for tomorrow. Page 64 in the Chinese Homework book had a list of fictional storybook characters written in the phonetic spelling symbols. While I could pronounce the names because I could read the symbols, I did not recognize most of the names. The first one was níuláng zhīnǚ (dictionary translation says: The Cowherd and the Weaving Maid). The object of this homework was to make a check mark next to the characters that we recognized. Teacher Wang looked at me and asked if I recognized the character. I smiled sheepishly and shook my head. Hu JiaXue looked at me and said in a sharp voice, "Yes you do! We had it in kindergarten last year!" Now I really felt sheepish. I smiled and ducked my head a bit. I did not know how to respond to this insistence on Hu JiaXue's part. Her tone was quite fierce and impatient.

This example illustrates two points. First, my advanced age did not guarantee a strong performance on academic tasks. I did not recognize the cultural reference to a Chinese children's storybook character even after consulting a dictionary. Second, my classmates expected me to share their peer-based knowledge. Hu JiaXue expressed her frustration at my incompetence on a topic she claimed we had covered in kindergarten. In short, she expected me to behave like an equal based on our shared school experience, and I performed as an incompetent member of the group based on my lack of cultural knowledge and apparently faulty memory.

Similar to kindergarten, the first-grade students also demanded that I adhere to the same academic rules and social standards to which the teachers held them. For example, each morning students showed the teacher that they had obtained a parent signature in the "Contact Books," which signaled the parents' knowledge of grades and classroom activities. When one boy noticed that I had not obtained a parent signature, he complained to the teacher about my behavior.

Field note 5: 10/24/2001, Where is your dad's signature?

Teacher Wang told me that she needed my Contact Book. Cai JiaWen was standing nearby and walked over to my backpack. He said, "I will help you get the book." He took the book out and flipped through the pages to the current week. He looked at the page and said to me, "You do not have a father's signature here." I told him that there was no way to get a signature. My father was in the United States. He took the book to Teacher Wang. Later Teacher Wang told me that Cai JiaWen talked to her about this issue further. He told her, "My father is far away, too." Teacher Wang told him that both of my parents are in the United States. He said, "She just has to "xiǎng bànfǎ" (think of a way)." Teacher Wang laughed at this a bit, and I did too. This was exactly what Teacher Wang told the students, "think of a way."

Teacher Wang's explanation for why I failed to follow the rule did not placate Cai JiaWen. Although he empathized with the fact that my father was far away, he still insisted that the excuse was not a sufficient reason for me to fail to obtain the signature. He insisted that I think of a method for solving this problem, showing that he expected me to do as he did regardless of my challenges. In short, he expected me to behave in the same manner as him and to receive equal treatment from the teacher when I failed to comply. Interestingly, Cai JiaWen used a phrase often employed by the teacher to describe the steps I should take to correct my shortcomings. Cai JiaWen demonstrated his position as expert knower, a position above mine as the poorly performing classmate.

I struggled with the problem of obtaining parental signatures throughout my time in the first-grade class. Early in the semester another boy in the class suggested a way that I could adapt to the situation and follow the rule. As I sat at my desk, Liu ShengYang turned to me and asked what my dad's name was. I told him "Tom Gold." He suggested that I could write that name in the space where the parent is supposed to sign our homework and Contact Book. Here Liu ShengYang recognized the problem I faced with no parent present to sign my book. He offered a concrete solution, suggesting that I simply write my father's name myself, thus meeting the teacher's requirement for all students in the class. It is possible that students suggested the forgery method to one another, but I never witnessed it. In fact, I did take his advice on several occasions after that so as to avoid further criticism from the students or teacher. Although Lui ShengYang demanded that I maintain peer-like standards, he suggested an option that was safe for a person who was not really a student. Perhaps he recognized the privilege I enjoyed as a person who could "afford" to forge a signature without facing serious sanction from the teacher.

First-grade students also monitored my social behavior just like they did to me and their peers in kindergarten. If I inadvertently broke a rule on the playground or during the daily flag-raising ceremony, student leaders reported my negative behavior as they did for their peers. One morning the class leader reported my misbehavior to the teacher, and she reported this to me.

Field note 6: 10/23/2001, reporting my disobedience

When I stood in line to have my Contact Book checked, Teacher Wang told me that Deng RenQuan, the class leader, told her that I was not "guāi" (obedient) during the flag-raising ceremony. She said that he told her this quietly. She laughed as she told me this, and I laughed a bit too. He never said this to my face.

Although the class leader did not criticize my actions directly, as he had on several other occasions, he disapproved of my disobedient behavior. If he thought of me fully as an adult, he would not comment about this since adults/teachers are not held to the same standards of behavior (sitting down, being quiet, not talking to others) during the flag-raising ceremony. As the class leader who was charged with monitoring his classmates' behavior, Deng RenQuan included me in his watch and reported the infraction of a standard he was charged to uphold. In fact, by exercising his school- and teacher-sanctioned authority over me, Deng RenQuan highlighted my incompetence as a participant who often knew less than the knowledgeable students.

While the first-grade teacher and students included me in all aspects of school life, they certainly noticed and occasionally commented on the differences between us. Several students asked me about the United States, my family, and even my education level. One boy asked why I would come back to first grade if I already went to college. Another pointed out our age difference by saying, "When I grow up, Katy will already be dead!" Nevertheless, I received many indications that the students accepted me as a special member of their peer culture both in kindergarten and first grade.

Gauging Acceptance: Age and Nationality as Resource and Barrier

As a least-adult participating with the children in a peer-like manner, I looked for clues to gauge how well the students accepted me as a member of their peer cultures. Acceptance is an important goal for the least-adult researcher because becoming a recognized and welcome member of the group facilitates richer data collection and deeper participation in activities that are important to the children themselves. In short, acceptance is the least-adult's means of gaining access to aspects of peer culture that children do not often share with "regular," authoritative adults. For example, in the kindergarten I witnessed and even was included in a range of child-created and child-directed word-play routines of which the teachers disapproved (Hadley 2003). As a least-adult, the kids actively taught and then included me in the routines, whereas they altered and even halted these routines in front of the classroom teachers.

Indeed, researchers who have studied children point to the importance of witnessing children's rule-breaking behaviors as a marker of acceptance (e.g., Eder, Evans, and Parker 1995). If children do not fear that the adult researcher will reprimand them or report these negative behaviors to authority figures, it is a signal that the researcher has gained a level of acceptance. I received one such message near the end of the second week of research in the kindergarten.

After playing in the sand on the playground one morning, the teachers directed us to wash our hands in a large outdoor sink before returning to the classroom. I stood near the back of the line and waited to wash my hands. By the time I reached the sink, the teachers were standing several feet away. As I bent to put my hands under the water, two boys stood up on the edge of the cement sink, pulled down their pants, and peed into the sink. On the one hand, I was impressed to witness such an event since the boys appeared unfazed that I was watching. On the other hand, I felt nervous that I would have to admit that I witnessed this clear episode of rule breaking once we returned to the classroom. A student did report this behavior to the teachers, and the two boys were reprimanded for their behavior. Luckily the teachers did not ask me what I saw, and I did not volunteer any information.

Although I felt accepted by the students both as a peer-like least-adult and as a lower-status, incompetent group member, the kids still commented on our differences, especially in terms of age and nationality. I found that the students did not question the legitimacy of my participation in classroom and free-play activities. In contrast, formal events designed to mark students' impending status change into first-graders did elicit brief discussions about my age and nationality status. After the members of the older class and I returned from a visit to one of the first-grade classrooms, Lan JinCai asked me if I was going on to first grade.

When I said "Yes," he responded, "Why? You're an adult. You already did that." I told him that I did not go to first grade in Taiwan and that I did not know what that was like. He said no more.

In this interaction, the students viewed my outsider status based on age as a barrier to my future participation in the group. My difference in terms of nationality, however, served as a resource for explaining my continued participation in their group. By directly pointing out my visible nationality difference and implicitly reminding them of my associated cultural incompetence, I used nationality as the reason for further and future inclusion in the students' peer cultures. Furthermore, by downplaying differences based on age and highlighting differences based on nationality, I framed my continued relationship with them as one between a novice (me) and a set of experts (the students).

In another interaction, the students used my nationality status as a tool of exclusion and effectively blocked my full participation in their peer cultures. As a group of students and I waited to take kindergarten graduation pictures, several kids questioned me about my future participation in the group.

Field note 7: 05/21/2001, taking graduation photos

As we stood in line waiting to take the photos, some of the kids turned to me and said, "You are graduating." Some of them asked, "Are you graduating?" Huang YingMing said, "You are going to first grade?" I nodded when the kids asked me these questions. I felt OK answering in the affirmative because I was participating in all their activities and I would go to first grade with them in the fall. Zhang XuanYi turned to me and said it's *jiǎ de bìyè* (fake graduation) for me. San JinWen told me that I cannot graduate because I am a *wàiguó rén* (foreigner), not a *zhōngguó rén* (Chinese person).

Here, students shared different opinions about the "reality" of my participation in the graduation. While several appeared to accept my participation based on my commitment to continue on to first grade, others denied that my graduation was real. One boy explained my inability to participate as an equal in the graduation based on my different nationality status. He marked me as an outsider, rendering my nationality a tool the students could use to exclude me from their shared peer experience as kindergarten graduates. Clearly, my differences based on age and nationality served both as resources and barriers to my peer-like participation. It was the students who closely managed those statuses. Sometimes the kindergarten students used my cultural incompetence to include me, and other times they refused to accept me as a full member of their group because I did not share their national identity as a Chinese person.

Because the students accepted me as a special member of their peer culture—that is, a member who shared an equal status at some times and who held a lower position at other times—they maintained control over the quality of our continued interactions. In short, the students had the power to let me in or leave me out. During the last four weeks of the semester, I felt like a real participant when one of the leaders in the class, Zhang XuanYi, "broke off" our friendship. One morning I sat in the classroom with several girls who were playing a game. We used the "rock, paper, scissors" hand-gesture method in order to decide who would take the next turn. When it was my turn I chose "paper." I held my hand out with the palm facing down and fingers together. Zhang XuanYi told me that I was holding my hand in the wrong way and demonstrated the correct, palm-up position. I tried to heed her advice, but as we played on I forgot on several occasions. When she continued to criticize my hand position, I finally asked her, "What does it matter?" Judging from her subsequent behavior toward me, Zhang XuanYi felt insulted when I questioned her authority.

To show her displeasure at my challenge, Zhang XuanYi held her pointer fingers together in front of my face and then abruptly separated the fingers in a downward chopping motion. She repeated this gesture and scowled at me many times over the next several weeks of the semester. Although it took me a while to learn the official name of this gesture, *qīe bā dùan* (break into eight pieces), the meaning Zhang XuanYi conveyed was clear from the first gesture. She was angry at me for the way I responded to her directive, and she showed me again and again by scowling and refusing to play with me further. This rejection hurt and reminded me of my own experiences in elementary school, where girls had behaved in a similar manner. Although this was an emotionally painful experience, it was also a revealing one in the sense that it demonstrated the power that the students had in shaping my least-adult role. In this case, Zhang XuanYi controlled my access to interactions with her by displaying her displeasure. In effect, she denied me access to her interactions with friends. In treating me as she would other students who upset her, I was denied access to interactions with some of the children in the kindergarten class. Once again, students served as important gatekeepers, accepting and sometimes rejecting my presence and inclusion in their interactions.

In kindergarten, I gauged my level of acceptance by observing rule-breaking events and fielding questions about my age and nationality. In first grade, I measured my acceptance by directly participating in minor rule-breaking actions and learning of others' concerns about my age and nationality. Snacks were forbidden during class time, but many first-graders brought cookies or crackers to school. There were many days when a student would offer me a tiny cookie or a piece of gum when the teacher was not looking. After checking carefully for watchful eyes, I extended my hand to take the small treat. While I feared discovery by the teacher, my greater concern was accepting the invitation for inclusion from the students. I looked forward to inclusion in these "secondary adjustments" (Corsaro 1985) and felt like a member of the peer culture. In addition, I frequently set aside my adult concerns about germs when accepting these treats.

My greatest germ test came on the day Teacher Wang handed out lollipops. As I stood in line with the kids at the end of the day, several talked animatedly about their lollipop flavors. Popcorn, blueberry, and cream soda were some of the favorites, and the students began to offer one another a lick on her or his lollipop. When one student extended a wet lollipop in my direction, I hesitated only for a second before taking a quick lick. My desire to participate as a member of the peer culture overrode my adult concern about sharing saliva-borne germs, and I tasted the lollipop. As Katriel (1987) pointed out in an examination of Israeli children's food-sharing routine, ignoring adult-like concerns about spreading germs brought kids together when they shared food with one another. This lollipop tasting was no exception, and I did not want to miss an invitation to participate by invoking an adult concern.

I also witnessed many examples of students hitting one another and committing other acts forbidden by the teacher. In fact, students even hit and kicked me on a few occasions. Although I did not want to call attention to these actions and get the students in trouble with the teacher, I did want the perpetrators to stop hurting me. In order to make the aggressors stop, I often resorted to the empty threat commonly used by students, "Do you want me to tell the teacher?" Luckily my threats worked, and the hitting stopped before I actually had to tell the teacher. As I learned from the kindergarteners and first-graders, the most painful experiences, both emotional and physical, revealed the type of acceptance I had achieved as a least-adult. If the students viewed me as an authoritative adult, they would have no reason to subject me to peer-like behaviors such as exclusion from their interactions, invitations to break a food-sharing rule, or even episodes of kicking and punching.

Interactions with other elementary-school students and teachers further highlighted the level of acceptance I had gained from members of First Grade Class One and a few other students in the school. For example, one morning as I rode the public bus to school, a Little Forest student from a different grade asked me some questions. He told me that he thought I was a teacher, and I explained that I was in First Grade Class One. When we walked in the school's front gate after the first bell rang, an older elementary student stood guard at the gate and asked all the tardy students to report their name and class. The older student ignored me but stopped the boy who walked in next to me. Teacher Wang told me later that the boy I rode the bus with that morning complained about the unequal treatment. He thought it was unfair that his name was marked as tardy but mine was not. I agreed with his reasoning.

Teacher Wang went on to explain that the teacher who supervised the student monitors was reluctant to encourage his monitors to treat me like any other student. In fact, this teacher had observed me "misbehaving" during the flag-raising ceremony when I held hands with another member of my class who had initiated the contact. He told Teacher Wang that he was unwilling to "scold" me for this infraction because I am an adult. Teacher Wang encouraged him to treat me like any other student, just as she did, but he never spoke to me about my behavior.

After that incident, I worked even harder to be obedient and follow the rules I knew because I did not want the other teachers to feel uncomfortable with my presence at the school. This episode showed that my teacher and the kids who knew me personally were the most accepting of my least-adult status, as evidenced by their willingness to point out my errors. My age status did not serve as a barrier for their equal treatment of me. In contrast, other adults in the school did not feel comfortable following Teacher Wang's lead, treating me as she did like any other student in her class despite my clear difference in age. This episode also highlights the continuous socialization process I experienced as a cultural outsider who constantly struggled to act like a competent member of the first-grade class. The students recognized the rules and the expectation of obedience to those rules. I strove to learn the rules so that I, too, could demonstrate my peer-like obedience to authoritative adult expectations.

The Least-Adult as an Equal Peer and a Lower-Status Novice

During my research in one kindergarten and one first-grade class in Taiwan, I adopted a least-adult role. I entered each classroom with the hope that I could create a complete participant role through my willingness to do what the students did, but I found that the teachers and students were largely responsible for shaping my peer-like experiences in both classrooms. The kindergarten teachers allowed me to participate in the children's activities as "Older Sister Katy." On the occasions when the teachers failed to include me in some aspects of student life, the students found ways to bring me into the fold. In first grade, the teacher included me even more fully into the life of the class. As just plain "Katy," I enjoyed all the privileges and responsibilities shared by every first-grader in her class. Again the students drew me into their interactions and held me to the same standards that teachers expected of them.

My novice status as a person who struggled to speak the language and who lacked taken-for-granted cultural knowledge contributed to my acceptance into the students' peer cultures. I brought few preconceived ideas about how to behave in the research setting, and I believe my participants also lacked clear expectations for my behavior. Our mutual curiosity and openness facilitated my relatively smooth entry into the students' lives. As a result, I spent much time engaged in activities that teachers and other adults rarely witnessed. Certainly the students never forgot our age and nationality differences. In fact, my shortcomings often contributed to my special status as a member of their class, in contrast to other adults in the school setting. The students used my weaknesses as teaching resources for themselves. As a result, they often became the experts who confidently guided me, the novice, into their peer worlds.

An important insight gained through the least-adult role is seeing the world through the eyes of at least some of these children. Students included me in a range of interactions both in and outside the classroom. I heard firsthand what interested them and observed what was important to them. I listened as the kindergarten students occasionally talked about going to elementary school, and I joined in the creative games that some first-graders adapted from the kindergarten peer culture. In fact, the teachers were unaware of many of the topics discussed and games that I observed and was asked to participate in both in kindergarten and first grade (Hadley 2003; Hadley and Nenga 2004). There was a downside, however, to achieving such a deep participatory role. Because I was so involved and included in small group interactions, it was hard to observe interactions of children outside the group I was with at any moment. Nevertheless, the depth of understanding I achieved over the course of two semesters outweighed the limited scope of some moment-to-moment observations. In the end, my position as least-adult placed me in a unique position from which to observe and even experience the students' daily activities as they made the transition from kindergarten to first grade.

Adopting a least-adult role requires the adult researcher to leave behind adult control over children and also over many aspects of the interactions themselves. Although teachers and other adult gatekeepers who govern children's worlds manage initial access to children's lives, the children themselves control the ebb and flow of the least-adult's participation in their peer cultures. Whether letting the least-adult into places "regular" adults rarely see or shutting out the least-adult who has already gained an insider status, children hold the ultimate authority over the adult researcher's access to their peer cultures. Fortunately, the Taiwanese students at Little Forest generously opened the gate to me both as Older Sister Katy and just plain Katy and showed me firsthand what it meant to be a student, a peer, and a friend.

NOTES

1. All names of persons, classes, and schools are pseudonyms.

2. Overall, the Blue Horse class was quite similar to other public kindergarten classes in Taipei City in terms of overall size of the attached kindergarten, class size, and student/teacher ratio (Ministry of Education 2002).

3. Following Farris's (1991) example, I use the *pinyin* romanization spelling system to romanize all Mandarin words and phrases. Although the Taiwanese often use the Wade-Giles romanization system, I am most familiar with *pinyin*, having learned it as a college student studying Mandarin.

4. Little Forest was small compared to other municipal elementary schools, with only two classes per grade, an average of twenty students per class, and fewer than three hundred students in grades one through six (Ministry of Education 2001).

REFERENCES

Bureau of Statistics. 1998. *Education in the Republic of China.* Taipei, Taiwan: Ministry of Education.

Corsaro, William A. 1997. *The Sociology of Childhood.* Thousand Oaks, CA: Pine Forge.

Corsaro, William A. 1996. "Transitions in Early Childhood: The Promise of Comparative, Longitudinal Ethnography." Pp. 419–457 in *Ethnography and Human Development,* edited by Richard Jessor, Anne Colby, and Roger Shweder. Chicago: University of Chicago Press.

Corsaro, William A. 1985. *Friendship and Peer Culture in the Early Years.* Norwood, NJ: Ablex.

Corsaro, William A., and Thomas Rizzo. 1988. "*Discussione* and Friendship: Socialization Processes in the Peer Culture among Italian Nursery School Children." *American Sociological Review* 53:879–894.

Eder, Donna, with Catherine Colleen Evans and Stephen Parker. 1995. *School Talk: Gender and Adolescent Culture.* New Brunswick, NJ: Rutgers University Press.

Farris, Catherine S. 1991. "The Gender of Child Discourse: Same-Sex Peer Socialization through Language Use in a Taiwanese Preschool." *Journal of Linguistic Anthropology* 1:198–224.

Fine, Gary Alan. 1987. *With the Boys: Little League Baseball and Preadolescent Culture.* Chicago: University of Chicago Press.

Fine, Gary Alan, and Kent L. Sandstrom. 1988. *Knowing Children: Participant Observation with Minors.* Newbury Park, CA: Sage.

Graue, M. Elizabeth, and Daniel J. Walsh. 1998. *Studying Children in Context: Theories, Methods, and Ethics.* Thousand Oaks, CA: Sage.

Hadley, Kathryn Gold. 2003. "Children's Word Play: Resisting and Accommodating Confucian Values in a Taiwanese Kindergarten Classroom." *Sociology of Education* 76:193–208.

Hadley, Kathryn Gold, and Sandi Kawecka Nenga. 2004. "From Snow White to Digimon: Using Popular Media to Confront Confucian Values in Taiwanese Peer Cultures." *Childhood: A Global Journal of Child Research* 11:515–536.

James, Allison, Chris Jenks, and Alan Prout. 1998. *Theorizing Childhood.* New York: Teachers College Press.

Katriel, Tamar. 1987. "'*Bexibudim!*': Ritualized Sharing among Israeli Children." *Language in Society* 16:305–320.

Liang, Chung-Hui. 2000. "Play in a Working-Class Preschool." Ph.D. dissertation, University of Illinois, Urbana-Champaign.

Mandell, Nancy. 1988. "The Least-Adult Role in Studying Children." *Journal of Contemporary Ethnography* 16:433–467.

Mayall, Berry. 2000. "Conversations with Children: Working with Generational Issues." Pp. 120–135 in *Research with Children: Perspectives and Practices,* edited by Pia Christensen and Allison James. New York: Falmer.

Ministry of Education. 2002. *Taiwan Education Statistics Information.* Available online at http://www.edu.tw/English/index.html.

Ministry of Education. 2001. *National Elementary School Statistical Profile: Acade-*

mic Year 2000–2001. Taipei, Taiwan: Ministry of Education Bureau of Statistics (in Chinese).

Ministry of Education. 1999. *Education Statistics of the Republic of China.* Taipei, Taiwan: Ministry of Education.

Thorne, Barrie. 1993. *Gender Play: Girls and Boys in School.* New Brunswick, NJ: Rutgers University Press.

Van Ausdale, Debra, and Joe R. Feagin. 2001. *The First R: How Children Learn Race and Racism.* New York: Rowman and Littlefield.

Chapter 7

The Outsider Lurking Online
Adults Researching Youth Cybercultures

Alyssa Richman

I prepared to begin this fieldwork as I did for my other youth research projects. I considered which details about myself and my project I would reveal and which I would withhold, and I brainstormed ways to minimize my adult status. I scouted out my locations and researched their rules and norms. And as my first official day of data collection approached, I felt well prepared.

At 5 p.m. on June 15, I entered my site, data recorder at my fingertips, prepared to begin my research. I stepped into the middle of a conversation that began long before I arrived and settled in to observe and acclimate to my new surrounding. I was instantly lost, unable to follow the multiple threads of conversation. The interaction was frenetic, as conversations were layered one on top of another, and I struggled to make sense of unfamiliar slang, shorthand, and symbols. I tried to jump in, but before I could get the words out, the conversation shifted and I missed my opportunity. I had just begun my fieldwork in an online chat room.[1]

As I struggled through my first few days of online fieldwork, questions about the ethics of my research (which primarily consisted of "lurking" on the message boards and chat rooms) began to arise. Additionally, the location of myself as a relative novice and outsider to the youth cyberspace I was researching became conspicuously clear. I came to realize that Internet research on youth necessitates addressing several key methodological considerations.

I was first drawn to Internet research while volunteering for an organization in which trained young people counseled other teens in an online chat room about relationships. During one such session, a white counselor was asked her race by the chatter. The counselor's response was "Italian." I was surprised by the relevance of race in this "anonymous" interaction and wanted to more thoroughly explore the meanings attached to race, gender, and class by young people online. However, as I began to search for other online research projects, I was shocked by both the dearth of information available on the methodologies used in previous studies and the absence of ethical guidelines that specifically addressed Internet research.[2] As a result, I was unprepared for my first journey into youth cyberculture as a researcher.

This chapter explores several considerations for adult researchers as they navigate online youth spaces in this historical moment marked by the emergence of the Internet as a social space largely populated by young people. First, we must consider the ways in which we are multiply located as outsiders: as adults and also as adults with no memories of a childhood mediated by Internet technologies. Additionally, we must consider the act of lurking and its implications (both positive and negative) for the quality of data we seek to collect *and* for the young people under study. Drawing from my own research project on the ways that young people take up race, gender, and class in online spaces and on my cyberspace fieldwork on message boards and chat rooms, I examine the benefits and limits of online research, specifically addressing the role of memory, the location of the outsider, and the politics of lurking when adults research young people.

Researching Youth Online

Recent years have seen a rapidly expanding body of research on the social aspect of the Internet, both as an element of contemporary youth cultures and as a medium through which young people experience that culture or are defined by it (Clark 1998; Heins 2002; Holloway and Valentine 2003; Mitchell and Reid-Walsh 2002; Turkle 1995). However, specific methodological issues that arise when conducting online youth research have not been fully examined. This emerging literature can be divided into historical analyses, which serve to locate youth in relation to the social and cultural meanings constructed around the Internet, and ethnographic studies, which attempt to understand the meanings youth themselves construct around these new information technologies. These studies raise a number of ethical considerations, such as the protected status of youth and the agency (or lack thereof) young people experience in online spaces, that are important problematics researchers must take into account.

Critically examining the ways in which definitions of youth shape public policy and commercial products aimed at protecting young people from the dangers of the Internet, Marjorie Heins (2002) makes visible the essentialist notions of childhood that inform the prevailing discourses about kids online. Ranging from child predators lurking in chat rooms to easy-access pornography, there is much to be feared online. Politicians have responded with proposed bills and other legislative efforts, while electronics companies have rushed to create new filtering and blocking software. In the meantime, parents unable to constantly monitor their kids' online activities and fearing the worst consume these new products in the quest for safety. Although more of a historical overview than a sociological analysis, Heins's work is most significant for its attention to the ways that these policing efforts not only rely on a specific set of situated values (which remain invisible) but also are explicitly linked to constructions of children as in need of protection (ibid.).

As many of us who research youth have already discovered, this definition of childhood shapes that research, from the restricted access to the multiple consent forms. Additionally, Heins's work highlights the fear of the outsider online—those adults "disguised" as children who lurk in darkened corners of cyberspace. This fear influences methodological choices for adults researching youth online, who must balance their own research interests with the perceived safety of youth cybersurfers. Lurking as a research tool falls under a veil of suspicion when located within a society that assigns children to a protected class of citizen.

John Springhall (1998) offers a historical context for the current fear surrounding computer games and the Internet, focusing on the phenomenon of "moral panics" that arise in response to youth culture. Although not limited to computers, his argument complements that of Heins by tracing the history of these panics. Springhall argues that the forms of amusement that adults choose for youth often rely on a romantic ideal of childhood, while the entertainment youth choose for themselves often challenge this ideal, making adults uncomfortable (ibid.). In addition, these "media panics can help to re-establish a generational status quo, that the pioneering cultural position of the young has undermined, by targeting violence or sex in teenage but not in adult forms of entertainment" (ibid.:7). Not only does this fear of computer games and the Internet reflect deeply rooted definitions of youth, but the panics that erupt in response serve to further reinforce the power imbalance between young people and adults.

Although Springhall is concerned with the social "moral panic" surrounding youth cultures and Heins specifically addresses the censorship of elements of those cultures, both authors highlight the ways that definitions of youth are situated within a larger cultural context of inequality. This dynamic is directly related to the hyperconcern for ethics when researching children and is magnified when that research is conducted online.

The historical analyses offered by Heins and Springhall set a critical stage for subsequent sociological studies that center on the meanings of the new Internet-based cultures from the perspectives of kids themselves. Although young adults (between the ages of eighteen and thirty) are the focus of the bulk of online research (Burkhalter 2000; Ignacio 2000; Kendall 2000; Turkle 1995), the following three studies specifically address the cultural space of the Internet for children and youth.

One of the most comprehensive studies of kids, computers, and the Internet, *Cyberkids: Children in the Information Age* addresses the ways that identity is shaped through interaction not only with other people but also with "things" such as the computer (Holloway and Valentine 2003: 9). Utilizing research with young people at home and school, this work situates computers and the Internet within the context of everyday life. Holloway and Valentine (2003) are attentive to the ways that computer-mediated communication is used by kids in quite sophisticated ways that may offer the possibility to complicate and renegotiate the boundaries between childhood and adulthood.

Interested in the emancipatory promise of online spaces, sociologist Lynn Shofield Clark (1998) researched the online dating that occurs between young people in chat rooms. Drawing primarily from interviews and teen-led focus groups, this study compares the experiences of Internet dating with "real-life" dating. Clark finds that these online spaces may offer greater freedom for girls, specifically the ability to (re)define the self, to use verbal skills, the ability to exercise aggression within a "safe" space, and the ability to construct (or reconstruct) their physical selves into more conventional ideas of beauty, thereby harnessing the power of self-presentation and authorship (ibid.). However, although there appears to be the potential for greater gender and sexual freedom online, more often than not the girls' work to author their own bodies actually became an exercise in the active reconstruction of their appearance to better fit traditional notions of (white, middle-class) beauty and heterosexuality (ibid.).

Whereas Clark was interested in the ways that young people interact with one another with the help of computer-mediated communication, Claudia Mitchell and Jacqueline Reid-Walsh (2002) were more interested in the ways that kids interact with websites themselves. Analyzing sites created for kids by adults and sites created by kids for other kids, Mitchell and Reid-Walsh found that the creation of websites has the most potential for young people to actively claim agency. "In the practice of 'creating' a website or homepage, the child is engaging in activities that undo the representation of children as cultural dupes. . . . the child is producing information, which is the prime cultural capital and monetary currency in the present-day information age" (Mitchell and Reid-Walsh 2002:169). More generally, these websites blur the boundaries between public and private spaces, as they are public sites often accessed from within a private bedroom. This boundary blurring "may enable children to enter the public domain as knowledgeable computer users, asserting their role as active agents" (ibid.:150).

Each of these studies points to the complex relationship between youth and online spaces. The Internet can be both a site of autonomy for young people as well as a space that upholds adult-youth power inequalities. This complexity mirrors the myriad methodological issues facing the adult who chooses to critically research youth cyberculture. Questions about the ethics of lurking, the role our own adult memory plays, and the quality of data collected by an outsider online must be worked through in the course of Internet research.

As the body of critical literature on young people online has expanded, there has been a parallel expanding interest in conducting general social science research online. The methodological literature that has grown out of this interest, though largely not youth-specific, begins to raise key questions about the validity and ethics of Internet research. Much of the early literature on Internet methods focuses primarily on quantitative practices and issues of validity (see Cho and LaRose 1999; Cook, Heath, and Thompson 2000; Daley et al. 2003; Dillman 2000; Tse 1998). These works are primarily interested in the Web as a tool for data collection and less as a site of social investigation in and of itself.

Other researchers, particularly in the interdisciplinary field of new media studies, do address methodological considerations when examining the Internet itself as a social and cultural space (Broad and Joos 2004; Mann and Stewart 2000; Paccagnella 1997; Wakeford 2004), and several take up the application of ethnographic and other qualitative techniques to the Web (Gaston and Zweerink 2004; Hine 2000). For example, sociologist Nina Wakeford (2004) is particularly attentive to the connected nature of the Internet as located within particular commercial and cultural networks and calls for research methods that allow for this context to emerge. Similarly, Christine Hine (2000) outlines a method of online ethnography that attempts to address the Internet both as a site of cultural production as well as a cultural artifact. Like Wakeford, Hine is concerned with methods that privilege the contextual nature of the Internet and offers an example of "online ethnography" with her study of a Louise Woodward online support site and its "real" consequences for the outcome of the trial and perceptions of that event.

Although these researchers address many of the methodological considerations that confront scholars interested in studying online cultures and social spaces, they are not specifically attentive to the unique ethical and epistemological challenges that arise when adults research youth online and youth cyberspaces. For example, in their "Handbook for Researching Online," Mann and Stewart address a number of practical and ethical considerations for conducting online qualitative research, but they only briefly mention researching young people in the context of a broader discussion of informed consent:

> This requirement [obtaining parental consent] could be simply addressed through the provision of extra electronic consent forms. However, given the difficulty of verifying the originator of electronic communication, the ethical researcher might consider that consent for research involving children should always be obtained from adults in paper form. (2000:54)

The issue of parental consent is central for those of us researching youth, but it is not adequately unpacked by Mann and Stewart and leaves us with many questions. For example, is lurking in youth spaces (and thereby not obtaining parental consent) an ethical practice, and what are the implications for the agency of young people? This chapter begins with these and other unanswered questions in an attempt not to offer definitive answers but to connect discussions of online methodologies with the practice of critical youth research.

Internet Ethnography: Doing Fieldwork
in Cyberspace

As mentioned, a number of sociologists and social theorists have begun to study the ways that children, youth, and young adults use the Internet (Clark 1998; Holloway and Valentine 2003; Ignacio 2000; Kendall 2000; Mitchell and Reid-Walsh 2002; Turkle 1995). However, their specific methodological approach was often only briefly mentioned or remained completely unstated. Despite the exponential increase in research on and about young people in cyberspace, there has been little reflexivity on the craft of research within this emergent social arena.

For example, Clark (1998) spent the least amount of time collecting data online, as most of her data came from face-to-face in-depth interviews and teen-led focus groups. However, she does state that she did "lurk" in teen chat rooms as part of her research process, but she offers no discussion of the ethical and methodological implications of this choice. On the other end of the spectrum, Emily Noelle Ignacio (2000) conducted all of her research online, as a participant in the newsgroup she researched. Interested in the ways that Filipina women negotiated and articulated their ethnic, racial, and gendered identities online, Ignacio was a participant-observer. As she explains, "Most of the time, I lurked, simply reading the debates; however, if a person wrote anything that I felt needed clarification, I entered the discussion by posting a response to the whole newsgroup" (Ignacio 2000:556). Although her method was clearly outlined, she provides little discussion of the issues it raised.

In her study of masculinity in an online forum, Lori Kendall (2000) conducted online research similar to Ignacio's. She joined and participated in the BlueSky forum and "gradually became a member of the social group, learning both technical aspects of online communication and social norms that enabled me to continue my participation" (Kendall 2000: 257). However, unlike Clark and Ignacio, Kendall made her role as a researcher known to the group and even solicited comments on her analytical interpretations from other members. Although this appears to indicate a more reflexive research process, Kendall does not explore the reasons for or implications of her research choices.

Outside of these three studies, I was unable to find specific examples or concrete rules for conducting online research with youth, making the development of my own methodology for this study a challenge and leaving a number of important questions unanswered. Drawing from the studies described above, available Internet ethical research guidelines (Ess et al. 2002), and my own expedition into youth cyberland, I developed a methodology that attempts to address the ways that young people construct, subvert, and reconstruct identities online. However, as my project progressed, three distinct but related methodological concerns became apparent and required thoughtful consideration throughout the research process: the role of adult memory, negotiating outsider status, and the ethics of lurking. Each of these complications has the potential to create problems for the quality of data, but if deliberately negotiated, all three may serve to enrich data and increase understanding of the ways young people make meaning online.

Memory, Reflexivity, and Online Youth

The concept of memory-work as a tool for qualitative research was first described by Frigga Haug and colleagues (1987) as a way to study the self. The method involves using subjects' memories, often captured through writing, to examine the ways that the self is socially constructed through reflection (Haug et al. 1987). I use the term in a similar way to capture the reflexive process involved in the recollection of memory, but I am more interested in the memories of the researcher as a variable in the research process between adults and youth.

The memory-work done by adults in the course of their research on youth has the potential to obscure the relations of power that truly situate adults as outsiders in relation to their research subjects. In her article "When Gender Is Not Enough," Riessman (1987) argues that although the researcher and the researched may share a social status, that alone is not always enough to guarantee complete understanding of the subjects' experiences and meanings. Similarly, adults' semi-insider status as former young people does not guarantee congruent life experiences and in no way ensures a more complete understanding of the meaning-making processes of the youth under study. In fact, adult researchers must actively work to reflexively acknowledge their own memories and experiences to prevent making assumptions about youth that may not reflect the actual experiences of those under study.

However, the relationship between memory and ethnography is complex, as described by Sari Knopp Biklen in her article "Trouble on Memory Lane: Adults and Self-Retrospection in Researching Youth":

> Memory is full of contradictions for ethnographers. The danger for narrators who construct their memories as links between their adolescent informants and the adult researcher who was once a youth rides on the implicit suggestion that the researcher can too easily access youths' perspectives. On the other hand, to represent memory as a form of bias that needs to be managed or overcome ignores the complexity and uses of the identity markers that fieldworkers bring to the research site and sidesteps the collective aspects of even our most personal memories. (2004:716)

Although researcher memory and the experience of youth informants should not be conflated, neither should memory simply be ignored or managed away, as we rely heavily on it to navigate research spaces.

Adult researchers bring memory baggage of our own time as young people with us into our sites. Many ethnographers acknowledge these memories; Barrie Thorne described moments during her early observations that led to a chain of memories of her own school experiences and forced her to recall the "emotional legacy" of her own elementary-school years (1993:26).

In the course of my own research, I must frequently work to recognize my own memories and their role in shaping my research in an attempt to not confuse my own memories of teenage life with a sense of authority on all youth experience. For example, it wasn't until collecting data from seven separate threads addressing feminism that I developed a curiosity about their apparent frequency. After reflecting on this finding and after several more days of data collection, I realized that feminism threads were not more frequent than other threads but that the probability that I would deem them interesting or potentially data-rich (and therefore choose them for analysis) was directly related to the contested space that feminism occupied in my own youth.

Although the online content frequently awoke my own memories of being a teenager, Internet research occupies a unique location at this moment in time. The study of youth and youth cultures *in cyberspace* complicates this nearly unavoidable experience of memory-work that occurs during the research process. Most social researchers today did not experience their youth online. The proliferation of computer-mediated communication technologies is a relatively recent event, and even as a young researcher currently in my twenties, I did not begin using email until I was a college student and never visited a chat room until I began this project in graduate school. As I conducted my online fieldwork, I was unable to rely on my own memories to navigate the space, and I had no intuitive knowledge about the nature of chat rooms and message boards.

Consider this excerpt from my field notes and observation comments from the first day of observation in a chat room (my screename is alygrl 2003):[3]

alygrl2003 joined the room.

championofsouthdakota joined the room.

u1c_ma joined the room.

patbuchanan2003 left the room.

dakota_davidson2001: thats good cause blacks are retarded *(Note: As soon as I enter the chat room it is clear that race is important in this space. I have no idea what this conversation is about or what the context of this comment is.)*

mahmoud_paradie joined the room.

ghost_thuglife23: means zeus in greek

jctsuperstar5: hi

dimple_htin joined the room.

dakota_davidson2001: dahhhh

dakota_davidson2001: hi

championofsouthdakota: hi everyone

alygrl2003: hi everyone *(Note: It has been only a matter of seconds since I have logged on but I'm already lost! I am having difficulty reading all the postings and typing my own.)*

ghost_thuglife23: no its the truth

jctsuperstar5: yea wuddup

foox2005 joined the room.

ghost_thuglife23: stop eatin meat

alygrl2003: whats up everyone? *(Note: I deliberately delete "what's" and re-type "whats" before I post it to eliminate the apostrophe. I am new to chat rooms, but I want to fit in and follow the conventions of this informal space. I am also actively working to present a younger persona.)*

u1c_ma: good day to all

In this example, I struggle both to keep up with the pace of the chat and to follow the conventions of this text-only space. I was unprepared for the speed of interaction in this chat room, as seen in the note: "It has been only a matter of seconds since I have logged on but I'm already lost! I am having difficulty reading all the postings and typing my own." In addition,

I was not yet practiced in the art of cyber-shorthand, as seen by my re-typing of the word "what's," and the constant self-editing took additional time. Conversely, many chatters appeared quite adept, making several entries before I was able to produce one.

Although my offline youth was not the sole cause of my lack of chatroom skills (as I am now quite adept in these online spaces), it did prevent me from immediately accessing the online youth experience from my own memory bank. I was forced to proceed with caution, slowly uncovering the rules of the space and the meanings youth themselves create there.

Our lack of memories of an online childhood may render less likely problems of assumption associated with a "been there, done that" mentality, but lacking these memories excludes us from the collective information about the ways youth navigate cyberspace. Although this may mean additional work is required to learn and understand the rules of the space, this can be a largely beneficial consequence. Our lack of memory necessarily locates us as outsiders online and can render even the most net-savvy adult a novice. Conversely, the youth informants are then positioned as experts, encouraging the desired dynamic between the researcher and her subjects. As Biklen writes, "Ethnographers of youth work to access how [youth] make sense of the world. Conceptualizing them as informants who can tell us about their perspectives of a particular culture helps researchers avoid thinking of them as unable to adequately describe their situations" (2004:722). Our lack of experiential knowledge of a youth online reinforces this relationship.

The Adult Novice and the Youth Expert: Negotiating Outsider Status Online

Adults who conduct research on or about youth complicate the insider/outsider debates, unable to be categorized by this dichotomous absolute. Attempting to answer the question "who can research whom?" these debates raise complex epistemological issues about the way knowledge is gained and the benefits and limits of in- or out-group associations. Supporters of outsider research believe that only as outsiders can researchers truly see the workings of the groups and access objective knowledge about the subjects, leading to better data. Alternatively, proponents of insider research argue that insider knowledge of the group will generate greater understanding, facilitate rapport, and ultimately lead to better data.

In her discussion of qualitative research of minority communities, Maxine Baca Zinn, a proponent of insider perspectives, argued that white researchers may be unable to transcend cultural or linguistic barriers, which could lead to incomplete or inaccurate interpretations of these communities: "field research conducted by minority scholars has some empirical and some methodological advantages. The most important one is that the 'lenses' through which they see social reality may allow minority scholars to ask questions and gather information others could not" (1979: 212).

In an examination of the study of Chicanos by white researchers, Americo Paredes (1978) argued that white researchers may misinterpret jokes or other performances by informants due to their lack of familiarity with the language and their outsider status in the group. Although both Zinn and Paredes outline the benefits of insider research, they each are also aware of in-group differences. For example, Zinn acknowledges her class and educational differences in relation to her informants but relies on their shared racial and ethnic locations. These scholars situate their work within the racial dynamics under which most social science research is conducted, namely, the majority of research that is conducted by white researchers on minority communities and the lack of researchers of color.

Complicating this debate, Catherine Kohler Riessman (1987) contends that a shared insider status may not always be enough to facilitate understanding or ensure complete and accurate data collection between researchers and subjects. Comparing two interviews conducted by a white researcher, one with a white woman and the other with a Puerto Rican woman, Riessman notes, "Although both were highly competent narrators, only the Anglo woman was fully understood by the white, middle-class interviewer. She was able to collaborate with this narrator and help her tell her story. In the case of the working-class, Hispanic woman, gender was apparently not enough to create the shared understandings necessary for a successful interview" (1987:173). In this example, despite sharing gender with her informants, this researcher remained on the outside, limiting the quality of data collected and ultimately the interpretations drawn from the data.

In many respects, adults research young people as outsiders. In their guide to conducting participant observation with children, Gary Alan Fine and Kent Sandstrom write, "Like the white researcher in black society, the male researcher studying women, or the ethnologist observing a distant tribal culture, the adult participant observer who attempts to understand a children's culture cannot pass unnoticed as a member of that group" (1988:13). We are not members of youth communities, and our everyday experiences are those of more privileged adults. In relation to our research subjects, adult sociologists hold social, economic, and cultural power that positions us differently than our informants.

However, adults are situated as former youth, previously occupying that less-powerful location. As Barrie Thorne writes about her fieldwork in an elementary school, "To learn *from* children, adults have to challenge the deep assumption that they already know what children are 'like,' both be-cause, as former children, adults have been there, and because, as adults they regard children as less complete versions of themselves" (1993:12). As adults, "youth" is the only category of oppression that we have all experi-enced and then left behind to become members of the more powerful, nontarget category of "adult." Although this complicates traditional no-tions of insiders and outsiders, adults who study youth cyberspaces do so largely as outsiders.

Positioned as outsiders because of memory and age (and likely other social categories as well), ethnographers of youth are forced to uncover the norms and rules of online youth spaces in order to fit in and understand the ways young people interact within these virtual spaces. As a result, the data collected are more likely to reflect the meanings youth themselves have assigned and created within their cyberspaces.

As an outsider online desperate to collect quality data for my master's thesis, I quickly realized that I was completely unfamiliar with the conven-tions of the spaces I had committed to researching for the next several months. I faltered and struggled to keep up while managing my youthful online persona. Early on, this proved to be a huge source of stress as I wor-ried about "outing" myself as an adult who did not belong on the youth boards. I would leave my field site after only an hour, exhausted from try-ing to keep up with the pace of the conversation. As I continued my field-work week after week, and made reflexive notations on the process, I began to recognize the benefits of my location as an adult outsider.

Consider the following notations from my field notes:

> **ghost_thuglife23:** in the original bible it was not a sin to have sex and many wives
> **sweet_r_heart** left the room.
> **alygrl2003:** how did the bible convo come up ghost? *(Note: I have decided to ask about this interesting conversation to see if I can find out more informa-*

tion. I receive no response to this question. This highlights the ability to
ignore or selectively respond to others in the room. This freedom is more dif-
ficult in face-to-face conversation.)

hothoneybunz172 left the room.

u1c_ma: ang laki laki ng bulaklak

jctsuperstar5: ang laki laki........

alygrl2003: dude—what ru guys talking about?

jctsuperstar5: nothin.........

alygrl2003: what ru doin tonight jc? *(Note: I am trying to make conversation.*
I am surprised that no one in this room is talking about television. This
seems strange since each room is specifically assigned a topic. I am also
actively trying to use the shorthand of the chat room so I appear to belong
here.)

jctsuperstar5: aint nobody talkin

In these notes, I am learning two important conventions of the site. First, the ability to ignore others or selectively respond is a powerful component of computer-mediated communication and suggests a level of agency that may not exist in offline sites. Second, although the topic of this chat room was television, there was little mention of television during the hour I spent there. Since I had specifically selected this site hoping to rely on my acquired knowledge of youth television, this was a sharp contrast from what I expected to find.

This example illustrates the way the position of the outsider may in fact enhance data collection by illuminating social rules of the space. Unintentionally situated in the role of the novice, I was able to uncover the unspoken laws that govern these chat rooms (and bulletin boards) that may have gone unnoticed by others with more extensive memories and experiences of this space.

Also revealed in this example is the expert status youth assume in this space. One of the key theoretical shifts that occurred with the rise of "new youth studies" was the recognition of young people as authorities on youth cultures and youth experiences. Because today's adult researchers have not lived their own childhoods online, it is impossible to even unintentionally draw from memories and make claims of "truth." For researchers who work to avoid situating the youth they study in disempowered positions, the researcher's location as a novice provides an opportunity for youth to preserve a sense of agency.

The text-only world of computer-mediated communication may also offer another form of agency for youth involved in online research. Much of my research involved collecting posts written by, for, and to young people. They authored their own text, with little or no interference from me. Although the process of analysis did involve my interpretation of these youth-authored texts, this type of online research makes the privileging of youth voices an easier objective to meet.

Lurking in Cyberspace: Ethical Considerations and the Implications for Data

As outsiders online, adult researchers are forced to learn the rules of the space from the participants directly. This learning process necessarily gives researchers access to the meanings *youth themselves* create within the space, thus contributing to better data and preserving a sense of agency for the youth participants. But what is the impact on this agency when adult researchers lurk around youth spaces?

Lurking refers to the process of visiting interactive sites (such as chat rooms and message boards) and reading the information there without participating in the discussions. It is a common practice used by Web surfers, and "despite real-life connotations to the opposite, [lurking] is an online practice which is ethical and sometimes wise" (Mann and Stewart 2000:14). In fact, lurkers are often welcomed into the online community if and when they "reveal" themselves and their previous lurking behavior (Kendall 2000).

"Real-life" lurking is a research strategy adopted by many ethnographers in public spaces, with little concern for ethical violations. However, the position of the lurker implies a particular element of power that comes from the observation of others without their knowledge, but unlike structural and institutional power imbalances that shape the relationships between adults and youth, anyone can choose to lurk in an online space.

Lurking can be an extremely valuable research technique; I would not have been able to collect the majority of my data without it.[4] Since the participants who posted on the message boards during the time of my data collection were unaware that their writings were being collected and analyzed, the convention of informed consent was obviously violated. However, this violation was mitigated by several factors: first, the public nature of the research spaces and, second, the publication aspects of bulletin-board postings.

Anyone with access to a personal computer connected to the Internet was able to access the sites in which I conducted my fieldwork. No type of payment or registration was required to view the message threads. Although registration was required to start a thread or reply to an existing thread, it was not required to "lurk" on the sites. By adopting the role of the lurker I was able to maintain my research goals without having to misrepresent myself.

In addition to the public nature of my research sites, the act of authorship and publication that accompanies these postings influenced my choice to use the message boards as a source of data. Implicit in and central to the concept of publication is the complementary concept of viewing. Unlike a personal diary or private correspondence, messages in a forum are authored, entered, and posted with the intention of being read and eliciting responses. Although this does not directly constitute consent for research or participation, it docs make the analysis of their contents less ethically ambiguous. Just as researchers may analyze newspaper or magazine articles, I have chosen to collect and analyze online publications. However, in order to more fully protect each participant, measures to ensure confidentiality and anonymity have been taken.

My research sits somewhere in between the two ethical conventions of confidentiality and anonymity. Screen names provide a certain degree of anonymity since I am unable to trace the online identity to a "real-life" person, but I acknowledge that many cybercitizens invest a great deal into their online identities (Turkle 1995). For this reason, all screen names were changed in published editions of my research in an effort to ensure complete confidentiality for all participants. In addition, the names and Web addresses of the research sites were changed. It would be very difficult to connect the postings cited in my writings back to a specific poster on a specific site because these identifying details obtained during my lurking have been omitted.

Lurking has yielded some rich and complex data, but collecting these threads and conversations without regard for their specific contexts limits their usefulness. Online research must be situated within the lived experiences of young people.[5] The primary limit of the lurker role is its inability to provide opportunities to ask for clarification or elaboration from posters. Supplementing lurker data with interviews and focus groups (conducted either on- or offline) becomes extremely important. As outsiders, we must be even more attentive to ensure that we are understanding the actual meanings created by those we study.

In this vein, I was curious as to how youth online would respond to my request for information about their experiences on message boards. I began a thread on the MusicVid site with the following post:

lyssgrl
ur experience on message boards
Hey there—I am a student and doing a project on message boards/forums/ etc and wanted some feedback from ppl who actually use them. Anyone want to tell me their experiences, what they like about them, what they don't like, or anything else important about bulletin boards. I am a recent addict and lurker but wanted to hear about why other ppl read/post on message boards.
TIA for your help!
Lyss

Several hours later I received the follow response:

crowbird586
RE: ur experience on message boards
Normally, I'd chew you out for going online to do homework. However, seeing how this pertains to the internet, I'll spare you a little.

I like message boards for the entertainment and intellectual value. Sure there is a host of stupidity and ignorance, but it comes with the territory. This place can be a learning experience if you let it. You have a wide range of people from all viewpoints and it helps make the boards lively. It's generally what keeps me coming back.

Now, do yourself and your project a favor, research some of your answers through actual students from your school. Just going to a message board (hopefully [MusicVid] isn't the only one you're looking into, skewed results my friend) and talking to random strangers won't help or provide a good project. Talk to your friends and classmates and seek out other boards. Good luck!

This post, written by a college sophomore, points to the limits of a research project derived solely from data collected while lurking. This poster suggests "research[ing] some of your answers through actual students from your school." By situating online data within the context of "real people," and creating the opportunity to better understand the online interactions and meaning-making processes, there is a greater possibility for more complete and valuable data.

The issues of lurking and memory do raise more-general concerns about the "colonizing" aspects of adults researching youth, namely, Who controls the knowledge obtained through this research? and Who is allowed to generate, publish, and disseminate knowledge about whom? These are the questions that have plagued the insider/outsider debates since their inception, and they continue to be relevant. The new technologies necessitating different approaches to research have not eliminated these questions; they have simply complicated them.

A reflexive research process becomes crucial to avoid potential pitfalls of memory and outsider status. Consistent and structured reflexivity should be built into various stages of the process. Activities such as journaling became central during the course of my research in order to peel back my own assumptions and beliefs from those of the youth online (although they were not always mutually exclusive).

In this moment of rapid technological change, young people are adopting new technologies and simultaneously shaping the social impact of these technologies. As a result of their unique relationship to computer-mediated communication and other new media, the young people who become the next generation of social scientists will bring their own methodological challenges to this discussion. However, as today's adults continue to conduct online ethnographies in youth cyberspaces, thoughtful considerations of lurking, memory, and the role of the outsider are necessary to generate theories that not only accurately represent young people and their experiences but that also work to ensure youth are not further disempowered by the research process and product.

NOTES

1. Online chat rooms and bulletin boards fall under the general term *computer-mediated communication* (CMC), along with email and instant messaging. Bulletin boards, also called message boards or forums, have been around since the early days of the Internet in the form of Usenet groups. These groups were structured around an initial posting by a single user to which other users would reply. As these additional postings build up, a thread is created. *Thread* refers to the strand of messages that build on one another around the initial posting. The thread then becomes a type of asynchronous conversation among many users.

Under any one topic on a bulletin board, there may be hundreds of different threads, each addressing a specific subtopic. Today, bulletin boards are popular interactive features on a variety of websites, and they were the site of my online research.

2. The Institutional Review Board at my own university offered no guidelines for Internet research, but I was able to find preliminary suggestions outlined by the Association of Internet Researchers Working Ethics Committee (Ess et al. 2002).

3. All other screenames have been changed to protect the anonymity of the chatters.

4. I collected postings from over one hundred individual users; obtaining consent from each one would have been time prohibitive, and it may in fact have been impossible to contact and receive replies from each person. This is not a reason in and of itself to forgo the convention of informed consent, but obtaining consent would have drastically changed the amount and variety of data I was able to collect.

5. Strong examples of lurking research contextualized with online interactions and offline interviews include Kendall (2000) and Ignacio (2000).

REFERENCES

Biklen, Sari Knopp. 2004. "Trouble on Memory Lane: Adults and Self-Retrospection in Researching Youth." *Qualitative Inquiry* 10(5), 715–730.

Broad, Kendal, and Kristen Joos. 2004. "Online Inquiry of Public Selves: Methodological Considerations." *Qualitative Inquiry* 10(6), 923–946.

Burkhalter, Byron. 2000. "Reading Race Online: Discovering Racial Identity in Usenet Discussions." Pp. 60–75 in *Communities in Cyberspace,* edited by M. Smith and P. Kollock. New York: Routledge.

Cho, Hichang, and Robert LaRose. 1999. "Privacy Issues in Internet Surveys." *Social Science Computer Review* 17(4), 421–434.

Clark, Lynn Schofield. 1998. "Dating on the Net: Teens and the Rise of 'Pure' Relationships." Pp. 159–183 in *Cybersociety 2.0: Revisiting Computer-Mediated Communication and Community,* edited by Steven Jones. Thousand Oaks, CA: Sage.

Cook, Colleen, Fred Heath, and Russel Thompson. 2000. "A Meta-Analysis of Response Rates in Web- or Internet-Based Surveys." *Educational and Psychological Measurement* 60(6), 821–836.

Daley, Ellen, Robert McDermott, Kelli McCormack Brown, and Mark Kittleson. 2003. "Conducting Web-Based Survey Research: A Lesson in Internet Designs." *American Journal of Health Behavior* 27(2), 116–124.

Dillman, Don. 2000. *Mail and Internet Surveys: The Tailored Design Method* (2nd ed.). New York: Wiley.

Ess, Charles, and the Association of Internet Researchers. 2002. *Ethical Decision-Making and Internet Research: Recommendations from the AoIR Ethics Working Committee.* Retrieved February 25, 2004, from www.aoir.org/reports/ethics.pdf.

Fine, Gary Alan, and Kent L. Sandstrom. 1988. *Knowing Children: Participant Observation with Minors.* London: Sage.

Gaston, Sarah, and Amanda Zweerink. 2004. "Ethnography Online: 'Natives' Practicing and Inscribing Community." *Qualitative Research* 4(2), 179–200.

Haug, Frigga, et al. 1987. *Female Sexualization: A Collective Work of Memory.* Translated by Erica Carter. London: Verso.

Heins, Marjorie. 2002. "Filtering Fever." Pp. 180–200 in *Not in Front of the Children: "Indecency," Censorship, and the Innocence of Youth.* New York: Hill and Wang.

Herring, Susan C. 1996. "Introduction." Pp. 1–10 in *Computer-Mediated Communication: Linguistic, Social, and Cross-Cultural Perspectives,* edited by S. Herring. Philadelphia: John Benjamins.

Hine, Christine. 2000. *Virtual Ethnography.* Thousand Oaks, CA: Sage.

Holloway, Sarah, and Gill Valentine. 2003. *Cyberkids: Children in the Information Age.* London: Routledge.

Ignacio, Emily. 2000. "Ain't I a Filipino (Woman)? An Analysis of Authorship/Authority through the Construction of 'Filipina' on the Net." *Sociological Quarterly* 41(4), 551–572.

Kendall, Lori. 2000. " 'Oh No! I'm a Nerd!': Hegemonic Masculinity on an Online Forum." *Gender and Society* 14(2), 256–274.

Mann, Chris, and Fiona Stewart. 2000. *Internet Communication and Qualitative Research: A Handbook for Researching Online.* Thousand Oaks, CA: Sage.

Mitchell, Claudia, and Jacqueline Reid-Walsh. 2002. "Virtual Spaces: Children on the Cyber Frontier." Pp. 141–170 in *Researching Children's Popular Culture: The Cultural Spaces of Childhood.* London: Routledge.

Paccagnella, Luciano. 1997. "Getting the Seats of Your Pants Dirty: Strategies for Ethnographic Research on Virtual Communities." *Journal of Computer Mediated Communication* 3(1). Retrieved January 11, 2006, from http://jcmc.indiana.edu/vol3/issue1/paccagnella.html.

Paredes, Americo. 1978. "On Ethnographic Work among Minority Groups: A Folklorist's Perspective." Pp. 1–32 in *New Directions in Chicano Scholarship,* edited by R. Romo and R. Paredes. La Jolla, CA: UCSD Chicano Studies Program.

Riessman, Catherine Kohler. 1987. "When Gender Is Not Enough: Women Interviewing Women." *Gender and Society* 1(2), 172–207.

Springhall, John. 1998. *Youth, Popular Culture, and Moral Panics.* New York: St. Martin's.

Thorne, Barrie. 1993. *Gender Play: Girls and Boys in School.* New Brunswick, NJ: Rutgers University Press.

Tse, Alan. 1998. "Comparing the Response Rate, Response Speed, and Response

Quality of Two Methods of Sending Questionnaires: E-mail vs. Mail." *Journal of the Market Research Society* 40(4), 353–362.

Turkle, Sherry. 1995. *Life on the Screen: Identity in the Age of the Internet.* New York: Simon and Schuster.

Wakeford, Nina. 2004. "Developing Methodological Frameworks for Studying the World Wide Web." Pp. 34–48 in *Web.Studies,* edited by David Gauntlett and Ross Horsley. London: Arnold.

Zinn, Maxine Baca. 1979. "Field Research in Minority Communities: Ethical, Methodological, and Political Observations by an Insider." *Social Problems* 27(2), 209–219.

Chapter 8

Racing Age

Reflections on Antiracist Research with Teenage Girls

Jessica Karen Taft

Issues of racial insider-outsider status have been explored by numerous field researchers (for example, Beoku-Betts 1994; Naples 1996; Twine and Warren 2000) and feminist ethnographers have written about a multitude of concerns and dilemmas of fieldwork (Abu-Lughod 1990; Reinharz 1992; Wolf 1996), but the impact of age in the research process requires increased attention from critical ethnographers and scholars. The growing body of scholarship on children and youth raises methodological questions that are inherent in qualitative research but with differences and additional considerations (some of which have been explored in, for example, Fine and Glassner 1979 and Mandell 1991). However, in analyzing age as a significant axis of power and difference, we must also be conscious of how it intersects in unique ways with gender, race, class, sexuality, and ability. Kathleen Blee notes the significance of multiple lines of commonality and diversity in the field, writing that "researchers can simultaneously be 'insiders' and 'outsiders' to the cultures and meaning systems of those they seek to study" (2000, 108).

In this chapter, I draw on the insights of critical race scholars and feminist methodology to explore just a few of these dynamics of similarity, difference, and unequal status in my own research experiences with two groups of teenage girls. My research on teenage girls' political selves has taken me to the Teen Women's Action Program (TWAP) in Washington, DC, which involves primarily Black and Latina girls, and to Ashema, a Girl Scout Camp in rural New England, which serves a largely White population.[1] By conducting field research, interviews, and focus groups in these two locations, I have been able to see some of the complex ways that age combines and interacts with other social identities in the research process. I spent half of my summer in each of these sites and moved very quickly between them (a two-day break between leaving TWAP and arriving at Ashema). In doing so, it was abundantly clear to me that my identity as a White, upper-middle-class young woman from New England was experienced and felt differently in these two locations. Not only was I conscious of the fact that my age influenced my research relationships in both spaces, but the configurations of racial similarity and difference also felt (and continue to feel) especially significant as I traveled between and wrote about these two spaces. Although there are numerous lines of commonality and difference that I experienced in the field and that mattered to the research relationships, including gender, class, and sexuality, this chapter focuses primarily on age and race dynamics and their intersections in my fieldwork. This is not to say that other identity patterns did not matter but simply that those of age and race were especially salient for me as I moved between these two contexts.

After describing my two research sites, this chapter will outline a few of the unique dynamics of age difference in my research relationships with girls. I will then go on to complicate these dynamics of age by looking at the role of race in my research and how racial identity influences the age-inflected process of rapport building, adult claims to knowledge and ignorance, and adult authority in the field. By racing age in this manner, I hope to indicate that in analyzing the methodological dilemmas of research with youth, it is crucial for researchers to consider how youth/adult is not a simple binary but is cross-cut with other aspects of researchers' and subjects' identities and locations. By starting with age and then incorporating race into the discussion, I do not mean to suggest that age is a more important category for analysis than race. Rather, I start with age as a unique element of research with youth (the focus of this volume) and then integrate race in order to demonstrate that although age is important to the methodological reflections of youth studies scholars, age differences do not operate separately from those of other identity locations.

Sites of Similarity and Difference

Teen Women's Action Program

When I arrived at the Teen Women's Action Program, it was the first day of the organization's 2002 summer program. During the school year, the TWAP office is a fairly quiet space, mostly used by the five to eight adult staff employed at a given time and, after school, a few of the paid, year-round teen staff members. Most school-year programs are conducted at local high schools, with TWAP adult and teen trainers going out to the schools for weekly group sessions, training hundreds of teenage girls on self-advocacy skills, peer support, reproductive health and sexuality, stress, dealing with violence and harassment, oppression, community needs assessment, and project development. In the summers, TWAP shifts to a summer employment program, and the eight-room office becomes filled with about twenty-five teenage girls (all from DC) and a handful of college-aged summer interns, in addition to the regular staff. Each room becomes crowded with anywhere from three to fifteen desks or tables, each with a welcome sign above it, personalized for the girl or woman who occupies that space. The walls in each space are covered with large pieces of cheap white paper with interpersonal advice, drawings of body parts, lists of skills to be developed in a session, and agendas and other visual teaching aids written on them in bright-colored marker.

Twenty-one girls, ages fifteen to nineteen, were involved in TWAP's 2002 summer program.[2] Fifteen members of this group identified as either Black or African American, and another five identified as Latina or Hispanic, including girls whose families were Mexican, Salvadoran, and Dominican. One young woman identified as mixed Black and West Indian. One young woman identified as bisexual; the rest did not name their sexual orientations. Three were teen mothers. All of these girls lived in Washington, DC, and most were from working-class or lower-middle-class backgrounds. Over the course of my few weeks at TWAP, I conducted three focus groups (involving all twenty-one participants) and semistructured individual interviews with thirteen teens.

Camp Ashema

Whereas TWAP is a distinctly urban organization, connected to city politics and city schools, and primarily serves Black and Latina girls, Camp Ashema is rural. Its programs focus on outdoor activities and enjoying nature, and the campers are almost entirely White girls from small towns in New Hampshire and Vermont. After spending several weeks at TWAP, I headed north to this very different girls' space. With more than three hundred acres of property, including forests, meadows, and a beaver pond, Ashema sits on the shores of a small lake and, at any one time, accommodates 125 campers between the ages of six and seventeen, as well as forty international and American staff members. Ashema's own private dirt road is marked by a green, pink, and blue sign clearly painted by children. The bumpy, curvy road through the woods follows the shoreline, passing treehouses built by campers and staff, a fire circle for camp gatherings, several cabins, and the beach/waterfront, with its wooden docks and boats. In addition to cabins scattered around the area, the camp also has several screened buildings for group activities, a few grassy fields, a large dining hall, and a crowded main office building housing administrators, the nurse, and a staff lounge.

Camp Ashema prides itself on "girl decision-making," meaning that girls select their own programs and activities, as a group. Unlike at some camps, where counselors offer different projects and girls simply individually choose among them, at Ashema the girls who live together collectively plan and organize their own activities and projects. There is no standard program in which all girls participate, but common activities include arts and crafts, swimming, hiking, cooking over fires, canoeing, and learning about science and nature. The camp's main goals focus on girls' individual development and growth, valuing teamwork, skill building, and trying new things.

Although there were 125 campers at Ashema while I was there, this study only included the very oldest girls at the camp, comprising all the girls who were participating in two leadership programs[3] and one group of campers who were involved in a wilderness-oriented project. I conducted one focus group with each of these groups, involving twenty participants. I then conducted one-on-one, semistructured interviews with fourteen of these teens. The age range of the Ashema members of my study was from thirteen to seventeen. All of these girls identified as either White or Caucasian. The group came from a variety of class backgrounds, ranging from working class to upper middle class. One girl identified as bisexual; the others did not name their sexual orientations. None were parents.

Navigating Age in Research Relationships with Youth

As a small (just over five feet), youthful-looking graduate student in my midtwenties who sometimes still gets carded for R-rated movies, I can easily "pass" for a teenager in some settings. However, this ability to look young and "fit in" is hardly guaranteed. And my previous work at both organizations meant that my status as an adult was established long before my arrival as a researcher. Furthermore, the fact that I look young does not mean that I am young, and it is, I would argue, crucial that adult researchers remember this in their research with youth. When researching youth, no adult researcher is ever a complete "insider" to the group. Although researchers of youth are necessarily outsiders, this should not be viewed as a tragic loss of a (false) "ideal" of complete inside status. Rather, the fact that those of us who study youth are always already outside could be seen as a starting point for thinking through the ways that our various positions are negotiated in the field.

Knowledge and Ignorance

Adult outsider status has a wide variety of implications on our research with youth, but I want to focus here on the unusual and unique dynamic that emerges from the fact that adults, despite being outsiders, often perceive themselves as having, in at least some way, "been there." That is, they have been youth; however, as youth experiences are shaped by gender, race, class, sexuality, ability, nation, location, religion, and a multitude of other factors, the youth of the researcher may have varying levels of commonality with the lives of the youth being studied. Adult memories of youth are also selective and mediated by our present-day perspectives (Biklen 2004), and historical change and generational differences lead to divergent experiences, even for researchers who return to their childhood homes (Kenny 2000b). The position that we have "been there" sometimes surfaces in researchers' claims about what youth should be doing or in thinly veiled "adults know best" sentiments. In addition to leading to dangerously presumptuous attitudes in both writing and in the field, these submerged beliefs about our own understanding of youth create some distinctive dynamics around claims to knowledge·and the building of rapport during the research process. Of course, as I will discuss below, researcher perceptions of having "been there" vary and are not racially neutral. My own feelings about how much I "knew what it was like" were highly mediated by the dynamics of racial similarity and difference at my two research sites.

The belief in adult knowledge, the dynamics of ageism, and a social context in which adults are expected to instruct and guide youth (as either teachers, mentors, or role models) can all make it difficult for adult researchers to admit our ignorance. Seeking to be some combination of wise and cool and believing (often subconsciously) that we already know what it is like to be a teenager, we may try to avoid acknowledging what we do not know. This is compounded, of course, by our desires to build rapport and forge meaningful connections with youth. On the other hand, as researchers, we have a variety of questions, and one of the benefits of admitting outsider status is that it can create an opening for learning about aspects of people's lives that are sometimes taken for granted. The more we admit ignorance and ask questions, the more youth explain their thoughts and actions. In my own research, I often felt conflicted between wanting to seem like I knew about the things the girls were interested in and admitting total confusion. At the beginning of the research process, girls used a lot of unfamiliar slang and talked about music groups I had never heard of. I rarely let on that I wasn't in the know about these things as I worked to build rapport. My competing desire to learn from these girls eventually convinced me to give up these attempts to be hip. I began to admit everything I didn't know and to acknowledge my ignorance, asking more questions about the references girls made. My willingness to do so shifted my relationships with the girls in some positive ways. Although I may have seemed less cool, my curiosity and obvious interest meant that girls began to teach me more about their lives, to see me as someone who would listen and value what they had to say. This is not to say that I stopped trying to relate to the girls or their interests but that I decided to let myself be an uncool and curious adult rather than a hip and wise one.

Admitting my ignorance was certainly helpful in some ways, but it may also have been risky—appearing too ignorant could have solidified my identity as another adult who would not or could not understand these girls' lives. And, if that was the case, why should they trust me to describe and interpret their experiences? I did not want to be *either* an adult who thinks they already know everything about youth nor an adult who just doesn't "get it." Therefore, making choices in the field about how to navigate my adult status was, in part, a question of balance.

Adult Authority

In addition to navigating adult outsider status, research with youth is also shaped by the dynamics of unequal social power and authority. Diane Wolf explores the complicated issue of constant power differentials in the research process and suggests that feminist fieldwork requires us to realistically grapple with our power. She writes, "although feminist researchers may attempt to equalize relationships while in the field through empathetic and friendly methods, these methods do not transform the researchers' positionality or locationality" (1996, 35). Good intentions and positive rapport do not erase the significance of our authority as adults and researchers.

My own adult authority was highlighted at both research sites by my assumed and actual connections to adults and staff members and the fact that I had once been a staff member at each. At TWAP I was able to maintain some distance from the position of "staff member" by making sure to never lead any activities or trainings, leaving the office for lunch rather than sitting with other staff or interns, and always introducing myself as a researcher. The other staff also worked hard to emphasize my nonauthoritative role. For example, I overheard one permanent staff member telling two teens, "She's not evaluating you." Although I made many efforts to dissociate from the staff and to emphasize my researcher/observer role, and thereby downplay my previous work role, having been known at one point as a staff member, however, probably did confer on me certain amounts of power, authority, and responsibility.

Although I was able to separate myself from the staff role to some extent at TWAP, this was nearly impossible at Ashema. When I arrived at Ashema, the camp was seriously understaffed, with several staff members having quit recently. The camp director, Tina James, was clearly excited by the arrival of an experienced counselor and program coordinator (my previous jobs over four summers at Ashema), but, as we both knew, I was not there primarily to do camp work. However, about two days into the session, while I was sitting at my laptop in the corner of the crowded office space and writing up some field notes, Tina and other camp administrators began holding a short meeting about how to deal with being so understaffed. As a former staff member, and someone who cares about Ashema and girls, I could not resist my feelings of wanting to help out and solve the staffing crunch. Earlier in the summer, Tina had asked me if I would be willing to spend some of my time at Ashema conducting some research with younger girls at the camp. Now, though, in the face of staffing issues and the daily difficulties of running camp, both Tina and I felt that this other research project was not the best use of my "extra" time. So, much as researchers working in schools are often pushed to assume some of the institutional burdens created by limited resources, I found myself taking on some work around the camp office, supervising a few staff members and assisting with the planning of some all-camp events.

Conscious of not wanting to become a direct authority over the girls involved in my research, the work roles that I took on at Ashema were largely oriented toward supporting the staff. When spending time with the girls, I tried to emphasize my researcher status. Since Ashema serves girls between the ages of seven and seventeen, and my research was focused only on older girls, I was able to do my "camp work" with different groups than my "research work." And by stressing that during interviews and focus groups I was not acting as a staff member and would not share what they said with their counselors or any other staff members,[4] in some ways I was unable to avoid being seen as an adult authority. One of the implications of this status as a staff member or former staff member is that at both organizations girls may have been less willing to share their criticisms of the organizations and may have avoided telling me things that they thought might "get them in trouble."

Even if I had never been a staff member at Ashema or TWAP, my adult status would have given me some power anyway. There are numerous things that teens do not want to tell adults for a variety of reasons. This was especially clear to me in my interactions with Janeen, a sixteen-year-old at Ashema. A White girl with long medium-brown hair and big eyes, Janeen had attended Ashema for five years, and I remembered her from a group a few years back as funny, playful, and a master of silly faces. However, she seemed both sad and bored at Ashema during the summer of my research. She was also causing a great deal of stress to her counselors because she was not eating, and they were concerned about her having an eating disorder. She met with the camp director about this and agreed to eat at least something at each meal. When I would see her around the camp, I would always smile at her and ask how she was doing. She would usually say "fine" then make a goofy monkey face, brushing off any attempts at seriousness. I liked Janeen a great deal and felt that she liked me too. However, this sense of "being friends" or "liking each other" did not minimize Janeen's reticence to talk to adults about her life. During our interview, she said "I don't know" as her first response to many of my questions, particularly those about her family or how she spent her free time. When I asked her about what websites she goes to, we had the following intensely awkward exchange:

JT: Like which ones do you particularly like?

Janeen: I don't know.

JT: Do you want to think about it for a minute?

Janeen: Sure.

JT: Okay.

Janeen: I don't know.

JT: You don't remember at all?

Janeen: Well, I do, but I don't.

JT: What does that mean?

Janeen: I don't know.

JT: Do you not want to tell me?

Janeen: Yeah.

JT: Okay.

Janeen: Yeah.

JT: Okay. So next time say you don't want to tell me, all right?

Janeen: Okay.

JT: Cuz that's fine with me, if you don't want to tell me. But don't say "I don't know," because then I keep asking questions to try to help you figure it out. So if there's something you don't want to tell me, just say you don't want to tell me. Okay?

Janeen: Okay.

She began to clarify her "I don't knows" but continued to be evasive. Later in the interview, she complained about the "shrink" her school made her go see, and I asked her if she felt like she had people to talk to in her life about how she feels about things. She said no, remarking, "it'd just get me in trouble." When I asked her what she meant by this, she said, "'cause they'd have to tell my parents." My reassurances about confidentiality were entirely insufficient to get Janeen to tell me, an adult, about her life because, as she put it, "adults have to tell my parents everything, or they get freaked out." In this instance, my adult status made me both suspect as a parent-informer and as someone who would possibly "freak out" about Janeen's experiences and feelings. What she would tell a peer, another teen, I don't know, but I am certain that my age made Janeen significantly less comfortable and open with me.

Adult authority, whether conferred on me because I was associated with staff or simply because I was an adult, can clearly create awkward and power-laden research interactions with youth. As adult researchers assist the staff of underresourced schools and youth organizations because we care about these programs and the young people in them, we may potentially be discouraging youth from sharing their criticisms of these institutions or experiences that they fear may lead to discipline. The patterns of adult intervention in teenagers' lives can also make adult researchers' questioning feel like another form of adult surveillance and supervision. We may be able to build rapport, connect with youth, and feel like we are part of their lives, but it is crucial to remember that we will not be seen as their peers and that this will shape what youth are willing to tell us.

Racing Age and Complicating Research Relationships with Youth

The preceding discussion points to a few of the ways that age difference matters in research with youth. Doing research with two contrasting groups of girls in the span of one summer has indicated how research with youth is not only shaped by age but also shaped by the dynamics of race. In the rest of this chapter, I will take some of the themes I have addressed (building rapport, knowledge and ignorance, and adult authority) and show how racial similarities and differences complicate each of these, creating distinct issues at my two research sites. I will attempt to analyze some of these issues, but it should be noted that the impacts of race on research relationships and outcomes are not fully transparent. I can make guesses about the ways that race mattered, but it is likely that it also mattered in ways that I do not fully recognize.

There have been numerous arguments both for and against racial matching of researchers and researched (see Twine 2000 for an excellent discussion of this debate), many of which were in my thoughts as I began my study of these two very different groups of teen girls. Anne Phoenix has argued,

> "Race" and gender positions, and hence the power positions they entail, enter into the interview situation, but they do not do so in any unitary or essential way. As a result the impact of "race" and gender within particular pieces of research cannot be easily predicted. Prescriptions for matching the "race" and/or gender of interviewers and respondents are too simplistic. (Quoted in Twine 2000, 13)

What is most significant for this chapter is the assertion that research is a racialized process whether it is conducted by racial insiders or racial outsiders, and both types of research need to be analyzed. Although it is perhaps more common to discuss the role of one's racial identity when researching racial "others," race also matters to the research process in spaces of racial similarity. Charles Gallagher (2000) suggests that for White researchers not to consider the racial dynamics of doing research with Whites is to allow whiteness to remain normative and unproblematized. Being White and talking to White girls and asking them about things that include racial politics requires as much consideration as being White and talking to Black and Latina girls. Therefore, in what follows, I will analyze the ways that race inflects the themes I have outlined about both of my research sites.

Amy Best writes that "as we do research, we are also actively doing race" (2003, 13). Like Best, I treat the research encounter, as with any social interaction, as a space in which race is produced, "negotiated, managed, and solidified" (ibid., 15). I analyze race and racial identity not as a fixed possession but as a historically and culturally situated product of interaction and social structure (Omi and Winant 1994). Furthermore, although I tend to divide my arguments into analyses of White-on-White interactions and interactions between myself as a White woman and girls of color, it is important to note that neither group of girls is homogeneous. I have tried to avoid essentializing any of these groups of girls, but when reading the following arguments it is important to keep in mind that White, Black, and Latina identities are all also cross-cut with other differences and can each be articulated and enacted in a variety of ways.

Speaking Race and Breaking/Building Rapport

In New Hampshire, I, like Lorraine Kenny (2000a), found myself in an almost entirely White space, a space of racial silence, attempting to address and study issues of race and racial politics. However, there are some important methodological differences between Kenny's work with White girls and my own. She was practicing primarily as an ethnographer, "attempting to follow the processes of disavowal and avoidance that go into making a White middle-class sensibility," and she therefore "couldn't name the unnamable without destroying the evidence" (128). In contrast to Kenny's ethnographic mapping of racial silences, I relied more heavily on interview and focus-group data, meaning that much of my research involved explicit conversations about race. Although the focus-group topics were open, with girls choosing most of the issues to be discussed, my interview protocol directly asked girls to discuss race, racism, and diversity in their towns and schools as social and political issues. This meant that, unlike Kenny, I was breaking the racial silence, raising race as an issue to be spoken about between a young White woman and White teenage girls. As Kenny's larger work (2000b) shows, this is not a "normal" occurrence in the lives of White girls in nearly all-White communities.

The abnormality of speaking about race in largely White spaces was also made visible in my research. When I would ask the New England White girls to describe the people who attended their schools, they never mentioned the racial breakdown of the student body. After they had finished describing the jocks, the punks, and other social groups, I would then ask them directly about the race/ethnicity of their fellow students. They would often become visibly uncomfortable and/or silent, pause for a significant time, and even sometimes "forget" this question right after I asked it. For example, after Elizabeth, a White seventeen-year-old, told me a bit about some of the different crowds at her schools, I asked her, "And how about race or ethnicity, and things like how much money do you think people generally have?" She replied, "It's pretty average school; I don't think anyone's really well-off or well-to-do. It's like average; everyone's pretty middle-class situation and then— [pauses] what was the first question you asked?" I repeated: "Race or ethnicity of the people there? Of the students?" She paused again, shifted a little, and said reluctantly, "It's almost all Caucasian." Like Elizabeth, many of the girls, after a brief break, would acknowledge that their schools (and towns) were almost entirely White but would express some dissatisfaction with this fact. Maryanne, for example, after describing her town, said she would like to "change, like, what kinds of races live there. 'Cause there's only White [people] and that's all." The following notes from my methodological journal, written after conducting several interviews, show how I experienced this:

> They don't like to admit to me that their schools, towns or friends are mostly White. It seems like they feel like it should be different, like they've been taught that multiculturalism and diversity are good, how things "should be." And, because of my questions, they have to acknowledge that their homes are not like this. But they seem to not really have an analysis of why—"it's just the area" [is something that I hear frequently from them].

In an almost all-White environment, my questions about race seemed surprising to these girls, breaking the rhythm of our conversations, creating silence and long pauses. Unexpected from a racial insider, my questions about race created temporary breaks in the rapport that I was working to build with these girls. Since the practice of whiteness is largely a practice of racial silence (Frankenberg 1993; Kenny 2000b), my questions about race placed me, an assumed racial insider, suddenly outside the norms of typical White behavior. By speaking race, I broke the rules of normal White-on-White interaction and indicated to these girls that although we were all White, I was doing whiteness differently. However, it was also my hope that even if my questions were unexpected, they were not overly threatening or uncomfortable and that girls did not interpret them as accusations about the lack of racial diversity in their social lives, because I too (as the girls knew) had grown up as a White girl in the area.

It is here that the dangers of assuming to have "been there" intersect with the experiences of shared whiteness. Despite my earlier comments warning about the assumptions that we know youth, as I conducted my research I still hoped that our shared upbringing, my "having been there," would help the girls to feel more comfortable sharing their thoughts on whiteness and race in small-town New England. Reflecting on this now, this hope seems somewhat foolhardy. Indeed, it is possible that our shared racial location and similar hometowns did not register with them as significant in these conversations. My questions about race may instead have been perceived as coming from a different historical moment, one with less talk about multiculturalism as an educational value. Whereas these girls had learned to speak about race indirectly through discourses of tolerance, diversity, and multiculturalism, I was explicitly asking them to talk about race. Without any experience with White antiracists who speak openly about race, they may have seen my questions as evidence of adult ignorance of the new way of addressing race (speaking about it only indirectly) or as racist. (See Best 2003 for a useful discussion of how questions about race can be perceived as racist by White research subjects.)

In addition to the possibility that girls' interpretations of my questions may have been shaped by their perception of my own *generational* ignorance about the "appropriate" way to discuss race, there is a significant issue with *age* to be addressed here. When I expected that girls would see me as someone who knew what it was like to grow up in primarily White New England, I was ignoring the fact that they may instead, because of my age, have seen my questions as a "test" of how well they had learned the lessons of racial tolerance. And if they thought I was testing them on these issues, they were not likely to be fully honest with me on this topic. Shared whiteness did not necessarily erase my age-based position as an outsider in this case. Julie Bettie correctly notes that "racial/ethnic sameness is not enough to lay claims to intersubjectivity" (2003, 25). Despite being a racial insider, I was an adult, and the girls' perceptions of my questions were likely to have been shaped by both of these identities. My questions about race not only indicated a divergent articulation of whiteness but also highlighted and solidified my age identity, thus doubly weakening my rapport with these White girls.

On the other hand, in Washington, DC, I felt that speaking openly about race and racism did more to build rapport than break it. As Julie Bettie found in her research with Mexican American girls in California, White researchers talking candidly about their own racial location and about race and racism is important in helping girls of color to develop their trust in us (2003, 21). This process of coming to be seen as an ally was made somewhat easier in my research by the presence of seven girls at TWAP whom I had worked with before. These seven teens were initially the most comfortable around me and proved to be crucial in legitimating my interest and convincing the other girls that I had good intentions and could be trusted. Since all interviewees had participated in a focus group before the interview, they were able to see from their peers' responses to me in the focus group that it was acceptable to discuss controversial topics with me, including racial politics. The teens who already knew me were nearly always the first ones either to introduce the themes of race and racism in the focus groups or to respond when I asked a question on these topics, signaling to the other girls that this was a safe space for discussion. In this sense, my prior role as a staff member proved useful in negotiating conversations across and about race, even though it also created distance between myself and the teens in terms of age authority.

Unlike the White New Hampshire girls, for whom my whiteness was an unremarkable fact and for whom talk about race indicated a rupture in what had been perceived as shared racial identity, the Black and Latina girls at TWAP routinely commented on my racial identity. One Black girl regularly told me that I had "a great butt for a White girl," emphasizing racial difference but, interestingly, bridging our age differences. This is not, I think, something she would say to an adult who looked or acted significantly more mature. Many of the girls also framed their comments on White people in such a way as to both include and exclude me from their statements. Mo, a Black nineteen-year-old, was careful to say to me "I don't mean no harm" in the middle of a statement on how White girls take their weight gain too seriously. Other teens also sometimes added disclaimers of "no offense to you" when mentioning or criticizing White people. These kinds of comments may be things they would say to any White person when discussing race, but the fact that I was a young adult and connected to staff members who they respected probably merited me more apologies than a peer would receive. So, in addition to marking me as a racial outsider, some (but not all) girls' comments on White people were inflected with an element of age-based distancing.

While serving to solidify my outsider status, girls' comments on whiteness also gave me an opportunity to both acknowledge my racial privilege and to make connections with these girls as a White antiracist ally. My responses to girls' comments about Whites and whiteness included everything from nods of understanding and statements of agreement, elaboration on their own points about White privilege, and collective laughter. In addition to responding to and engaging with their comments on whiteness and White privilege, and asking direct questions about race, I also expressed my solidarity when girls would talk about their experiences with racial discrimination and their analyses of institutional racism. For example, when Mo told me a long story about being mistreated by her boss because he was racist, I agreed that the situation "was crazy" and paused on that point for a little while before moving to the next question. Or when girls would talk about being followed by store employees when they went shopping, I regularly noted how "messed up that whole thing is" and would nod in agreement at their assessments of the racist character of various social structures and institutions. This kind of overt expression of agreement is not standard interviewing procedure and is not something I do regularly. Rather, for the sake of building rapport, solidarity, and trust, I intentionally chose to respond to and validate these statements explicitly.

Washington, DC, is a highly segregated city, and most of the teens discussed with me the patterns of school and neighborhood segregation. The girls told me that there is really only one public high school that has a sizable population of White students and that their interactions with White peers are fairly infrequent. And although there are increasing numbers of Whites moving into their neighborhoods, leading to concerns about gentrification and rising rents, most of the DC girls' interactions with young White women are with their teachers or with other White staff members at TWAP. Their stories about interactions with White strangers tended to focus on White people's misperceptions of them. And although some of them had one or two White teachers who would talk about race and racial discrimination, these conversations were usually abstract and impersonal. The TWAP staff members (including two White women) addressed racial identity, racism, and White supremacy in several different lessons with the teens, but talking about race with White adults was still a fairly unusual occurrence in their lives.

I do not want to suggest here that these girls trusted me fully or that my whiteness did not influence our conversations. Rather, what I want to point to is the ways that being a White woman talking about race with girls of color served to build rapport, whereas talking about race with White girls tended to break rapport. If we focus only on building rapport with youth as a process of fitting in, we are missing the ways we may need to break the normal modes of interaction (or normal social science method) in order to achieve our research goals. And if we only consider the age dynamics at work in rapport building, we will miss the ways that racial identity and the production of race may interact with age to either highlight or obscure our adult status at different moments and the ways that our adult status may make talking about race more or less difficult in different contexts.

Knowledge, Ignorance, and the Racialized Other

The feeling that we have "been there" is a unique dynamic in research with youth, but it is also a dynamic that varies based on other lines of similarity and difference. Researchers' claims to knowledge and ignorance are shaped not only by age but also by race and other factors as well. Although I saw myself as moderately ignorant in both research sites because of my age (I did not know the musical groups that either group of girls was talking about, and the like), I did feel somewhat more knowledgeable about the Ashema girls' social context. This sense of my own greater expertise in this space means that I inevitably left some valuable questions unasked because I thought I knew the answers or made false assumptions based on my own experiences. The other side of this, of course, is the recurring fear that I did not know enough about the lives of the girls of color in DC and would therefore either misunderstand or misinterpret them. Having read the extensive literature on White women's problematic representations of women of color, I was cautious about either assuming too much shared experience or overemphasizing and essentializing the Black and Latina girls' "Otherness." Keeping these concerns present as I conducted my research meant slightly different things at my two research locations: reminding myself to act somewhat less knowledgeable at Ashema and a bit more knowledgeable at TWAP than my original instinctive responses.

Despite having a different sense of how ignorant I was in each of these spaces, I did, as I noted earlier in this chapter, try to position myself as at least a partial novice in both locations. Interestingly, locating myself as a fairly ignorant outsider had different implications at each site based on the dynamics of racial similarity and difference. As Amy Best argues, White researchers taking on the novice role in interviews with girls of color expand both their and our sense of racial/ethnic difference. She writes,

> A series of seemingly unremarkable, ordinary comments from an experienced interviewer—"What do you mean?" and "Can you clarify that?"—aren't so ordinary at all. These comments can be seen as performing an action—positioning me as an outsider. In this particular instance, then, the novice role, realized through talk, served to affirm or resignify a set of racial/ethnic dynamics rooted in "difference," widening the distance between us and cementing our racial identities. (2003, 10)

While responding and engaging with Black and Latina girls' comments about race and racism positioned me as an ally, novice-style questions that may have appeared from the girls' perspective to indicate a lack of understanding solidified not only my location as an adult (which it did in New Hampshire as well) but also my status as a racial outsider. In this way, the research encounter itself produced and reproduced girls of color as the complex, difficult-to-grasp "Other." In contrast, positioning myself as a novice in New England helped me to destabilize my assumptions about what I already knew and highlighted, for both myself and the girls, my difference in age.

Much as I moved through my two sites with different ideas about how much I knew, the girls at each location also made different assumptions about my knowledge. White girls often left things unsaid in our conversations, taking for granted that I knew what they were talking about when referencing everything from the names of their hometowns to the social groups in their schools (jocks, punks, hicks, and so on). They would primarily clarify points that they felt I might not understand because of my age (particularly various popular culture references). In contrast, the DC girls were more likely to explain in greater detail a wider range of things that they thought I would not know about, such as their school buildings' states of disrepair and the importance of family in Salvadoran culture. These explanations were, I think, largely based on perceptions of my racial ignorance more than my age ignorance.

Perceptions of my lack of knowledge about their lives may have encouraged the DC girls of color to make their everyday practices more visible to me, but there were probably also topics that they were less comfortable discussing with me, as a racial outsider. For example, I think my whiteness played a significant role in how girls of color discussed racial solidarity and social change. Kevona, for example, a Black girl who, as she put it, was "really into Black authors and other, like, Black things," spoke in the focus group about how "Black people need to get together and be united more. That is something that I would like to get into, like uplifting my people." This statement was prefaced by her disclaimer, "not to be racist or anything." Interested in this, I asked her, "Why did you say, 'not to be racist'? Why do you think you might be perceived as racist?" She responded by saying, "Well, because people might, like, get that feel from me, because, like, why are you just trying to help your people?" Whether or not Kevona would have begun with her disclaimer if she were talking with a Black interviewer remains unknown. But I would imagine that my status as a White woman, someone not in "her people," shaped how carefully she expressed her views. Similarly, Lamaya, a dark-skinned sixteen-year-old with long dark hair with bleached-blond stripes who alternately identified herself as Hispanic and Dominican, also began her commentary on racial inequality with a disclaimer: "Not trying to be sounding all racist and stuff . . . but I think that'd be good—somebody Black or somebody Hispanic should be in a higher level than a White person and see how that makes them feel."

Black and Latina girls in DC often made critiques of systems and structures of racial inequality and were very vocal about how they think White people stereotype them, but they were more cautious with me in their talk about racial politics and challenging racial hierarchy. Thus, they recognized my whiteness or privileged position in the racial structure of the United States and how it might affect the way I heard their comments. Their own visions for racial justice were, perhaps, something that they felt I might, as a White person, take the wrong way. And because I was an adult and had connections to the staff, they may have felt that they needed to be respectful and not offend me too much. This, then, may have encouraged these girls to be more careful, cautious, and sometimes apologetic when making statements about how they want to help their own people or have people of color be "higher" than Whites sometimes. My status as both an adult and a racial outsider were probably acting in tandem here as the TWAP teens considered issues of group and individual privacy and made choices about how to talk about racial politics in my presence.

Antiracist Intervention and Adult Authority

One of the ways that adult authority can emerge in the field of youth research is through adult researchers' desire to educate or teach the youth in their studies about any number of subjects. In my case, it was a belief in the idea of White-on-White research as a site of antiracist intervention that most often seduced me into the educator role. Charles Gallagher suggests that we might find some ways, as researchers of whiteness, to encourage our subjects to "think of the structural advantages that accrue to them because of their skin color" and thus contribute to antiracist projects (2000, 86). Because I was more likely to see myself as in a position to engage in antiracist education at Ashema than at TWAP, this section focuses especially on Ashema, rather than discussing both sites. This is not to say that there were no intersections of age authority with race at TWAP. Instead, I use the example of antiracist intervention at Ashema to highlight and discuss in depth one of many possible ways that race and age authority can interact in the field.

At Ashema, racial similarity and age difference intersected in my own hope to inspire these girls to become more aware of their racial privilege. Because we had some significant similarities, I found myself wondering if these girls saw me as a potential role model, an example of a White woman who talks about racism and White privilege. Even if they did not see me as a role model, I certainly thought about myself in this way at various times. I frequently found myself considering the possibilities for raising girls' consciousness about race and racism through the research encounter. My sense of myself as an antiracist activist led me to want to respond to some of the girls' statements about the nonimpact of their racial identities in their lives, to make White privilege visible to them, and to challenge them to think more about institutionalized racism. However, the desire to do this kind of antiracist education frequently conflicted with my commitment to avoiding "adults know best" behaviors and expressions of age authority whenever possible. Although it would not be impossible to tread a path through this complex tension, I certainly felt that, in this case, I could not *easily* act on both my antiageist and antiracist politics.

Interestingly, several girls at Ashema did seem to be trying to shift their own racial discourses as the research progressed. As I noted earlier, the fact that I was an adult may have led them to feel like I was testing them on their multiculturalism and racial tolerance. Therefore, I do not know if they were simply trying to give me the correct answers, or wanted to prove that they were not "racists," or if they were actually reconsidering the issues based on my "example." Nellie, a White fifteen-year-old, provides an interesting example of a girl whose racial discourses shifted during our interview. She was initially confused about my question of how she would identify her race or ethnicity, asking "my what?" and needing me to explain the question. And, like many other girls, she did not seem to want to talk about the racial breakdown of her school, town, or friendship networks. But as the interview progressed and I continued to ask her questions about race, she began to try to demonstrate an antiracist identity. When I asked her if she thought all people were treated equally in society, she said, "by certain people they are, but by a good amount of people they aren't. Like, I think we still have a lot of racist people in our town and stuff, but there's a good amount of people that aren't racist. So that's good." And when I asked her to describe her ideal community, she responded, "I guess it would be a place where racism doesn't exist." She also made sure to distinguish herself from her brothers, who "can be pretty racist at times," saying, "I don't believe it and stuff, and if, like, they say something that I think is not true, and I'll try to, like, you know, say, 'hey, you shouldn't say that kind of stuff,' and stuff like that." Nellie was not the only girl who, late in the interviews, would talk about wanting a world without racism or wanting their community to be "more diverse." I may hope that this shift in girls' racial discourse indicates the development of an antiracist politics through the research interaction. However, it is also likely that their discursive shifts are, at least in part, a response to my authority as an adult and evidence of their desire to give me the "right answers" to my questions. Research with White participants as antiracist intervention is thus complicated by the dynamics of adult authority and age difference. And the researcher's desires to avoid taking on adult authority are also certainly complicated by desires to intervene in conservative articulations of whiteness and the production of White privilege.

"Scientific Knowledge" and the Intersection of Age and Race

Addressing and exploring the dynamics of similarity, difference, and power in the research process are important tasks for researchers of youth interested in challenging both ageism and racism. The danger of what Donna Haraway (1988) calls "the god trick," the portrayal of research as objective and without the influence of the researcher, is of course present in research with youth. Unfortunately, some still assume their ability to portray the complete truth of "what it means to be a teenager today." In research on youth, these claims reinscribe the power of adults to define what youth are like and what they should be like. Thus, by enacting the authority of the scientist, these researchers also enact and reproduce the authority of the adult. The epistemological claims are, in this way, translated into a political stance of ageism and adult power. Exploring and writing about the issues of similarity, difference, and power—in short, being reflexive—is not simply a theoretical concern but a political one. Researchers of youth who are committed to addressing inequality and challenging injustice have a responsibility to consider the ways that age operates in the field. However, as this chapter has shown, age does not operate separately from other social identities and forces.

At both research sites, I tried to build rapport without pretending to be something that I am not. I attempted to avoid adult presumptions of knowing more than youth but also the appearance of being totally unable to understand where these girls were coming from. I also tried to remain conscious of my adult authority and the ways that it would prevent girls from telling me certain things about their lives. However, teenage girls are not a uniform category, and the dynamics of race intersect with the dynamics of age to create the divergent situations I have described in this chapter. As the second half of this chapter indicates, these themes of building rapport, balancing knowledge and ignorance, and dealing with adult authority are also infused with racial meaning-making and my own racial identity as a White woman. Therefore, in analyzing the methodological dilemmas of research with youth, it is also, I would argue, crucial to consider the ways that youth/adult is not a simple binary but intersects with other aspects of researchers' and subjects' social identities and locations.

NOTES

1. This material is based on work supported under a National Science Foundation Graduate Research Fellowship and drawn from my larger study on U.S. teenage girls' political consciousness and activities.

2. There were three teen women involved in TWAP who were eighteen and one who was nineteen. Although I generally use eighteen, the age of majority, as the defining feature of the distinction between woman and girl, and would consider these participants "young women" more than "girls," they were still located primarily as "teens" or "girls" by the practices of the organization, rather than as "staff" or adults. Clearly, the line between child and adult, girl and woman is a shifting and complicated one, with many teenagers feeling like they are at one moment a girl and at another a woman. In the case of this research, the unifying characteristic of "girls" as opposed to "women" is largely their location in these sites as participants. However, the girl/woman distinction is far from clear, which should be remembered in what follows.

3. These are the counselors-in-training, who learn skills to become a counselor, and the camp aides, who volunteer around the camp, taking care of the children of staff, helping in the kitchen, and so on.

4. I did, however, inform them that if they told me of any abuse, I would have to report this information.

REFERENCES

Abu-Lughod, Lila. 1990. Can There Be a Feminist Ethnography? *Women and Performance* 5: 7–27.

Beoku-Betts, Josephine. 1994. When Black Is Not Enough: Doing Field Research among Gullah Women. *NWSA Journal* 6: 413–433.

Best, Amy. 2003. Doing Race in the Context of Feminist Interviewing: Constructing Whiteness through Talk. *Qualitative Inquiry* 9: 895–914.

Bettie, Julie. 2003. *Women without Class: Girls, Race, and Identity.* Berkeley: University of California Press.

Biklen, Sari Knopp. 2004. Trouble on Memory Lane: Adults and Self Retrospection in Researching Youth. *Qualitative Inquiry* 10: 715–730.

Blee, Kathleen M. 2000. White on White: Interviewing Women in U.S. White Supremacist Groups. In *Racing Research, Researching Race: Methodological Dilemmas in Critical Race Studies,* ed. F. W. Twine and J. W. Warren, 93–109. New York: New York University Press.

Fine, Gary Alan, and Glassner, Barry. 1979. Participant Observation with Children: Promise and Problems. *Urban Life* 8: 153–174.

Frankenberg, Ruth. 1993. *White Women, Race Matters: The Social Construction of Whiteness.* Minneapolis: University of Minnesota Press.

Gallagher, Charles A. 2000. White Like Me? Methods, Meaning, and Manipulation in the Field of White Studies. In *Racing Research, Researching Race: Methodological Dilemmas in Critical Race Studies*, ed. F. W. Twine and J. W. Warren, 67–92. New York: New York University Press.

Haraway, Donna. 1988. Situated Knowledges: The Science Question in Feminism and the Privilege of Partial Perspective. *Feminist Studies* 14: 575–600.

Kenny, Lorraine Delia. 2000a. Doing My Homework: The Autoethnography of a White Teenage Girl. In *Racing Research, Researching Race: Methodological Dilemmas in Critical Race Studies*, ed. F. W. Twine and J. W. Warren, 111–133. New York: New York University Press.

———. 2000b. *Daughters of Suburbia: Growing Up White, Middle Class, and Female*. New Brunswick, NJ: Rutgers University Press.

Mandell, Nancy. 1991. The Least-Adult Role in Studying Children. In *Studying the Social Worlds of Children: Sociological Readings*, ed. F. C. Waksler, 38–59. Bristol, PA: Falmer.

Naples, Nancy. 1996. A Feminist Revisiting of the Insider/Outsider Debate: The "Outsider Phenomenon" in Rural Iowa. *Qualitative Sociology* 19: 83–105.

Omi, Michael, and Howard Winant. 1994. *Racial Formation in the United States: From the 1960s to the 1990s*, 2nd ed. New York: Routledge.

Reinharz, Shulamit. 1992. *Feminist Methods in Social Research*. New York: Oxford University Press.

Twine, France Winddance. 2000. Racial Ideologies and Racial Methodologies. In *Racing Research, Researching Race: Methodological Dilemmas in Critical Race Studies*, ed. F. W. Twine and J. W. Warren, 1–34. New York: New York University Press.

Twine, France Winddance, and Jonathan W. Warren, eds. 2000. *Racing Research, Researching Race: Methodological Dilemmas in Critical Race Studies*. New York: New York University Press.

Wolf, Diane L. 1996. Situating Feminist Dilemmas in Fieldwork. In *Feminist Dilemmas in Fieldwork*, ed. D. Wolf, 1–55. Boulder, CO: Westview.

Chapter 9

"What If a Guy Hits on You?"

Intersections of Gender, Sexuality, and Age in Fieldwork with Adolescents

C. J. Pascoe

"Yeah, she's writing a book on River guys," said sixteen-year-old Ray as he introduced me to a few of his friends in River High School's bustling main hallway. Don, a tall, lanky basketball player, leaned casually against the stone pillar next to me. "Damn," he said, smiling down at me, "I was gonna hit on you." Six months into my research I had grown more accustomed to, although certainly not comfortable with, this sort of response from boys at River High School. During my time in the field I often heard similar comments from boys interested in dating me, my advice on their sexual adventures, or information about my own sex life. In this chapter I discuss the unique challenges encountered by female researchers when studying adolescent boys. I focus particularly on how the boys infuse our interactions with sexual content and how I manage these interactions so as to maintain rapport while simultaneously enforcing a professional distance (and maintaining my own dignity) through the creation of what I call a "least-gendered identity."

The role of sexuality is understudied in ethnographic research in general, and thoughtful analysis of the role of sexuality in methodological discussions of ethnographic research among youth is nearly absent. Although teenagers are almost obsessively studied as sexual actors, most research focuses on sex education, "at-risk" behaviors, or nonnormative sexual identities (Kulkin, Chauvin, and Percle 2000; Medrano 1994; Strunin 1994; Waldner-Haugrud and Magruder 1996), rather than on the ways in which sexuality constructs daily lives. In researching teenage boys I have found that sexuality is not just a set of behaviors studied by researchers but is part of the very research process itself in that it mediates, complicates, and illuminates researcher-respondent interactions. This chapter shows how masculinizing processes in adolescence do not just take place between peers but also occur between a female researcher and male respondents (Arendell 1997). As a female researcher I was drawn into a set of objectifying and sexualizing rituals through which boys constructed their identities and certain school spaces as masculine. In the end I was not just studying their sexual identities, but I also became part of the very process through which they constructed these identities.

In researching how teenage boys positioned themselves and others as masculine, I found that boys created masculine identities through tandem processes of repudiating homosexuality and femininity and enacting a sexist heterosexuality (Eder, Evans, and Parker 1995; Epstein 1997; Hird and Jackson 2001; Kehily 2000). They demonstrated heterosexuality through sexual rituals such as talking about their sexual desires, engaging in storytelling contests about their sexual histories, and verbally or physically demonstrating their physical dominance through sexualized interactions with girls.

River High boys directed these rituals at their female peers and occasionally at me. In response, I tried to manage this use of me as a masculinity resource by creating a "least-gendered identity," positioning myself as a woman who possessed some masculine "cultural capital" (Bourdieu 1977). I carefully crafted my identity and interactional style to show that I was a woman who knew about "guy" topics and could engage in the verbal one-upmanship so common among boys at River High. That said, at times I accepted their use of me as a potential sexual partner or sexual object in order to maintain rapport, as I did when Don said he wanted to "hit on" me. At other times, I responded differently to the boys by establishing an insider/outsider position in terms of age, gender, and sexuality. This liminal stance, and specifically my attempts to create a least-gendered identity, allowed me to maintain a good relationship with the boys. This relationship yielded more information than I would have gathered had I reacted like an offended, judgmental adult or a giggly, smiling teenage girl. However, this strategy stopped short of actually challenging the sexist practices in which boys engaged to craft masculine identities.

Project

This chapter is drawn from a project entitled "'Dude, You're a Fag': Masculinity, Sexuality, and Adolescence," in which I argue that masculinity is recognized by students at River High School as the exercise of sexualized will, either by male or female youth. I conducted fieldwork for this project at a suburban high school in north-central California, which I call River High. River High is a working-class, suburban fifty-year-old high school located in a town called Riverton. With the exception of the median household income and racial diversity (both of which are elevated due to Riverton's location in California), the town mirrors national averages in the percentage of white-collar workers, rate of college attendance and marriage, and age composition (according to the 2000 census). It is a politically moderate to conservative, religious community. Most of the students' parents commute to surrounding cities for work.

On average, Riverton is a middle-class community. However, students at River are likely to refer to the town as two communities: "Old Riverton" and "New Riverton." A busy highway and railroad tracks bisect the town into these two sections. River High is literally on the "wrong side of the tracks," in Old Riverton. Exiting the freeway, heading north to Old Riverton, one sees a mix of fifties-era ranch-style homes, some with neatly trimmed lawns and tidy gardens, others with yards strewn with various car parts, lawn chairs, and appliances. Old Riverton is visually bounded by smoke-puffing factories. On the other side of the freeway, New Riverton is characterized by wide sidewalk-lined streets and new walled-in home developments. Instead of smokestacks, a forested mountain, home to a state park, rises majestically in the background. The teens from these homes attend Hillside High, River's rival.

River High is attended by two thousand students. Its racial/ethnic breakdown roughly represents California at large: 50 percent white, 9 percent African American, 28 percent Latino, and 6 percent Asian (as compared to California's 46, 6, 32, and 11 percents, respectively, according to census data and school records). The students at River High are primarily working class. Lauren Carter, the guidance counselor, described the school as an archetypical American high school with its focus on tradition, sports, and community. She illustrated this focus by telling me of the centrality of football to the social life of both Riverton and River High. The principal, Mr. Hobart, had played on the football team when he had attended River. "There's all these old-timers who come out to the football games. Which I think is pretty funny. It's like Iowa. This school could be straight out of Iowa." Lauren told me that Mr. Hobart's career path was a common one: "You go to River. You go to Carrington State for college. You come back to River and teach." She also told me that the historically industry-based economy of Riverton was faltering, and thus poverty rates were rising.

I gathered data using the qualitative method of ethnographic research. I spent a year and a half conducting observations, formally interviewing forty-nine students at River High (thirty-six boys and thirteen girls) and one male student from Hillside High, and conducting countless informal interviews with students, faculty, and administrators. I concentrated on one school because I wanted to explore the richness rather than the breadth of data (for other examples of this method see Bettie 2003; Eder, Evans, and Parker 1995; Ferguson 2000; MacLeod 1987; Willis 1981).

The initial interviews I conducted helped me to map a gendered and sexualized geography of the school, from which I chose my observation sites. I observed a "neutral" site—a senior government classroom, where sexualized meanings were subdued. I observed three sites that students marked as "fag" sites—two drama classes and the Gay/Straight Alliance. I also observed two normatively "masculine" sites—auto shop and weight lifting. I took daily field notes focusing on how students, faculty, and administrators negotiated, regulated, and resisted particular meanings of gender and sexuality. I attended major school rituals such as Winter Ball, school rallies, plays, dances, and lunches. I would also occasionally "ride along" with Mr. Johnson (Mr. J.), the school's security guard, on his battery-powered golf cart to watch who, how, and when students were disciplined.

Given the importance of appearance in high school, I gave some thought as to how I would present myself, deciding to both blend in and set myself apart from the students. In order to blend in I wore my standard graduate student gear—comfortable, baggy cargo pants, a black T-shirt or sweater, and tennis shoes. To set myself apart I carried a messenger bag instead of a backpack, wore no makeup, and spoke slightly differently than the students by using some slang but refraining from uttering the ubiquitous "hecka" and "hella." I took my rainbow sticker off my car because I was afraid of ruining my fieldwork or being asked to leave the school because I was gay.

The importance of the ethnographic process in gathering data for this sort of project cannot be overstated. I had gathered my previous data through interviews. These were one-on-one situations with teenage boys, interactions that, while relaxed, were more formal than the rough-and-tumble ones I found myself involved in while gathering data in the high school itself. When recruiting for interviewees during an earlier project, I presented my research and asked for interview volunteers during class time with a teacher present. The students remained in their seats, politely raising their hands to ask questions or comment on the research. I was recognized by them and by the school authorities as, and I felt myself to be, a researcher from a respected educational institution, coded as an adult, an authority, and, in some ways, an expert. My method of gathering personal information furthered the impression of my role as objective, detached social scientist when I requested that they fill out their names, phone numbers, ages, and parent signatures on special permission forms. I continued to present myself as a detached social scientist as I asked questions from an official sheet of paper on a clipboard when interviewing the boys. These research practices served to reinforce identities of researcher and the researched—physically, intellectually, and temporally. Regardless of this sort of hierarchical, sterile, traditional scientific approach to research, I had assumed that the information I was getting from the boys in my interviews told me what they thought masculinity was. From their words, and not from our interactions, I drew conclusions about definitions of contemporary American adolescent masculinity.

But listening to boys talk in a formal interview setting about gendered norms, expectations, and practices was very different from engaging with them as they lived these norms, expectations, and practices. I experienced this change as I began to engage in participant observation for this project. I was no longer a detached, scientific questioner. I was a live, flesh-and-blood girl, sitting next to them in their classes, waving "hi" across campus, lurking around the edges of the dance floor, and lending them money for sodas at lunch. Through these sorts of interactions I became part of the boys' masculinizing processes by engaging in and responding to their treatment of me as a masculinity resource. In the fifty interviews I conducted while I engaged in this participant observation, I never saw or heard the same sort of behavior or treatment of me as a potential sexual conquest or a less-gendered outsider that I experienced during interacting with boys during my observations.

Going Back to School: Negotiating Intersections of Age and Gender

The first methodological challenge I encountered when researching adolescents was not exactly what I had expected: going back to high school. I had assumed that since I had already researched adolescents, it would be simple to do the same for this project. However, I had not anticipated the difference between interviewing and actually existing among teenagers in their social worlds. I realized that this project was going to be different the first day I walked onto the River campus to begin conducting research at 8:00 a.m. on a warm Monday morning. I walked out of the office in front of the school, having just signed in to the guest log and grabbed my visitor pass. The visitor pass, a blue and white rectangle sporting my name and VISITOR across the top, was supposed to be worn in a conspicuous location. Not wanting to highlight my temporary and outsider status, and possibly feeling some of that high school pressure to "fit in," I stuck it in my bag. Striding down the open-air hallway to my first classroom observation I heard a deep voice booming out behind me, "Hey You! Hey! Hey You! You! Who are you?!" Frozen, having sudden flashbacks to my own high school experience, and remembering narrow escapes while ditching classes and enduring threats of detention, I turned around. A fifty-something African American gentleman built like a linebacker loomed over me, looking down through his glasses, asking, "Who are you?" Recovering quickly and remembering that I was finishing up my twenties, not my teens, I looked up, smiled, and, in a way I hoped was charming, said, "I'm C. J., a researcher here." I showed him my slip, and he said "Okay, as long as you have that with you." He explained to me that he was the school's security guard. His name was George Johnson, but I soon called him Mr. J., just like the rest of the kids at River did. Later, as I became a more familiar sight at the school, Mr. J. engaged in many of the same sexualizing processes as the boys did, often saying flirtatious things to me like "Well, my day suddenly got much brighter since *you* got here!" followed with a wink.

That moment of misidentification was the first of many: teachers thought I was a student, students thought I was a new student, a teacher, or worse, a parole officer. Early in my research as I sat in the back row of the auto-shop class, a tall, lanky blond boy with spiky hair and a relaxed demeanor turned to me as the rest of the boys in the class zinged from one side of the room to the other and asked, "You new here?" I laughed and said, "Sort of. How old do you think I am?" "Uh, seventeen?" he answered. I laughed, explaining, "No, I'm a researcher. I'm almost thirty. I'm writing a book on you guys." He told me he hoped it was a good book.

The students often could not decide whether I was a new student, someone's mother, a teacher, or a parole officer. Soon after that tall, lanky blond thought I was a new student, I found myself standing at a table with the "High School Democrats" as they tried to recruit students to their club. I stood next to the vice president, Trevor, as he summoned David, the president, over to introduce me. David looked at me quizzically as he walked over, and I, responding to his questioning look, said, "Who do you think I am?" David paused, looked at Trevor, and said, "His mom?" I burst out laughing, as did Trevor. Somehow I had gone from late teens to late thirties in a matter of hours. I told him no, I was a researcher from Berkeley, and I was writing a book on boys in his school.

I found I was anxious not to let the students know my actual age, fearing that I would lose some of the cachet inherent in my role as a Berkeley researcher. My concern about age reflected in my clothing choices as well. I did not want to dress like their teachers because I did not want to be seen as an authority figure. However, because I did not wear the extremely low-slung pants that the girls tended to wear and possibly because I walked with more confidence than did most teenage girls, students often mistook me for a teacher. Even though I wore baggy pants and a black T-shirt, one day as I was walking down the hallway one of two boys who had been joking around and using swear words looked at the other and said, "Shhhh! She's a teacher."

Like these two boys, other students were wary of me, thinking I was there to report on their behavior. I spent one afternoon early in my fieldwork hanging out at Bob's, a small, yellow burger shack around the corner from school, where kids ordered their food from a window and congregated around the eight picnic tables separated from the sidewalk by a tall wrought-iron black fence. The "bad" kids hung out here. Most dressed in dark, baggy clothing, and many smoked. Frankly, some of them with their spiky hair and multiple piercings intimidated me. I had never hung out with these sorts of "bad" kids when I was in high school and still felt like I might be punished for associating with them. Thinking about this fear of punishment, I asked a large white boy in a red and black plaid shirt and baggy pants, with earrings and a slight mustache, if kids ever got in trouble for smoking. He said, "No. Every once in a while the cops would come by and tell us to put it out, but not usually." I told him I was writing a book on River, and he looked a little surprised. He took me over to another group of boys, three of them, one with a skateboard. The one with the skateboard looked at me and asked, "Who are you?" I responded by asking, "Who do you think I am?" He said, "P.O." I immediately thought "participant observer" and laughed to myself. In explanation, he offered "parole officer." I laughed out loud at this point. "No, I would probably make more money being a parole officer. Do they really come around here?" "Yeah, all the time," he answered.

I finally settled on telling the students I was "almost thirty." I tried to make it seem that I was an adult but not too much older than they were, more of a mediator between the adult world and their world. I negotiated a "least-adult" identity (Mandell 1988), in which I was simultaneously like and not like the teens I was researching. Barrie Thorne, in her research on elementary-school children, provides vivid examples of how to enact a least-adult identity across generational lines (Thorne 1993).

In establishing and maintaining a least-adult identity, I had to repeatedly promise the boys that they would not get in trouble for the things they told me. J.W., for instance, walked out of the weight room to ask what I was writing down in my notebook. I said I took notes on everything they do. He asked if I wrote about a fight that had occurred the day before. I said yes and asked him if he was worried that he was going to get in trouble. He nodded. I told him that everything I wrote down was confidential, that I could not get him in trouble at all. He said he was worried that I was going to tell his teacher. I told him, "No, I don't tell teachers about stuff that I saw that could get kids in trouble." I continued by saying that maybe if "*I* were in the middle of a fight or got hurt then I might tell somebody." J.W. asked, "What if a guy hits on you?" I laughed and said that I did not tell teachers about that either. J.W., in this early interaction, began to lay the groundwork for later comments he would make about my body and sexuality, by ensuring that he would not get in trouble for saying them.

Once the boys got used to the fact that I was going to be hanging around and writing about them, they took pains to make sure I was writing down what they thought was important. It took them a while to realize that I would not tattle on them. They tested me on this claim by breaking the rules in front of me and then looking at me to see if I disapproved. One day I proved my mettle by refusing to tattle on them as they monkeyed around on the cable machine in the weight room. Mike, J.W., and Josh set the pin to lift the heaviest weights on the cable machine. This meant that the cables were so heavy that none of them had the strength individually to pull the weights off the ground. As Billy and I watched, Mike, J.W., and Josh all tried to perform chest flies with this absurd amount of weight. They aided each other by holding the lifter's arms in place while another boy placed the handle on the lifter's arm. As they tried out the cables, they discovered, much to their delight, that the weight was so heavy that if a boy kept ahold of the cables, he would be lifted off the ground. When J.W. tried to perform a chest fly, he lost the battle with the weights, allowed the cables to pull him up, and executed a back flip as they did so. As he performed more flips, the boys in the class gathered in a half circle around him, urging him on.

I asked Jeff what he thought this gymnastic/weight-lifting performance was all about. He told me, "Proving masculinity. They're only doing it because they're guys and they're around other guys. They prove how strong they are, and then when everyone sees how strong they are, they don't mess with them." As if realizing that he did not want to be messed with either, soon after making this pronouncement Jeff walked over to join in. By this time the crowd was so large that they kept looking to make sure Coach Ramirez was not paying attention. A group of boys helped Jeff grab on to the cable handles, and he tried desperately to hold on to them. The weights yanked the diminutive Jeff quickly into the air as he easily performed a back flip. He kept trying to do a front flip, which no boy had yet performed, but when he was unable to complete it, he let the weights fly down as he let go. They clanked down so hard that the pin snapped in half. The boys scattered, yelling, "He broke it! He broke it!" Josh, standing next to me, started laughing, "Write it down! Write about guys doing dumb stuff!" Instead of fearing that I would tattle on them to Coach Ramirez, they wanted me to document their misdeeds. Thankfully teachers never put me in the position to report on student behavior either, with the exception of one teacher who left me in charge of her class while she left for half an hour.

Many of the boys in auto shop and the weight room came to pride themselves on their status as research subjects. Brook took a look at my big pad of paper, which I happened to be carrying that day because I had filled up the small one I usually carried with me. He cried, "She came in with the big notebook today!" Darren chimed in, "She knows we do too much to put in the small one!" Arnie said, amazed, "I can't believe you filled up a whole notebook." I said, "Yeah, between you guys and weight lifting." Arnie replied, "Yeah, *they're* really bad." The boys frequently equated "badness" with masculinity. They knew I was there to study masculinity and as a result thought that what I wrote down was "bad" stuff. For instance, Ryan said to me, "Your book is a lot today." I said, "Yeah, lots of good stuff." To which he responded, "About Josh?" Josh was pegged as one of the most masculine boys, because he was one of the "baddest"; thus, Ryan assumed that I wrote more on the days he acted up.

This constant documentation helped to define me as an outsider, albeit a privileged outsider, an expert, someone who knew more about the boys than they knew about themselves. The boys highlighted my outsider status in auto shop when a substitute was engaging in futile attempts to calm the class down. The substitute, Mr. Brown, stated, for the tenth time, "Okay guys and girls. Settle down guys and girls." Brook responded, "Uh, it's all guys." Jeff said, looking at me, "except for her." Brook countered, "She's an outsider. She takes notes." Both looked at me, and we laughed. Brook and Jeff highlighted my liminal status—I wasn't *really* a girl because I was an outsider. All of these instances show that negotiating age and authority differences are important when studying adolescents. I had to leave my "adultness" behind and refrain from admonishing them for behaving like teens. Their impressions of me were in themselves a source of data, as boys projected onto me adultness, femaleness, and the ability to punish them.

Creating a Least-Gendered Identity

Although I did not lift weights with the boys or work on cars with them, I did engage in gender practices that marked me as less like the girls in their peer groups. I was not easily categorized, creating what I thought of as a "least-gendered identity." Establishing a least-gendered identity required drawing on masculine cultural capital such as bodily comportment, living in a tough area, and displaying athleticism, an inability to be offended, and a competitive joking interactional style.

I first attempted to create a least-gendered identity by dressing and carrying myself differently than teenaged girls. Most girls at River High wore tight, fitted pants baring their hips or navels. I, on the other hand, routinely wore low-slung baggy jeans or cargo pants (pants with multiple large pockets), black T-shirts or sweaters, and the puffy vests or jackets favored by those who identify with hip-hop culture. Similarly, I "camped up" my sexuality. I performed what might be identified as a soft-butch lesbian demeanor. I walked with a swagger in my shoulders, rather than in my hips (Esterberg 1996). I stood strong-legged instead of shifting my weight from one leg to the other. I used little flourish in my hand motions, instead using my arms in a traditionally masculine way—hands wide with stiff wrists. I smiled less. I also sat with my legs wide apart or crossed ankle over knee, rather than knee over knee.

This appearance allowed my difference to be less marked, and I was let in to boys' worlds and conversations, if not as an honorary guy, then at least as some sort of neutered observer who would not be offended. For instance, in auto shop, Jay bragged about how he was going to turn eighteen soon and lamented that he would not be able to "have sex with girls under eighteen then. Statutory rape. Younger girls, they lie. Stupid little bitches." He laughed menacingly and then said, "God, I hate girls." At this point he saw the female teacher's aide on the other side of the classroom and said loudly enough so that she could hear, "They're only good for making sandwiches and cleaning house. They don't even do that up to speed!" She looked at him and shook her head. Jay started throwing licorice at her and yelling, "I agree, her sister is a lot hotter than her! Make me a sandwich!" It was as if it did not occur to him that I, the only other "girl" in the room, might be offended by such a pronouncement. Although Jay seemed to quickly forget my gender status, other boys never forgot my outsider status. As soon as Jay finished insulting the classroom aide, Brook quickly looked at me and said, "Write that down!"

My athletic ability and interests also contributed to my least-gendered status. Boys and I often spoke of mountain biking and the numerous injuries I had sustained during my mountain-biking adventures. We would sometimes get into injury-comparison contests, trying to one-up each other with the grossest and most outlandish sporting incident—me talking about my concussions and revealing my scars, boys showing their stitches and scabs. The weight-room teacher, Coach Rodriguez, inadvertently helped establish my sporting identity when introducing me to his weight-lifting class. We had spoken on the phone before I had come to observe his class, and during our discussion we talked about lifting weights, something I did on a regular basis. This helped me establish rapport with him because he was passionate about weight lifting and strength training. When he introduced me to the class, he told the boys I was a "weight lifter from U.C. Berkeley who has some things she wants to talk to you about." He encouraged them to ask me questions about weight lifting and form. I think this gave the boys the impression that I was a weight lifter from Berkeley in some official capacity, as opposed to a graduate student who went to the gym several times a week and lifted weights in order to stay fit.

Although boys did not come running to me for advice, I did tease them about their form (which, more often than not, was horrible), and we were able to joke back and forth about it, thus establishing rapport. This sort of masculine cultural capital—both the teasing, a hallmark of masculinity (Kehily and Nayak 1997; Lyman 1998), and the knowledge—allowed me to attain somewhat of an inside outsider status.

Sharing my address with boys at River High also bolstered my least-gendered status. I lived off a main thoroughfare in Oakland, California, famous for drug deals, prostitution, and gang fights. Indeed during the time of my research a man was gunned down on the street outside my apartment. This actually helped entrée with some groups of boys, especially African American boys, who were slightly less willing to talk with me, regarding me as just another white member of the administration who could discover their real addresses and send them back to the "bad" school in the nearby "Chicago" school district. Once, when I was standing outside the weight room watching a bunch of boys I had not spoken with yet, J.W. turned to them to introduce me, saying, "She lives in East Oakland." A chorus of "ooohs," "aaaahs," and "no ways!" followed this announcement. One of the boys in that group, Mike, later introduced me to a group of his friends, all African American boys, by pointing at me and saying, "She live in East Oakland." One of the boys in the group said, looking over short, blond, female me, "No she don't." Mike challenged him, "Ask her." So Dax did, in disbelief, "You live in East Oakland?" I smiled and said, "Yeah, between East 18th and East 14th." Talking about a recent murder, Rakim said, "She lives two blocks from where that guy was killed." The boys still look skeptical. I asked Dax, "Why don't you believe that I live in Oakland?" "'Cause it's ghetto," he replied. I agreed, "Yes, it is ghetto." They all laughed uproariously as I said the word "ghetto." Then they clamored, asking where I was *really* from. I told them that I was born in Orange County, a famously white, conservative area in Southern California. This seemed to make much more sense to them. They seemed to be picking up on a raced and classed ethnicity—a whiteness that was at odds with my residence in such a tough neighborhood. Much as the boys perceived badness as masculinity, my living and surviving in a "bad" area helped me to establish credibility with them. From this point on, this group of African American boys was much more likely to let me into their circles. Again, this sort of knowledge allowed me to be an insider in multiple ways, in terms of street credibility, racial identity, and age.

As I established a least-gendered identity, I disrupted the common understanding of sex/gender correspondence. Like many women who gain access to all-male domains, I distanced myself from more conventional forms of femininity (Herbert 1998). I purposefully distinguished myself from the other women in these boys' lives: mothers, teachers, and, most importantly, other teenage girls. I did not wear makeup or tight clothing or giggle. I also purposefully selectively shared information about myself, emphasizing attributes such as mountain biking, weight lifting, guitar playing, and bragging about injuries. I intentionally left out topics that would align me with femininity, such as my love of cooking, my feminism, and my excitement about my upcoming commitment ceremony. Like the boys, I distanced myself from femininity; however, I did not, like the boys, actively demean femininity. In this sense, creating a least-gendered identity involved a deliberately gendered research strategy.

Negotiating Sexuality

I was not consistently successful in maintaining this least-gendered identity. Some boys insisted on positioning me as a potential sexual partner by drawing me into the sexualizing and objectifying rituals central to the maintenance of a masculine identity at River High. Being used as an identity resource in this way left me feeling objectified, scared, angry, and unsettled. As a strong, assertive woman who socializes primarily with other feminists, it was disconcerting to have boys leer at me and ask invasive questions about my sex life. Despite my efforts to create a least-gendered identity, some of the boys set up a heterosexual dynamic between us, trying to transform me into a girl their age who may or may not be a future sexual conquest. It was as if, by making me concretely feminine, they could assert their masculinity as a socially dominant identity. I had power over the boys in a variety of ways—my age, my knowledge about them, my economic status—and by emphasizing my sexual availability boys were able to assert their control over me as a female outsider (Horowitz 1986).[1]

The first time that this happened I was startled, and looking back at how I described the incident in my field notes, I now have a hard time describing why I knew that I was being positioned as a sexual object. During my second day of research at River High, I had presented my research to the auto-shop class, saying to a room full of boys,

Hey, you're probably all wondering what I'm doing here. I'm writing a book on teenage guys. And I'm researching the guys at your school. I'm gonna be a doctor in two years; that's what this book is for. I'm gonna be at your football games, dances, and lunch and school etc. . . . for the next year. And I'll probably want to interview some of you.

A bunch of boys in the back of the room yelled out, "Rodriguez will do it! Rodriguez will do it!" Rodriguez said lasciviously with a leer, "Yeah I *totally* will." His comment served as a warning. I felt warned that these boys were in a process of building dominant identities and that I, as a woman, was central to this process. As a result, I knew early in my research that I would have to figure out ways to deal with this sort of treatment by the boys while maintaining my rapport with them.

On a few occasions I felt physically intimidated by the boys, as they invaded my space with their sheer size and manipulated my body with their strength. At one point during the junior prom, David ran up and started "freaking" me. Freaking is a popular dance move in which students grind their pelvises together in time to the music as if to simulate sex. David was probably six feet tall (as compared to my five feet and two inches) and the size of a grown man, not a wiry adolescent. I had never been grabbed by a man in such a way and responded with a bit of panic. I tried to step back from him, but he wrapped his arms around me so that I could not escape his frantic grinding. I put my arms on his shoulders and gently pushed back, laughing nervously, saying I hoped he had a good night. I was desperately hoping no administrators saw it because I did not want to get in trouble for sexually accosting one of the students. Researching teens requires maintaining rapport with two groups that often have different interests: students and administrators. I needed administrators to see me as a responsible (and thus nonsexual) adult while simultaneously appearing accessible, but not too much so, to the teens on the dance floor. Similarly, at another dance a boy I did not even recognize ran up to me, tightly grabbed both my wrists, and pulled me toward the dancing throng, saying, "Come on! You want to dance!" as a statement, not as a question. Again, I tried to hide my fear and exit the situation by laughing, but I had to struggle to pull my wrists out of his grip.

Other boys were even more physically aggressive, especially in all-male spaces. In auto shop, Stan, Reggie, and J.W. kept grabbing each others' crotches and then hurriedly placing their hands in a protective cup over their own, while giggling. After watching them for a while I finally asked J.W. what they were doing. He explained, "It's cup check. Wanna play?" I must have looked shocked as he extended his hand toward my own crotch. Trying to maintain my calm, I said, "no thanks." Looking slyly at me, he tried again, saying, "Wanna play titties?" and suddenly shoving his hands toward my chest and twisting them around. I shook my head, dumfounded. He turned and walked away as Stan and Reggie defensively put their hands over their genitals. I felt especially violated because he did not just ask, "Want to play cup check?" He followed this question with a specifically gendered proposal, reaching for my breasts. In order to protect myself from their violating touches, while at the same time maintaining a relationship with them, I laughed to mitigate discomfort and quietly exited the situation. In these instances I found no way to maintain some sort of least-gendered identity but, rather, tried to escape their sexualizing and objectifying processes without looking offended or flattered.

Josh was one of the boys whose actions I found most troubling. He often stood too close to me, eyed me lasciviously, and constantly adjusted his crotch when he was around me. He was constantly seeking masculine positioning by talking about women's bodies in sexist ways. I had forged a decent relationship with his off-again/on-again girlfriend, Jessica, a striking blonde. She came up to me one morning in drama class to tell me that she and Josh had been talking about me on the phone the previous night. I looked surprised as she continued, saying that he told her how he liked older women and that he would like to "bang" me. After hearing this, I felt exceedingly awkward and, frankly, quite vulnerable. It had not occurred to me that conversations about me were going on in my absence. I also realized that I was in a vulnerable position, not just in terms of sexual advances but also in terms of any stories these boys might choose to tell about me. Throughout my research, Josh continued to make allusions to me as his sexual partner. In auto shop one day, I rose from my seat to use the restroom in the school office. Josh yelled out, "You leaving already?" I looked at him and said, "Bathroom." He pointed to the grimy bathroom/ changing room the boys used and said, "There's one here." I replied, "I don't think so." As I walked away, Josh looked around, adjusted his crotch, and followed me out, saying, "I'll be back fellas," implying that he was going to follow me and that something sexual was going to happen. Of course, he had adjusted his crotch with a greasy hand; so, falling back, he said, "My nuts are greasy!" and stopped following me. Using the strategy I had by that time perfected, I just ignored him.

When I could not escape or ignore my involvement in these sexualizing and objectifying processes, I sometimes tried to respond as neutrally as possible, while encouraging boys to continue to talk about their feelings. One day in the weight room, J.W. was looking pensive, sheepish, or moping—I could not tell which. He finally sidled up to me and asked, in a saccharine, bashful voice, "Can I ask you a personal question?" Of course, this question always gave me pause. I had been asking them all sorts of personal questions and following their every word and deed. As a result, I felt that I should reciprocate, to a certain extent, with information about myself. I responded, "Sure," thinking I could talk myself out of inappropriate questions about whether or not I was married or single, gay or straight, which was usually the vein these types of questions were in. Instead he surprised me with a question I did not fully understand but knew was inappropriate: "Have you ever had your walls ripped?" Frantically, I thought, "I must stall for time," as I figured out how to respond to what I knew must be a lewd question. I assumed, given the context of the boys' previous discussions about making girlfriends bleed by "ripping" their walls, that it had something to do with their penises being so large that they ripped bloody tears in their girlfriends' vaginal walls. I tried to respond with a relatively neutral answer, asking, "What do you mean, walls ripped?" J.W. stammered a nonsensical answer, looking around desperately for help, asking other guys to help him define it. Since it was not really possible to rip a girls' walls as often and as harshly as they bragged, none of them really explained what it meant. The boys all looked at him as if to say, "You've gotten yourself into your own mess this time," and laughed at him as they shook their heads no. Finally, unable to continue to embarrass him and feeling incredibly awkward myself, I said, "I know what it means. Why do you want to know?" He responded, "Cuz I like to know if girls are freaky or not. I like freaky girls." I felt awkward at this point because it seemed that I was being categorized as a potential sexual conquest. Instead of following that line of talk, I redirected the question and asked him, "Have you ever ripped a girl's walls?" J.W. responded proudly, "Hell yeah." So I asked him, "How does it make you feel?" He spread his legs and looked down between them, gesturing, "I feel hella bad because they are bleeding and crying. It hurts them." This strategy of redirecting the offensive statement back toward the boys had the effect of producing rich data. While trying not to reveal information about myself or appear offended, I furthered the discussion by trying to get J.W. to talk about his feelings, which he did to the extent that he was able.

By the end of my research, I frequently copied some of the boys' masculinizing strategies in my interactions with them, specifically the ways in which boys established themselves as masculine through discursive battles for dominance in which they jokingly insulted one another (Kehily and Nayak 1997; Lyman 1998). These battles usually took the form of a "fag discourse" (Pascoe 2005), in which boys insulted one another by calling each other fags. I began to engage in a similar strategy when the boys would begin to make sexualized comments to me. Although I did not invoke the "fag discourse," I tried to verbally spar with them in a way that was both humorous and slightly insulting. For example, in auto shop, Brook asked for some grease to lubricate an engine part. In response, Josh looked at me and commented lewdly, "I got white grease, baby." Fed up with Josh's incessant comments and no longer needing to establish rapport, I mimicked the boys' interactional style. I looked at him and said scathingly, "What does that mean, Josh?" The surrounding boys looked stunned and then burst out laughing. Brook looked down at me and said, "I'm startin' to like you. You're okay!" Josh, angry, ran across the yard yelling, "Faggots!!! I'm not talking to any of you!!!" I had "won" this exchange and the respect of some of the boys by interacting in their masculinized manner. Josh did not stay angry at me, but he actually did tone down his comments during the remainder of my time at River.

As with Josh, I finally became so weary of J.W.'s continual propositions that I responded to him with a similar sort of verbal insult. In the weight room, I tried to walk past J.W. to get to the back of the room. Looking at me, he put his leg up on a weight bench to prevent me from walking past. I said, without a smile, "Very funny J.W.," and turned to walk around him. Quickly he put his other leg up. I was now trapped between both of his legs. I felt harassed and ensnared. He looked at me and smiled as if he expected me to smile back. I tried my usual strategy of invoking humor and challenged him: "But can you put both legs up like that at the same time?" He said, loudly for the entire class to hear, "You'd like that wouldn't you?!" Ticked off and embarrassed that my approach had not worked, I said, witheringly, "You know, I was a teenager once, and I dated teenage boys then. They weren't impressive then, and they aren't now." The other boys laughed loudly, jumping in with their own insults. J.W. hung his head in embarrassment. I felt that I had linguistically wrested sexual and gendered control of the situation from his grasp.

With both of these boys, I engaged in the sort of verbal sexual one-upmanship that boys engaged in with one another. They tried to pull me into their objectifying rituals, but I had to deny them that control without raising my voice, condemning the sex talk, or revealing my own sexual preferences. Instead, I had to either highlight the illogic of what they were saying, as I did with Josh, or make it clear that they were immature. I refused to engage in the feminizing verbal war of the "fag discourse" that the boys used to define themselves as masculine. As a result, I had few other options with which to encourage their respect and avoid becoming a victimized girl, appearing flattered by their obscene overtures, or looking like an authority figure by scolding them. Deploying this competitive joking strategy worked when my least-gendered identity failed and I was pulled into their objectifying rituals.

A Feminist Challenge in Adolescent Masculinity Research

Crafting a researcher identity when researching teens is difficult because adolescence is such a chaotic life period. When conducting research with adults, a researcher most likely has a general sense of the ways in which he or she is defined. Interacting with adults, even in social worlds very different from one's own, usually involves age-defined shared categorizations, ways of interacting, and manners. Although doing fieldwork across lines of difference can lead to misunderstandings and unintended interactions in any setting, age differences bring up a unique set of issues (Baker 1983; Weber, Miracle, and Skehan 1994).

In adulthood, the self is relatively settled. It is not so in adolescence. The self is so much in flux during the teenage years that psychologist Erik Erikson called adolescence a time of "normative crisis" (Erikson 1980 [1959]). An adolescent's task, according to developmental theorists like Erikson, is "identity consolidation." This task requires that teens they figure out "who they are." As teens categorize themselves, they categorize others as well. The researcher, in this setting, becomes part of their meaning-making systems and identity work. As a researcher, I was not necessarily perceived by them according to the way I tried to present myself, which is generally the way I am perceived by adults. Rather, I became one of the resources they mobilized to create identity and make meaning.

When I simply performed interviews, as opposed to gathering data through observations, less identity negotiation was required of me. My identity was more or less firm. I was a researcher, tied to a prestigious university. However, as I spent much of the boys' daily lives with them, they challenged my own assumptions about my identity, and I had to meet those challenges with my own identity strategies. During my time with them, my identity was ever shifting, and I had to adapt to different identities. However, I was not always in control of my own researcher identity. As Ruth Horowitz documents, a researcher's identity, especially in a setting that allows for very few identities, is actively negotiated between the respondents and the researcher (Horowitz 1986). Sometimes these identities suited my purpose, but other times I was stuck in a role I did not want. I was alternatively a teacher, a mother, a girl, an outsider, a note taker, an author, a student, a potential sexual partner, or a confidante.

Being mobilized as an identity resource was quite jarring. As boys positioned me as a potential sexual partner, none of them seemed concerned about my thoughts or desires about my own sexual availability. In trying to create a least-gendered identity or responding by copying their joking strategy, I was able to maintain rapport with them, maintain my own self-respect, and earn some of theirs. I distanced myself both in terms of gender and age from being a "girl" or a "boy" by refraining from the giggling and squealing commonly associated with teenage girls joining in boys' objectification of girls, a strategy that would not likely have worked for me. I also distanced myself from recognizably adult behaviors by refraining from expressing disapproval of dirty talk, expressing offense, or disciplining them. Instead, I struck a balance by not joining in with this sort of talk and not reporting it to school faculty. By occupying a less-gendered and less-age-defined position I was able to maintain rapport with the boys while also unfortunately helping to preserve some of the more troubling aspects of gender inequalities in this school.

Using the masculine capital I had at my disposal often meant that I did not challenge the sexist and homophobic behavior among the teenage boys. This is a challenge for feminist research into adolescent masculinity: maintaining rapport with boys while not necessarily validating their belief systems and gender prejudices. I walked a tightrope in managing my feminist allegiance to teenage girls and the need to gather data from the boys who mock them. When I could, I used masculine joking strategies to best other boys, without simultaneously invoking feminizing or homophobic insults. Similarly, I had to maintain a balance between distancing myself from femininity and not belittling it. Although I may have challenged gender stereotypes by decoupling sex and gender in utilizing masculine interactional strategies and cultural capital, this research approach failed to challenge the sexist underpinnings of masculine identities at River High.

Researchers' own subjectivities are central to ethnographic research, as feminist methodologists have long demonstrated (Arendell 1997; Borland 1991; Harding 1987). Paying attention to my own feelings and desires as the boys drew me into their objectifying and sexualizing rituals helped me to recognize processes of masculinity I otherwise may have missed. In this way, my own feelings and experiences were central to the data I gathered. My own horror at being involved in these processes led to a gendered identity strategy that both elicited information from the boys and frequently stopped short of challenging their sexism.

NOTES

1. Horowitz (1986) documents a similar phenomenon in her research with Chicano gang members in Chicago. The members initially saw her as a desexualized "lady," but as her research continued and her knowledge of them deepened they recast her as a "chick." In this way they tried to counter what they saw as her threatening presence in their organization.

REFERENCES

Arendell, Terry. 1997. "Reflections on the Researcher-Researched Relationships: A Woman Interviewing Men." *Qualitative Sociology* 29:341–368.

Baker, Carolyn. 1983. "A 'Second Look' at Interviews with Adolescents." *Journal of Youth and Adolescence* 12:501–519.

Bettie, Julie. 2003. *Women without Class.* Berkeley: University of California Press.

Borland, Katherine. 1991. "'That's Not What I Said': Interpretive Conflict in Oral Narrative Research." Pp. 63–76 in *Women's Words: The Feminist Practice of Oral History,* edited by Sherna Berger Gluck and Daphne Patai. New York: Routledge.

Bourdieu, Pierre. 1977. *Outline of a Theory of Practice.* Cambridge: Cambridge University Press.

Eder, Donna, Catherine Colleen Evans, and Stephen Parker. 1995. *School Talk: Gender and Adolescent Culture.* New Brunswick, NJ: Rutgers University Press.

Epstein, Debbie. 1997. "Boyz' Own Stories: Masculinities and Sexualities in Schools." *Gender and Education* 9:105–115.

Erikson, Erik. 1980 [1959]. *Identity and the Life Cycle.* New York: Norton.

Esterberg, Kristin G. 1996. "'A Certain Swagger When I Walk': Performing Lesbian Identity." Pp. 259–279 in *Queer Theory/Sociology,* edited by Steven Seidman. Cambridge, UK: Blackwell.

Ferguson, Ann. 2000. *Bad Boys: Public Schools in the Making of Black Masculinity.* Ann Arbor: University of Michigan Press.

Harding, Sandra G. 1987. *Feminism and Methodology: Social Science Issues.* Bloomington: Indiana University Press.

Herbert, Melissa S. 1998. *Camouflage Isn't Only for Combat: Gender, Sexuality, and Women in the Military.* New York: New York University Press.

Hird, Myra J., and Sue Jackson. 2001. "Where 'Angels' and 'Wusses' Fear to Tread: Sexual Coercion in Adolescent Dating Relationships." *Journal of Sociology* 37: 27–43.

Horowitz, Ruth. 1986. "Remaining an Outsider: Membership as a Threat to Research Rapport." *Urban Life* 14:409–430.

Kehily, Mary Jane. 2000. "Understanding Heterosexualities: Masculinities, Embodiment, and Schooling." Pp. 27–40 in *Genders and Sexualities in Educational Ethnography,* edited by Geoffrey Walford and Caroline Hudson. Amsterdam: JAI.

Kehily, Mary Jane, and Anoop Nayak. 1997. "'Lads and Laughter': Humour and the Production of Heterosexual Masculinities." *Gender and Education* 9:69–87.

Kulkin, Heidi S., Elizabeth A. Chauvin, and Gretchen A. Percle. 2000. "Suicide among Gay and Lesbian Adolescents and Young Adults: A Review of the Literature." *Journal of Homosexuality* 40:1–29.

Lyman, Peter. 1998. "The Fraternal Bond as a Joking Relationship: A Case Study of the Role of Sexist Jokes in Male Group Bonding." Pp. 171–193 in *Men's Lives,* edited by Michael Kimmel and Michael Messner. Boston: Allyn and Bacon.

MacLeod, Jay. 1987. *Ain't No Makin It: Aspirations and Attainment in a Low-Income Neighborhood.* Boulder, CO: Westview.

Mandell, Nancy. 1988. "The Least-Adult Role in Studying Children." *Journal of Contemporary Ethnography* 16:433–467.

Medrano, Luisa. 1994. "AIDS and Latino Adolescents." Pp. 100–114 in *Sexual Cultures and the Construction of Adolescent Identities,* edited by Janice M. Irvine. Philadelphia: Temple University Press.

Pascoe, C. J. 2005. "'Dude, You're a Fag': Adolescent Masculinity and the Fag Discourse." *Sexualities* 8:329–346.

Strunin, Lee. 1994. "Culture, Context, and HIV Infection: Research on Risk Taking among Adolescents." Pp. 71–87 in *Sexual Cultures and the Construction of Adolescent Identities,* edited by Janice M. Irvine. Philadelphia: Temple University Press.

Thorne, Barrie. 1993. *Gender Play: Boys and Girls in School.* New Brunswick, NJ: Rutgers University Press.

Waldner-Haugrud, Lisa K., and Brian Magruder. 1996. "Homosexual Identity Expression among Lesbian and Gay Adolescents: An Analysis of Perceived Structural Associations." *Youth and Society* 27:313–333.

Weber, Linda, Andrew Miracle, and Tom Skehan. 1994. "Interviewing Early Adolescents: Some Methodological Considerations." *Human Organization* 3:42–47.

Willis, Paul. 1981. *Learning to Labor: How Working-Class Kids Get Working-Class Jobs.* New York: Columbia University Press.

Part III

Activating Youth
*Youth Agency, Collaboration,
and Representation*

Chapter 10

Trouble on Memory Lane
Adults and Self-Retrospection in Researching Youth

Sari Knopp Biklen

Like it or not, ethnographers who study youth often travel down memory lane to revisit their own adolescence. In many ethnographies of youth, authors refer to their own youthful experiences in their narratives. More common than uncommon, these references reaffirm an adult's status as a former youth. With such a status, narrators announce that they are not complete strangers to their informants. Rather, these narrators bring to bear on their projects some experience that increases their interpretive authority. Memories of youth also signify the narrator's social location in relation to the research, reflecting the importance of articulating the vantage point from which the ethnographic story gets told (White 1987). And perhaps most directly, memories of youth map a gaze, providing a way of seeing the informants through a particular understanding of youth and youthful experiences. Ethnographers deploy memory as a narrative strategy to heighten their authority, to distance themselves from their informants, to authenticate their speaking positions, and to trouble their field-work approach.

Memory is full of contradictions for ethnographers. The danger for narrators who construct their memories as links between their adolescent informants and the adult researcher who was once a youth rides on the implicit suggestion that the researcher can too easily access youths' perspectives. On the other hand, to represent memory as a form of bias that needs to be managed or overcome ignores the complexity and uses of the identity markers that fieldworkers bring to the research site, and sidesteps the collective aspects of even our most personal memories. Memories are not just individual but are also part of a "social imaginary" (Klein 1997) that is rooted in national and cultural traditions and implicated in the larger relationship between youth and adults. Memory's contradiction for ethnographic work in the field connects its danger and desirability.

Women who study men, gay people who study bisexual people, or deaf people who study blind people—in other words, researchers who study others—must always negotiate difference. Adults have to negotiate difference, too, when they study youth, but they also have to engage connection since every adult was once a youth. When we do ethnographic research on youth, we engage a group that is familiar in an experiential sense but that is historically and, hence, significantly different. This situation of having once been a member of the informant group, broadly defined, means that when adults write about youth, we engage a group of which we once were members but are no longer and can never be again. Although adults cannot "go back" to being youth, those who study young people seem to place their recollections of adolescence into the matrix when they do fieldwork, analyze data, and write about it. Whatever happens in the process of doing fieldwork or analyzing data, the effect of citing personal memories in the written text is to authenticate the narrator's privileged speaking position.

It is a common practice for narrators in ethnographies of youth to describe their own adolescence in relation to the youth they study. Most of the narrators illustrate how these memories increase their access to the youth, their knowledge of the culture, and their abilities to relate to or accurately understand their informants. Foley narrates how his memories of his rural upbringing in Iowa enabled him to act "naturally" in the Texas agricultural area he studied and reported on in *Learning Capitalist Culture*, increasing his rapport with everyone (Foley 1990). In *Our Guys*, a study of the rape of an adolescent girl with intellectual disabilities by the popular athletes in Glen Ridge, New Jersey, Lefkowitz (1997) uses his memories of his geeky boyhood to reinforce the authenticity of his knowledge of the rapists, because during his own adolescence he had closely observed popular and athletic boys from his position as an outsider. Fordham (1996) tells the reader in *Blacked Out* that her observations of African American high school girls for her study of race and achievement brought back with immediacy her own experiences of adolescence. She felt she could have been them, she knew them so well. In *Bad Boys*, a study of public schools' construction of black masculinity, Ferguson describes how she had to "freshen" her memory "of what it meant to be a 'child' in a world of total and arbitrary 'adult' power" (2001:14). So, to connect to feelings of powerlessness, she called on less-distant memories of being a graduate student, when she was treated as a "blank slate" whose "accumulated knowledge counted for nothing." There are multiple other examples as well (e.g., McRobbie 1991; Passerini 1996; Proweller 1998; Walker 1988). Whereas most of these other examples rely on but do not deconstruct memory as a narrative strategy, only Thorne directly addresses memory as a conceptual aspect of this kind of research with young people. Memory, she argues, is both "obstacle and resource in the process of doing fieldwork with kids" (1993:7). It is an obstacle when adults conceptualize young people as incomplete, as "learners of one's own culture" (12). Thorne highlights memory's usefulness when she describes how it enabled her to see that her own experiences in elementary school pushed her to notice particular children and ignore others. She connected her extensive note taking on one popular girl to her own position at that age: "Then I realized the envy behind my note-taking and analysis and recalled that many years ago when I was a fourth- and fifth-grader of middling social status, I had also carefully watched the popular girl, using a kind of applied sociology to figure out my place in a charged social network" (24). Social status configurations are influential in youths' social groups and remain influential later. Realizing that she was still drawing on her "standpoint as a girl in the middle of the social hierarchy" (26), Thorne used this memory work to focus more of her attention on students on the margins. She came to realize that there is more interaction between genders than she had noticed when her attention was drawn to the more popular children. So she changed her strategies of observation. The significance of these examples is that when adults study young people, we are not just interacting with another group about which we know little from personal experience. Rather, we often find it difficult to resist the imaginary position of "been there, done that," though we may be interested in the differences between current and earlier constructions of adolescence.

This chapter explores memory as a problematic for qualitative studies of youth. It is not a rejection of memory as a feature of research, nor is it an argument about memory's contribution to bias in ethnographies. People have memories, and these memories inevitably influence adults when we conduct research about young people. As Sturken writes, "memory forms the fabric of human life, affecting everything from the ability to perform simple everyday tasks to the recognition of the self" (1997:1). Rather, this is an exploration of the complications memory contributes to adults' ethnographic scholarship on youth, emphasizing how memories, when unselfconsciously employed, increase the authority of the adult researcher over the adolescent informant, with sometimes negative effects. These effects include, particularly, an overemphasis on defining the perspectives of our informants in relation to an adult sense of "what is happening," with inadequate attention to the informants' legitimacy and authority as interpreters of their experiences. This chapter examines some of the ways scholars currently conceive of memory, addresses youth as a category of informant, and offers an example from a research project on youthful informants for illustration.

Memory

If memory were just a "store" (Jedlowski 2001) that warehoused our recollections of experiences, then individual memories would rest there waiting to be consumed by recall. Lying still on the store shelves, memories would be stable, discrete representations of different things that happened to us. When called up, or consumed, in the process of remembering, they would spring to life for a while and then, like the rejected T-shirt that the shopper does not want to buy, be placed back on the shelf. Although researchers once understood memories in this manner, they no longer seem to imagine them in this kind of discrete, static form. Even neurologists who examine how the brain produces and stores memories acknowledge the social aspects when they write that to understand the relationship of memory to identity, memories must be seen as "systematized" and "organized" (Damasio 1999:17–18).

From psychologists who study autobiographical memory (e.g., Rubin 1996) to social anthropologists to cultural studies scholars, researchers in multiple fields assert the intimate relationship between memory and identity. Anthropologists Cattell and Climo, for example, emphasize its centrality:

> Without memory, groups could not distinguish themselves from one another, whether family, friends, governments, institutions, ethnic groups, or any other collectivity, nor would they know whether or how to negotiate, fight, or cooperate with each other. From the simplest everyday tasks to the most complicated, we all rely on memories to give meaning to our lives: to tell us who we are, what we need to do, how to do it, where we belong, and how to live with other people. (2002:1)

Cultural studies scholar Sturken has used similar language:

> Memory forms the fabric of human life, affecting everything from the ability to perform simple, everyday tasks to the recognition of the self. Memory establishes life's continuity; it gives meaning to the present, as each moment is constituted by the past. As the means by which we remember who we are, memory provides the very core of identity. (1997:1)

Though there is agreement on the significance of memory to identity in multiple fields, the huge range of perspectives different disciplines and theoretical positions use to approach memory is visible in its multiple representations. Robins sees the differences as discipline based: "Where the discipline of psychology has tended to define memory as a product of the biological or cognitive processes of the individual, cultural studies has conceptualized memory as a product of social processes whereby the past is represented through cultural forms" (1995:201). Many psychologists today, however, see these "biological or cognitive processes" as socially connected and interactive to some degree. Rubin, for example, examines the "components" of autobiographical or personal memory, but finally insists that these memories are constructed: "This does not mean that they are either accurate or inaccurate, but that they are not encoded, stored, and retrieved as wholes but rather are created at retrieval using components like the narrative, imagery, emotion division used in this introduction" (1996:4).

Others have looked at the social construction of memory. "What we call 'memory,'" says sociologist Paolo Jedlowski, "is a complex network of activities, the study of which indicates that the past never remains 'one and the same,' but is constantly selected, filtered and restructured in terms set by the questions and necessities of the present, at both the individual and the social levels" (2001:30). In addition to analysis of how memories are shaped by contemporary experience, Antze and Lambek look at "the disciplines through which the very idea of memory has been constructed" (1996:viii), and Swanson (2000) explores how our current understanding of memory rests on the division between public and private that developed in the nineteenth century. Our memories are connected to identity construction and to their social markers. They are not representations of our earlier lives that we can bring in or leave out at will, because our memories are not just "there." As Bal writes about cultural memory, it "is an activity occurring in the present, in which the past is continuously modified and redescribed even as it continues to shape the future" (1999: vii). Bal calls on the work of Pierre Janet, one of Freud's colleagues, to argue that "memory is an action: essentially, it is the action of telling a story" (ibid.:ix). Memories, then, are not just recalled events.

One way to think of memories is that they are fashioned by us over the years into a narrative so that different parts of our memories are connected to each other. Whether "memories exist as traces that are continually re-worked in the present" (Robins 1995:204) or whether they can only be seen in the "trails" they leave (Klein 1997), they are a narrative, as Louisa Passerini says, that "speaks from today" (1996:23).

Another way to think about memory is that it is performative. Holiday celebrations such as Fourth of July fireworks and parades, Veterans Day marches, and Martin Luther King Day ceremonies muster memories for particular understandings of history and for particular social goals. In this way, memories are used to have the United States viewed and understood in certain ways. Research on trauma, such as slavery or the Holocaust, not only puts people's stories into the public realm but also promotes particular understandings. Antze and Lambek describe some of the performative aspects of memory: "When memories recall acts of violence against individuals or entire groups, they carry additional burdens—as indictments or confessions, or as emblems of a victimized identity. Here, acts of remembering often take on performative meaning within a charged field of contested moral and political claims" (1996:vii). Though it is complex, this performative aspect of memory is connected to "identity construction" in certain situations, for example "when we offer particular stories about ourselves in order to make a certain kind of impression" (ibid.:xvi).

The relationship of performative memory to identity is significant in relation to authority. Since memories are continually reworked into a narrative, this narrative marks out the stance that the researchers take, and from which point they make sense of the youth they study. Authors construct identities for themselves as narrators when they share memories of their childhood, positioning themselves in particular relation to their informants.

These memories are not just resources for sense making; but in a Foucauldian sense, they also regulate what we hear. When American students talk of their proms, for example, American researchers may think back on our own proms to make sense of what we hear and who the other person is. When a student talks of easy access to money and material goods, we may label the student as privileged when we compare their resources to our own at that age. I am not arguing that researchers are thoughtless interpreters of the lives of young people. In fact, many researchers have usefully drawn on their experiences as outsiders in the culture to point out what gets taken for granted in particular communities (e.g., Bettie 2003; Proweller 1998). Memory, approached in these multiple ways, gives us access both to memory's power to construct our current approach to others and to be constructed by it.

Mannheim, for example, points to the stabilizing power of generations and their control over young people. In "The Problem of Generations," he suggests that memories of one's early experiences tend to "stabilize" themselves "as the natural view of the world" for each particular generation (1952). Adults, then, see their view of the world as the stable, "normal" view and approve or disapprove of the next generation's approaches. Adults employ collective memories "to validate the view of the past that has become important to the individual or group in the present" (Teski and Climo 1995:3). The very act of noticing or seeing can be generational in what is visually captured, when both the youth and the adults who know them may be from different genders, classes, and races. Think of older people paying particular attention to how the young dress or mark themselves. They may notice the navel piercings or cropped shirts of informants or students. This is an observation from a particular location that normalizes one look and exoticizes another. Meanwhile, other young people looking at those same youth might notice the type of jewelry piercing the navel, to see whether it is straight or bent barbells, captive bead rings, or labrets. Foucault looked for ways that official memories, continually reproduced through mass media, do not account for how marginalized people want to tell the stories of things. And Frigga Haug (1987) and her colleagues in working on female sexualization employed "memory work" to account for women's inserting themselves into particular social relations, relations that construct their femininity in certain ways.

The relationship of memories to power is publicly meaningful in relation to who speaks them: "the purposes and uses of memories are determined by who I is that voices them. The 'who' of the memory voice is often a question of power" (ibid.:2). Groups and individuals come into conflict over whose memories are the right ones and over the differences between official and unofficial memories. Hence, connecting memory as performative with its relationship to power, memory is "an active production of meanings and interpretations, strategic in character and capable of influencing the present" (Passerini 1983:195, quoted in Radstone 2000:10).

Adults have memories of many events, feelings, and interactions that we bring with us and rework when we research youth. These memories might be of fireworks after Fourth of July picnics, of having to wait to get water because the "colored fountain" was broken, of pain at the death of a parent, of experiences in the wind-swept internment camps for Japanese Americans during World War II, or of being excluded from the cool groups of kids. Our memories are related to our race, class, gender, and generational positions, that is, to powerful identity markers; they are both personal and cultural.

People are born within particular political climates, climates that can shape the shared values of many in a generation. When generations talk to each other, there are barriers that must be crossed in order to communicate. Think of discussions between second- and third-wave feminists, between civil rights activists and their children, between professors and students. When adults from one generation approach informants from another, we produce particular memories in the course of the work, and then we also employ particular memories for narrative goals when writing up the research.

Youth

Ethnographers of youth work to access how their subjects make sense of the world. Conceptualizing them as informants who can tell us about their perspectives of a particular culture helps researchers avoid thinking of them as unable to adequately describe their situations. The dangers of the filter of a developmental approach lie in its framing adolescents as hormone driven or, to use Nancy Lesko's phrase, "acting their age" (2000). The phrase "acting their age" implies that adults do not act our age. The need to listen carefully, or to find a way to take seriously the words of youth, depends not only on methodological issues but on theoretical ones as well. If we view youth as incomplete adults, then that "less-than" perspective will shape how we approach them. "Less than" is different from recognizing, as part of a structural analysis, that youth occupy a less powerful status than adults. There is a strong methodological and theoretical history of taking a particular stance when less powerful groups are studied. In the field of disability studies, for example, Bogdan and Taylor (1994) assumed, in their study of people labeled mentally retarded, that their informants could speak meaningfully, authoritatively, and informatively about their lives. This was a radical assumption. The researchers positioned themselves to learn from their informants, when most others did not imagine that people with intellectual disabilities could communicate with any thoughtful or reflective competence about their lives.

Ethnographers apply the methodological guideline that researchers should position themselves to learn from their informants, but although this research approach means that all informants should be our teachers, it does not take into account the unequal power differences between adults and youth. "Studying up" and "studying down" may rely on the same principle that researchers must learn from informants, but the strategies differ in how to take the other seriously. One of these strategies includes taking the position that youth are knowledgeable about their lives and able to understand social meanings.

Youth occupy a less powerful position in relation to adults, as a variety of writers including Grossberg (1992), Lesko (2000), Wyn and White (1997), and many others have noted. Grossberg has argued that the category of youth serves adults rather than the youth themselves (1992:176). Ferguson, who studied the construction of black masculinity in public elementary schools, said that when she began her study, she "underestimated the enormous chasm of power that separated grown-ups and young people" (2001:13). One of the ways this power differential occurs is through the social construction of adolescence as a transitional period between childhood and adulthood (Wyn and White 1997). The formative quality of this depiction, for example, means that youths' words will be taken to represent them at an incomplete stage of life. Mayall (1996) and Alldred (1998) discuss some of the implications of treating young people as "cognitive incompetents." These include underestimating young people's abilities to describe with any authority their own subjectivity. Narrators who address power dynamics foreground youths' lack of power in relation to adults rather than their status as incomplete adults.

In describing youths' low social status in relation to adults, I do not romanticize them. Certainly, as David Buckingham describes, young people are "increasingly seen as threatened and endangered" and at the same time "also increasingly perceived as a threat to the rest of us" (2000:3). However contradictory young people's social representation, the low status of adults who work with them, the lack of access young people have to represent their perspectives in the public realm, and the amount of time they spend in institutional settings under the control of adults all mark their place in the hierarchy.

Appadurai's (1992) discussion of the significance of hierarchy in relation to "natives" as used in anthropology is a helpful metaphor for describing this concern. Appadurai argues that we do not use the word "native" "uniformly to refer to people who are born in certain places and, thus, belong to them" (34). He says that, rather, "natives are not only persons who are from certain places, and belong to those places, but they are also those who are somehow *incarcerated*, or confined in those places" (35, emphasis in the original). Appadurai analyzes the multiple ways that this confinement works but emphasizes that the "critical part" is that natives "are confined by what they know, feel, and believe. They are prisoners of their 'mode of thought'" (35). Appadurai's description of "natives" and their intellectual confinement is similar to youth, and their confinement, either by their hormones, immaturity, or lack of experience. It is this confinement that makes them lower on the hierarchy. Ethnographic studies of youth must confront this problem of hierarchy.

Discussion

To summarize thus far: first, ethnographers have adolescent memories that engage them when they either do fieldwork or analyze their data; also, ethnographers employ memories to particular narrative and rhetorical effect. In other words, placed in the text, these memories increase the narrative authority of the researcher. Additionally, ethnographers' own memories of youth infiltrate their fieldwork and their developing conceptions of the youth they are studying. Furthermore, adolescents occupy a status that is hierarchically lower than adults with regard to power, and this relationship is problematic.

What do these concerns mean for ethnographic scholarship on youth? Ethnographers need to name and interrogate the memories that we face when we research young people. There are multiple ways to do this interrogative work, including asking the relationship of individual memories to particular identity markers, questioning their ideological foundations, and looking at the effects on one's thinking about data or students. The following example comes from a research project on youth.

In a study of college women's understanding of the vocabulary of gender, I used focus groups as part of the method of studying how these informants' understanding of gender shifted when they went to college and majored in particular fields. The young graduate students who were researchers with me on the Vocabularies of Gender project and I found ourselves using our memories of adolescence when we discussed what our informants said. This tactic was both a resource and a barrier. The filters we used to hear their comments differed, but many of our discussions during data analysis evoked talk of "when I was their age." Class was a significant issue in the focus groups for multiple reasons. The site of the case study was a private university where a number of upper-middle-class students attended. Consumer goods were also significant codes for constructing and reading identities. And these women talked a lot about "things," their stuff.

In this example, a Greek American student from a strict family spoke of a significant topic, the hegemony of particular fashion codes. Mallory defended her shopping patterns:

Sometimes my friends are on me like, "I can't believe you spent $40 or $50 on that shirt" or something. And like, that's fine that they want to say that. . . . But, like . . . when I was in high school, like, the Gap was the store that was right next to, like, all of our houses. So, pretty much everyone wore Gap clothes. And now that I'm at Upstate U., it's, like, K. Johns is the thing that's, like, right down the road from you, and if you don't have the money, or if you have the money, you're still going in there. Because people, like, if you're, if you're with a group of friends that go in there, then you're going to go in there. And if you like something from there, then you're, then you're going to want to buy it. So, like, I just think that coming here maybe I've become a little bit more materialistic, but I don't, I don't think that has to do with the fact that I'm watching other girls and the way they're dressing. I think it's that, like, the resources here and, like, the, the access for clothing here is a lot, is different than it was at home. [Pause] 'Cause, like, I don't really appreciate when people tell me that they think I'm, like, a snob or something like that just because I'm wearing a shirt that I like, really liked, and decided to get that instead of spending my money on something different. I, I kinda realized that as I began this year. And it's just not, like, it's not because I like what other girls are wearing or am jealous of them. But it's like I have my own style, and I, if I like something, I'll get it.

Mallory shared what she took for granted as she discussed her style, her situation, and how this understanding shifted over the two years she participated in the focus groups. Mallory was a "good girl" in the sense that she always wanted to please us at the project, so she worked to engage with our questions even if they were not concerns that occupied her without our prodding. She tried to answer our questions descriptively, not to give us what we wanted but to engage fully.

Often, when she spoke, or particularly later when we coded data, I thought back on my own experiences struggling with fashion and identity when I was younger. I started adolescence with two skirts, a navy pleated skirt, and a plaid pleated skirt. Since we had to wear skirts to school, my wardrobe was limited. At college, I was on such a limited budget that I can count on the fingers of one hand the number of times I bought clothes. It is not that I did not want them; it was that I did not think I could afford them. So when I heard Mallory describe her thinking process about buying clothes—that when you go into a store, whether you have the money or not, you might buy something—I invoked memories of my contrasting adolescence. The research assistants also drew on their memories to make sense of Mallory's assumption that every penny does not count. Their memories of being working-class high school students made Mallory's assumption about her peers' privileges being the norm stand out for them. They saw her defense of "if you go into the store with your friends, you're going to buy something" as a reflection of how invisible her privilege was to her. What were the differences between the researchers' and informants' college years? Is it that she had much more money than we ever did? Was it that Upstate University was more deeply enmeshed in a consumer-driven culture than my former university? Was I less concerned about my image because of my counterculture attitudes? As I asked myself these questions I saw that looking at my memories took away my focus from Mallory's struggle to negotiate her identity in relation to shopping, consuming, and fashion.

This is one of memory's dangers for ethnographers of youth. It takes us away from our informants' understandings of the world and turns us back in on ourselves. This turning is not always negative, because it can help researchers become more thoughtful about the data. In our case, for example, it led to discussions about privilege, the current nature of consumption, what cues college women employ to read each other, and other topics of significance. But it is something that must be worked through. It is not enough to say the times, consumption patterns, and the world are all different now. For this is how memories creep in and perhaps take us away from important questions that need to be asked. What ways of thinking does Mallory draw on to make sense of her presentation of self in relation to others? When she conducts surveillance on others, or others do this to her, what does it mean? How much does she participate in it? How does Mallory's class position push her to see her patterns of consumption in particular ways? How does Mallory understand the tension between the individualist emphasis present in the possibility of having her "own style" and the pressures of a consumer economy that push her to go to a boutique because her friends are going? What kind of observer is she of Upstate University culture? How does she articulate her struggles?

Conclusion

My argument here is that although memories may be used to help researchers and teachers access informants on the margins, there is a great danger that they will be used to solidify the adult narrator's or the adult teacher's authority in relation to young informants. Ann Ferguson also struggles with this problem in *Bad Boys*. She describes herself having to make the switch from "learning about boys" to "learning from them" (2001:14). This required a shift in power dynamics, partly accomplished by having one of the "difficult" students she studied become her research assistant. The Vocabularies of Gender researchers also tried to accomplish this switch by asking the informants in the focus groups to become research consultants.

This chapter has spent less time articulating the significance for youth of adults' memories. There are many examples of the noteworthy role that adults' memories have for helping young people confront complicated situations, figure out actions, and present the possibility for a future, as well as providing impetus for a research agenda. Since personal, cultural, and social memories are interconnected, when adults tell young people stories of their lives, these stories can be important for social change because they add in what is often left out. Even though groups and generations contest memories, it is commonly said that without a history a group has no future, so that the process of naming memories and their contributions to history is particularly important as marginalized groups reconstruct knowledge. Carolyn Steedman's *Landscape for a Good Woman* was significant in making space for a particular kind of working-class autobiography that had not yet been recounted (Steedman 1987). In *Lucky*, Alice Sebold's searing memoir of her rape while a student at Syracuse University, the author reports an exchange with her professor, the poet Tess Gallagher:

> Somehow I ended up telling her my story. And she listened. She was not bowled over; not shocked, not even scared of the burden this might make me as her student. She was not motherly or nurturing, though she was both those things in time. She was matter-of-fact, her head nodding in acknowledgement. She listened for the pain in my words, not to the narrative itself. She was intuiting what it meant to me, what was most important, what, in that confused mass of experience and yearning she heard in my voice, she could single out to give back. (Sebold 1999:98)

In the description of this conversation, we might interpret Gallagher's response as significant to Sebold because Gallagher can focus on her student, rather than on her own reaction. Yet Gallagher uses her own experiences, or memories of them, to respond. It is what enables her to respond this way.

I have not emphasized the significance of memories because I have focused on the adult researcher (and narrator) and the youthful informant (and subject). The logic of youthful views, even with critique, needs to occupy the central space in a study of youth. But in other relationships such as teacher-student, parent-child, older friend–younger friend, and adviser-mentor, memories can build and enrich both the relationship and social views. These issues are beyond the scope of this discussion, but I want to underscore that this argument is not a critique of memory in human relationships. Rather, it is an analysis of how memories work in ethnographic texts about youth.

There are more issues to be explored. First, there is the question of the identity of the narrator whose memory enters the text. Does the racial or gender identity of the researcher make a difference in relation to the function of the memories? This is the question of the relationship of memory to identity markers. Does the identity marker's relationship to power relations matter? For example, when an informant in the Vocabularies of Gender study referred to herself as lower middle class or "not rich" but described objects that she owned in high school, a young researcher used memories of her own working-class high school experience to interrogate this description. Does this use of memory enable analysis of privilege? Or researchers of color may draw on memories of their high school experiences to highlight informants' skin privilege. Is memory in this case a resource for understanding racism?

Second, would it be useful to think of adults doing ethnographic studies of youth as cross-cultural researchers? The novelist Graham Greene referred to childhood as a different place when he wrote that adults are "emigrants from a country we remember too little of" (quoted in Sherry 1989:6). If we speak with youth because they represent a particular location from which to view the world, then we need to imagine them as people with varying degrees of expertise on this world. In cross-cultural work, we see informants as capable of being articulate about their lives. This is a stance that adult researchers of youth need to take. This does not mean that adult researchers have to agree with youth. It does mean that we have to take their views seriously. Perry studied high school students' views of whiteness and described the significance of studying high school students to learn about how people make meaning of whiteness:

> Contrary to common stereotypes, teens are bold and resourceful human beings with keen insights into society that are too often dismissed. Moreover, adolescence is an excellent age for observing and analyzing identity formation. It is the time when youth must face the fact of impending adult status and embody the rules, values, and roles the society calls them to fulfill. (2002:10)

Perry illustrates her respect for young people while acknowledging the pressures of social expectations they face. Rather than view youth as transitional or inadequate observers of American culture, we can also see them as knowledgeable observers of identity formation.

Sturken argues that "it is important not to allow discussions of memory to bog down in questions of reliability. Memory is crucial to the understanding of a culture precisely because it indicates collective desires, needs, and self-definitions. We need to ask not whether a memory is true but rather what its telling reveals about how the past affects the present" (1997:2). In the case of ethnographies of youth, researchers need to ask how their own memories affect their "ways of seeing" (Berger 1973). Memories are not a form of research bias in the sense that without them the research would be more pure. Memory is intrinsic to ethnographic work because memory is part of the human experience, and humans are the "research instrument" (Bogdan and Biklen 2003) in this kind of research. But an ethnographer's memory can romanticize or demonize youth.

Adult memories written in ethnographies of youth tend to pull the narrator toward the center of the story, emphasizing the "I was there" orientation and the narrator's authority. Performed in this way, memory serves as another of multiple ways that researchers increase their narrative authority in texts. As such, it emphasizes the power differential between adults and youths rather than the logic of youthful views. This argument does not mean, obviously, that when adults study youth they should not be critical of some of their views. Lefkowitz (1997) employs a useful analysis of the middle-class athletes and popular boys who raped a girl with intellectual disabilities in Glen Ridge, New Jersey. But because he emphasizes the role of his memory of himself as a high school student who knew the popular kids because he was not one of them, he has no strategy to explain his narrow and medicalized understanding of the girl who was raped. Could we say that because schools did not practice inclusion when he was in high school, he has no memories of kids with disabilities and hence fails to portray her with any of the complexity that he does the boys? Had he approached the girl to teach him about her perspectives as he did the boys, he might have been able to resist some of the more conventional understandings that infiltrate the work. Because all adults were once youth, when adults study youth the issue of memory is a significant power dynamic in the research process.

NOTE

This chapter has appeared previously in *Qualitative Inquiry* and is reprinted here.

Many people commented on different versions of this work. Special thanks to Lesley Bogad, David Buckingham, Norman Denzin, Kathleen Weiler, Gaby Weiner, and Lyn Yates. Earlier versions of this chapter were presented at La Trobe University, Melbourne, Australia, 1999; Youth, Popular Culture, and Schooling Conference, Syracuse, NY.

REFERENCES

Alldred, P. (1998). Ethnography and discourse analysis: Dilemmas in representing the voices of children. In J. Ribbens and R. Edwards (eds.), *Feminist dilemmas in qualitative research*, pp. 147–170. London: Sage.

Antze, P., and Lambek, M. (eds.) (1996). *Tense past: Cultural essays in trauma and memory.* New York: Routledge.

Appadurai, A. (1992). Putting hierarchy in its place. In G. Marcus (ed.), *Rereading Cultural Anthropology,* pp. 34–47. Durham, NC: Duke University Press.

Bal, M. (1999). Introduction. In M. Bal, J. Crewe, and L. Spitzer (eds.), *Acts of memory: Cultural recall in the present.* Hanover, NH: Dartmouth College and the University Press of New England.

Berger, J. (1973). *Ways of seeing.* New York: Viking.

Bettie, J. (2003). *Women without class: Girls, race, and identity.* Berkeley: University of California Press.

Bogdan R., and Biklen, S. (2003). *Qualitative research for education,* 4th ed. Boston: Allyn and Bacon.

Bogdan, R., and Taylor, S. (1994). *Inside out: The social meaning of mental retardation.* New York: Teachers College Press.

Buckingham, D. (2000). *After the death of childhood: Growing up in the age of electronic media.* Cambridge, UK: Polity.

Cattell, M., and Climo, J. (2002). Meaning in social memory and history: Anthropological perspectives. In J. Climo and M. Cattell (eds.), *Social memory and history: Anthropological perspectives,* pp. 1–36. Walnut Creek, CA: AltaMira.

Conway, M. (1997). The inventory of experience: Memory and identity. In J. Pennebacker, D. Paez, and B. Rime (eds.), *Collective memory of political events,* pp. 21–45. Mahwah, NJ: Lawrence Erlbaum.

Damasio, A. (1999). *The feeling of what happens: Body and emotion in the making of consciousness.* San Diego, CA: Harcourt.

Ferguson, A. (2001). *Bad boys: Public schools in the making of black masculinity.* Ann Arbor: University of Michigan Press.

Feuer, L. S. (1969). *The conflict of generations: The character and significance of student movements.* New York: Basic Books.

Foley, D. (1990). *Learning capitalist culture.* Philadelphia: University of Pennsylvania Press.

Fordham, S. (1996). *Blacked out: Dilemmas of race, identity, and success at Capital High.* Chicago: University of Chicago Press.

Grossberg, L. (1992). *We Gotta Get Out of This Place.* New York: Routledge.

Haug, F. (ed.) (1987). *Female sexualization.* London: Verso.

Ishino, I. (1995). Memories and their unintended consequences. In M. Teski and J. Climo (eds.), *The labyrinth of memory: Ethnographic journeys,* pp. 185–202. Westport, CT: Bergin and Garvey.

Jedlowski, P. (2001). Memory and sociology. *Time and Society* 10(1): 29–44.

Klein, N. (1997). *The history of forgetting: Los Angeles and the erasure of memory.* London: Verso.

Lambek, M., and Antze, P. (1996). Forecasting memory. In P. Antze and M. Lambek (eds.), *Tense past: Cultural essays in trauma and memory,* pp. xi–xxxviii. New York: Routledge.

Lefkowitz, B. (1997). *Our guys.* Berkeley: University of California Press.

Lesko, N. (2000). *Act your age.* New York: Routledge.

Mannheim, K. (1952). The problem of generations. In K. Mannheim (ed.), *Essays in the sociology of knowledge*, pp. 276–321. London: Routledge and Kegan Paul.

Mayall, B. (1996). *Children, health, and the social order.* Buckingham, UK: Open University Press.

McRobbie, A. (1991). *Feminism and youth culture.* Boston: Unwin Hyman.

Passerini, L. (1996). *Autobiography of a generation.* Hanover, NH: Wesleyan University Press.

Passerini, L. (1983). Memory. *History Workshop Journal* 15 (Spring).

Perry, P. (2002). *Shades of white: White kids and racial identities in high school.* Durham, NC: Duke University Press.

Proweller, A. (1998). *Constructing female identities: Meaning making in an upper-middle-class youth culture.* Albany: State University of New York Press.

Radstone, S. (2000). Working with memory. In S. Radstone (ed.), *Memory and methodology*, pp. 1–22. Oxford, UK: Berg.

Robins, T. (1995). Remembering the future: The cultural study of memory. In B. Adam and S. Allan (eds.), *Theorizing culture: An interdisciplinary critique after postmodernism*, pp. 201–213. New York: New York University Press.

Rubin, D. C. (ed.) (1996). *Remembering our past: Studies in autobiographical memory.* New York: Cambridge University Press.

Sebold, A. (1999). *Lucky.* Boston: Little, Brown.

Sherry, N. (1989). *The life of Graham Greene,* vol. 1. New York: Viking.

Steedman, C. (1987). *Landscape for a good woman.* New Brunswick, NJ: Rutgers University Press.

Sturken, M. (1997). *Tangled Memories: The Vietnam War, the AIDS Epidemic, and the Politics of Remembering.* Berkeley: University of California Press.

Swanson, G. (2000). Memory, subjectivity and intimacy: The historical formation of the modern self and the writing of female autobiography. In S. Radstone (ed.), *Memory and methodology*, pp. 111–132. Oxford, UK: Berg.

Teski, M., and Climo, J. (eds.) (1995). *The labyrinth of memory: Ethnographic journeys.* Westport, CT: Bergin and Garvey.

Thorne, B. (1993). *Gender play.* New Brunswick, NJ: Rutgers University Press.

Walker, J. C. (1988). *Louts and legends: Male youth culture in an inner-city school.* Sydney, Australia: Allen and Unwin.

White, H. (1987). *The content of the form: Narrative discourse and historical representation.* Baltimore: Johns Hopkins University Press.

Wyn, J., and White, R. (1997). *Rethinking youth.* Sydney, Australia: Allen and Unwin.

Chapter 11

Power-Puff Ethnography/Guerrilla Research
Children as Native Anthropologists

Elizabeth Chin

I have learned that, in order to alter this society, we have
to forge covenants with those who have been cast out.
—Jim Hubbard, *Shooting Back from the Reservation*

For decades now, anthropologists have attempted to unhinge our discipline from its colonialist frames. Challenging constructions of both
"native" and "anthropologist," many have collaborated with research "subjects" or embarked on autoethnography in order to critically examine
what it is that we do. In collaborations with children, my own work has
endeavored to engage in just this type of imaginative repositioning, a project that is equally political and intellectual in its aim. In this chapter, my
interest is in thinking about the potential of collaborative research with
children for shifting the ways in which we as anthropologists view our
own work, its importance, and its purpose. Drawing upon Vygotsky's notion of the "zone of proximal development," my aim is to show how collaborative research with children allows both researcher and researched to
reach new understandings about their worlds. Much discussion has already taken place regarding the merits and limitations of so-called insider
or outsider perspectives; in contrast, the question of age—and more specifically adulthood—as it pertains to researcher/experts has not been well
articulated. In anthropology, the powerful normativity of research as adult
remains fundamentally unquestioned. Doing collaborative research with
children challenges the assumption that to be an anthropologist is also to
be a grown-up. In retooling research processes and products themselves so

as to be accessible to and created by children as native anthropologists, there is much to learn about our own discipline and the ways in which it continues to construct its objects.

Vygotsky: Practical and Theoretical Concerns for Developing the Discipline

For me, the apparent inability of many to think of children as competent, thinking, aware beings is key to understanding the problems we face in creating an anthropology of children and, more specifically, an anthropology (and body of social theory more generally) that *takes children seriously.* Here I mean not the *idea* or the theory of children, but children themselves. Defining the child is notoriously difficult, even slippery. It is a category diversely understood to be positional, generational, legal, chronological, and developmental.

The developmental theories of Russian psychologist Lev Vygotsky are particularly useful for anthropologists and an anthropology of children because rather than viewing individual development as self-contained, Vygotsky understood it to be a profoundly social process. According to Vygotsky, it is through social interaction that certain important developmental spaces are in fact created, an idea exemplified by his Zone of Proximal Development (ZPD). The ZPD is a conceptual space that emerges in problem-solving interactions between experts and novices. In the ZPD, Vygotsky theorized that novices are capable of doing things above their individual developmental level: in other words, in social interaction we are capable of more than we are individually. This idea has been tremendously influential for reshaping understandings of children's development, in particular because it emphasizes the active engagement of children as social agents. Moreover, Vygotsky's dialectical approach lays the groundwork for understanding development as inherently dynamic and transformative in ways that most dominant developmental theories do not. Here I want to focus (uncharacteristically for me) on the transformative and developmental effects on adults who step into the ZPD with children.

Vygotsky viewed development as featuring what he termed "crises," which can be described as sudden developmental leaps. For him, development is not a smooth, accumulative process. Rather, he argued, as van der Veer explains, that "small quantitative changes lead to abrupt qualitative changes," an idea illustrated metaphorically by the example of water that heats gradually but then abruptly changes to steam (van der Veer 1997:5). If child development is typified by crises and leaps, then retooling adult-oriented disciplines to be accessible to children as collaborators similarly requires crises of its own. This is the adult side of the dialectical developmental relationship, and an aspect that has been neglected: entering the ZPD challenges the expert as well as the novice. Like any sort of teaching, teaching children to be anthropologists is much more complicated than simply downscaling adult-sized efforts for (supposedly) pint-sized minds: what novices learn is not a miniaturized version of the "real" thing. From the adult side, then, I argue that retooling our own competencies so as to be approachable by novices requires us, as experts, to expand our own capabilities. Inherent in such expansion is a developmental crisis in Vygotsky's sense, and one that results in important and high-level learning for experts. This effect is amplified as the developmental distance between experts and novices grows: it requires more cognitive sophistication and reimagining to teach ten-year-olds to be anthropologists than it does to attempt the same thing with college students.

Let me provide an example from a different field. In my other life I am a dancer, and teaching dance illustrates perfectly the problem of so-called simplification: slowing something down does not necessarily make it easier. When teaching complex, syncopated body rhythms, slowing them down for novices is a tricky task. The dance step is not the same when it is slowed down; the relationship between the parts is transformed, and the steps are usually more difficult to do slowly than they are to do at the proper tempo: it is physically impossible to do a jumping turn in slow motion, and syncopated foot movements done slowly must be coordinated completely differently than when done at speed. Experienced dancers learn new things about dancing through the slowness required to teach beginners; this is one reason that teaching is an important part of almost any dancer's career. This is true of social science research as well, and this is why we have so much potentially to learn from researching with kids and not just about them. As we slow down and take apart what we think we already know, we are likely to move into new territories. Amy Chak (2001), in a discussion of adult "sensitivity" to children in the ZPD, notes that adults entering the ZPD with children must use high-level abstractions, distancing, and other specific cognitive tools to evaluate what it is they are doing. This process requires a bringing to consciousness, even the verbalization, of much that is taken for granted or unexamined about the problem at hand. It is this process of abstraction and bringing-to-consciousness that challenges and expands the expertise of the expert. In engaging with beginners, especially children, anthropologists must break down and examine much about the discipline that goes unsaid and even unthought. It is the interaction itself, then, that provokes new ways of thinking about and entering the anthropological field. Certainly, the kind of knowledge that child native anthropologists can produce is not the same as that produced by adults. Ten-year-olds can hardly be expected to generate complex statistical models and conduct multivariate regression analyses (something I am incapable of doing myself, by the way). Nor would we expect them to masterfully wield the latest neo-Marxist or post-modern theories in exploring the world around them. However, children can and do produce knowledge that is worth paying attention to exactly because it is not the sort of knowledge we tend to produce ourselves. In my experience with kids as ethnographers, the intense interaction that was required during the training and research process yielded much that was unexpected, in terms of both children's educational process and my own pursuit of ethnographic knowledge.

Children as Native Anthropologist

In 1970, Delmos Jones argued that the use of native anthropologists has not led to the development of a native anthropology (1970:20). For Jones, native anthropology is specifically non-Western in its precepts and as-sumptions (21). What he was getting at is the problem that incorporating "them" (say, a black anthropologist like himself) into the practices and ideas of anthropology is not the radical move it might seem, particularly because it does not involve change in the discipline's intellectual assump-tions. Jones did not advocate that anthropology as a discipline go native; rather, he was interested in having the discipline engage with and make use of ideas that were non-Western. Jones was proposing that anthropol-ogy should move beyond assimilating otherness to a Western intellectual mode for understanding difference and become fully anthropological by the creation of truly multi- or transcultural intellectual and investigative practice. Drawing from such notions, the idea of having children as native anthropologists strikes me as necessary in part because it can offer a view-point that is specifically nonadult in its precepts and assumptions—even though it could also be practiced by adults. Like Jones, I do not have in mind the complete reworking of anthropology as we know it, but I am convinced that thinking of a children's native anthropology allows us to reimagine the anthropological endeavor in important ways.

This idea seems particularly radical—even crazy—in part because the construction of the academy as a child-free zone is nearly unassailable. Kids in the academy are anomalous, and the occasional child genius who enrolls at MIT at the age of nine is a freakish occurrence. My idea is not that children should go to college or that there is no difference between kids and adults. I am a proponent of recognizing children's agency, but I take issue with those advocates of children's agency who claim any exercise of adult power or limit-setting with children is a hegemonic attack spawned solely by oppressive social relations. Children do need adult guidance, though the ways in which such guidance is offered is indeed quite often hegemonic. Legions of street children worldwide attest to the ability of even very young children to live independently, but few would argue that this is an ideal or desirable state of affairs.

What adults can do, however, is to approach interactions with children with the expectation that kids are capable of a great deal (Christensen and James 2000; Corsaro 1997; Schwartzman 2001). This has been seen, for example, in studies recognizing the importance and generativity of children's peer cultures (Corsaro 1997; Corsaro and Nelson 2003), their capacity for independence (Hecht 1998), and their capacity for social action (Fine, Roberts, and Torre 2004; King 1994). As children and adults together create zones of proximal development, both are likely to explore surprising new territories, each from their unique positions and in relation to their unique interaction. This interaction, as anthropologists studying youth have pointed out, may be understood along two axes: child-adult and insider-outsider, in which child and anthropologist are both expert and novice. It is for these reasons that it does not seem to me to be far-fetched to insist that anthropological collaborations with children are eminently possible and deeply valuable. When I was thinking about the place of children in social theory, and the place of children in the scholarship about children, I was struck by the degree to which we as scholars are invested in studying and theorizing children but are not invested in allowing them to participate in that process, despite more recent attempts to give voice to children in much qualitative work. Our power to allow (or not) children to appear, to be heard, is a power that we have, and it is a power we exercise more often than not, and it is a power we depend on to secure our own positions in the academy. Thus, we mistake it for who we are: if we are not in control of the research and writing, what sort of expertise might we claim? How will we get jobs or get promoted or finish our degrees if our voices and ideas do not trump those of the people we study—especially if they are children?

The researched are often disenfranchised by a research process that excludes their active participation because they are understood as uninformed or uninitiated. Children, because they are widely thought to be developmentally incapable of really understanding the complexities of research, are further disenfranchised. Children are generally understood to be beneficiaries of the knowledge produced by the experts that later "helps" them somehow. The result is a model of research that by its very design profoundly limits our understanding of the children with whom we work. We have seen with the development of feminist theory and research methods that research can be severely hampered by faulty assumptions about the researched (Lawless 1992; Stacey 1998). With children, such faulty assumptions continue in force, relatively unnoticed.

Our dominant research models give highest value to research designed primarily to perpetuate the academy and the hierarchies of knowledge and position that sustain it. As practitioners of feminist methodologies have illuminated so well, even so-called liberal or radical research can still be caught up in the reproduction of paternalistic, hegemonic power structures (Abu-Lughod 1990). Developing strategies for conducting social science research that does not reproduce those power structures is intensely difficult in part because it is delegitimated from the beginning: if it does not reproduce the power structure by conforming to "the rules," then research is labeled as, well, not research. From much experience, I know that most scholars still consider absurd the notion of children anthropologists and of an anthropology conducted by children. Jones's charge of the lack of a native anthropology in the terms he describes is as valid today as it was over thirty years ago. We should always be suspicious of agendas, articulated or not, that make the claim that so-and-so is not capable of doing whatever-it-is competently. My proposal, then, is this: it is not the kids who are incapable of doing the anthropology; it is the anthropology that is incapable of incorporating the kids.

Some Examples

Up to this point I have painted the grimmest picture possible in order to starkly outline the problem. There is, after all, a growing group whose members advocate children's participation in social change and in social research. They come from disparate settings and backgrounds and do not as yet often come together to exert collective pressure on disciplines or communities. Shooting Back Inc., based in Washington, D.C., and the Institute for Community Research (ICR), based in Hartford, Connecticut, are two such examples. Both these organizations illustrate the kind of extraordinary work that young people can turn out if given the time and the resources to do so. Although guided by different philosophies and approaches, both organizations share a child-centered process that hands the control of work and research over to the young people themselves.

Jim Hubbard of Shooting Back is a photojournalist who has been working with children since 1989. At that time, he was shooting a photo essay on life in a homeless shelter in Washington, D.C. He decided to teach some of the children how to take photographs themselves, and this ultimately led to the founding of Shooting Back Inc., an organization that recruits professional photojournalists to volunteer their time with kids, teaching them how to take pictures using 35 mm cameras (not the point-and-shoot kind), develop film, and make black-and-white prints. Later, Hubbard organized national and international shows of the children's work, and he has published several books as well, including *Shooting Back* (Hubbard 1991), a book of those first children's photos, and *Shooting Back from the Reservation* (Hubbard 1994), photos taken by Native American children from communities as far flung as Arizona, New Mexico, Minnesota, and North Dakota. One of the most powerful aspects of this work is the purposeful way in which photography has been used and interpreted by all involved as a way for disenfranchised children (black, poor and homeless; or Native American, poor and rural) to speak about their worlds. The visions and voices are tremendously powerful. The seriousness with which the books and exhibitions were presented underscores the important point that children's work can stand on its own and is worth examining for its own sake. In all of this, Hubbard takes on the role of editor, not impresario. The books begin with short introductions, no more than five or six pages of text, in which Hubbard explains the genesis of Shooting Back and offers some of his own thoughts on what the work has meant to him. After this, his voice is silent. The pages are dominated by the photos taken by children, photo captions, and commentaries by the photographers or, in some cases, comments by children who viewed the photographs on exhibition.

The very basic act of putting real cameras into kids' hands was (and is?)

relatively radical. (Won't they break them? Aren't 35 mm SLR cameras too complicated for kids?) The photographs themselves belie such fears, demonstrating kids' competency in taking what are often extraordinarily good pictures and demonstrating the sometimes more important point that their perspectives are emphatically their own. The scope and range of photos (even after realizing that the images included in the books are chosen by Hubbard) do not reproduce the schemas and obsessions of the journalistic or academic gaze on these children's worlds. Many of the images in the books are accompanied by commentaries of the children who took them. Some discuss the process of taking the photos; others offer their interpretations of the finished photograph or explain why they took the picture in the first place. The cover photo of *Shooting Back* is of a young boy suspended in the midst of a back flip: he is arched in midair, stomach to the sky, hands and feet suspended, miraculously, at equal levels from the sidewalk. In explaining how he took the photo of the flip, the photographer recounts that they had to do it over and over again to get the photo right. The person who took the photo is a young, black homeless boy. Poor, African American children are generically portrayed as delayed, impulsive, undereducated, and uncritical. The picture itself challenges these assumptions: it is the result of careful planning, determination, aesthetic vision, practice, expertise, desire, creativity, and knowledge.

It is also worth thinking theoretically about the ways in which the images are the result of the subjects' interaction with the photographers. One of my favorite photos from *Shooting Back from the Reservation* is of an elderly Native American man who is not staring stoically into the distance, or into the camera, but mischievously crinkling up his eyes and sticking out his tongue (75). This photo seems clearly to be a playful moment between a grandfather and grandchild, an elder and a young person from the community, a moment that inverts and toys with age-appropriate roles. The photo speaks of an intimacy that exists because of that specific relationship, a relationship seen, shared, and captured by that particular fifteen-year-old who took the picture. It is probably not an exaggeration to insist that the picture *required* that particular relationship. The idea of the photo, with its frame, is an apt metaphor for ethnography, and the Shooting Back books show the degree to which adult-specified frames sometimes reproduce orthodoxies of knowledge and interpretation; children's perspectives can and do challenge those orthodoxies but too often lie outside our frames of reference. The method has since been used by such organizations as Save the Children, which conducted a project in Vietnam, called Visions of Children Who Can't Hear, that used photographs and photography as a way for hearing-impaired youth to speak about their lives (Theis, Pickup, et al. 1999). As it stands, of course, the Shooting Back work does not quite constitute ethnography. But as an example of how sophisticated children's output can be, Shooting Back provides much food for thought.

The Institute for Community Research (ICR) is located in Hartford, Connecticut, one of the poorest cities in the United States. The Institute takes on an array of policy-related and community work and in recent years has initiated an institute of youth research where the staff is made up of high-schoolers recruited from area public schools. Most of them are African American and Latino, from the troubled urban neighborhoods that make up most of the city of 130,000. ICR describes its approach as Youth Participatory Action Research, or Youth PAR. Central to the ICR approach is the insistence that youth (primarily teens) are capable of intelligent independent research and that what they need most is a structure and support in which to develop their capacities. Implicit in the ICR approach is an important element missing from most research with/about children: that youth are citizens too. ICR's approach not only treats youth as citizens but has as its aim expanding youths' ability to take on the work of citizenship in their communities by first putting them in charge of a research effort on a topic identified by youth themselves and then facilitating not only the research but also the formulation of actions designed to move toward positive solutions. In the process, youth researchers not only analyze the world around them but may also transform their perceptions of it and themselves. In a city where only an estimated 30 percent of ninth-graders graduate from high school, ICR's work with Youth PAR is politically and socially forward-thinking.

In a recent Youth PAR study on youth hustling, forty paid ICR youth staff members were augmented by seven "senior youth" who had participated in the previous year's project (Morgan, Pacheco, et al. 2004). ICR strategies specifically emphasize having youth take stock of themselves and other team members in addition to learning such research methods as interviewing and conducting pile sorts. Training includes attention to various aspects of identity including race, class, and gender, and youth researchers are urged to use this knowledge to help the research team to work more effectively. Participatory research methods have been around for several decades, gaining ground in a variety of settings, but their use with youth is relatively recent. Through their work with youth researchers,

ICR is at the forefront of developing effective models for Youth PAR. Their work shows just how effective it can be to take kids seriously as researchers. In part because the ICR strategy makes use of summer employment as a way to recruit and compensate youth, ICR's focus is on older youth and teens. Their methods, with some adjustments, can also be effectively used with younger children. Involving elementary-school children as researchers remains a much rarer project, in part because of logistical barriers—it is a very time-consuming enterprise—and in part because of lingering beliefs on the part of many that younger children are not capable of conducting research. My own experiences in working with fifth-graders in New Haven and Los Angeles have shown me that such assumptions are spurious. There is, of course, some lower limit where enlisting children as researchers is likely to be untenable. Rather than putting that limit in place primarily through a lack of imagination, we ought to vigorously explore worlds with children to locate that limit.

Investing in Crisis

Teaching children how to be anthropologists has, in turn, taught me a great deal about anthropology, and particularly about the questionable boundaries we maintain between "us" and "them." The hierarchy of power between the researcher and the researched parallels all sorts of other power structures and relationships to which kids are subjected on a regular basis, most obviously those of student/teacher or parent/child. As adults who have graduated away from the kids' table, we have a lot invested in maintaining our positions, particularly since it took so long to attain them in the first place. Kids, too, are invested because they have spent most of their lives so far learning the costs of *not* supporting the status quo. But if we do not disrupt it just a little bit—and perhaps only temporarily—we miss things. As I have been finding out, even the attempt at disruption is terribly instructive.

Among the trickiest things is allowing children to take the lead, and then to follow it. First, children must be convinced that this is actually a viable dynamic. Most of their time is spent being dictated to and responding "appropriately," which generally means guessing what the adult wants and producing the correct behavior or response. This is especially the case in schools. Moving away from this dynamic is not always easy to accomplish: in one warm-up exercise I led while studying fifth-graders in an urban public school, we played a version of the game duck, duck, goose, in which people would make up any pair of words as they went around the circle patting heads: cup, cup, saucer; sun, sun, moon; and so on. One boy, when it was his turn, took about three full minutes to choose his word pair, and his distress at having to choose for himself was only alleviated when he ended up choosing a word pair a previous child had already used.

Putting children in charge need not mean entertaining utter chaos, but it does go against the grain of most adults' and children's experiences. The degree to which this is true depends a great deal on class and culture. In the urban public schools where I have worked with fifth-graders, open-ended activities were especially unfamiliar. Allowing children to construct their own interview guides, for instance, can provide a window into ideas and issues that kids themselves find important or interesting. On the whole, such ideas may not reproduce adults' expectations or assumptions about children's points of view. Thus, children's suggestions for questions to consider become a sort of data, even as they are instruments for collecting information. For me, the most productive dynamic has been to monitor and keep track of my own expectations. The distance between my assumptions and children's own interests is often rather large, and as the questionnaires take shape, the tension between my own ideas of what constitutes a proper question and what it is that children really want to know again becomes a rich source of information about the anthropological enterprise.

In work I did with children who would be considered "inner city" in both New Haven, Connecticut, and Los Angeles, California, putting children in charge allowed them to integrate skills that are usually treated (and tested) discretely in the classroom. As they gained skills and confidence, some children often struck out on their own. In my New Haven work, for instance, one girl began taking field notes documenting classroom activities. Later, a group of children who had participated in the New Haven project went out and designed and implemented a study (Chin 2001). The study emerged as the children found themselves needing to do some problem solving. Having received a large number of dolls that they had decided to donate to local daycare centers, members of the class realized they needed a way to decide which dolls to give to which place. The children who had learned to be anthropologists volunteered to figure it out, visiting each center to count and categorize the dolls they already had, seeing the numbers of boys and girls, and figuring out from there which toys would make the best contribution at each site (Chin 2001).

That the children I had taught conducted a study of their own both stunned and humbled me. In having the confidence to solve a problem using anthropology, they had truly become anthropologists. In applying it to a problem in their own worlds, in their own neighborhood, they made anthropology their own, or at least a little piece of it. This is perhaps the element of the work I find most important: its potential to allow children to demonstrate and wield their expertise in a way that expands their human potential. However, this also requires that I as the anthropologist and expert relinquish my stake in being the arbiter of knowledge.

Time restrictions in my Los Angeles work meant that we were not able to proceed quite as far with data analysis and report writing as we had in New Haven; nonetheless, over the course of fifteen weeks, a number of the children became quite adept interviewers. One child, Jose, impressed us all with his confidence and his strengths as both an interviewer and note taker. Arriving on Occidental University's campus to conduct interviews with a soccer coach and an art professor, he spent nearly an hour with each of them, engaged in conversation and furiously taking notes. His confidence, curiosity, literacy, and social skills are not what we might originally have expected, given that he was an "at-risk" child with a disordered home life and performing poorly in school.

This example illustrates an important aspect of teaching children anthropology. The skills required of these native anthropologists are often different from the skills rewarded in classroom settings. In my experience working with kids it is this rich and complex interweaving of skills that seems to result in their moving into new territories, making knowledge their own, and doing so in surprising ways.

This kind of collaborative work does take more time than if it were all conducted by experienced professional social scientists. Children, youth, and teens can conduct quality research but usually not in the time frame or scale that "we" might expect. Many academic researchers do not think the additional time and effort are worth it, in part because their own job security often rests on pumping out an almost inhuman amount of work that is going to be evaluated by other academics. This pressure militates against the kind of time-intensive work required to collaborate with young researchers, but it does not support the idea that such research is always and absolutely of poor quality. In fact, as I discussed in my example about generating interview questions, it is often the *process itself* that produces the most interesting and useful knowledge, rather than the product (data sets) being the most valuable outcome.

The problem is in thinking about what counts in research: what is important, good, useful, and worthwhile. If we value only what adults do, and define the worthwhile as being fundamentally adult, we have created a field of value from which children are barred by definition. In my own work with developing child researchers, I have had to seriously rethink the relationship between researcher and researched and critically understand my own investment in maintaining my expertise as a source of power and control over my young colleagues. Such reflection has not always been pleasant, though it has been extremely valuable. My own understanding of the dangers of being too invested in my own expertise has led me to important reevaluations of what it means to be expert or novice and reawakened my own commitment to upending the hierarchies that inevitably seep into research and teaching relationships.

Children are not novices at everything, either. They are certainly the experts on being children; adults may be former children, but memories of past childhoods are a poor substitute for the actual experiences of current children. The common trope of anthropologist-as-child shunts aside living children who are both culture learners and contemporary citizens, proper members of their communities in ways that anthropologists are not. From this point of view, then, it behooves us to understand development as a task for everyone, not just children. In developing our own perspectives as anthropologists, critically engaging with the expertise of children regarding the worlds they know and understand best is just good old ethnographic practice.

Final Incident (or the Straw That Broke the Camel's Back)

When presenting these ideas at a conference in New York in spring 2001, I was asked, "But why don't you do this kind of work with a group of people who can really benefit from it, like women?" Frankly, I was stunned: after twenty minutes of what I had thought was very cogent discussion of the importance of taking children seriously, my female questioner had absolutely dismissed them as unworthy of concern. That dismissal was a symptom of the very problem I seek to address. My answer then remains the same today: it is hard for me to imagine how collaborating with the disempowered and marginalized can be the wrong thing to do. Children, being profoundly disempowered and marginalized in research and in a host of other arenas, can hardly be understood to be undeserving of the transformative attention and work that social justice efforts imply wherever they are implemented.

Vygotsky is concerned with how the more practiced person can facilitate the learning of the novice. The process of teaching in the service of research has forced me to learn more and think more about my work, as well as about those with whom I am engaged, and to do this in ways that I would not have if I had used another model or method of research. Particularly when the activity entails a mutual exploration of unknown territory, zones of proximal development are opened up for all participants: the experience is not one simply of the novice moving toward the position occupied by the expert. As in any dialectical process, the process itself creates change, flow, and transformation so that, as the work proceeds, the very territory in which it takes place is remapped, redrawn, and re-experienced.

To return to the epigraph to this chapter: I have learned that in order to alter this society we must forge covenants with those who have been cast out. For those of us who view social change or social justice as one of the goals of our work, it is time to forge covenants with those who have been cast out: the children who lie at the very heart of our endeavors.

NOTE

An earlier version of this chapter was presented at the conference "Off the Grid" at New York University and at the conference "Children in their Places" at Brunel University in London. The research was supported by grants from the National Science Foundation and the John and Dora L. Haynes Foundation. Thanks to Amy Best, Maria Avila, Maria Lorena Nunez, Kat, Det. Bob Lopez, Deputy City Attorney Jeanne Kim, Jim Anderson, Jean Schensul, Marlene Berg, and all the former fifth-graders. Beryl Langer and Donna Maeda forced me to clarify myself at key moments. Jenna Lippe-Klein, ever admirable, set me a fine example for everyday activism.

REFERENCES

Abu-Lughod, L. (1990). "Can There Be a Feminist Ethnography?" *Women and Performance: A Journal of Feminist Theory* 5: 7–27.

Bloch, M. (2004). "A Discourse That Disciplines, Governs, and Regulates: The National Research Council's Report on Scientific Research in Education." *Qualitative Inquiry* 96(10): 96–110.

Chak, A. (2001). "Adult Sensitivity to Children's Learning in the Zone of Proximal Development." *Journal for the Theory of Social Behaviour* 31(4): 383–395.

Chin, E. (2001). *Purchasing Power: Black Kids and American Consumer Culture.* Minneapolis: University of Minnesota Press.

Christensen, P., and A. James, eds. 2000. *Research with Children: Perspectives and Practices.* London: Falmer.

Corsaro, W. (1997). *The Sociology of Childhood.* Thousand Oaks, CA: Pine Forge.

Corsaro, W. (1985). *Friendship and Peer Culture in the Early Years.* Norwood, NJ: Ablex.

Corsaro, W., and E. Nelson. (2003). "Children's Collective Activities and Peer Culture in Early Literacy in American and Italian Preschools." *Sociology of Education* 76(3): 209–227.

Fine, M., R. Roberts, and M. E. Torre. (2004). *Echoes of Brown: Youth Documenting and Performing the Legacy of Brown v. Board of Education.* New York: Teacher's College Press.

Hecht, T. (1998). *At Home in the Street: Street Children of Northeast Brazil.* New York: Cambridge University Press.

Hubbard, J., ed. (1994). *Shooting Back from the Reservation: A Photographic View of Life by Native American Youth.* New York: New Press.

Hubbard, J., ed. (1991). *Shooting Back: A Photographic View of Life by Homeless Children.* San Francisco: Chronicle Books.

Jones, D. (1970). "Towards a Native Anthropology." *Human Organization* 29(4): 251–259.

King, D. (1994). "Captain Planet and the Planeteers: Kids, Environmental Crisis, and the Competing Narratives of the New World Order." *Sociological Quarterly* 35(1): 103–120.

Lawless, E. (1992). "'I Was Afraid of Someone Like You. An Outsider Would Misunderstand': Negotiating Interpretive Difference between Ethnographers and Subjects." *Journal of American Folklore* 105: 301–314.

Morgan, D., V. Pacheco, et al. (2004). "Youth Participatory Action Research on Hustling and Its Consequences: A Report from the Field." *Children, Youth, and Environments* 14(2): 201–228.

Schwartzman, H. 2001. *Children and Anthropology: Perspectives for the Twentieth-First Century.* Westport, CT: Bergin and Garvey.

Stacey, J. (1998). "Can There Be a Feminist Ethnography?" *Women's Studies International Forum* 11(1): 2–27.

Theis, J., K. Pickup, et al. (1999). "Visions of Children Who Can't Hear: A Photography Project by Young People with Hearing Impairments." Save the Children.

van der Veer, R. (1997). "Some Major Themes in Vygotsky's Theoretical Work: An Introduction." In *The Collected Works of L. S. Vygotsky,* vol. 3, *Problems of the Theory and History of Psychology,* ed. R. W. Rieber and J. Wollock, pp. 1–7. New York: Plenum.

Chapter 12

Performing Youth

*Youth Agency and the
Production of Knowledge in
Community-Based Theater*

Stephani Etheridge Woodson

"Stephani, I need to pick up the camera. Uhm . . . do you have a moment? . . . Can I talk to you?" One of my graduate students stood hesitantly in the door to my office. Looking up, I nodded my head.

"Sure, come on in. What's up?"

She moved into the office looking at everything but me. "We're meeting with Richard today to interview him on camera, and I'm worried about it."

This student in my community-based drama class was working with me on a Place: Vision & Voice project with long-term-care foster youth in the metro-Phoenix area. Since 2000, Place: Vision & Voice (PVV) has operated under my direction as a community-based performance and digital arts residency program focused on youth participants at the Herberger College of Fine Arts at Arizona State University. During residencies—which typically last anywhere from one to ten months—the adolescent youth and I (plus assorted graduate students) collaboratively create and edit multimedia performance collages (digital storytelling pieces) incorporating performance, music, interviews, digital graphics and images, creative movement, creative writing, and theatrical presentations. These artworks are then brought back into the youths' communities to spark democratic dialogue and youth feedback on critical issues. I generally conduct residencies in the youths' space—working in schools, community centers, libraries, and parks. In this instance, however, the youth were also coming to the college campus. Structured as a two-hour workshop once a week, with additional off-campus time in small groups to work in alternate environments, the residency lasted, in total, twenty-five hours.

Richard was an uncommunicative—if not downright surly—fourteen-year-old with severe emotional and behavioral disabilities and a moderate developmental delay. I could understand the graduate student's nervousness. Her job was to help Richard express himself—to communicate—through the medium of the art. Richard was never late to our workshops and never missed a class, but he had yet to participate willingly in any activity. As the rest of the group played games, created improvisations, told stories, and shared inner thoughts, Richard isolated himself both physically and emotionally. He communicated, if pressed, in monosyllabic grunts and refused all eye contact. He was also functionally illiterate, so during writing activities facilitators would transcribe his words for him. Richard had been adopted out of the system around age four but had been brought back into the system several years later when his behavioral difficulties became too tricky for his adoptive parents to handle.

What we had discovered, though, is that Richard loved the cameras. He adored setting them up and would meticulously level the tripods, adjusting them for both his tall, lanky form and for those of us much shorter. Although he hated appearing in front of the camera, he blossomed behind it.

> "Richard hates being in front of the camera. I don't know what to do."
> "Are you sure he wants to create an "'I am . . .' digital poem?" I asked.
> "Yes, that's the weird thing. He already has the places set out for us to visit. We are picking him up at his group home and going to a park. He wants to interview one of the staff at the home, and he also wants some footage on a busy street."

The practice of community-based theater and performance is a relatively old field, known globally by multiple names: grassroots theater, community cultural development, applied theater, theater of the oppressed, community arts, *animation socio-culturelle* (community animation), theater as social intervention, theater for development, and several others. The multiple names reflect a large and diverse practice that can best be understood through specific examples than through what is a wide range of approaches and politics. Using my own experiences in the Place: Vision & Voice projects, I argue that community-based performance practices with youth hold multiple implications for critical youth studies, ethnography, and sociology, particularly in terms of methodology, understandings of youth agency, and the production and dissemination of knowledge. Through this type of collective art making, groups can explore how performance transmits, reflects, and constitutes identity, cultural memory, and power.

As a community-based artist and scholar, I have been struggling with both the theory and the practice of representation, ethics, and the Other. I am interested in exploring youth roles in culture, youth agency, and childhood as a performed social construct; I am also interested in questions relating to how we know about youth worlds and youth themselves, that is, epistemological and methodological questions that revolve around the study of youth. I consider my arts practice as an applied theory of the social construction of childhood and youth identity worked out in cooperation with youth themselves. Art created in this way directly addresses the fluid nature of identity as situated in space and time and through multiple languages and communicative structures. Art becomes a "research" methodology as well as a complex process and product of culture, space, time, and individual/community identity formations.

I began PVV, in fact, to address my growing frustration with the "traditional" research understanding of the social construction of childhood in North America. As a researcher, I analyze youth-oriented media, paying particular attention to the performed construction of childhood. I am interested in how we interpolate young people into cultural and behavioral tropes, like the child as cute, the child as cool, the innocent child, the dangerous child, and so on. I work to understand how real young people negotiate within the landscape of childhood marked by boundaries of power, class, gender, and skin color. In practice, however, I have often felt that my research too easily conflated children with childhood, creating further coercive structures and denying children agency. Place: Vision & Voice expands on my previous theoretical work of deconstructing the social performance of childhood by addressing young people's own perceptions, identity constructions, and articulations through the use of performance—moving children and childhood from the object of study to active participants in the pursuit of understanding. This is a conceptualization of art as a process and product of mutual discovery.

Using specific examples drawn from Place: Vision & Voice projects to ground the underlying theory behind my community-based performance practice with youth, I foreground three specific, although deeply interconnected, implications of community-based performance as a theory and a method to direct critical youth studies.

1. The performance paradigm allows for complex community explorations of how performance transmits, reflects, and constitutes cultural memory and power structures.
2. Community-based performance practices with youth address the fluid nature of identity as situated in space and time and through multiple languages and communicative structures.
3. Community-based arts practices are processes and products of mutual discovery, interpretation, and integration.

These three propositions together address undeniably key issues for all youth work, particularly in terms of methodology, understandings of youth agency, and the production and dissemination of knowledge.

To return to my specific example for a moment: in my conversation with my worried graduate student, and perhaps in my own mind, I needed to transform Richard from an object or a label (foster youth, developmentally delayed, behavioral disorder, troublemaker) to a collaborator. In the end, the graduate student took two cameras to her meeting. She gave one to Richard and used the other to capture their interview (using questions collectively devised by the youth participants). For his part, Richard captured remarkably sophisticated imagery on his camera. For example, he constructed striking images of a broken van window. The shot begins with the camera focused in extreme close-up on a single piece of darkly tinted safety glass. Slowly, with care and a steady hand, Richard pulls the focus out and brings into being the jagged line of the dark black glass on the screen, tracing the toothed edge with slow and gentle motion. While in a local park, Richard played with his camera while swinging, creating a nauseating motion. He also captured the swing's moving slowly on its own, echoing his previous motion in ever-decreasing arcs. What I find striking about this work is how the two camera tracks work together. As I viewed the footage, it became clear to me that although Richard could not clearly articulate in words his answers to the interview questions, he was using his camera to record his answer in performative visual imagery. The question "What does it mean to be a foster kid?" was answered clearly with concentration and a level of abstract thought that I found surprising. Verbally, Richard's only comment was, "It sucks." But the fractured glass and shadowed interior of the ubiquitous group-home white van symbolically articulated his experience in foster care. Richard's conceptualization of his own identity could only be showcased in the melding of verbal and artistic languages through the performative landscape.

The Performance Paradigm

The term "performance" has been almost unilaterally co-opted to metaphorically describe nontheatrical manifestations of social interaction. Theorist Marvin Carlson describes performance and performativity as "ubiquitous tropes" that "owe allegiance to no particular field or discipline" (1996:193). Performance studies as a field (or an antifield) is indebted, however, to the many diverse disciplines that developed performance as both metaphor and analytic tool—in particular, cultural studies, which theoretically decentered as objects "text," "identity," "play," and "performer" (plus a host of other formerly solid structures) and reconceptualized them as complex products and processes of cultural (inter)play. Culture, here, can be considered a type of code necessary to the understanding of practically everything else. I want to differentiate, however, between understandings of culture as textual—or clusters of phenomena to be read or interpreted—and understandings of culture as something that is performed, created, and by extension, consumed. As Dwight Conquergood put it, "Only middle-class academics could blithely assume that all the world is a text because texts and reading are central to their lifeworld, and occupational security" (quoted in D. Taylor 2003:27). A primary difference in the two interpretations concerns agency, and only the second conceptualization of culture allows for and even promotes active cultural agents. A related difference can be found in how one understands the "real." In a textual interpretation of culture, one starts first with language, which can be peeled away to reveal deep layers of fundamental core "truth." But culture understood broadly as and through performance places "truth" squarely in public acts. Erving Goffman, for example, notes that "a 'performance' may be defined as all the activity of a given participant on a given occasion which serves to influence in any way any of the other participants" (1959:15). This broad definition opens out modernistic understandings of behavior as outward manifestations of inward realities and turns behavior on its head. Brissett and Edgley note, "the theatre of performances is not in people's heads, it is in their public acts. People encounter each other's minds only by interacting, the quality and character of these interactions comes to constitute the consequential reality of everyday life" (1990:37).

In my work, I am interested in the ebb and flow of cultural beliefs and experiences about childhood identity as seen in art, mass media, cultural practice, and bodily performance. I do not consider it a particularly large leap to conceptualize performance as a *type of research* with unique abilities to explore and to map the diverse discourses constituting and reconstituting childhood in formal and informal practices. Theorist Diana Taylor states, "Instead of focusing on patterns of cultural expression in terms of texts and narratives, we might think about them as scenarios that do not reduce gestures and embodied practices to narrative descriptions" (2003:16). Artistic practice combines both discovery and the process of interpretation. As with all research, the goal of work like this is to add to cumulative knowledge in substantive ways.

My own work in performance with youth investigates children's culture(s) as a series of performed (embodied) relationships constantly negotiated and refined, "permeat[ing] every aspect of social life" and indeed psychological life (Cox 1996:5–6). In this, I align myself with Shannon Jackson, who believes that "at its best . . . performance function[s] as a vehicle for understanding the big questions. Whether conceiving performance as practice, as paradigm, or as epistemological location, it [is] . . . the most useful place from which to speculate upon the nature of identity, space, temporality, and social interaction" (2000:v). I use performance to explore the social communications that produce childhood as both a space and a temporality that inscribe identity onto and into youth. Theoretically, then, performance functions as both the object/subject and the interpretive grid to explore childhood(s) and the collective and embodied practices of social memory and individual identity formation—thinking with, thinking through—both theory and practice in one.

Taylor's concept of "scenario" as patterns of meaning making needs to be further explored. Her use of the term far outweighs traditional conceptions of narrative or plot to include the physical, emotional, psychic, and contextual landscape of the scene or situation. Scenarios have the traditional elements of dramatic action, but they also contain the bodies and souls of the "performers" themselves, including their attitudes, body language, and emotive expressions that cannot be reduced to words. "Simultaneously setup and action, scenarios frame and activate social dramas" (Taylor 2003:28). Perhaps even more interesting is Taylor's suggestion that scenarios are frameworks in which individuals and communities make and remake understandings of lived life. These frameworks can be honored, transformed, subverted, and transferred into new situations, milieus, and cultural contexts. Sharing something of the same shape as tropes, scenarios are larger than written metaphors or metanarratives. Scenarios also bear the accumulative weight of history. As Taylor notes, "The scenario makes visible, yet again, what is already there: the ghosts, the images, the stereotypes" (28).

Let me provide an example to ground this theory. In addition to my CPS Foster Children project, I have been artist-in-residence at the Ira H. Hayes Memorial Applied Learning Center on the Gila River Indian Community since 2002. Each year, I am in residence at the school with a team of graduate-student teacher/artists. We work with any interested youth currently enrolled in the school to create a collaborative digital performance piece delving into a central question decided on by the youth. All told, residencies typically last 260 hours. In the second year of the program, 2003/2004, we created a piece about families that we titled "A Window into Family." As you can imagine, the central metaphor was a window through which we showed glimpses of the youths' feelings, family structures, difficulties, and joys. We interpreted "family" broadly to include place as well as people, exploring the more dispersed conception of identity typical to the indigenous youth. We were extremely conscious of creating scenarios or meaning-making paradigms that transform depending on whether one looks from the inside or the outside of the "window."

In the opening of the piece we used the windows (interpreted broadly) of abandoned mud houses to frame each young artist who contributed to the piece (fifteen teens and seventeen elementary-school children). During Raul's segment (he was more commonly known as Roo), the young man enters into the frame of the window from the darkness of the house interior. He looks out into the distance and then turns and directly acknowledges the audience. He then moves closer into the window's frame, slinging one arm up and over the sill, turning his profile to us, and giving a characteristic chin lift, nodding acknowledgment to his audience and to his own performance of self. When we show this piece to audiences, there is a striking difference between audiences of Native Americans and all others. Indigenous audiences react with laughter and a type of bashful pride in Roo's performance that travels in an almost physical wave over their bodies. White, middle-class audiences rarely react at all. What is different here is the manner in which the audiences translate the given scenario.

To most audiences, Roo appears to be nothing more than a teenage male, staged in a stereotypical Southwestern environment. His body language acknowledges both his pride and his discomfort, but neither is particularly remarkable. Indigenous audiences, however, seem to recognize not only the way in which Roo manipulates male posture and typical gestures but also how he plays with the tension of performance itself—the aggregate of imperialistic U.S. history held in this moment. Roo is aware of how the scenario "stages the Indian," and he plays with that tension, slyly referencing stereotypes of the stoic warrior through posture, gesture, and expression.

Performance exists both as a powerful method of sensual and embodied reproduction of hegemonic social and cultural structures and as a material and temporal practice highlighting the very vulnerability of dominant social structures to re-production. This duality locates both the potential and the peril of community-based performance practice. Ultimately my practice with youth rests on the belief that by engaging in the arts as an epistemological system, by mastering, communicating, exploring in and through the arts, participants bring to consciousness the deep and structural (structuring) significance of experience and culture(s). And by bringing these deep meanings to the surface, participants can become aware of their own power as cultural makers and (re)makers, putting into practice the strength of an authentic voice—actively engaging the authority of experience. But this type of performance practice can also re-create structures of domination, inculcate ideologies, and replace one type of domination with another based on leftist identity politics and superficial understandings of power and agency.

Communicating and Exploring the Fluid Nature of Identity

At once a turning out and a turning in, community-based performance allows a group to express its way of life, interests, and anxieties both to outsiders and, not least of all, to itself. Sociologists have long acknowledged that community depends as much on exclusion as inclusion. In many ways, then, community-based theater works as strategic performance of self and other. This, however, highlights the necessity of directly and procedurally addressing the moral principles of authenticity and ownership. As Suzanne Lacy reflects, "We want to believe in the unassailability of direct experience" (2001:n.p.). Theater, however, is predicated on the belief that one individual can step genuinely and holistically into another's subjectivity. Who can and should speak for whom? What stories should and should not be told? How does and how can performance negotiate the dangerous line between validating direct experience and negating expressions of empathy?

Performance understood in this manner, as both theory and practice, troubles essentialized understandings of identity and experience, which makes distinctions of the authentic, or an outward seeming of the inward, difficult if not impossible to resolve. Which of the multiple performative identities Roo performs in his brief introductory moment stage the "real" Roo, the "authentic" Roo? Is there even such a creature? The paradox is that "authentic voice" remains a, if not the, hallmark of community-based arts work, as well as of much of critical youth studies, especially in ethnographic work. This hurdle is doubly present in youth-focused community-based arts centered on identity issues, as is the Place: Vision & Voice program. Adults working in these environments must be able to honestly negotiate the grid of difference and power disparity with a hyperawareness that the process of community-based theater and performance almost unavoidably will reproduce hegemonic power structures and the social injustices that characterize public life and civic discourse in the United States. In my own practice, for example, I will always be Other to the youth with whom I work. Yes, my Otherness is strikingly clear in my work on the Gila River Indian Community, but as an adult, I am Other to all children and youth by virtue of my age. I also am an insider to the power of language, scientific discourse, and academic worlds. This situation, then, highlights power and control in ways both obvious and subtle.

There is no easy answer to this predicament. I personally answer this difficulty with a commitment to negotiating difference by reproducing the very multivocality that characterizes collective endeavors: I commit procedurally and aesthetically to structures that place performances of self and other in patchwork form, highlighting the fluidity of identity by using forms of pastiche or collage. In this way, the artwork foregrounds the differing understandings of "truth" and disrupts singular linear narratives. This is not a universal solution, however. Questions of authenticity and ownership remain a problem that must be solved no matter what question is being explored or what methodology is being used. Again, community-based performances like those in the Place: Vision & Voice project function as strategic performances of self and other, which seats this type of work decisively in the realm of the political. From my experience, the very commitment to reproducing multiple voices, perspectives, and subject positions can become threatening even to the community in which the work is created.

The limits and promise of collage structure are well illustrated in another experience I had working on the Gila River Indian Community (GRIC). In the 2002–2003 school year, I conducted a residency for ten months at the Ira H. Hayes Memorial High School with ten Akimel O'Otham (Pima) students. Together with my graduate student and teaching partner, Megan Alrutz, the twelve of us collaborated on a forty-minute video piece called "The River People." This piece has been showcased in multiple festivals and conferences including several juried events. The work circles around the youths' exploration of the term "heritage" and what that word means to each of them. Their creation is deeply honest, sometimes difficult to watch, and emotionally evocative. The dominant image of the piece is that of a bridge over the dry Gila riverbed. The piece begins and ends with the youth on the bridge, returning repeatedly to the idea of place as both a time and a space, with the youth suspended between the two. We made the choice to structure the piece as a collage that circles around the question of heritage in multiple ways, returning again and again to similar questions and answering them in a variety of ways. Musically, we began and ended the piece with a drumming song traditionally sung at the end of powwows and festivals—the "going home" song. We chose to use the song in both its traditional context and a less traditional one because we wanted to stress the circular nature of the piece and of the youths' explorations. They were in fact going home through the entire process. This choice and other artistic choices came under fire when we showcased the piece for the tribal council. Although for the most part positive, a few council members made several strongly worded recommendations to change sections of the piece to reflect a unified political position and subjected me personally to an informal legal investigation as to whether I even had permission to be on the reservation. Ultimately, we made no changes.

The council, though, was responding from their experiences as a people within a structure that systematically silences them, a people who must speak with a unified and strong voice in order to be heard by those in power. Our piece, though almost uniformly loving, does contain some troubling moments. Bruce McConachie points out in his essay "Approaching the 'Structure of Feeling' in Grassroots Theater" that community as an idea functions "to provide symbolic unity in the face of real differences within the group" (2001:17). The form of pastiche or collage can trouble essentialized notions of community—especially a practice, like mine, that is committed to multivocality—but toward what end? And is multivocality always an appropriate and/or principled choice to make? I do not pretend to have the answers to these questions. I am not so sure safe answers are even possible. But I continually and recursively struggle with questions of authenticity, and ownership, and my ethical responsibilities to the youth, to the school, and to the community. Adults who work in critical youth studies must set aside (or at least become wholly aware of) their own discourses and their own narrative structures in order to authentically negotiate the youths' direct experiences in nuanced ways. At the same time, however, we cannot forget that communities depend on their children for their continued existence.

In the GRIC project, I was ultimately able to transform what could have been a frustrating experience for all involved into a conversation about choices and consequences in art and in life, a conversation that probably was one of the most significant discussions of the entire year's process. We were able to talk about the different institutional frameworks structuring each of our lives and how those frameworks limit our performances, our behaviors, our scenarios. The council members are political and social leaders focused on issues of sovereignty, tribal rights, and the significant power of words and images to affect public opinions. As a university professor, I was working in an institutional framework more often at odds with the tribe than not, a frame that often denies subjectivities in favor of quantitative data and can relegate the lived life of indigenous people to dilettante status in favor of white anthropologists. Who creates knowledge? How is knowledge defined? Who owns the stories? Currently, in the U.S. Enlightenment framework, "objective" knowledge is valued much more than so-called experiential or organic knowledge. As a Western artist, I was working in an institutional framework that values individual creative expression above almost all else. As tribal youth, the young people worked from within tightly nested frameworks of childhood, family organization, tribal structures that esteem elders, and particularized cultural heritage, among others. The youth were also moving from within the U.S. youth culture that valorizes resistance, media, and glossy surfaces.

What this experience crystallized for me, though, is that adults working in critical youth studies must develop reciprocal relationships with both the community and youth where they work. Trust is a fragile thing that ultimately is multilayered. William Cleveland's 2002 study of successful community-based programs found that "practitioners say over and over that their most important resources are relationships. Effective community-based work is about partnership" (n.p.). Artists and scholars, of course, need to invest the time and energy in researching and understanding the community and the community's unique perspectives. That research must be combined, however, with an attitude of respectful deference. Knowing and understanding are not the same thing. Artists and scholars must give up the "expert mode" and allow the individuals with whom we work to be the primary informants of their own existence. This is an especially important implication of using a performance-studies paradigm with youth, as childhood itself functions as a cultural space of memory into which communities heavily invest. This is a critical point that I want to further discuss.

Childhood is structurally important in creating and continuing community kinship. As Paul Connerton argues, "The narrative of one life is part of an interconnecting set of narratives; it is embedded in the story of those groups from which individuals derive their identity" (1989:21). And the act of remembering creates meaningful narrative structures— stories we tell ourselves about ourselves. This remains particularly true of childhood. Childhood functions as a site of remembrance, or what Joe Roach calls "genealogies of performance," which "document—and suspect—the historical transmission and dissemination of cultural practices through collective representations" and recollection (1996:25). This highlights childhood itself as a performative structure that often relegates children themselves to roles as spectators to the accumulation of cultural memory. Culture depends on memory both as a social cement (Gross 2000:78) and as a way to connect the past to the future through occasion or, as Kant states, "to connect, in a coherent experience, what no longer exists with what does not yet exist through what is present" (1974 [1797]: 57). The collective representation/performance of culture organizes itself around absence or that which is no longer here but only apprehended through the processes of memory—for example, traditions, history, customs, genealogy. "Death," starkly claims Gary Taylor, "is the foundation of culture" (1996:5). When we look into the faces of our children we see the future, the present, and the past. And as a cultural site of memory, childhood circulates both social and political memories (e.g., compulsory schooling, habits of comportment) and personal ones (e.g., the definition of "mother"). Childhood is a space through which communities negotiate communal structures of feeling.

Communities are invested socially, emotionally, and psychologically in conceptualizing the structure of childhood and the future of their children in powerful ways. But we must ask ourselves, What kinds of knowledges are privileged or displaced when performed (adult) experience becomes a way of childhood knowing? For one thing, childhood as a site of memory is most often seen through the lens of nostalgia. As Herbert Blau points out, "the bottomless source of the future is the inexhaustible past . . . [and] the only real paradise is the paradise that is lost" (1987:140). There is also a paradox created because although adults were children, as adults they have "no direct . . . only represented . . . access to that experience" (Stainton-Rogers and Stainton-Rogers 1992:19). So although we all have lived experience within childhood, we (re)construct childhood, even our own, through narrative discourses—through memory. There is the added difficulty that youth are often understood as having no memory but, rather, are in the process of building memories—adults must inculcate tradition, knowledge, and understanding of the world before the so-called malleability of childhood hardens into static adult minds. In effect, this structures children and youth as blank slates that must be inscribed by adults.

Childhood exists as a site into and onto which we perform personal and social memories, since childhood functions as a type of "universal" social reference while occluding race, gender, and class. The simple fact remains that all adults were at one time or another children. Unlike the categories of race, culture, or gender, all individuals have shared in the temporality of childhood. Thus, childhood exists as a location to which everyone has ties—emotional, foundational, physical—memories and thoughts. An investigation of the presentation of childhood *as performance,* however, highlights scenarios of meaning and the grounded nature of "culture" in metaphorical and material space while privileging the body as a site of knowing. In effect, this reinscribes youth agency and situates young people as knowledge producers. To go back to Goffman for a moment, the performance paradigm turns memory on its head, moving from the outside in rather than from a stable internal landscape.

Process and Products of Reciprocity

I believe that the performance studies paradigm—performance as research, research as performance—opens out aesthetic structures for use in critical youth studies. Art is a process of questioning and proposing, giving makers the ability to juxtapose and connect items, thoughts, and emotions in new and unique ways. Art also provides nonlinear, nondiscursive space in which to think in deep, messy, and meaningful ways. Thinking aesthetically is also about crafting, negotiating, and manipulating the relationship (for the makers, the perceivers, during the process, and in the product) between intellectual and emotional engagement. Rethinking research of any kind as a type of performance highlights the process of research as well as the product while accentuating the emotional and intellectual components of inquiry. Methodologically, critical youth studies can benefit from the balance of process and product. Form becomes a key question, not a necessary given. Like life itself, my practice in community-based performance with youth depends as much on process as product, and that process can be messy, contradictory, frustrating, unpredictable, and magnificent. Concerned adults must be able to negotiate this morass effectively and with a willingness to change directions in midstream. And what is more, if the community artist has done his or her job appropriately, people will question the aesthetic, the process, and the final product—how frustrating and frightening, and how glorious. In the end, community-based practice reconfigures the artist-artwork-audience equation, spinning it from monologue into dialogue. This parallels recent calls for more dialogic and collaborative forms of research within the qualitative research tradition.

Balancing process and product demands flexibility from concerned adults. Art as the practice of dialogue depends on a willingness to remain open, to hear what others have to say and even what they are not saying. As Patricia Romney states, "real dialogue presupposes an openness to modify deeply held convictions" (2003:n.p.). Resident artists must also be willing to engage in the practice of their art form without knowledge of where they will end up. In order to truly collaborate with participants, my residencies must remain open-ended, as the substance needs to be dictated by the participants rather than being imposed by the facilitator. Artists/scholars must be able to balance the needs of the process with their hope for the product. The nature of collaborative work is that it is messy and variable.

Secondarily, community-based practice is at heart a practice predicated on reciprocity, partnership, and mutual creativity. For too long, children and youth have been the object of study rather than participants in understanding. But the reality is that children are social actors with their own unique narrative understandings who can and should participate in the telling of their stories (O'Kane 2000:136–141). Again, by paying just as much attention to the process of work with young people, artists and scholars working with youth can provide helpful structures to maximize participant agency. As is so clearly illustrated in Richard's story, the process—as difficult as it was—revealed something meaningful when connected to the product (his filming). Also, community-based theater and performance is a process of positive youth development, with the artistic product a visible and celebrated victory providing youth access to public space and dialogue. When possible, I believe that all research with children should function in the same manner. bell hooks calls this process "coming to voice." She says, "Coming to voice is not just the act of telling one's experience. It is using that telling strategically—to come to voice so that you can also speak freely about other subjects" (1994:144).

To work in critical youth studies is to engage in the political, cultural, and ethical landscape of a socially constructed childhood. In my own practice, I have found that only a truly transparent process that attempts to balance the needs of the youth participants, the needs of the community group, and the needs of the artist/scholar provides me a sensitive ethical framework to contain this work. Part of that sensitivity includes an intensive exploration of my own beliefs and frames of reference, including issues of rank, race, and privilege, along with a willingness to share that exploration both as a form of modeling and as a response to others' stories. Remaining totally and emotionally open throughout the process is quite difficult, but it is a necessary requirement to building relationships of trust. These ethical and procedural concerns parallel similar discussions in other research fields including insider versus outsider status, observation or participant-observation, action research or laboratory research. And again, as in most fields, these questions remain unanswered and perhaps even unanswerable except in direct contextual practice. They cannot, however, be ignored. In fact, I strongly suggest that all adults engaged in critical youth studies attempt to make the difficult nature of these process negotiations transparent within the performance/report itself to greater and lesser degrees. This is not an easy prospect, however. Suzanne Lacy makes clear the ramifications of a transparent process: "All assumptions within a transparent process are open to challenge: dominant cultural assumptions about what makes a good story—choice of subject, narrator's voice, the style, shape, and choice of medium; the availability of economic resources, ownership of venues, and choice of audience; the methods of entering a community, researching, enlisting support, and consensus building (2001:n.p.).

Part of balancing process and product includes creating a safe environment in which to risk. The feeling of ensemble goes a long way toward allowing youth both ownership and social cohesion (in so much as that is possible given each community's unique situation). Part of the adult's responsibility then is the creation of positive social bonds among participants. That is not to say that conflict will not or even should not occur. Conflict is a natural part of the process of communal expression of lived life—both internal and external discontent (Adams and Goldbard 2001: 64). I would argue, actually, that solving problems within a powerfully reciprocal environment allows young people to learn some of the many skills needed to navigate in a democratic environment. For one, they learn how to be responsible for one another. They learn that each of their choices has consequences, and they learn that real life is more often provisional than static. Learning how to disagree without being disagreeable is a necessary skill for anyone living in a deliberative democratic environment. Adult scholars, researchers, and artists must develop strategies, then, for how to help negotiate conflicts and how to avoid misuse of the process itself. Listening to and acknowledging problems goes a long way toward diffusing potential difficulties. A constructive outcome of creating positive social bonds and ensemble is that the adult is not alone in having to solve problems. I have found that the group functions as a much more powerful problem-solver than I could ever hope to be.

Practically, I have found that providing a flexible workshop structure of graduated risk-taking helps develop participants' belief in their own ability to succeed. For example, I almost always begin residencies with theater games. In particular, games that allow youth to participate without risking themselves work quite well. One of the standard games I use is called Kitty Wants a Corner. In this game all players stand in a circle with one person in the center. The center individual moves from person to person asking, "Kitty wants a corner?" Players on the outside of the circle reply, "Try my neighbor." As "Kitty" travels from person to person, those on the outside of the circle attempt to exchange places without letting Kitty "steal" their spots. There is no talking in this game beyond the single question and response. Players who wish to exchange spots must come to agreement to do so through the use of nonverbal communication only. This allows youth who do not want to participate to simply stand in the circle and deny all attempts to move to their spot. This lets individuals like Richard, for example, belong to the group without immediate risk of failure or embarrassment. In balancing process with product and securing authentic youth participation in my work, I also have discovered that I must provide tangible results as a consequence of participation. For example, in the first year of my GRIC residency I attempted to spend the first several weeks teaching the youth how to manipulate the media and the technology separate from our work generating performative content. I failed miserably. The students were bored, and I was frustrated. I did not provide the youth material understandings of the possibilities of multimedia performance work. When I began structuring the workshops in such a way as to provide the youth multiple and tangible results (what commercial films call "dailies," for example), all of a sudden the work blossomed. In effect, I had been structuring the workshop in such a way that the youth were merely consumers of my advanced knowledge of video and performance. When, however, I transformed the workshop to structurally place the youth at the center of production, as knowledge producers rather than consumers, the import of the events radically transformed.

The performance studies paradigm also opens out methodological issues and highlights questions of reciprocity. Frankly, I do not buy the argument that the search for knowledge is its own justification. Academics traditionally go into communities to perform their fieldwork and leave repackaging their information to other researchers—building their careers by moving their fields forward. But the communities often never hear from the researcher again. I question the ethics of that practice. So we know what the researcher gets from the relationship, but what about what the researcher gives to the participants? I think that anyone performing fieldwork should think seriously about what they can exchange for access. Can they teach their skills in observation and analysis, for example? I think it might be interesting to give workshops in field research to the young people, as some researchers have attempted to do. This could have the effect of opening out young peoples' learning experiences and giving them insight into possible processes prior to the exchange of informed consent. A school might want to have the researcher give a career talk or share previous research. All this might sound pie-in-the-sky, but the point is to build mutual relationships based on trust and complex understandings. Practitioners must give constant and faithful attention to the ethics of their work with and for youth, with particular awareness toward representational authenticity and questions of ownership. Who owns the stories we tell and how we negotiate the telling itself should be primary questions throughout.

At the very least, we should involve young people in the process and product as much as is possible and feasible. Different situations will call for different solutions. But a commitment to "coming to voice" admits that the performance of self and social world is primarily strategic for both youth *and* for the researcher/artist. Another way to respect the lived experience of being young is to honor the cultural capital of our young people in the reporting of research about their lives—meaning a considered manipulation of populist cultural forms and symbol systems directly addressed to the young people involved. Graphic novels, poetic or musical form, or short documentaries are all fascinating ways in which to report back to (or with) young people. There are quite a few academics who are currently working in ethnographic performance, primarily with autobiographical forms but also including longitudinal case studies. I recognize that alternative forms will never replace traditional academic writings, but I do believe that they can and should supplement them. We have a responsibility not only to our own intellectual communities but also to the young people and their communities. And that responsibility is not completed after the residency has ended or the dissertation has been written and approved. I also believe that it is important to close the discussion circle once the artwork or research project is finished. Reporting back to the community is just as important as reporting back to an academic institution. For example, "The River People," the first performance piece of the Hayes Memorial High School project, has been touring all over the GRIC reservation and has been shown at multiple film festivals and several academic and social welfare conferences. Where possible, the youth themselves frame the piece and later discuss their work with the audience. This provides opportunities for the youth to acquire and hone the many social, intellectual, and performative skills needed to negotiate public space. This also imbeds the artwork further into a shared process, opening dialogue between the children and the adults in their community by providing a unique and nonthreatening forum focused on the assets, strengths, and experiences children bring. All research with and on children and childhood should attempt to bring the youth voice into public/adult spaces.

NOTES

This article expands on and theorizes some of the questions I presented in 2004 on the Community Arts Network Website, http://www.communityarts.net/reading room/archives/2004/05/place_vision_an.php.

In order to protect privacy, I use pseudonyms chosen by the youth.

For more on the history of the field, I suggest the following references: Jan Cohen-Cruz, *Local Acts: Community-Based Performance in the United States* (New Brunswick, NJ: Rutgers University Press, 2005); chapters 1 and 2 in Sonja Kuftinec, *Staging American: Cornerstone and Community-Based Theater* (Carbondale: Southern Illinois University Press, 2003); Don Adams and Arlene Goldbard, *Creative Communities: The Art of Cultural Development* (New York: Rockefeller Foundation, 2001); and Baz Kershaw, *The Politics of Performance: Radical Theatre as Cultural Intervention* (London: Routledge, 1992).

REFERENCES

Adams, D., and Goldbard, A. (2001). *Creative communities: The art of cultural development.* New York: Rockefeller Foundation.

Blau, H. (1987). *The eye of the prey: Subversions of the postmodern.* Bloomington: Indiana University Press.

Brissett, D., and Edgley, C. (1990). The dramaturgical perspective. In D. Brissett and C. Edgley (eds.), *Life as theatre: A dramaturgical sourcebook,* 2nd ed. New York: Aldine de Gruyter.

Carlson, M. (1996). *Performance: A critical introduction.* New York: Routledge.

Cleveland, W. (2002). "Mapping the Field: Arts-Based Community Development." Community Arts Network Website, www.communityarts.net/readingroom/archive/intro-develop.php, accessed 10 December 2003.

Connerton, P. (1989). *How societies remember.* New York: Cambridge University Press.

Cox, R. (1996). *Shaping childhood: Themes of uncertainty in the history of adult-child relationships.* New York: Routledge.

Goffman, E. (1959). *The presentation of self in everyday life.* New York: Doubleday.

Gross, D. (2000). *Lost time: On remembering and forgetting in late modern culture.* Amherst: University of Massachusetts Press.

hooks, b. (1994). *Teaching to transgress: Education as the practice of freedom.* New York: Routledge.

Jackson, S. (2000). *Lines of activity: Performance, historiography, Hull-House domesticity.* Ann Arbor: University of Michigan Press.

Kant, I. (1974 [1797]). *Anthropology from a pragmatic view.* Trans. M. J. Gregor. The Hague, Netherlands: Martinus Nijhoff.

Lacy, S. (2001). "Seeking an American Identity: Working Inward from the Margins." Animating Democracy Website, www.AmericansForTheArts.org/Animating Democracy/resource_center, accessed 12 December 2003.

McConachie, B. (2001). Approaching the "structure of feeling" in grassroots theater. In S. C. Haedicke and T. Nellhaus (eds.), *Performing democracy: International perspectives on urban community-based performance*. Ann Arbor: University of Michigan Press.

O'Kane, C. (2000). The development of participatory techniques: Facilitating children's views about decisions which affect them. In P. Christensen and A. James (eds.), *Research with children: Perspectives and practices*. New York: Falmer.

Roach, J. (1996). *Cities of the dead: Circum-Atlantic performance*. New York: Columbia University Press.

Romney, P. (2003). "The Art of Dialogue." Animating Democracy Website, www .AmericansForTheArts.org/AnimatingDemocracy/resource_center, accessed 22 November 2003.

Stainton Rogers, R., and Stainton Rodgers, W. (1992). *Stories of childhood: Shifting agendas of child concern*. New York: Harvester-Wheatsheaf.

Taylor, D. (2003). *The archive and the repertoire: Performing cultural memory in the Americas*. Durham, NC: Duke University Press.

Taylor, G. (1996). *Cultural selection*. New York: Basic Books.

Chapter 13

Beyond "Straight" Interpretations
Researching Queer Youth Digital Video

Susan Driver

Traditionally, the body for youth has been one of the principal terrains for multiple forms of resistance and as a register of risk, pleasure and sex. It has been through the body that youth displayed their own identities through oppositional subcultural styles, transgressive sexuality, and disruptive desires. The multiple representations and displays of the body in this context were generally central to developing a sense of agency, self-definition, and well-placed refusals.

> —Henry Giroux, "Teenage Sexuality, Body Politics, and the Pedagogy of Display"

It's the requirement that we define ourselves so that everything will run smoothly, so that we can be categorized before we're even born. So that we're constantly searching for the answers to your questions

> —Natasha Pike, "Untitled," Queer Youth Digital Video Project

When I tell people about my research project on queer youth sexualities, I am struck by the arousal, fear, and discomfort this topic elicits. I think that it is my passionate interest and the directness of my approach that triggers surprise and embarrassment. Connections between sexuality and girlhood have become a locus of whispered titillation and moral condemnation, but rarely do we candidly address our own and others' feelings and attitudes about this taboo realm of experience. Even feminist academic researchers have learned to translate the intensities of flesh-and-blood teen worlds into safely packaged knowledges. The very categories of "girl" and "boy" remain distinct and clear, erasing those who identify as both/and or neither. I have been quietly warned to stay away from messy embodied relations of young queer lust, suggesting unpredictable and dangerous elements of youth culture. Yet it is not only the unruly threat of physical sexual pleasures and blurred genders that scares rational thinkers away; it is also the dangers of exposing and promoting voyeuristic longings on the part of adult authorities positioned to regulate and police the young. An impasse emerges that separates critical research off from active articulations of desire by, for, and about girls/boys/trans youth, inscribing rigid academic boundaries in an effort to avoid ethical risk-taking and self-questioning. Rather than avoid such risks, I am convinced that active engagement with the research dilemmas of sexuality is an important step toward a more inclusive and open understanding of young peoples' lifeworlds. Sexual complexity is an inextricable part of the negotiations youth face on a daily basis, and so the methodologies we devise to listen and respond to them call for thoughtful and challenging strategies.

Within a social context that increasingly exploits sexualized images of tweens and teens, open discussion about how young people feel, think, and act as sexual subjects becomes a vital element of counterhegemonic representation. This is especially the case when binary sexual ideals and norms are disrupted and spaces are opened for specificity and differences. Qualitative research into queer youth that seeks to articulate the transience and diversity of experiences comes up against social and ethical boundaries defining the sexual status of childhood and youth. This work demands a rethinking of myths that construct universal notions of girlhood "innocence" and boyhood "aggression" while also questioning how experiences become framed so as to avoid reinscribing queer youth as deviant, guilty, or heroic. Studying queer youth compels reflexive forms of knowledge that implicate the identities and interests of researchers in a process of dialogue, interpretation, and activism. At stake is a willingness to broach the pain and pleasures of girls' erotic desires for other girls, boys' desires for boys, and boys and girls desiring and being desired in ways that exceed the comfort of expected categories. The horizons of queer youth are in flux and ambivalent. This calls on researchers to read the detailed languages of sexuality through which youth decode media messages and communicate with each other in changing contexts. In this chapter I will discuss the joys and difficulties of developing a methodology based on an exchange of vulnerable memories, visual images, fictional stories, and lived experiences. I seek to problematize the force of institutional ideals along with the powerfully eccentric longings of queer youth who give rise to inventive alternatives to mainstream media representations. I try to combine theoretically informed textual analysis with community-based media advocacy that stresses the cultural and individual value of youth-centered production.

My argument builds on reflexive feminist narrative approaches to reading girls' experiences in their everyday environments that criss-cross public/private, educational/familial, pleasure/work social boundaries. At the same time I draw on queer theoretical work on performative representations of sex/gender/sexuality, calling attention to the need for nonlinear, transitive ways of understanding desire beyond dichotomous gender identities. I elaborate queer feminist interpretive strategies to help me approach do-it-yourself media projects that enable young people to produce their own creative visions of sexuality as an empowering and difficult practice of self-representation. In the midst of hypercommercialized media cultures targeting youth through sexual appearances and heterosexist ideologies, I argue that it is ethically and politically important to develop research that provides queer youth with room to experiment with verbal and visual languages of desire as a means of self-consciousness and public recognition. Research does not become a mirror of preexisting social relations but rather is central to a dialogical process of changing heteronormative conditions of youth embodiment by according youth the power to return the gaze and speak back. This is a risky endeavor that includes the possibility that in the end many queer youth may choose to leave the researcher out altogether as they build their own supportive and imaginative communities. Yet such risks are vital to a research project aimed at unlearning the arrogance of adult scrutiny while encouraging youth to direct a conversation that enables researchers to respect their ambivalence and encourage their autonomy.

Feminist Researchers Listening to Girls' Desires: Challenging Commodified and Moralistic Frames of Reference

Parents and educators believe that we protect our daughters by exacerbating their vulnerability, by instilling them with what we know are the perils of sex: fears of victimization, of pregnancy, of disease. Those fears are, of course, all too real, but so is desire, and we do not teach girls that. (Orenstein, 1994:54)

Unfortunately, girls are often denied the very possibility of desiring agency by teachers, parents, researchers imposing desexualized moralistic rhetorics in their attempts to assert protective control over girls' bodies. Educator Michelle Fine notes that "the naming of desire, pleasure or sexual entitlement, particularly for females, barely exists in the formal agenda of public schooling on sexuality" (1988:33). Fine argues that there is a missing discourse of desire in relation to girls' embodied subjectivities, an absence of recognition of the complex ways young people live out sexual power and ambivalence. Most institutional discourses deny the very possibility of sexual awareness and the means to articulate that awareness to youth, characterizing them as either passive victims or as precocious kids vulnerable to adult manipulations. In many ways this is the crux of heteronormative powers shaping girlhood, intensified by mass-media discourses that either valorize the spectacle of girls showing off their nubile bodies for the male spectator or purify girls as modern-day saints. All the while, traditional sites of church, family, and school continue to demonize "bad" girls for unruly behaviors that suggest a lack of sexual control. Liz Frost writes that "girls whose sexuality is active, who are 'unfeminine' in that they are 'mouthy' or argumentative at home or at school, are likely to be interpreted as a problem and as 'at risk'" (2001:121). Indeed, fear of losing control and being demonized as a "slut" pervades narratives recounted in feminist research on girls (Orenstein, 1994). Yet even those girls marked out as "sexual trouble" are contained within frameworks of heterosexuality that render them manageable. Girls negotiate contradictory fields of vision in which feminine sexual elusiveness is essential to popular identity, while girls who go too far are prohibited and punished. A clear boundary is drawn between sanitized images and acts of impropriety that produce fear and silence. Surface appearances dominate contemporary values of girl sexuality, leaving little room to perceive and recognize interactions that might interrupt the uniformity of visual icons and perhaps even offer up an alternative visual economy of girl desire. Frost writes,

schooled by almost all available sources that it is their prime duty to be as visually attractive as possible . . . girls are apportioned the responsibility for controlling a male sexual "drive" which they have been warned is threatening, if not actively dangerous. "Look sexy," "act sexy" . . . "but don't be sexy." (2001:121)

Responding critically to the double standards of media and educational discourses, feminist researchers have attempted to ask girls intimate questions about the details of their sexual behaviors and feelings as part of a broader process that includes a "voice-centered, relational method within which researchers become listeners, taking in the voice of a girl, developing an interpretation of her experience" (Tolman, 1994:327). This approach makes it clear that the way girls are addressed—communicative languages, styles, formats, contexts—are key processes shaping their social status and self-perceptions as sexual subjects. Communicative dynamics are taken seriously by psychologist Deborah Tolman when she argues that "asking these girls to speak about sexual desires, and listening and responding to their answers and also to their questions, proved to be an effective way to interrupt the standard 'dire consequences' discourse adults usually employ when speaking at all to girls about their sexuality" (1994:340). What is remarkable about this approach is the candid and flexible method of following the narrative responses of girls who are rarely given opportunities to talk with others about their sexual excitement, fears, and conflicts. Most of the girls interviewed in Deborah Tolman's studies say that they are used to keeping their fantasies and memories quietly to themselves. Being given the opportunity to name and share difficult experiences within a research context enables girls to reflect and to construct their own identities while getting feedback and support.

Feminist research on girls' sexuality points to the importance of reflecting on the very assumptions through which sexuality is deemed legitimate to scholarship. Much of the present work on girls focuses on self-esteem, negative body images, and sexuality, and although studies point to serious problems that need to be addressed, the one-sided emphasis on normalized discontent and pathology fails to grapple with those features of girls' desires that do not fit into heteronormative models of sexual health, beauty, and happiness. In other words, it becomes important to think beyond the taken-for-granted languages of sexual development and normalcy in order to read girls' experiences. Not only do feminist theoretical paradigms reproduce "straight" interpretations, but so do the interview methods used to collect, organize, and interpret data. Although the conscientious aim of feminist ethnographic work on girls' sexuality is to remain responsive to the ideas presented by girls, the interview models tend to be limited to semistructured interview forms that call for transparent and direct naming of empirical experiences. Though providing some room for unpredictable fantasies and loose narrative lines of dialogue, feminist social science texts tend to be rigidly marked by the authoritative inquiry of an adult positioned as the knower-interpreter who decides and guides who, what, and how representations become institutionally relevant and valid.

Within most social science research, when a girl is asked if she has felt desire and she responds with silence, uncertainty, and caution or with dizzy enthusiasm, answers tend to be directed to fit into a linear academic text. Hesitations and doubts become rechanneled into familiar codes of heterosexual feminine identity, even when those codes are critiqued as historical effects of dominant ideologies and powers. What strikes me is the tendency to discount or devalue interruptions to a coherent narrative of desire, to smooth over contradictions or ephemeral traces of unconventional pleasures. Very few texts leave room for those loosely structured, wandering, and discordant moments of speech that remain unintelligible according to social scientific categorizations. The perimeters of controlled definition and comparison tend to exclude those features of desire that remain unintelligible within the conventional codes of academic knowledge. It seems to me that this is the crux of heteronormative discursive powers: they render ambiguous, indirect, and unstable ways of signifying desire invisible to the social analyst. What needs to be theorized are the very means through which the contested desires of youth become noticeable and meaningful to researchers. This seems especially important with regard to queer subjects, whose embodied and psychic differences tend to defy conventional codes and strategies of representation. Provocative questions emerge: What means of signifying desire might allow for queer girls to convey their experiences beyond the "straight" codes and methods? Does this undermine the fixity of the category "girls"? Is gender indeterminacy representable within the social sciences? What about the poetic, embodied, or visually articulated moments of sexual subjectivity that are not easily transcribed into interview models? How might nonverbal communications by and about queer youth sexuality become textualized? What modes of nuanced reading and representation would help to shift not only dominant mass-media norms of feminine heterosexuality but also academic protocols of rational coherence?

I argue that the very methodologies used to explore and understand embodied desires need to be substantively rethought to include grassroots projects that involve youth in a creative process of translating their sexual differences using multiple styles, media, and venues. The expansive media presence of youth sexuality has both increased visibility and reinforced binary norms of identity and desire. At the same time, proliferation of visual cultures and textual languages through which sexuality is represented has also generated some volatile possibilities for unruly queer girl meaning making. It is notable that alternative media formats such as zines, ezines, video art, music, performance, and poetic fictions have been the primary means by which queer girls have actively sought to represent themselves publicly. The emergence of productive do-it-yourself self-representations that use and transform media through the active involvement of youth enables strategies of engagement and interpretation at the level of grassroots creative cultural practices. This calls for situated and diverse research practices that elicit, gather, and reinterpret images and stories of girl desire in close correspondence with styles and media through which they choose to express themselves. Before I move on to elaborate a specific example, I want to explore queer theoretical issues as the backdrop to redefining youth research. As changing historical discourses that shape embodied narratives, visual icons, and conceptual categories, queer theory enables new ways of thinking about the intersection of girls and sexuality. The very status of sexual desire is up for grabs as always already constituted through the languages employed to understand diverse subjects. Ethical, cultural, and political issues emerge in relation to research on girls informed by queer theories that throw into crisis the ground on which sexuality is knowable while at the same time providing an affirmation of contextual and bodily signifying practices that refuse scientific generalizations.

Theorizing Queer Girl Desires: Toward Performative Methodologies

The Poststructuralist theories of sexuality articulated around the label "queer theory" problematize how one might form or claim sexual identity and thus dominant understandings of adolescence as the formation of sexuality. . . . If adolescence locates (as yet) unfixed sexual identities, it can only with difficulty be assigned a gay or lesbian identity, and it may be labeled "queer," then it is only insofar as all adolescence would be queer. (Driscoll, 2002:161)

Catherine Driscoll elaborates the ways in which adolescence is marked by a striking fluidity, as a passage in-between, a state of flux that defies clear-cut labels. She notes that although the uncertainties of girls' sexual selves are most often evaluated in terms of immaturity and passivity that negatively contrasts with the norms of the adult male subject, there is also the potential to explore the transformative openness of this subject position. Driscoll refers to Judith Butler's declaration "It's a girl" as exemplary of the performativity of sex/gender, a linguistically enacted category that inscribes its "transitive" formation through repetition in various times and places. It is precisely this unsettling reiterative activity, of signifying sexual subjectivity without certainty or closure, that shifts attention away from a heterosexual teleology of sex/gender/sexual development and onto the dynamics through which images and narratives configure youths' desires in social contexts. Confounding any ontological division between original and copy by suggesting the imitative status of all sexuality, Judith Butler analyzes performativity as an active and modifying formation of gendered subjectivity rather than substantive essence or truth. Butler writes,

> performativity is thus not a singular "act," for it is always a reiteration of a norm or set of norms, and to the extent that it acquires an act-like status in the present, it conceals or dissimulates the conventions of which it is a repetition. . . . Within speech act theory, a performative is that discursive practice that enacts or produces that which it names. (1993:12–13)

Butler's writings indicate heterosexuality as a defensive imitation of its own unattainable ideals that repeat themselves over and over again. Performative approaches to language are shown to support nonessentializing gender notions through citational acts that both repeat and displace historically sedimented sexual dichotomies.

Framing verbal and bodily enactments of gender identification and desire as an ongoing process of resignifying words, images, and narratives within specific contexts of embodiment, performative paradigms allow for productive openness while remaining cognizant of the legacies and powers of meanings out of the past. It is the very possibility of dynamic articulations of self in the midst of hegemonic forces of exclusion that situates queer performativity as an ambivalent and unstable practice. Performativity allows for an indeterminate space between representation and experience, speech and embodiment that defies rational control. Butler writes,

Performativity is not just about speech acts. It is also about bodily acts. The relation between them is complicated, and I called it a "chiasmus" in *Bodies That Matter*. There is always a dimension of bodily life that cannot be fully represented, even as it works as the condition and activating condition of language. (2004:198–199)

Leaving room for those ephemeral elements of experience that exceed conscious symbolic control, theories of performativity make it possible to recognize and value subjects excluded within dominant modes of knowledge. Performative enactments not only reveal the normative pressures that reproduce conformity but also enable transformations, drawing attention to unpredictable and changing facets engendering selves and relations.

Within deconstructive methods of queer theory, it becomes important to situate the embodied emotional struggles that propel performativity out of childhood experiences of exclusion and devaluation. Eve Sedgwick's essay "Queer Performativity: Henry James's *The Art of the Novel*" presents a reading of the ways in which sexuality becomes configured through performative utterances such as "shame on you." Using shame as exemplary of the enactment of queer subjects, Sedgwick avoids collapsing queerness into prescribed narratives of homosexual depravity while at the same time unfolding the bodily and emotional impact of painful words of abuse. It is precisely because of psychosocial, embodied, and linguistically interactive processes that subjects are able to perform queer affirmations of difference through interpellations of "shame." Sedgwick writes, "If queer is a politically potent term, which it is, that's because, far from being capable of being detached from the childhood scene of shame, it cleaves to that scene as a near-inexhaustible source of transformational energy" (1993:4). Sedgwick refers to processes of shaming as an exemplary instance of queer performativity, which enables her to avoid imputing any substantive content to queer identity while theorizing it as "a strategy for the production of meaning and being" (ibid.:11). By tracing signifiers of suffering, social withdrawal, and communicative struggles for recognition in response to shame, Sedgwick renders queerness a dialogic, cultural process rather than a rigid identity: "the emergence of the first person, of the singular, of the present, of the active, and of the indicative are all questions, rather than presumptions, for queer performativity" (ibid.:4).

Both Butler and Sedgwick challenge abstract conceptual celebrations of sexual fluidity and contingency that work to erase the more painful experiences of queer youth who bare the psychic burdens of heteronormativity. When applying queer theory to the lives of girls coming out as lesbian, bisexual, and transgendered, it becomes crucial to balance poststructuralist notions about the performative mobility of adolescent desires and identifications with detailed accounts of how they look, act, speak, and feel in specific times and places. Creative affirmations of difference coincide with degrading experiences of being named and othered as sexually "perverse" or deviant. Against tendencies to romanticize the sex/gender/sexual polymorphism of youth shaped by adult projections and fantasies, it is vital to consider how girls and boys maneuver in-between hegemonic norms of heterosexual femininity and masculinity and their own culturally mediated and corporeally lived selves. The question of where and how to begin researching queer youth differences calls for attentiveness to the performative contours through which youth negotiate who they are and want to become through embodied acts of self-representation. In this way, queer theories provide a set of tools for practical learning and engagement rather than a prescribed set of ideas. Deborah Britzman writes, "I have found it useful to read queer theory not as a set of contents to be applied but as offering a set of methodological rules and dynamics useful for reading, thinking and engaging with the psychical and social of everyday life" (2000:54).

Developing a performative method for interpreting queer youth, I shift attention away from seemingly transparent statements of sexual identity such as "I am a lesbian" toward layered experiential stories, fictions, and fantasies that emerge out of the communicative initiatives of youth using a range of cultural forms and media. What becomes challenging is to learn how to approach gender and sexual minority youth beyond the formulations of adult expectations, while at the same time rendering them intelligible. Susan Talburt asks,

> Rather than containing youth in adult narratives, how might we avoid repeating identities? How can we encourage practices that do not depend on the intelligibility that dominant adult narratives presume to be necessary? How might adults come to see the identities we and youth adopt as creative rather than as evolving copies? (2004:35)

Performativity becomes a useful conceptual tool through which to frame not only the signifying activities of youth but also endeavors to read and interpret them. In this way, a researcher's own production of discourse becomes part of a reflexive and relational process of representation that engages intimately with languages used to understand queer youth.

Coming to know queer youth as articulate subjects of desire, I am compelled to utilize practices of meaning making through which narratives and memories unfold gradually, provisionally, and indirectly, refusing to start out with conceptual guarantees or establish a stable endpoint or finalizable meaning. Patti Lather's elaboration of a "postpositivist praxis," in which research is undertaken within a performative and participatory frame of action becomes useful for studying queer youth sexualities and cultures. In this perspective, research is thought in terms of productive enactments of desire and power among various subjects that need to be interrogated in a direction of democratic inclusion and social transformation rather than inscribed as a single authorial truth. Within a moving field of social relations in which gender, race, class, nationality, ethnicity, and sexuality simultaneously constitute subjective desires, multiple versions provide partial representations of shifting social encounters, effecting exclusions that need to be addressed as part of a persistent reflexivity. Lather highlights performative dimensions of research texts, displacing the exactitude of social categories and facts through ongoing signifying relations. Data becomes a basis for telling stories that might disturb and alter people's consciousness and provoke actions. Lather writes,

> Data might be better conceived as the material for telling a story where the challenge becomes to generate a polyvalent data base that is used to vivify interpretation as opposed to "support" or "prove." . . . Turning the text into a display and interaction among perspectives and presenting material rich enough to bear re-analysis in different ways bringing the reader into the analysis via a discursive impulse which fragments univocal authority. (1991:91)

Lather reconstructs data as socially meaningful narratives, offering several versions and reading them against each other. Research data are used "demonstrably, performatively . . . to condense, exemplify, evoke, to embellish theoretical argument rather than to collapse it into an empirical instance where data function as a 'certificate of presence,' a buttressing facticity" (ibid.:150).

Following Lather's cue, my goal is not to pin down and decipher the essence of queer youth or to analyze exactly what a particular representation means but, rather, to open up spaces in which to listen for culturally mediated and imaginatively embellished communications. I am an active part of the dialogical movement of ideas without laying claim to any grand gesture of theoretical synthesis. Involved as a key cultural participant, a situated and desiring queer researcher, I engage with both media texts and queer girls, looking and listening for momentary confluences and disjunctions of meaning. The goal is to open up passages through which young people can be understood as creative cultural subjects while paying attention to how media representations become constituted and invigorated by them. I do this without forgetting that I am an integral part of what Lather calls "vivifying interpretation." I try to show how queer youth themselves are continually theorizing identity and power as they struggle to recognize and speak themselves through personal and collective discourses. In this sense, I join my theorizations with the ongoing representational practices of youth rather than imposing metaconcepts onto what often gets belittled as unformulated empirical data. This is not to discount my power and limitations as a researcher but to complicate the ties between myself as an adult theorist and youth participants. One of the most challenging facets of researching queer teens is learning to respect the ways in which young people name who they are and what they like in nonlinear, oblique, and informal dialogues.

Lather's performative approach makes it possible to develop research projects that are analytically and ethically responsive to the innovations of youth cultures arising in the 1990s, which stress do-it-yourself strategies of media production and interaction over passive consumption. As Mary Celeste Kearney argues, a substantial increase in girls' involvement in cultural production includes "the rise of girls' advocacy in response to reports of female adolescents' problems with self-esteem, the popularization of a 'girl power' ethos, and the formation of adult-run media education programs organized specifically for female youth" (2003:18). Research into queer youth needs to be tied to advocacy and support for accessible arts and media projects through which youth cultural production is facilitated. Examining the self-representational contours of queer youth video, I try to integrate queer theoretical insights through a performative flux of desire in language in relation with emotionally passionate and socially situated uses of media through which youth make sense of themselves and talk back to dominant heterogendered discourses.

Performing In/visible Pleasures of Queer Youth: Reading "Untitled" from the Queer Youth Digital Video Project

For queer youth, media compels tricky negotiations with commercialized heterosexist ideals, interweaving elements from pop culture, imagined connections, and experiential narratives. Challenging conceptions of youth as passive consumers, queer youth actively positioned themselves as creative producers. For example, Sadie Benning began using Super 8 film as a queer teen to document her everyday family and social environments; through her films, she explores her subjective perspectives. Benning's experimental work details the quirky intimate moments of growing up as a lesbian in the late 1980s, confronting simplistic assumptions of femininity with bold visual statements that humorously show up intelligent desires and ways of seeing the world. Her intimate films circulated in film festivals across North America, spurring interest in the process of filmmaking for queer girls as a dynamic mode of personal and political self-representation. Kearney writes that

> Benning's videos, most of which she produced in her room, are clearly from a teenager's perspective, yet they debunk the stereotypical notion of girls' "bedroom culture" as a cheerful space of heterosexual awakening and commercial consumption. Instead, Benning presents herself as both a lesbian and an active cultural producer who is anxious about the alienating and often violent society in which she lives. (2003:22)

Sadie Benning's films exemplify the emergence of local media production by, for, and about teens struggling to define their identities in complex and flexible cultural ways. It is through creative practices of image making alongside the memory work of storytelling that youth convey their sexual subjectivities as provisional and composite. A critical dimension of such do-it-yourself youth media is the refusal to dichotomize the private/public, psychic/political, individual/collaborative, commercial/alternative relations of representation. By enacting the signs of dominant cultures over and over again in ways that always come to mean something else, young artists go beyond uniform visual codes and surfaces to what Teresa de Lauretis calls a "semiosis of experience" (1994) that includes bodily, emotional, political, and analytical engagements with sexual discourses to produce unique self-representations. This interplay between public images and personal expressions is an especially important move for queer girls under pressure to silence and conceal their sexual desires and identities for fear of social rejection and violence. Exploring the experiential languages and meanings of queer girl sexualities requires the researcher to take account of the impossibility of transparency in coming to see and hear the sexual histories of marginalized youth, acknowledging the ethical primacy of indirect, partial, dialogical, and invested ways of knowing. In this way, the goal is not to fix definitions of queer girls by rendering their narratives into generalizable data but to explore the contexts through which youth "do" representational work alongside interactive readings that implicate the desires of researchers as advocates and interlocutors. This activates meanings as they are constituted in the productive texts of youth and become part of intergenerational conversations that address gender and sexual specificity.

Paying attention to creative initiatives of youth as a starting point for qualitative research is a useful way to decenter adult authoritative knowledges away from institutionally bound methods, following the lead of youth to affirm the mediums, communicative styles, and social arenas connected to their everyday worlds of experience. Such an approach attentively seeks out subcultural spaces and community programs where youth find symbolic and material encouragement to represent themselves. This raises the issue of the relationship between academic interpreter and queer youth: Who is best suited to bridge these positions? How should this relationship be oriented and developed? Although research on youth subcultures has in many ways ignored these difficult questions, those grappling with the specific conditions of queer youth have begun to frame this problem in terms of shared alliances built on mutual interests and goals. Judith Halberstam refers to

> an alliance between the minority academic and the minority subcultural producer. Where such alliances exist, academics can play a big role in the construction of queer archives, and queer memory, and, furthermore queer academics can and some should participate in the ongoing project of recoding queer culture and interpreting it and circulating a sense of its multiplicity and sophistication. (2003:n.p.)

Halberstam frames the relation between researcher and queer subcultures in terms of motivated reciprocity, as an ongoing struggle for inclusive and diverse public representations by and about queer lives. This suggests the importance of analyzing the commonalities, divisions, and

shared stakes between academics and queer youth who are in the process of crafting visual stories of themselves. Working against a detached
voyeuristic gaze, such investigation demands a vulnerable willingness by
researchers to speak about their own histories of sexual marginalization
and erasure, as well as a recognition of their interests in exploring what
youth have to say in the here and now. A dialogic structure of exchange
becomes especially useful in a media environment that objectifies and
treats teens as something to be sexually commodified for the pleasure
of adult spectators. The point is to align the self-representational acts of
young people with academic and community activists working on multiple fronts to expand the range of ways through which youth articulate
their lives. Toward this end, a willingness to turn reflexively back upon the
self is important to help understand how a researcher's location and identities impact on interpretive relations with youth. Reflexivity provides tex-
tured emotional insights into how the fears, desires, and social experiences
of the researcher mark all aspects of a process of interacting with and theorizing queer youth. Awareness of the partial and limited scope of any
research text becomes the basis for reaching out and learning from youth
without imposing totalizing authority. This process does not stop at personal reflexivity but must also use this knowledge of the specific stakes
and boundaries of learning to outreach toward coalition building with
other youth researchers and advocates as a way of bridging the partial
perspectives of multiple subjects and groups. Both reflexivity and collec-
tivity work together to enable responsible and constructive methodological practices.

My own research attempts to interweave self-reflections of my expectations, memories, and longings. I am challenged through queer youth
image-making to question the limits and biases of my thinking. Here, I
present a case study that grew out of my own experiences as a queer
woman attending the Toronto Lesbian and Gay Film and Video Festival
and becoming amazed by the intricately stylized explorations of sexual
identity within the youth program. Collective queer youth initiatives such
as the Queer Youth Digital Video Project provide occasions for creating
personal visual messages as part of a broader organizational movement
to hear from marginalized youth. The layered and temporally complex
stories constructed by youth within these videos provide rich sources of
material for qualitative research that are grounded in young people's life-
worlds. Here, queer youth frame the questions and select the issues that
matter to them without prescribed notions of what a researcher wants to

ask. The youth digital video project promotes the accessibility of media production and reception as a means to empower and educate young people, while also encouraging a diverse range of representations through which to gather and interpret histories of growing up queer. Research on queer digital video needs to become integrally connected to the promotion of community-based media projects through which youth reconstruct their relationships and fantasies as public texts. It also requires attentive readings of the works produced by queer youth, staying close to the images/words/narratives used to compose video shorts.

I am going to focus on an example from the 2002 Queer Youth Video program. My reading will highlight some innovative representational strategies adopted by a queer youth videomaker and also a process of interpretation that I enact as a way of bridging our life-worlds. There is nothing objective or detached about my methodology here. I was blown away by the candid brilliance of Natasha Pike's video "Untitled," which stood out in its singularity and its linkages with the other video pieces in the program. Watching Pike's video I was struck by how rare it is to see and hear accounts of growing up queer, especially those that artistically mediate hidden childhood pleasures and struggles. Pike's two-minute short drew me in as a vulnerable viewer in need, invested in witnessing its bold recollections, pushing me to reflect on the gap between my own femme queerness and Pike's representation of transgender boyhood. I approach Pike's text as a chance to learn about another's experience, while turning back on my own desires to signify alternatives out of the past and in the present. This is qualitative research at the threshold between self and others, genders and generations. It is not meant to pin down evidence or categorize data. It is a practice of tracing the performative dimensions of youth identifications in the context of a locally operated media collective. I am not interested in tightly structuring my analysis but, rather, in fostering nonlinear commentary that catches arbitrary and fragmented signs of desire and responds with curiosity, interest, and care. What I offer is a small glimpse of my reading and writing process that pays close attention to how youth convey meanings in autobiographical and fictional audiovisual performances of queer desire. It is meant to propose a dialogic style of listening and responding to youth sexuality without regulating and prescribing differences.

Natasha Pike's "Untitled" offers a creatively stylized reminiscence of childhood told from the perspective of a transgendered youth. It begins with a television screen frozen with visual static; we are left waiting for a message, caught in an uncomfortable space of a transmission impasse that marks the media invisibility of queer youth. Suddenly, an ordinary, seemingly "innocent" picture of a child appears. Using what seems to be family video footage of Pike as a young girl, s/he overlays a counternarrative voiceover that opens with the following statements:

> When I was a kid I was this guy named Steve.
> Sometimes he managed a video store.
> Sometimes he was a biker.
> Sometimes a baseball player.
> Talking about it scares me.

Feelings and fantasies of queer beginnings are performed as a flow of video images that elicit ideals of childhood normality, interrupted by narratives of gender subversion. Riddled with bold assertions of becoming "boy" while appearing as a little "girl," images and words bump up against each other telling the viewer to be wary of expectations. The quiet little girl sitting in a chair is paired with a voice claiming, "I feel like a boy." This voice continues with shots of a kid in a row boat: "I never told anyone that I used to stuff balled up socks in my pants and look in the mirror." A dancing girl in a frilly dress becomes the background to the words, "TV has never been as good as when I watch it in my boxers with my legs spread casually apart." The dissonance between what we see and what we hear is a reminder that "experience" goes beyond surface appearances, that fantasy is a powerful element of children's lives capable of rupturing myths of gender and sexual conformity. I am taken back to my own silenced gender transgressions, realizing that they are also traceable through the forms of sporadic memory work enacted within Pike's video. I wonder how I might gently recover these sites of queer trauma and erasure through cultural research capable of embracing tentative and incomplete images/stories.

Pike depicts queer sexuality as a conflictual aspect of identity that can only be reiterated through momentary fragments of desire and shame, becoming simultaneously sources of empowering difference and embodied frustration. An anonymous video clip of aggressive physical intercourse is digitally integrated into the personalized coming-of-age tale of transgender sexual identity. The need for past secrecy and present queer affirmation is interwoven in a confession of ambivalence: "No one knows that the first time I made love with a penis strapped to me I thought I was flying. And no one knows just how badly I wish I could have felt it, really felt it." Sexual initiation into strap-on sex is introduced through emotional re-membrance in a context of emerging transgender awareness, defying at-tempts to desexualize or heteronormalize young people. It is the reflexive consciousness of a youth crafting memory, as both a disruptive and a re-constructive tool of representation, that challenges objectifying categoriza-tions of gender and sexuality. Pike turns the gaze on the viewer:

> I despise searching for a definition of what those things are.
> But I don't need one until you ask.
> The problem isn't me
> It's you . . .

The viewer is confronted by the narrator, who refuses to be patholo-gized. Addressing the audience with the problem of "definition" opens up a space for thinking about how this video will be interpreted: what expec-tation, assumptions, questions will I bring to my readings? Am I seduced by Pike's butch honesty? How does my own position influence the ways I view Pike's video? Do I identify? Am I bothered by this refusal of neat cat-egories? Is strap-on sex too edgy for youth studies? How will I avoid con-ceptualizing Pike's message in binary ways? What is my role and respon-sibility as an academic researcher analyzing this work? Displaying sexual-ity as a problem of naming, which at the same time is made into a visual and verbal puzzle that calls for active deciphering, Pike positions queer youth sexuality as an ongoing interpretive practice.

Inviting the viewer to reflect on the ways in which queer children and youth are ignored, noticed, and comprehended, "Untitled" becomes framed as a politicized collective struggle. My viewing becomes directed to look beyond this specific video into a broader mediascape of popular cul-tural icons and grassroots responses. Pike extends the problem of repre-sentation beyond individual acts of interpretation, toward the broader cultural environment that constitutes shared languages for understanding queerness. Suggesting that possibilities are emerging that "fall outside of a) or b)" as prescribed choices, Pike flashes television and film images evoking queer desires: "of course we're luckier than many others. These days there's c), d), e), f), g)." Examples include clips of butch-femme cou-ples, queer punks kissing, gay male sitcom stars, transgender fictions, and talk-show spectacles. Listing evidence of queers in mainstream media, Pike sets up a popular cultural vocabulary with which to name historical changes that impact back upon how youth see themselves.

Pike ends her video with the direct gaze of her own eyes, having framed her own representation as a television show that she controls through a converter, and she turns it abruptly off. Pike is simultaneously performer, producer, and consumer. S/he gestures at the importance of actively making images that expand the visions through which queer youth make sense of their lives. "Untitled" is a critical experimental text, throwing notions of girlhood into "crisis" through an experiential/fictional/documentary mix of representational forms. As a viewer and a researcher I remain uncertain of what is fabricated and what is real, compelling me to wonder why I need to make such distinctions in the first place. Using video art as a basis for research renders realist notions of "experience" problematic; the very languages through which the lives of youth are meaningful become the foreground of analysis. I am able to engage with Pike's video nót as static data or information to be coded but as a process through which I recompose and interpret fragments of stories and images into my own partial narrative of queer youth self-representation. In other words, my research is an open-ended reconstruction of stories, folded through diverse self-fictions of youth, working to critically challenge heteronormative ways of thinking while also providing affirmative discursive space for alternative modes of representation. Situating Pike's single video piece along with many others by queer youth expands the dialogue in several directions. Pike reveals the limits of her representation as she turns on and turns off her story as a televised "show." Stay tuned for more to come . . . and quickly the next video emerges as part of this year's program.

Studying these videos across heterogeneous subjects, years, and topics enables me to respect the unique passages of queer youth sexuality. I have little control over the questions being asked or the directions each videomaker sets out on. My authority as an adult researching becomes humbled without being entirely erased. It is my job to be receptive and attentive to the variability of styles and contents, to mark my discomforts and to guide my speculations with caution. This is a wildly unsettling terrain for understanding identity and knowledge, and that is precisely the point. As the horizon of creative expression expands to include youth creating images out of complex social intersections of race, class, gender, and sexual relations, realms of youth "experience" being documented grows impossible to generalize and unify. The end result of working on queer youth video is a gathering of cultural practices that refuse systematic closure, insisting on the renewal of readings over and over again. Although my own research here has followed the productive media output of an established community group, other possibilities might involve the design and activation of a digital-video-making project as part of a research project. A crucial lesson emerging out of my study revolves around the value of facilitating youth media while learning from their texts as a process of reflexive engagement. More important than consolidating institutional knowledge about queer youth is the chance to watch them negotiate and re-create the cultural signs that inscribe queer youth lives with the confidence to tell us when and how we might be useful to them. Engaging with queer youth video as a researcher stretches me to accept that my role is bound by what I am able to give back, working to provide the symbolic and material conditions that encourage and support queer youth to tell us what they need and want.

REFERENCES

Britzman, Deborah. (2000). "Precocious Education." In *Thinking Queer,* ed. Susan Talburt and Shirley Steinberg. New York: Peter Lang.

Butler, Judith. (2004). *Undoing Gender.* New York: Routledge.

———. (1993). *Bodies That Matter.* New York: Routledge.

———. (1989). *Gender Trouble.* New York: Routledge.

de Lauretis. (1994). *The Practice of Love: Lesbian Sexuality and Perverse Desire.* Bloomington: Indiana University Press.

Driscoll, Catherine. (2002). *Girls.* New York: Columbia University Press.

Fine, Michelle. (1988). "Sexuality, Schooling, and Adolescent Females: The Missing Discourse of Desire." *Harvard Educational Review,* 58(1), 29–53.

Frost, Liz. (2001). *Young Women and the Body.* New York: Palgrave.

Halberstam, Judith. (2003). "What's That Smell? Queer Temporalities and Subcultural Lives." *Public Sentiments,* 2(1). Available at http://www.barnard.edu/sfonline/ps/halberst.htm.

Kearney, Mary Celeste. (2003). "Girls Make Movies." In *Youth Cultures,* ed. Kerry Mallen. Westport, CT: Praeger.

Lather, Patti. (1991). *Getting Smart.* New York: Routledge.

Orenstein, Peggy. (1994). *Schoolgirls: Young Women, Self-Esteem, and the Confidence Gap.* New York: Doubleday.

Sedgwick, Eve. (1993). "Queer Performativity: Henry James's *The Art of the Novel.*" *GLQ,* 1(1), 1–16.

Talburt, Susan. (2004). "Intelligibility and Narrating Youth." In *Youth and Sexuali-*

ties: Pleasure, Subversion, and Insubordination in and out of Schools, ed. Mary Louise Rasmussen. New York: Palgrave.

Tolman, Deborah. (1994). "Doing Desire: Adolescent Girls' Struggles for/with Sexuality." *Gender and Society,* 8(3), 324–342.

About the Contributors

Amy L. Best is Associate Professor of Sociology in the Department of Sociology and Anthropology at George Mason University. She is author of *Prom Night: Youth, Schools, and Popular Culture* (2000), which was selected for a 2002 American Educational Studies Association Critics' Choice Award, and of *Fast Cars, Cool Rides: The Accelerating World of Youth and Their Cars* (2006).

Sari Knopp Biklen is Laura and Douglas Meredith Professor of Teaching Excellence; Professor of Cultural Foundations of Education; and Professor of Women's Studies. Her recent books include *School Work: Gender and the Cultural Construction of Teaching* (1995); *Qualitative Research for Education*, with Robert Bogdan (1998); *Gender and Education*, with Diane Pollard for the National Society for the Study of Education (1993); and *Changing Education*, with Joyce Antler (1990).

Elizabeth Chin is Associate Professor of Anthropology at Occidental College in Los Angeles. She is author of *Purchasing Power: Black Kids and American Consumer Culture* (2001), which was a finalist for the C. Wright Mills Prize. Her current projects include implementation of a gang intervention program in collaboration with the Los Angeles Police Department, the Los Angeles City Attorney's Office, and the Los Angeles Public Schools; an autoethnography of her consumer life; and working as artistic director of the Haitian folkloric dance group Troupe Ayizan.

Susan Driver is Assistant Professor in the Contemporary and Communication Studies program at Wilfrid Laurier University. She is completing a book on queer girl cultures and is editing a collection on queer youth. She has published articles on queer mothering and feminist theories of sexuality. She teaches courses analyzing media representations, youth culture, and girls in popular culture.

Marc Flacks is Assistant Professor at California State University, Long Beach. His research focuses on young people's engagement with social, political, and cultural institutions and has included studies of rock music practices, gangs and skinheads in the military, military enlistment decisions, and student engagement with their universities. He is currently writing a book examining how films figure into the process of identity formation of emerging adults.

Kathryn Gold Hadley is Assistant Professor of Sociology at California State University, Sacramento. Her research interests in the peer cultures of young children spanned two continents when she conducted ethnographic research in an American preschool and a Taiwanese kindergarten and first-grade classroom. She has published a number of articles on children's peer culture. Her next research project will investigate the peer cultures that Asian American kids create while attending Chinese-language schools.

Madeline Leonard is Reader in the School of Sociology and Social Policy, Queen's University, Belfast. Her main research interest is in the sociology of childhood and particularly the relationship between work, gender, and childhood. She has published a number of articles and reports on children's experiences of paid work, housework, and care work. Her most recent research involves examining and illuminating the experiences of Catholic and Protestant children living beside the peace lines in Belfast.

C. J. Pascoe received her Ph.D. in sociology from the University of California, Berkeley. Her research and teaching interests center on qualitative investigation of sexuality, adolescence, masculinity, and culture. She is currently a postdoctoral researcher with the MacArthur Foundation's Digital Youth Project and is focusing on how youth create online communities. Her book *"Dude, You're a Fag": Masculinity, Sexuality, and Adolescence* is forthcoming from University of California Press.

Rebecca Raby is Assistant Professor in the Department of Child and Youth Studies at Brock University, Ontario. Her research interests include constructions of childhood and adolescence, particularly how such constructions are experienced by children and adolescents themselves; theories of youth resistance; and children and youth as active participants in research. She is currently investigating secondary-school dress and discipline codes in the Niagara and Toronto regions, particularly how they are perceived and experienced by students.

Alyssa Richman is a doctoral student in the Department of Sociology at Temple University. Her research interests include youth, racial and gender identity formation, and popular culture. She is currently working on a qualitative research project that looks at class and racial identity formation among rural youth.

Jessica Taft is a doctoral candidate in the Department of Sociology at the University of California at Santa Barbara. She is currently writing her dissertation, a multisite political ethnography of teenage girl activists in the Americas and their participation in social movements for global justice and against neoliberalism.

Michael Ungar is Associate Professor and Undergraduate Program Chair at the School of Social Work, Dalhousie University, Halifax, Canada. He is the author of *Playing at Being Bad: The Hidden Resilience of Troubled Teens* (2002), *Nurturing Hidden Resilience in Troubled Youth* (2004), and *Strengths-Based Counseling for At-Risk Youth* (2006), and he is the editor of *Handbook for Working with Children and Youth: Pathways to Resilience across Cultures and Contexts* (2005).

Yvonne Vissing is Professor of Sociology at Salem State College in Salem, Massachusetts, where she is also the Coordinator for its Center for Child Studies. Dr. Vissing is a pediatric sociologist who has written extensively about homeless children. A National Institute of Mental Health Post-Doctoral Research Scholar, she is also an expert in child abuse, especially verbal and emotional abuse of children. Her most recent book addresses the issue of how safe children are when they are in the care of other people such as clergy, day-care providers, and camp counselors.

Stephani Etheridge Woodson is Assistant Professor in the Department of Theatre at Arizona State University, where she teaches in the MFA and Ph.D. programs. Her research and creative interests focus on the social construction of childhood through performance and the group creation/performance of original work. She is the author of several articles for such journals as *Youth Theatre Journal, Journal of American Culture, Stage of the Art, Research in Drama Education, Arts Education Policy Review,* and *Bad Subjects.*

Index

paternalism in universities, 72; analyzing data about, 79; Arnett and, 65, 80; civic engagement, 61, 70–71; cliques, 74; collective or social outlets from, 66; "committed youth," 66; conceptualization and theorization of, 62–63; declining significance of youth subcultures, 73–78; definition, 62; discomfort with narrow social identifications, 74; enlistment in the military, 61–64, 65, 80; epistemological fallacy, 78; escape from, 65; events making up, 64; feeling trapped and stifled by prolonged adolescence, 68; films depicting, 80; generalized terms for, 78; "generation effect," 74; "Generation X," 61, 63; global context, 81; historical and social structural factors in, 65–66; "infantilization" of American youth, 72; late capitalism, 66, 67; "lifecourse effect," 74; meaning ascribed to, 67; "moratorium" on adulthood, 65, 67–68; qualitative social research methods, 80; relational nature of youth, 67, 79–80; representations in popular culture, 80; social diversity, 74; sociological understanding of, 66–67; subjective factors, 66; "twixters," 80, 81; voting behavior, 70 (*see also* Student Experiences in the Research University in the 21st Century)

Enlistment in the military: childhood resilience, 91; emerging adulthood, 61–64, 65, 80; suicide bombers, 91, 92–93

Epstein, D., 142–143

Erikson, Erik H., 65, 243

Ethnicity and roles available to adult researchers, 23

"Fag discourse," 242

Farris, Catherine, 179n3

Feagin, Joe, 11

Fellow worker role, 51

Ferguson, Ann, 252–253, 259

Fieldwork with Children (Holmes), 5

Fine, Gary Alan: accessibility of young people's lives, 46; adult authority, 12, 22–23; children's sense of researchers as potential friends, 142; on conducting participant observation with children, 161, 193–194; impression management by children, 138; *Knowing Children* (with Sandstrom), 5, 26; roles available to adult researchers, 22–23

Fine, Michelle: criticism of self-other

dichotomy, 87; desire in girl's education, 307; social struggle of the exploited/subjugated, 54; working the hyphens, 7

The First R (Van Ausdale and Feagin), 11

Flacks, Marc, 19–21

Flom, B. L., 95–96

Focus groups, 197

Foley, D., 252

Food-sharing routines, 176

Fordham, S., 252

Foucault, Michel, 13, 18, 257

France, Alan, 48

Fraser, M. W., 86

Fraser, Sandy, 5, 42, 44

Freire, Paulo, 53

"Friend" role, 22, 51, 161

Frosh, Stephen, 50

Frost, Liz, 307–308

Fundamentalism and childhood resilience, 91

Furlong, Andy, 66–67

Furstenberg, Frank F., 64–65

Gallagher, Charles, 213, 221

Gallagher, Tess, 264

Gangs and childhood resilience, 89

Garbarino, J., 96–97

Garber, Jennifer, 23

Gatekeepers, 133–156; adopting child-friendly roles, 141–142; adult-pupil relationship, 138; adults as, 25, 134, 147; anonymity, 146–147; children as, 136, 137–139, 152, 158, 165–172, 175–176; child's right to dissent, 153; confidentiality, 144–146; continuous negotiation with, 136–137, 152–153; definition, 135; within educational establishments, 135–136; gender, 140–141; informed dissent, 138; during initial access stage of research, 141; knowledge about powerless *vs.* powerful people, 137; layout of the interview room, 142; outward appearance to, 141; parental consent, 136; powerful gatekeepers, 136; quasi-adult-quasi-child researcher role, 140–144; researchers as, 25, 134, 147–148, 153–154; right to withdraw from research, 139; role of, 133–134; students as, 158, 165–172; superiors' disregard for subordinates, 137–139; teachers as, 25, 158, 163; term-time employment, studies of, 134, 138, 145, 148–149; transfer test (11 plus exam) in Belfast, studies of, 135, 149–150; types of, 23; youth as, 25, 46; in

Pike, Natasha, 304, 319–322
Place: Vision & Voice project (PPV), 284–287, 292
Placement, 98
Pole, Christopher, 54
Politics. *See* Civic engagement
Pollack, Gary, 27
Post-traumatic stress, 90
Power, 12–17; adolescence, 47–48; adult authority, 12–17; in adult-pupil relationship, 138; of adults, 7, 138, 153; disempowerment and marginalization of children, 281–282; empowering marginalized voices, 95–96; feminist methodologies, 54; gulf between adults and children, 46, 47–48, 153; imbalance between adults and youth, 7, 259–260, 266; imbalance between employers and employees, 139; imbalance between teachers and pupils, 139–140; imbalance in research, 12; knowledge about powerless *vs.* powerful people, 137; memory, 257–258; memory-work, 189; the minority-group child, 47; participatory research, 97; qualitative social research methods, 7; in relation to "natives," 260; the socially constructed child, 47; "studying down," 12; of youth, 7, 138, 153, 259–260
"The Problem of Generations" (Mannheim), 77, 257
Prout, Alan, 44–47, 51
Proweller, Amira, 51
Public spaces, 23

Qualitative social research methods: age of the sample, 8–9; anticipated futures, study of, 80; benefits, 92–97; "catalyst" questions, 103; childhood resilience, 87–88, 89, 92–97; consciousness of researcher standpoint bias, 97; contextualization, 89, 94–95, 98; core considerations, 8–9, 17; critical parts of, 6; discovering health among those assumed to be unhealthy, 96; discovering unnamed processes, 94; divisions within, 8; emerging adulthood, 80; empowering marginalized voices, 95–96; International Resilience Project, 100–101; memory-work, 189; nonexploitative research, 7–8, 12–13; power imbalances, 7; quantitative social research methods and, 97–98; questions addressed in this book, 8–9; researcher's role, 6; social

dimensions of research practice, 6; social dynamics in the field, 21; in studying adolescent boys, 229–230; in studying homeless children and youth, 115; in studying minority communities, 193; thick descriptions, 96; transferability across contexts, 96–97, 99; working the hyphens, 7; young children *vs.* young adults, 9; in youth studies, 6–9
Quantitative social research methods: cultural myopia, 92; marginal discourses among youth, 96; qualitative social research methods and, 97–98; in studying homeless children and youth, 115
Quasi-adult-quasi-child researcher role, 140–144
"Queer Performativity" (Sedgwick), 312–313
Queer youth digital video, 304–324; alliance between minority academics and minority subcultural producers, 317–318; community-based media advocacy, 306, 315; counter-hegemonic representations, 305–306; do-it-yourself media production, 15, 315, 316–317, 322–323; do-it-yourself self-representations, 310; girls' sexuality, 307–310; heteronormativity, 308, 309, 313; memory-work, 316; nonverbal communications, 309–310; performativity of gender, 311–315; Queer Youth Digital Video Project, 318–319; researching queer youth, 313, 315; shame, 312; storytelling, 316; strap-on sex, 321; Toronto Lesbian and Gay Film and Video Festival, 318; "Untitled" (Pike), 304, 319–322
Queerness and identity, 312
"Quiet friend" role, 161

Raby, Rebecca: adult authority, 18–19; insider-outsider distinctions, 13; roles available to adult researchers, 22–23
Race: adult authority, 221–223; age-based distancing, 217; applied research as a racialized process, 212; balancing knowledge and ignorance, 218–221; building rapport, 213–218; claims to intersubjectivity, 216; data collection, 13–14; generational ignorance of ways to discuss race, 215; matching race of researchers and researched, 212–213; roles available to adult researchers, 23; talking about it with black girls, 218; talking about it with white girls, 214–216, 218, 222; in youth studies, 204, 212–223